D1489729

NT

THE

CONCEPT OF

POLITICAL

JUDGMENT

Peter J. Steinberger

THE UNIVERSITY OF CHICAGO PRESS
Chicago & London

PETER J. STEINBERGER is professor of political science at Reed College, Oregon. Among his previous books is *Logic and Politics: Hegel's Philosophy of Right* (1988).

The University of Chicago Press, Chicago 60637
The University of Chicago Press, Ltd., London
© 1993 by The University of Chicago
All rights reserved. Published 1993
Printed in the United States of America
02 01 00 99 98 97 96 95 94 93   1 2 3 4 5

ISBN: 0-226-77191-1 (cloth)
         0-226-77193-8 (paper)

Library of Congress Cataloging-in-Publication Data

Steinberger, Peter J., 1948–
      The concept of political judgment / Peter J. Steinberger.
         p.   cm.
      Includes bibliographical references and index.
      1. Judgment.   2. Political science.   I. Title.
   JA74.S675   1993   92-45707
   320'.01'1—dc20   CIP

CONTENTS

FOUR

Judgment as Intelligent Performance
211

FIVE

Toward a Theory of Judgment in Politics
281

Index   305

PREFACE

B OOKS, LIKE MOST OTHER THINGS, may be different in appearance from what they are in fact. Sometimes the discrepancy is attributable to deficiencies of the author, sometimes to the peculiar sensibilities of the reader. But sometimes it is simply an intrinsic and unavoidable feature of the book itself.

The present book is an essay in political philosophy, but at times it may appear to be something quite different. In the second chapter, for example, a great deal of attention is paid to issues in modern aesthetic theory, and political matters are either ignored altogether or treated only in passing. Similarly, the third chapter focuses on the philosophy of language and interpretation, and discusses virtually nothing of direct political consequence. The reader who has encountered the political thought of Machiavelli, Tocqueville, and Nietzsche in Chapter 1, and who is expecting more of the same in succeeding chapters, may be perplexed by what appears to be a long and arbitrary detour into the world of taste and purposiveness, utterance and implicature, prejudice and perception.

I believe that political judgment—the topic of this essay—is merely a species of the larger category of judgment itself. Judgment is, by hypothesis, the mental activity in virtue of which we predicate universals of particulars. When this activity occurs in a political setting with respect to universals and particulars of a political nature, then we have political judgment. I conclude that in order to understand *political* judgment, we must pursue in some depth the notion of judgment *sans phrase*. Much of the present book is devoted to such an inquiry, and this will often take us far from the standard topics and literatures of political philosophy. My hope and claim is that all of these excursions do indeed bear in important ways on the question of political judgment which is, and remains throughout, the focus of the work.

I take it that philosophy is primarily an inquiry not into the meaning of life, the structure of the universe, or the ultimate source of being; it is, rather, an inquiry into the nature of our concepts about these and other things. In this sense, my ambitions are directly and exclusively philosophical. The aim is to construct and present an account of a concept, the concept of political judgment, hence to uncover and clarify what we really mean when we say that this or that person has, or this or that action was the product of, good judgment. While the chapters that follow treat a wide variety of materials representing a diversity of intellectual traditions, they do so not for historical or exegetical reasons but simply and solely to advance the argument.

In my view, most arguments about concepts at least implicitly take a certain form. Of a particular concept *F*, they ask the question, What is *F*? or, more precisely, What is the meaning of *F*? They pursue this question by casting about for alternative theories. Typically, they encounter theories that differ from one another in substantial ways, yet seem each to have something important to contribute. Philosophical arguments seek to reconcile such theories, to describe what is valuable in each, and to show how their differences can be at once eradicated and rehabilitated, annulled and preserved, in a more comprehensive and compelling theory about the meaning of *F*.

The present essay undertakes an argument of this sort. It asks about the meaning of our concept of political judgment, considers differing and seemingly incompatible approaches to that concept with reference to the idea of judgment per se, and attempts to discover how those differing approaches in fact reflect various aspects of what is, in the end, a single and coherent notion. Such an argument inevitably involves a tendency to refer to itself, to circle back constantly upon itself, and consider anew what has already been considered, to restate conclusions at a more advanced level that seemed to have been well established earlier on; and this, in turn, may make the argument appear to be repetitive. It is, of course, up to the reader to decide whether or not the chapters that follow reflect faithfully and with appropriate parsimony the discursive requirements of a conceptual analysis. But I take solace in what I believe to be true, that the risk of appearing to be repetitive is inherent in any inquiry that purports to be in some sense dialectical.

This is a comparatively short book composed of comparatively long chapters. Each chapter is intended to present a discrete and coherent position in a more or less complete way, and this has required chapters of a length sufficient to permit in each case a relatively extensive and integrated exposition. Despite this, and despite the diversity of materials that these chapters treat, the book as a whole is designed to trace out a single, unified argument. In this sense, the various chapters are, at least by intention, not at all independent. The later chapters entirely presuppose the earlier ones, while the earlier ones acquire their true character only in the context of the whole.

Chapter 1 seeks to establish in detail some of the intellectual history surrounding the problem of political judgment by considering a variety of influential ideas about the nature of politics itself: politics as *virtu* and deliberation, as an aesthetic enterprise, as the characteristic form of human action, and as the pursuit of intimations. The discussion examines, seriatim, three iterations of a thesis about political wisdom. It critically evaluates these iterations, and thereby lays the groundwork for a more satisfying approach to the general issue of judgment and politics.

The second chapter retreats from political matters to take up the problem of judgment *simpliciter*. It explores what I call the *dichotomy* of judgment—some judgment is inferential, some not—and considers this dichotomy with respect to certain classical theories of ethics and certain modern theories of art. On the basis of this analysis, I construct a rationalistic model of judgment. This model embraces and reflects many of our standard and widely held views. But the model itself is seriously inadequate, and this means that the truths it contains, if they are to be fully recognized and appreciated as such, must be isolated from the model and incorporated into a quite different and more compelling theory.

The third chapter examines selected themes in the contemporary philosophy of language and interpretation with a view toward specifying the importance of intuition and inference for human cognition, at least as we understand it. It considers approaches to judgment that vigorously reject the rationalistic model and offer a sharply alternative picture of what it means to judge. Again, the very real insights that we discover here are obscured by serious theoretical deficiencies, and must therefore be reformulated in the light of a theory that does more justice to our own underlying conceptual apparatus. In Chapter 4, I propose the philosophical sublation of the dichotomy of judgment. Relying on an explicit account of intelligent performance, I suggest a notion of judgment that dissolves many of the problems and perplexities discovered in earlier chapters, and thus represents a fair reconstruction of our own intuitions about the judging process. The fifth and final chapter returns to political matters. It maps the findings of the previous chapters onto questions of politics, explicates the sense in which political judgment reflects the notion of judgment in general, and considers some of the practical and moral implications of a theory which places judgment at the very heart of political practice.

As the foregoing would suggest, my discursive strategy is to present a variety of positions on the question of judgment in general and political judgment in particular, to examine these positions critically in the light of one another, and to discover thereby the elements of each that belong properly to a complete and satisfying conception of judgment. The underlying form of the argument is thus dialogic. Particular perspectives, each of some historical significance, are made to confront the others in a kind of conversation about judgment. The criterion for evaluating these particular viewpoints is the criterion of coherence. I assume that we approach the notion of political judgment on the basis of a conceptual apparatus—a universe of discourse—that both shapes and reflects our deep intuitions about the world. Particular views of political judgment are assessed in terms of the degree to which they comport with, and help to justify, those intuitions. The result is an account of what we really mean when we speak of good judgment, an account that we cannot articulate and make explicit until a variety of alternative hypothetical interpretations have been investigated, juxtaposed, and evaluated.

My method of inquiry is, in large part, a matter of examining some important texts in philosophy and political theory. While these texts emerge out of different circumstances and often speak to different concerns, I assume that they nonetheless address some very basic questions in ways that can and must be compared. This is certainly how the authors themselves saw it. Kant did not write in ignorance of Plato; Hobbes argues as much against Aristotle as against his contemporaries. I am far from wishing to decontextualize such writings. Indeed, my view is that their differences often reflect differences in basic assumptions, but that these latter do not at all prevent us from analyzing the texts with a view toward specifying, clarifying, and ultimately enriching our own ideas about judgment in politics. All of these texts compose, among other things, a part of our conceptual heritage. Their different background assumptions necessarily resonate in our thoughts, for we are their intellectual heirs.

Throughout, I worry that a long and laborious argument has been mounted in support of conclusions that are at once unexceptional and self-evident. On the other hand, I worry too that the argument itself fails to support those conclusions adequately, and that readers will remain unconvinced. In the face of these doubts, I have, of course, relied on my own judgment, understanding full well my responsibility to reconstruct that judgment rationally, should the occasion arise.

This book covers at least some of the territory treated previously in three fine books by Vollrath, Beiner, and Bernstein.[1] I have learned a great deal from each of these authors; in a certain sense, my argument emerges out of a serious engagement with their work. On the other hand, the mere fact that I have written a book about political judgment suggests substantial dissatisfaction with its predecessors. I have chosen not to remark at length on this dissatisfaction, which will be clear to anyone who takes the time to examine the issues in question. Suffice it to say that I disagree sharply, though in different ways, with each of these books on the most basic matters of substance and method. Such disagreements, however fundamental, do not in any way diminish my genuine admiration for authors who have considered in a serious and systematic manner issues that I know to be difficult and believe to be important.

I am most grateful to Richard Flathman for his generous and helpful reading of the manuscript. As would be expected, his reactions were uncommonly interesting and challenging, and forced me to clarify and strengthen the argument at several key points. Our doctrinal differences, which have only now become fully apparent to me, do not in any way diminish my great admiration for his own work and intellect. I am similarly grateful to Marion Smiley, who offered extremely useful suggestions that led to a number of important revisions.

William Peck, Peter Schwartz, and Richard Wolin all read the entire manuscript and provided the kind of ongoing stimulation, serious criticism, and friendship that help to make the intellectual life so deeply satisfying. Morris Lipson and C. D. C. Reeve were extraordinarily generous with their time, and offered painstaking and hard-nosed criticism at several key points in the text. Jean Elshtain and John Stanley also provided especially useful reactions to selected argu-

---

1. Ernst Vollrath, *Die Rekonstruktion der politischen Urteilskraft* (Stuttgart: Ernst Klett Verlag, 1977); Ronald Beiner, *Political Judgment* (Chicago: University of Chicago Press, 1983); Richard J. Bernstein, *Beyond Objectivism and Relativism: Science, Hermeneutics, and Praxis* (Philadelphia: University of Pennsylvania Press, 1983). See also Ernst Vollrath, *Grundlegung einer philosophischen Theorie des Politischen* (Würzburg: Königshausen & Neumann, 1987), especially Chapter 10; and Allessandro Ferrara, "On Phronesis," *Praxis International* 7 (Winter 1987/8), pp. 246–67.

ments. My lengthy and peripatetic conversations with Neil Thomason were, as ever, a source of great insight and inspiration.

This project was written with the support of a year-long fellowship from the National Endowment for the Humanities, and also with the help of numerous grants, both major and minor, from Reed College. A small part of Chapter 1 originally appeared, in rather different form, as "Hannah Arendt on Judgment," *American Journal of Political Science* 34 (August 1990). Sections of Chapter 2 reflect the argument, though not the precise text, of "Ruling: Guardians and Philosopher-Kings," *American Political Science Review* 83 (December 1989). I am grateful, finally, to be a part of Reed College, which is perhaps unique in providing an atmosphere that recognizes and celebrates above all the intrinsic value of intellectual endeavor.

ONE

Three Iterations of a Thesis

I N S EPTEMBER OF 1987, at the height of the controversy surrounding Robert Bork's nomination to the United States Supreme
Court, Anthony Lewis wrote the following in the *New York Times:*

Judge Bork's extraordinary five days of testimony left the sena-
tors with a task that [Former Attorney General] Katzenbach
stated sensitively. "Were I in your position," he told the committee, "the central question I would be asking is this. Is Judge Bork
a man of judgment? Not intellect, not reasoning, not lawyering
skills, not ideology, not philosophy—simply judgment. Is he a
wise person?" There is something deeply troubling about a judge
who seeks certainty in abstractions: who discovers a grand theory
that will solve all the problems, then turns to another when the
theory fails—as it must. All of us make mistakes, as journalists
surely know. But Robert Bork's pursuit of theory has led him to
profound misjudgment on great legal and moral issues, and to
unconvincing changes. That is why this intelligent and engaging
man should not sit on the Supreme Court.[1]

The particular merits of Robert Bork's candidacy are of little or
no philosophical interest. What is of interest is the nature of the argument that Lewis and Katzenbach bring to bear on the issue. It is a
kind of argument that most of us will find familiar and serious, at least
at first blush. We recognize that there is often a very great difference
between being wise and being knowledgeable, that persons of substantial analytical strength are not always persons of prudence and good

---

1. Anthony Lewis, "Question of Judgment," *New York Times,* September
27, 1987.

judgment, that the skills and habits of the intellectual are quite different from those of the practitioner. We all know of people who dwell
in the world of ideas—the mathematical prodigy, the scientist in an
ivory tower, the befuddled, absent-minded professor—and who are,
at least by reputation, seriously lacking in what is commonly called
common sense. Our literary tradition amply reflects and sustains this
awareness.[2]

The argument presupposes, of course, not simply a distinction
between abstract intellectual activity and practical activity but also an
image, however inchoate, of the prudent or practical person. Presumably, Anthony Lewis and Nicholas Katzenbach think that some individuals are in fact suited to service on the Supreme Court and that the
world does produce, therefore, people of good judgment and practical
wisdom.[3] Few of us would deny this, and our literary/historical tradition is replete with putative exemplars—Pericles, Trajan, Cromwell,
Washington, to name but a few—whose evident lack of purely theoretical achievement or ability is more than compensated for by, is perhaps
part and parcel of, a certain talent for acting successfully in the world
of affairs.[4]

It is, moreover, precisely this latter world, the political realm, with
which we shall be particularly concerned. Prudence or practical wisdom is not the peculiar property of political activity; all of the practical
arts have their standards of good judgment and common sense. But
it is certain that such standards have played an especially prominent
role in the Western political tradition, and that images of political
leadership, statesmanship, and citizenship have often been connected

---

2. See Plato's *Republic,* 516e–517e. One also thinks of such more recent
but otherwise disparate works as Mary Shelley's *Frankenstein,* Thomas Mann's
The Magic Mountain (especially the Leo Naphta/Georg Lukacs character),
James Joyce's *Ulysses* (Stephen Daedelus as intellectual ingenue), Heinrich
Mann's *The Blue Angel,* Norman Mailer's *The Naked and the Dead,* and Edward
Albee's *Who's Afraid of Virginia Woolf.*

3. Here and throughout, I will often mention political judgment and practical wisdom together. In fact, I believe that although good judgment in politics reflects a certain variety or a certain application of practical wisdom, the
scope of practical wisdom is not limited to the political realm.

4. For example, few historians would deny that Washington was a better
president than either John Adams or Madison, whose "intellectual" achievements were, of course, quite substantial.

in important ways to notions of judgment and practical wisdom. The question of judgment is, thus, a central problem for political philosophy.

It is also certain that the views of Lewis and Katzenbach, far from being heterodox or novel, are in fact utterly unexceptional. They reflect intuitions that most of us share, albeit in varying degrees. Indeed, for convenience sake we may refer to our Lewis/Katzenbach text, suitably elaborated, as the First Iteration of an initially plausible and quite widespread thesis about *political wisdom*—a thesis sufficiently commonplace that it can be offered by two noted opinion leaders as something of a self-evident truth.

Now the First Iteration is certainly incomplete. For obvious reasons, it leaves many of the most important questions unanswered. But if we try to tease out its implications and reconstruct the way in which it would answer some of those questions, we encounter a perspective that is puzzling and unsatisfying in some very complex ways.

We might begin, for example, with terminological issues. On the one hand, good judgment or political wisdom is contrasted with "intellect," "reasoning," "philosophy," "abstraction," and "theory," among other things, as though the meanings of these latter terms were reasonably clear. In fact, they are not clear at all. Each of them could be, at least in principle, the subject of considerable philosophical discussion. The First Iteration thus employs in a casual and offhand manner difficult and challenging words and notions that in fact demand the closest and most careful consideration. For certain purposes this may be perfectly satisfactory, but for ours it is not.

Moreover, I believe that even a cursory and preliminary attempt to clarify some of these terms would suffice, in and of itself, to raise grave doubts about the coherence and plausibility of the First Iteration, and of the views that it represents. Consider "intellect." According to the First Iteration, intellect is one thing, judgment quite another. Does this mean that judging is in no sense an intellectual activity? Does it imply that the prudent person is not using intellect when making a decision? Does the First Iteration hold that common sense is somehow a thoughtless attribute? Presumably, none of these claims would be very attractive. Perhaps then the relevant distinction is not at all between intellect and judgment but between different kinds of, or different uses of, intellect. Exactly what those might be is hardly self-evident. But, more important, to collapse the distinction between intellect and judgment would be to undermine the First Iteration itself, for such a distinction is precisely what that iteration is all about.

Similarly, do we imagine that political wisdom involves no "reasoning" whatsoever, that it has no connection at all with "philosophy", contains no "abstractions," is utterly non-"theoretical?" Again, none of that seems very plausible. But then, what is the precise distinction that the First Iteration wants to establish?

Problems of terminology apply equally to the other side of the equation. Deciding whether or not an intellectual as such lacks "judgment," "common sense," and "political wisdom" requires that we know what those things are. On the one hand, the authors of the First Iteration seem to be fairly confident that they can recognize a good intellectual or theoretician when they see one; that's what Lewis/Katzenbach claim to have found in Robert Bork. Evidently they have access to some roughly reliable test or standard of intellectual distinction— prestigious academic appointments, publication in learned journals, the ability to sustain complex arguments, and the like. But how would Lewis/Katzenbach identify a person of good judgment or political wisdom? What are the telltale marks of common sense? Without a clearer account of what certain key terms mean, it is unlikely that one could derive from the First Iteration any useful criteria for deciding who has judgment and who does not.

These terminological and conceptual problems are, I think, self-evidently troublesome, but they also give rise to some otherwise hidden theoretical difficulties. For the First Iteration may be thought to imply that it "takes one to know one," that there is no procedure—no test or method—for identifying the person of political wisdom and that, to the contrary, it is only by having wisdom ourselves that we can come to recognize it in others. This kind of circularity may not be troubling to the authors of the First Iteration, but to anyone who seeks a more explicit and rigorous account of concepts and conclusions, it cannot be very satisfying.

Now it may be that the First Iteration is not really criticizing intellectuality per se but, rather, the kind of intellectuality that aims at "grand theory," that is, the impulse to seek "certainty" in a single, overarching principle. In such an account, theories are fine as long as we realize the inevitability and desirability of theoretical pluralism. The complexity of the world of affairs, together with the limitations of the human mind, means that there will always be competing theo-

ries that are likely to be variously useful, depending on the circumstances. The person of good judgment is one who can accept this
pluralism with equanimity and who has the good sense to utilize a
variety of theories in a perspicuous and effective manner. That person
might well be an intellectual, but if so, he or she is the kind of intellectual who abjures and rejects as wrongheaded any interest in grand
theory.

I think such an argument cannot be very persuasive. All theories
are judged at least in part on their comprehensiveness; the better the
theory, the more it explains. The intellectual in pursuit of knowledge
aspires necessarily to the greatest possible generality, and to certainty
as well; hence he or she aspires to create, if possible, a grand theory. We may acknowledge the unlikelihood that such an effort could
ever be finally and definitively successful, but this would not alter the
fact that generality and certainty are constitutive goals of theorizing
per se.

It is surely true that we often have to deal with a plurality of
competing theories, but this simply raises for us the question of how
we should choose among them. It seems that there are only two possibilities: either we have some higher principle or theory for making
such a choice, or we do not. The former case is effectively the same
as having a grand theory, a single (though perhaps very complex)
principle that somehow orders and subsumes all of the others, so that
we can decide when they are useful and when they are not. In the
absence of such a comprehensive principle, we presumably must rely
entirely on good judgment or common sense in order to make choices.
This situation, which the First Iteration implicitly regards as our actual
situation, would preserve, of course, the alleged gap between theoretical speculation and practical wisdom. But it would also leave us with
our terminological problem completely intact: What is that gap, and
how can one make sense of it?

At this point, we should note that the question of intellect and
judgment is not, as the First Iteration might imply, simply a matter
of theory versus practice, for there are many accounts of practical
activity—for example, those that rely on notions of instrumental rationality or technique—that conceive of practice as simply the application
of specific and identifiable principles, procedures, and routines to various real-world problems. In this sense, practical ability is essentially a
matter of (more or less) hard work guided by appropriate rules and
methods, hence nothing very mysterious. On the other hand, common

sense, or political wisdom, as envisioned by the First Iteration, is a mysterious business indeed, irreducible to explicit principles and procedures, hence fundamentally inexplicable. Good judgment is a trait that one either has or does not have and is ultimately impervious to analysis and explanation. What is at issue, then, is not practice per se but a particular kind of practical ability that cannot, allegedly, give a systematic account of itself. Again, the question is how to demonstrate even the existence of something so unaccountable.

These various problems suffice to show that the immediate theoretical implications of the First Iteration are at best troubling and incomplete. But its perplexities actually go much beyond this, for the First Iteration suggests not simply that intellectuality and political wisdom are distinct but that they are, in fact, mutually incompatible. Intellectuality, whatever it may be, is not merely an insufficient qualification for good judgment or political wisdom; it is, more strongly, a virtual disqualification. Lewis writes that Bork is fickle "when the theory fails—*as it must*"; he attributes Bork's lack of judgment precisely to his "pursuit of theory." The implication is that some feature of the world requires that a person who deals in "theory" and in "abstractions" is, for that very reason, unlikely to be a person of common sense and practical wisdom. It is hard to imagine exactly what that feature of the world might be; the First Iteration offers no clue. But Lewis/Katzenbach seem to be saying that intellectual endeavor, of its very nature, can make no sustained, reliable contribution to practical life.

It is, of course, one thing for the First Iteration to presuppose that certain selected kinds of abstract or intellectual achievement are insufficient for or unconnected with practical wisdom; it is quite another to suggest that all such achievement is equally insufficient and unconnected. There is no prima facie reason to suppose, for example, that an accomplished literary critic would be in any special way suited to a life of politics. Literary criticism, as a speculative/theoretical manner of thinking, is, arguably, politically useless. But there may be other manners of thinking, equally theoretical in nature, that are peculiarly appropriate for the affairs of the public realm. According to some readings of the *Republic*, Plato thought this to be the case. The philosopher's awkward stumbling in the shadows of the cave, in the world of affairs, is only a temporary condition ultimately overcome by the intellectual habits and skills provided by a philosophical education. The First Iteration, by implication, would deny this for no very obvious reason. A life of theoretical speculation and a life of political wisdom are simply assumed to be conceptually distinct, empirically separable, and even mutually antipathetic.

It should by now be clear that, in my opinion, the First Iteration does not stand up very well to critical scrutiny. But despite this, despite serious intellectual deficiencies, the fundamental and underlying premises of the First Iteration continue to have for us a strong prima facie plausibility. We share with Lewis/Katzenbach the intuitive belief that abstract intellectual endeavor does not translate comfortably or straightforwardly into the world of affairs. We believe that judgment in politics is not reducible to, is perhaps not even correlated with, the ability to understand, formulate, and evaluate arguments of theoretical or analytical substance. This belief, although widely held, is also typically ill defined, and is not at all self-evidently true. In order to assess it adequately, and to evaluate thereby the constitutive presuppositions of the First Iteration, we would require, above all, a thoroughgoing *analysis* of judgment, common sense, and political wisdom as these things relate to, and differ from, the theoretical intellect.

To be sure, the very appropriateness of such an analysis will be doubted. For, as we have seen, many of those who would insist on the distinction between intellectuality and practical wisdom would insist also on the ineffability of the latter; insofar as it is something quite different from analysis, it is itself resistant to analysis. Indeed, the very project of this book—to provide a systematic theoretical account of judgment in politics—will be regarded by some as a kind of category mistake, a theoretician's attempt to explain that for which no theoretical explanation is possible.

In my view, however, purchase on the question of judgment requires, at the very least, something better than the First Iteration. It requires, that is, a more compelling iteration that allows for a clearer grasp of the kinds of questions we have encountered thus far. How are certain key terms—"intellect," "theory," "judgment," "common sense," "political wisdom," among many others—to be understood? Exactly what is the putative distinction between theoretical reason and practical or political wisdom, and can this distinction survive critical analysis? Do such notions as judgment, common sense, and political wisdom describe a unique and specifiable feature of human thought? What role can or should abstract speculation play in matters where good judgment seems necessarily to be paramount? Does the distinction between judgment and theoretical speculation mean that the former is somehow unavailable for philosophical analysis? The First Iteration raises questions such as these, but does not provide satisfying answers to them.

I suspect that very few people hold exclusively to the First Iteration, but again, I am convinced that it accurately evokes a variety of views that many of us do hold from time to time. Moreover, these views have been articulated by thinkers of great historical importance, and presently enjoy a good deal of philosophical currency, at least in certain circles. Some such perspective, emphasizing the distinction between the habits and criteria of the theoretical intellect and those of practical common sense, is deeply embedded in Western political culture and merits something more serious than the rather laconic and undisciplined account that we have considered thus far. Our immediate goal, then, is to discover or develop a more satisfying version of this general point of view, and it is with this in mind that we begin by turning briefly to certain influential and enduring themes in the history of political thought.

I

A central feature of Platonic philosophy is the distinction between knowledge and right opinion. While this distinction receives explicit treatment in only certain of Plato's works—for example, *Phaedo* (64d–66a), *Republic* (476d–480b), *Meno* (85c–86d)—I think some such notion is at least implicit in a great many of the dialogues, not simply in the rather treatiselike efforts of the (presumably) later period but also in those early elenctic and aporetic inquiries that ask the question, What is *F*? When, for example, Socrates pursues with Euthyphro the question of piety, or with Laches the question of courage, or with Protagoras the question of virtue, it is clear that the goal is not simply to be correct but to be correct because one has genuine knowledge. Perhaps it really is pious for Euthyphro to bring his father to trial, but it seems that there will be always something unsatisfying about the deed until and unless Euthyphro himself comes actually to *know* that it is the pious thing to do.[5]

Some such distinction between knowledge and mere opinion has been an important feature of Western thought since the classical age,

5. For a general discussion of Plato's thought in this regard, see Nicholas P. White, *Plato on Knowledge and Reality* (Indianapolis: Hackett, 1976).

as reflected above all in the philosophical tradition.[6] That tradition, moreover, gives us reason to think that the distinction is at once ever-present, apparently self-evident, and yet painfully elusive. Recent and recurrent controversies surrounding the so-called Gettier cases, for example, suggest strongly that we think we know quite well what genuine knowledge is but are, nonetheless, hard-pressed to provide a satisfying account of it that distinguishes it clearly from, say, true justified belief.[7]

For our purposes, these thickets can be happily avoided. It will suffice to say that the distinction in question involves the notion that knowledge, as opposed to right opinion, is in principle capable of giving a compelling account or justification of itself; that such an account proceeds in terms of intellectual standards of right and wrong having some kind of privileged status; that those standards are associated with notions of demonstration and proof; that a demonstrated or proven proposition is to be regarded as true insofar as it describes accurately some feature of reality; and that the accuracy of such a description is thought to be not purely accidental, but the result of a genuine understanding of how things really are. In this sense, the possibility of knowledge is often thought to presuppose at least the following: (1) there is a real world sufficiently stable and accessible to permit its being known; (2) some humans have faculties that allow for access to that world; and (3) there are therefore and in principle certain reliable and indubitable data that provide secure foundations upon which all particular knowledge claims can be based. Such foun-

---

6. My present focus is on knowledge of propositions—*knowing that*—rather than *knowing by acquaintance* ("I know John") or *knowing how* ("I know how to drive a car"). These distinctions are complex, and to the degree that *knowing that* in fact subsumes the other two, they are of course covered by what follows. As the reader will discover, the difference between *knowing that* and *knowing how* will be central to the argument of Chapter 4.

7. See, for example, Edmund L. Gettier, "Is True Justified Belief Knowledge?" *Analysis* 23 (June 1963), pp. 121–123; Michael Clark, "Knowledge and Grounds: A Comment on Mr. Gettier's Paper," *Analysis* 24 (December 1963), pp. 46–48; Ernest Sosa, "The Analysis of 'Knowledge that p,'" *Analysis* 25 (October 1964), pp. 1–3; Keith Lehrer, "Knowledge, Truth, and Evidence," *Analysis* 25 (April 1965), pp. 168–175; Alvin I. Goldman, "A Causal Theory of Knowledge," *Journal of Philosophy* 64 (June 1967), pp. 357–372; Fred Dretske, "Conclusive Reasons," *Australasian Journal of Philosophy* 49 (May 1971), pp. 1–22; and Marshall Swain, "Epistemic Defeasibility," *American Philosophical Quarterly* 11 (January 1974), pp. 15–25.

dations are frequently thought to include sense perceptions and the laws of thought or logical inference, though on some accounts they may also include religious revelations (as in St. Thomas's treatment of divine law) and certain immediate, necessary, indisputable intuitions (as in Descartes's *cogito*). Knowledge is objective, context-free, and non-solipsistic to the degree that we can presuppose foundations of this kind.

Now it seems certain that most of the major authors of the Western political tradition—or, rather, those whose works make up the presently accepted canon of political theory—are foundationalists in at least two respects. First, they see political life as properly governed by knowledge rather than opinion and conclude, therefore, that those who engage in political activity ought to do so knowledgeably. Second, they see political thought itself, that is, their own theoretical enterprise, as equally so governed. The paradigm case here is Plato (at least as traditionally interpreted), for whom the principles and procedures of philosophy apply both to philosopher/kings and to those philosophers or dialecticians who engage in discussions about philosopher/kings. But in Hobbes as well, the indubitable observations and deductions that produce the correct principles of a commonwealth are also the means by which political actors—citizens and sovereign—are to establish and carry out their civic obligations or prerogatives. In each case, the theorist and the practitioner, whatever their differences, are conceived of as operating in terms of the general foundations of knowledge, such as they may be; theoretical speculation and political action are, in this quite restricted sense, of a piece. Classical teachers of natural right, stoics, medieval casuists, utilitarians, theorists of positive liberty, scientific socialists, social Darwinists, contemporary moralists interested in justice and liberalism—nearly all such writers have insisted on or presupposed some kind of foundationalism for both political thought and political life.

There are, however, certain important exceptions, authors of substantial influence who have engaged in elaborate and sustained thought and writing about political matters but who have tried to do so without relying on, and perhaps even in explicit defiance of, foundations of knowledge. These authors have pursued the notion that there is a very great difference between having systematic knowledge and having political wisdom. Either they have presupposed that there are no foundations of knowledge and hence no truly knowledgeable people, or else they have presupposed that for some reason such foundations simply do not obtain in the world of political and social affairs. In either case, they view politics as an activity that must be undertaken to some degree without reference to and without relying primarily on traditional forms of theoretical speculation. It is an activity that proceeds in ways that cannot be reduced to the standard methods of science and philosophical inquiry, that operates not at all in terms of fixed and defensible rules or algorithms, and that necessarily lacks the reliability or certainty characteristic of genuine knowledge.

Politics may be the queen of the sciences, but it has also been theoretically parasitic, understood in terms of human endeavors that seem somehow more basic, more secure, and more easily comprehended. Not surprisingly, the dominant foundationalist traditions assimilate politics to one or more of those various other enterprises that depend upon and presuppose some kind of objective knowledge, for example, philosophy (as for Plato), theology (St. Augustine), mathematics (Hobbes), empirical science (Condorcet), behavioral science (Bentham), and the like. The antifoundationalist authors that we now have in mind similarly describe politics in nonpolitical terms; but they look to a quite different array of human endeavors from which to derive images or models of—metaphors for—political life. Three such images in particular seem to stand out: politics as a *quest for glory*, politics as *deliberation*, politics as *aesthetic*. Together these images can help us generate a quite complex and challenging iteration—a Second Iteration—of the notion that judgment, common sense, and political wisdom constitute a distinct and autonomous sphere of human life, independent of and largely unrelated to the realm of the theoretical intellect. It will be useful now to examine briefly this iteration in each of its three forms in order better to understand the thesis in question and also to provide some sense of its historical importance. The exposition will be ultimately critical, since I believe that the philosophical (though not historical) significance of the Second Iteration resides primarily in its failure to provide a persuasive and satisfying account of political judgment.

Perhaps the most important efflorescence of the idea of *politics as a quest for glory* occurred among the Italian city-states of the *quattrocento*, reaching a quite full and complete expression in the early part of the following century. There is some debate among scholars about how and why this took place, and the exact timing is itself a matter of dispute. That it took place, however, is quite clear, and there is considerable agreement that it represented a genuine break with orthodox medieval thought.

According to that orthodoxy, politics is a matter of making laws, and that, in turn, is a matter of utilizing human reason to discover and imitate laws of nature, which reflect and describe necessary truths about the world. The human lawmaker performs his function properly only if he has knowledge of those necessary truths, and this kind of knowledge is something that humans, as creatures of reason, can aspire to. It is true, according to St. Thomas's account, that the actual making of human laws is a practical matter, concerned with things that are "singular and contingent," and as a result cannot have "that inerrancy that belongs to the demonstrated conclusions of sciences." But this hardly leads to the irrationality of lawmaking. Though fallible, lawmaking nonetheless properly strives to achieve the certainty of science and is to be judged good or bad to the degree that it is based on a genuine knowledge of natural law.[8] The result has been aptly called an "intellectualistic" approach to public law and politics.[9]

This intellectualistic approach runs into problems, however, when confronted with the thesis that the world is perhaps not so orderly, that history unfolds not according to some discernable plan, and that those "singular and contingent" things that St. Thomas referred to do not in fact accommodate the idea that the world of affairs is part of an all-encompassing, rational, and systematic structure. One certainly finds an awareness of such problems in the medieval period itself. The orthodoxy that I have described is only arguably that. Thus, mirror-for-princes writings, such as the *Policraticus,* as well as the related rhetorical tradition, exemplified by the work of Brunetto Latini, do indeed reflect a genuine appreciation of the particular and the ineffable in politics. But a systematic and self-conscious approach to such questions only begins to emerge clearly, I would argue, in the work of a transitional figure like John Fortescue. If the change in political perspective from the Middle Age to the Renaissance was not altogether radical and abrupt, a certain important shift of emphasis, reflected in Fortescue's thought, was nonetheless both characteristic and quite decisive.

8. St. Thomas Aquinas, *Summa Theologica,* Q. 90, A.1; Q. 91, A. 2 and A. 3. See also, *On Princely Government,* Chapters 1 and 2.

9. A. P. d'Entrèves, *The Medieval Contribution to Political Thought* (New York: Humanities Press, 1959), pp. 21ff. Also, A. P. d'Entrèves, *Natural Law* (London: Hutchinson University Library, 1970), pp. 45ff.

As a theorist of English constitutionalism, Fortescue was naturally inclined to consider not just timeless principles of law but also issues peculiar to England and its history. It is true that his basic views on knowledge are deeply rooted in a kind of Thomistic foundationalism. Specifically, for Fortescue the truth of any claim is proven by showing that it is a necessary logical consequence of some indubitable principle or set of principles. Such principles, moreover, are "universals . . . acquired, as it is taught in the second book of [Aristotle's] *Posteriora,* by induction through the senses and the memory." Thus, all rational knowledge is entirely a matter of objective, reliable inductions along with their logically deduced consequences or implications, and according to Fortescue, this is as true for law and jurisprudence as it is for mathematics.[10]

But Fortescue's *De Laudibus,* a dialogue between a Prince of Wales and a Lord Chancellor of England (an office Fortescue held), is largely devoted to a systematic comparison of English law with Roman or civil law; it is an important early effort at comparative jurisprudence. As such, it focuses naturally on the idiosyncrasies and peculiar, "praiseworthy" virtues of English law, that is, those very aspects that resist a universal, rationalistic justification. Indeed,

> Customs and statutes together make up the particular laws of any nation. Now if these are to claim rational justification they must be rationally deducible. . . . [B]ut it is not their deducibility or their rationality which gives them their particular character. To understand wherein the laws of England differ from those of Rome or France, we must investigate not their rationality—since therein they are identical with those of other nations—but the ways in which the principles of justice have in them been applied to the special character and circumstances of England. In short, English law contains—as does the law of any nation—an element other than the purely rational.[11]

---

10. Sir John Fortescue, *De Laudibus Legum Anglie* (Cambridge: Cambridge University Press, 1942), Chapter 8. My discussion follows that of J. G. A. Pocock, *The Machiavellian Moment* (Princeton: Princeton University Press, 1975), pp. 10–11. Fortescue's debt to St. Thomas is explicit. See *De Laudibus,* Chapter 9, and also his *The Governance of England* (Oxford: Oxford University Press, 1926), pp. 109–110, 117.

11. Pocock, *Machiavellian Moment,* p. 13

The implications for political theory are substantial:

> [T]here exists in his [Fortescue's] thought an inexpugnable level
> at which it appeared that English law was not rational, in the
> sense that it could never be reconstructed by the performance of
> any deductions. Other forms of intelligence than the philosophi-
> cal, which took longer to learn because they were based on expe-
> rience rather than study, had been at work in its making. . . . It
> is therefore hard for Fortescue's prince to legislate, for the reason
> that there is no scientific method of determining what particular
> laws will suit particular peoples or particular situations.[12]

The problem is to provide an account of what those "other forms of
intelligence" might be, and this is a problem that rests at the center of
political thought during the Italian Renaissance—a world generally
"unruffled by religious upheavals" and hence comparatively well
suited to "the exploration of new realms of inquiry without the distrac-
tion of endless religious polemics."[13]

Political thought in this setting emerged out of a stark and troubling confrontation with "fortune's capricious tyranny."[14] The traditional Christian view that the world is created and guided by a divine
intelligence and is therefore meaningful, orderly, and rational ceased
to have much plausibility for many Renaissance writers on politics.
Instead, things were thought to operate in large part through *fortuna*,
through arbitrary and unpredictable chance. The political actor and
political thinker face a world of "random movements" and "inherent
instability,"[15] and this in turn deflects attention away from universal
principles and general historical patterns and toward the peculiar features of singular and discrete events and institutions located in particular historical settings.[16]

It would be wrong to overstate this sense of aimlessness and caprice. Pitkin's formulation seems especially plausible:

12. Ibid., pp. 17–18.

13. Sheldon Wolin, *Politics and Vision: Continuity and Innovation in Western
Political Thought* (Boston: Little, Brown, 1960), p. 197.

14. Quentin Skinner, *The Foundations of Modern Political Thought*, vol. 1
(Cambridge: Cambridge University Press, 1978), p. 96.

15. Wolin, *Politics and Vision*, pp. 213 and 221.

16. Pocock, *Machiavellian Moment*, p. 53.

Machiavelli presents a political universe that is neither a fixed, sacred order nor a meaningless accident. We face neither eternally valid abstract standards of right that it is our duty to try to approximate, nor inevitable forces moving to predestined goals, nor yet a randomness that defies understanding and effort. . . . [I]t is like dealing with a person—a difficult, unpredictable, even sometimes malevolent person, to be sure, and one larger and more powerful than ourselves, but nevertheless a being with personality like ours, intention like ours, moods and foibles like ours, open to influence to some extent and in some ways, just as we are, yet never wholly within our control.[17]

At the same time, it would be wrong to underestimate the degree to which such views created a set of considerations dramatically different from those confronting medieval political theorists. How could one say anything intelligible and reliable in a world where "all human affairs are in constant motion and cannot remain fixed"? Where fortune "blinds men's intellects when she does not wish them to check her gathering might"? Where "men are able to assist Fortune, but not to thwart her"? Where the insatiability of human desires necessarily leads to "unending discontent" and relentless political instability? Where the intractable, perpetual flux of human affairs "renders all policies doubtful"? Where chance is "the mistress of one half our actions," while the other half come about through our own undetermined, perhaps inexplicable free wills? Where events are governed by a capricious, often malevolent force "who has no lack of ways for aiding her friends and thwarting her enemies"? Where political life is ever at the mercy of this "unstable and fickle goddess [who] often sets the undeserving on a throne to which the deserving never attains"? Where (to give Guicciardini his say) the fool is often successful and the wise man often unhappy and tormented, and where "there can be no determined truth of future contingencies."[18] How indeed could

17. Hanna Pitkin, *Fortune Is a Woman: Gender and Politics in the Thought of Niccolo Machiavelli* (Berkeley: University of California Press, 1984), p. 292.

18. Niccolo Machiavelli, *Discourses*, Book 1, Chapter 6; Book 2, Chapter 29; Book 2, Introduction; *The Prince*, Chapter 21; *Prince*, Chapter 25; *History of Florence*, Book 6, Chapter 4; *Tercets on Fortune*, 34. Here and elsewhere I rely on *Machiavelli: The Chief Works and Others*, ed. and trans. Allan H. Gilbert, 3 vols. (Durham, N.C.: Duke University Press, 1965). Guicciardini's remark is from his *Maxims and Reflections* (New York: Harper, 1965 [1530]), series C, nos. 60 and 58.

one theorize about and act in a "world having precious little in the way of a firm foundation for knowledge"?[19]

The most powerful response, of course, was to talk about *virtu* and to characterize *virtu* in terms of the quest for glory. While chance and caprice typically rule the world, some humans do have the capacity, at least for short periods, to gain the upper hand, to master *fortuna*, however briefly, and to establish in the political realm some kind of order which, though ultimately doomed to fail, nonetheless provides for a while something like the good life and thus stands as a monument to the extraordinary powers of the human spirit. To have built such a monument over and against fortune is to have earned glory, and that is about the most important thing that a person can achieve.

Exactly what such glory actually amounts to is, as we shall see, not entirely clear. But it is clear, at least according to the best-known account, that *virtu* is very different from traditional notions of moral virtue. Here, in part, is where we can locate Machiavelli's departure from the standard mirror-for-princes literature.[20] More important, *virtu* is also largely unrelated to, and certainly does not depend upon, orthodox philosophical speculation. Given that the world of affairs was thought to provide no foundation for knowledge, it is not surprising that political writers would denigrate those who aspire to any kind of speculative or theoretical certainty; and indeed, such a denigration—a denigration of the traditional life of rational contemplation—is central to the politics of *virtu*.

Thus, for example, in the famous fifteenth chapter of *The Prince*, Machiavelli seeks to distance himself from the methods of the philosophical tradition, complaining that "many have imagined republics and principalities which have never been seen or known to exist in reality" while insisting on his own intention "to go to the real truth of the matter" by examining how we actually live rather than how we ought to live. In the *Discourses* (Book 1, Chapter 10), when assessing those kinds of individuals who deserve praise and who should be imitated, intellectuals are ranked well below men of action, for example,

---

19. Wolin, *Politics and Vision,* p. 212.

20. See Felix Gilbert, "The Humanist Concept of the Prince and *The Prince* of Machiavelli," *Journal of Modern History* 11 (December 1939), pp. 449–483; Eugenio Garin, *Italian Humanism: Philosophy and Civic Life in the Renaissance* (Oxford: Basil Blackwell, 1965), p. 64; and Skinner, *Foundations of Modern Political Thought,* vol. 1, pp. 48 and 129ff.

founders of republics or kingdoms and men of military distinction. In the *History of Florence* (Book 5, Chapter 1), he calls philosophy itself an "honorable laziness" that infects cities with "great and dangerous deception" and sows the seeds of disorder and ruin. He supports this opinion with a story:

> When the philosophers, Diogenes and Carneades, came to Rome, sent by the Athenians as ambassadors to the Senate, Cato thoroughly realized this [the danger]; hence, seeing that the Roman youth began to follow them with admiration, and knowing the evil that such honorable laziness might bring upon his country, he made a law that no philosopher should be received in Rome. By such means [i.e., philosophy] countries come to ruin.

One doubts that Machiavelli, an active and industrious man, would find any kind of laziness to be truly honorable. Be that as it may, his view is that when philosophy enters the world of affairs, the consequences are necessarily woeful. Either philosophers know nothing or else their knowledge is, at best, useless. Some such opinion is shared by Guicciardini:

> How different theory is from practice. So many people understand things well but either do not remember or do not know how to put them into practice. The knowledge of such men is useless. It is like having a treasure stored in a chest without ever being able to take it out. (*Maxims and Reflections*, Series C, No. 35)

The more modest interpretation here is that such views simply privilege the *vita activa* over the *vita contemplativa*, thereby embracing the legacy not of Greece but of Rome, where "the impulse to soar above temporal events was never present."[21] The detached intellectual is engaged in "largely trivial enquiries" and is basically incapable of dealing effectively with real social and political issues.[22] The stronger version is that philosophy and theoretical speculation are utterly irrele-

---

21. Mark Hulliung, *Citizen Machiavelli* (Princeton: Princeton University Press, 1983), p. 132. See also Pitkin, *Fortune Is a Woman*, pp. 103ff. For the historical background, see Hans Baron, *The Crisis of the Early Italian Renaissance* (Princeton: Princeton University Press, 1966), Chapter 3; also, Garin, *Italian Humanism*, Chapter 3. For a rather different view, see Leo Strauss, *Thoughts on Machiavelli* (Glencoe, Ill.: The Free Press, 1958), pp. 291ff.

22. Skinner, *Foundations of Modern Political Thought*, vol. 1, pp. 106–107.

vant and even dangerous to political life, and that political man—both actor and thinker—must operate entirely without the benefit of abstract, universal truths, that is, "without constructing or even presupposing a philosophy."[23]

Either way, the man of *virtu* finds himself alone, so to speak, in his battle with *fortuna,* able to rely only and entirely on his own practical resources. How does he do it? On what does he base his decisions, his judgments? Deprived of theoretical or speculative knowledge, how does he know what is the prudent thing to do? Given his apparently inevitable ignorance, how can he select the most effective policy, distinguish what works from what does not, make those choices that will control the excesses of fortune, at least for a while? To repeat our earlier question, are there "other forms of intelligence" whereby the political actor, though lacking in systematic, rational knowledge, can nonetheless act wisely?

I believe that there are two general answers to this question, neither of them very satisfying. The first involves simply the brute assertion that to have *virtu* is by definition to have a certain kind of political wisdom, that is, a certain foresight and a certain insight that enable one to act effectively in the world of affairs. The true prince is one who just *knows* when to go to war and when not, when to crush his opponents and when to coopt them, when to be merciful and when to be cruel. Such knowledge is not sufficient for *virtu;* it must be wedded to other traits, including courage, boldness, energy, imagination, resilience, ambition, and the like.[24] Nonetheless, it is a necessary condition. For without *fore*sight (the ability to intuit consequences) and *in*sight (the ability to penetrate beyond the surface appearances of persons and events), the man of action would hardly be in a position to know how and when to utilize prudently his other remarkable attributes; hence, he wouldn't really have *virtu* at all. This formulation simply asserts, then, that the man of *virtu* by definition has "it," but it also fails to provide any independent account of what "it" might be.

23. Wolin, *Politics and Vision,* p. 211. Of course, it would be absurd in the extreme to say that this kind of anti-intellectualism was characteristic of Italian Renaissance culture in general. See, for example, Garin, *Italian Humanism,* Chapter 6.

24. See John Plamenatz, "In Search of Machiavellian *Virtu,*" in *The Political Calculus,* ed. Anthony Parel (Toronto: University of Toronto Press, 1972), pp. 157–178.

How does one acquire this kind of political wisdom? In what does it consist? How does it compare with other, more familiar types of knowing? How can one be sure that one really does have it? At times, Machiavelli seems to imply that the proof of the pudding is in the eating; success itself is adequate evidence of *virtu,* a sufficient indication that one has that special knowledge. But of course, Machiavelli also recognizes and emphasizes that many successes arise not from *virtu* but from pure luck. Given the lack of an independent description of the kind of knowledge found in *virtu,* it is hard to know how one would be warranted in making such discriminations.

The second answer to the question of other forms of knowledge involves notions of experience, history, and imitation. Though he was many things, Machiavelli was importantly a historian, and it seems that he felt a study of history could provide the kind of knowledge required of princely *virtu.* History, after all, is replete with tales of greatness and of folly. One need only examine the events of the past in order to uncover some of the ways of mastering *fortuna.* In part, then, political wisdom comes through imitation: "A prudent man will always choose to take paths beaten by great men and to imitate those who have been especially admirable, in order that if his ability does not reach theirs, at least it may offer some suggestion of it" (*The Prince,* Chapter 6). But history also yields a knowledge more systematic than this, for a thorough study of the past can generate not simply exemplars but also principles for governing effectively. In a sense *The Prince* is nothing other than a compendium of such principles: a ruler should listen to advice only on matters he explicitly asks about, militias are always better than mercenary armies, princes should not worry about being called miserly, and the like. The sum of these precepts may be said to comprise Machiavelli's new "political science," a truly realistic and useful kind of inquiry based not on airy musings about virtue but on a deep acquaintance with history. Of course, actual experience is probably the best teacher. But experience is not easy to come by, and often the lessons it teaches come too late to be of use. A systematic study of history can generate examples to be imitated and rules to be followed, all of which provide a kind of wisdom or knowledge that, although less good than actual experience, is still far superior to that offered by philosophy, at least with respect to public affairs.[25]

25. For a striking treatment of Machiavelli's "political science," especially with respect to the role of the scientist or advisor, see Harvey C. Mansfield,

It is at this point, of course, that the knowledge of the political actor and that of the political thinker dovetail. The thinker—the historian—can convey the lessons of history with particular clarity and insight, so that the actor can come to see what it is that should be imitated. But indeed, theory and practice are actually even closer than this. We know that Machiavelli himself was a man of action and that he "refused to permit himself the dissociated so-called detachment of the intellectual."[26] His own historical inquiries were informed by and bound up with the insights he gained as a political actor. Thus, the wisdom or knowledge involved in *virtu* can only be generated by the historically inclined actor and/or the action-oriented historian. Again, the result in each case is a set of exemplars and precepts which together provide the kind of knowledge necessary for ruling.

It is not easy to know what to make of this position. If the study of history is to generate principles of effective political action, then one needs at a minimum some procedure by which the events of the past can be apprehended, classified, and understood accurately, and this in turn would seem to presuppose a method and a theoretical vocabulary according to which particular cases are identified reliably as being of this or that type. The truths of history are not self-evident. Some princes succeed through *virtu*, others through mere luck. How does the historian confidently distinguish the one case from the other? Presumably one utilizes concepts that are or ought to be defined in such a way that their features can be observed in particular instances, and presumably these instances offer data the relevant features of which can be observed accurately and known truly. But in the case of Machiavellian *virtu*, we have neither useful concepts nor useful data. Let us consider this more closely.

Conceptually, *virtu* is importantly a matter of learning from history. If Lorenzo di Medici is to be a true prince, this means in part that he will learn the lessons of Francesco Sforza. But if Sforza was a true prince, he presumably learned the lessons of some previous true prince who, in turn, had learned the lessons of some previous true

---

Jr., "Machiavelli's Political Science," *American Political Science Review* 75 (June 1981), pp. 293–305. On Machiavelli's privileging of history over philosophy, see Bruce James Smith, *Politics and Remembrance: Republican Themes in Machiavelli, Burke, and Tocqueville* (Princeton: Princeton University Press, 1985), pp. 96ff.

26. Pitkin, *Fortune Is a Woman*, p. 18.

prince, and so on. Those who learn from history are those who learn from those who learn from history. We are in a vicious circle. Exactly what is it that is learned? What are the lessons? Of course, one can assert that *virtu* is a matter of courage, boldness, energy, and the like, and that these are what history teaches. But without a clear and *independent* account of such things, it is most unlikely that we would know how to look for and recognize them. It is doubtful that one can find such an account in the pages of Machiavelli.

As for data, Machiavelli seems to have thought that the life of Sforza, among others, provides a clear, observable case of *virtu*. But was Sforza really a man of courage, boldness, energy, and the like? How would we make such a determination? To the degree that the elements of *virtu* are simply defined as "the kinds of things characteristic of Sforza," we face a tautology in the most pejorative sense. To the degree that they are not independently defined at all, we have no way to answer our question. In either case, it is not clear that Machiavelli provides a sufficient justification for conclusions about Sforza in particular and about history in general; again, the truths of history are not self-evident.

Machiavelli claims that one should imitate the man of *virtu*. But how does one know exactly whom to imitate? To answer this question adequately would surely require some general account or theory of princely *virtu*, a method of analysis, and an epistemological warrant for correctly identifying and distinguishing particular cases. But all of this could emerge only from a study that would be highly speculative, involving abstract, universal principles, and hence would be the result of a contemplative endeavor not very different from the kind of thing that Machiavelli, following Cato, would want to ban from cities as subversive. Indeed, such an endeavor would be, in effect, a philosophical/scientific inquiry roughly as understood and practiced by Plato, who developed a sophisticated theory of ruling based on a rich conceptual apparatus that could then be used as a standard against which to judge particular cases accurately. Of course, Machiavelli claims to be doing no such thing, and we can well believe him. He claims further that the political world, governed as it is by the whims of *fortuna*, does not permit a reliable, accurate analysis of that sort. But then the question persists: Exactly what kind of knowledge does he have, and what kind of knowledge can the man of *virtu* acquire?

Doubts of the sort expressed by Hannah Arendt appear to be persuasive: "In my opinion the scientific character of Machiavelli's theories is often greatly exaggerated."[27] Indeed, one is led to the conclusion that the true prince does not have rational knowledge at all but has, rather and at best, some kind of inexplicable gift or knack, a peculiar genius that defies analysis, an awareness that resists discourse.[28] In a standard (albeit arguable) formulation, a person has knowledge if the following three conditions obtain: (1) there is a fact about the world, *p;* (2) the person believes that *p;* (3) the person is justified in having that belief.[29] In Machiavelli's account of *virtu,* conditions 1 and 2 might hold, but condition 3 does not, since princely "knowledge" seems to defy anything that would qualify as justification.

The result is a kind of mysticism. The image is of a world filled with "occult signs and mysterious portents, decipherable by auguries, and haunted by unpredictable *Fortuna* . . . a political universe inhabited at its very center by magic."[30] No mere philosopher, no rational human, could operate successfully in this kind of world. Politics is an "art," and the actor who would decide wisely must have the inexplicable, miraculous gifts of a great artist. Indeed, what is required is a hero having virtually superhuman abilities that, as such, resist rational analysis. According to Pocock, this is clearly true of the prophet and the legislator, each of whom is attempting "a task beyond normal human powers." But a supernatural or occult ability of some sort seems to be required for *virtu* and political wisdom per se, for "it could be that since, as some philosophers hold, the air about us is full of intelligences—and these through their natural abilities foreseeing future things and having compassion on men—these spirits warn men with such signs, so they can prepare for resistance" (*Discourses,* Book 1, Chapter 56). If in fact the man of *virtu* has knowledge, it is a type of knowledge that relies on no discernable foundations, and hence transcends any kind of coherent, rational description.[31]

How then can the political thinker, convinced of the fundamentally ineffable character of political knowledge, nonetheless formulate

27. Hannah Arendt, "What Is Authority," in *Between Past and Future* (New York: Viking, 1959), p. 136. See also, Hulliung, *Citizen Machiavelli,* pp. 155ff.

28. Wolin, *Politics and Vision,* p. 216.

29. See Jonathan Dancy, *Introduction to Contemporary Epistemology* (Oxford: Basil Blackwell, 1985), p. 23.

30. Wolin, *Politics and Vision,* pp. 210–211. Also, *Discourses,* Book 1, Chapter 56.

31. Wolin, *Politics and Vision,* p. 216.

and convey at least some notion of what that knowledge is all about? One plausible line of thought argues that Machiavelli in effect has no philosophical or discursive pretensions, properly understood, and that his method of presentation—his method of thought—is primarily imaginative, figurative, and literary. If politics is an art, then the political thinker—the true political connoisseur—must be an aesthete. Thus, we are told that "Machiavelli is an artist as much as he is an historian."[32] His writing is steeped in metaphor, in allusion, and in irony.[33] His methods are fundamentally literary, and his precise intentions are often "obscured by his love of paradox."[34] Indeed, "he was less concerned with the explanation of facts than with making an impressive argument."[35] According to Federico Chabod, Machiavelli relied on "the sudden flash of intuition, identical with that of the great poet, who in any single event detects the ever-recurring workings of a universal process that is part and parcel of the human story."[36] And further,

He is not, then, primarily a logician, working from principles from which, by a continuous process of reasoning, rigorous and slavish, he deduces a complete "system." He is first and foremost a man of imagination, who sees *his* truth in a flash, with blinding clarity. . . . Machiavelli, in common with the greatest politicians— who, like him, so resemble the artist in that their logic and their dogma are completely subordinate to their intuition—has what may literally be termed initial inner "illuminations," immediate, intuitive visions of events and their significance. . . . Such, then, is the genius of Machiavelli—a potent genius, peerless in the realm of political thought, consisting entirely of sudden, immedi-

---

32. Strauss, *Thoughts on Machiavelli,* p. 45; see also Joseph Kraft, "Truth and Poetry in Machiavelli," *Journal of Modern History* 23 (1951), pp. 109–121; and George Feaver, "The Eyes of Argus: The Political Art of Niccolo Machiavelli," *Canadian Journal of Political Science* 17 (September 1984), pp. 555–576.

33. See Skinner, *The Foundations of Modern Political Thought,* vol. 1, p. 131; and Hulliung, *Citizen Machiavelli,* p. 98.

34. Skinner, *Foundations of Modern Political Thought,* vol. 1, p. 131.

35. Felix Gilbert, *Machiavelli and Guicciardini: Politics and History in Sixteenth-Century Florence* (Princeton: Princeton University Press, 1965), pp. 166–167.

36. Federico Chabod, *Machiavelli and the Renaissance* (Cambridge: Harvard University Press, 1958), p. 129.

ate flashes of insight, coupled with an almost miraculous natural dynamism and the manner and imagery of a great poet.[37]

When confronted with a world bereft of natural law, steeped in particularity, and ruled by capricious fortune, the political thinker/ political actor seeks glory in miracles—in inexplicable flashes of insight and sudden illuminations that far transcend the "slavishness" of logic. Presumably, such illuminations constitute a special kind of wisdom or knowledge. It is a knowledge that emerges out of the exceptional ambition for glory that is a mark of *virtu*. But as such, it is also a condition for the attainment of glory; and that attainment is, indeed, the other mark of *virtu*.

For those who believe in miracles, this view may have its appeal. But those whose interests are philosophical must look elsewhere for a satisfying account of prudence and political wisdom.

II

In the notion of politics as a quest for glory, one often finds intimations of those other images embraced by antifoundationalist traditions, namely, politics as deliberation and politics as aesthetic. With respect to the latter, we have now seen how the life of *virtu* can be likened to a life of artistic creativity and, similarly, how a treatise or discourse on *virtu* can be compared to the work of a "great poet." Machiavelli himself wrote poems in the conventional sense; and if his poetry is not outstanding, there are many indeed who would rank *Mandragola* and *Clizia* among the great comedies. It is not surprising then that he would produce accounts of *virtu* rich in the kinds of figurative or metaphorical materials that the subject matter itself seems to require. If the very notion of *virtu* demands a fundamentally aesthetic formulation, Machiavelli was evidently quite well prepared to provide it.

As for deliberation, there is also the undeniable fact that Machiavelli was in some sense, and at some point, a republican. Exactly how far his dispositions went in this direction is of course a matter of considerable dispute. In some interpretations, he was fundamentally agnostic on all such questions, essentially indifferent as between monarchy and republicanism, a professional political operative willing to

---

37. Ibid., pp. 142–147, passim. Chabod's view is endorsed by Gilbert, *Machiavelli and Guicciardini*, pp. 322ff.

work for whomever was in power. Others demur, claiming that his deep loyalty was to republicanism and that *The Prince* was an aberration produced by a man desperate to return to the world of affairs, however that world may have been governed. At least one recent essay claims that *The Prince* was actually an ingenious and artful effort of republican inspiration to overthrow Lorenzo de Medici by secretly and intentionally giving him terrible advice.[38]

Be that as it may, it is clear that Machiavelli's greatest work, his *Discourses on Livy,* is written about and for republics, and that part of its goal is to translate the notion of princely *virtu* and political wisdom into terms compatible with republicanism. One result, of course, is the historically important idea of civic virtue or civic humanism. This notion harks back to selected themes in Aristotle's *Politics,* and its reemergence in the Italian Renaissance preceded by some time the arrival of Machiavelli. We should also say that Machiavellian republicanism does not comport in all respects with more modern notions; its picture of the good citizen attributes to him little more than a simple sense of patriotism and a willingness to fight for his polity. Still, there are at least hints that a sound republican regime requires an active and engaged body of citizens involved in, among other things, *deliberation* upon social ends and political means.

Thus, in one reading, Machiavelli "at his best" emphasizes

> the activity of struggling toward agreement with and against each other, in which citizens take active charge of the historical process that would otherwise direct their lives in hidden ways. And that activity is no mere courtly dialogue, but a genuine conflict, in which needs and important interests are at stake. Without passion and struggle there can be no liberty, but only reification, habit, and drift. . . . The struggle must be kept open and public, rather than clandestine and private. It must involve a genuine appeal to principle, to what is reasonable and what is just.[39]

Another commentator claims that the *Discourses* show a genuine "appreciation on Machiavelli's part of the political capabilities of the masses."[40] Renaissance thought in general presupposed that the polity

38. Mary Dietz, "Trapping the Prince: Machiavelli and the Politics of Deception," *American Political Science Review* 80 (September 1986), pp. 777–799.

39. Pitkin, *Fortune Is a Woman,* p. 300.

40. Wolin, *Politics and Vision,* p. 229.

is "composed of interacting persons rather than of universal norms and traditional institutions"; it "depicted human social life as a universality of participation [whereby] one's virtue depended on cooperation with others."[41] In this sense, republicanism denotes not simply, or even primarily, a constitutional arrangement of powers and offices characteristic of a mixed regime. Rather, it embraces the idea of politics as rooted in a process of citizen participation, interaction, and deliberation undertaken by loyal and uncorrupted patriots exploring with one another different views about what does and does not conduce to the public interest.

These notions—politics as deliberation and politics as aesthetic— find no very explicit formulation in the Renaissance.[42] It may be that the time was not ripe for the articulation of such visions and that conceptions of interactive deliberation and art as unique and identifiable categories of human endeavor were not yet developed with sufficient clarity and depth. In any event, such notions certainly appear much more distinctly in quite later eras, for example, in the period following the triumph and tragedy of the French Revolution. With respect to political thought, there is of course an implicit if limited analogy between this period and the Italian Renaissance. In the earlier case, new, antifoundationalist images of political life—*virtu* and the quest for glory—emerged amidst the ruins of an older theological consensus, a consensus that had presupposed and insisted optimistically on the capacity of human reason to apprehend in some fashion important and ultimate truths about the world. In the other case, the optimism of Enlightenment rationalism in all of its various permutations had been shattered, or at least seriously shaken, by the extraordinary facts of the Terror and its aftermath; again, one result was the development or rediscovery of certain antifoundationalist notions of what political life was or ought to be like: for example, politics as deliberation and politics as aesthetic. In each case, the aim was to provide an account of politics and political wisdom that separates it from—renders it independent of and unconnected with—the habits,

41. Pocock, *Machiavellian Moment,* pp. 74–76, passim.

42. Thus, Pitkin's account, quoted above, in fact strikes me as rather generous. She actually presents little hard evidence to show that Machiavelli held such views about civic participation. Her findings are, perhaps, more in keeping with the spirit rather than the letter of Machiavelli's writings.

dispositions, rules, and assumptions of the abstract, theoretical intellect, now discredited.

The most substantial modern formulation of the republican ideal emphasizes *politics as deliberation,* understood as a distinctive process of human interchange aimed at generating a reliable and defensible consensus regarding the public's interest. One important model for this kind of activity was thought to exist in the New England town of the early nineteenth century, an association "so perfectly natural that, wherever a number of men are gathered, it seems to constitute itself as a town (*commune*)."[43] According to the ideal of the New England town, decisions are made through an ongoing process of mutual consultation. Officials explain to their fellow citizens the particulars of an issue; the urgency of the case and the various means of dealing with it are discussed and debated; a decision is made through a democratic process in which each citizen "is an equal part of the sovereign entity and participates equally in the government."[44] The New England town thus embodies in a particularly vivid way what Tocqueville elsewhere calls "the general theory of association," which conceives of civil and political organizations not simply as intermediaries between people and central government but as communities that develop in citizens the skills and habits of discussion and public-spirited cooperation. In such voluntary associations, "feelings and ideas are recruited, the heart is enlarged, and the human spirit is developed only by the reciprocal action of men upon one another. I have shown that this action is almost nonexistent in democratic countries. It must therefore be artificially created. And this can only be accomplished by associations."[45] Indeed, in the New England town, otherwise unrelated people become, in effect, friends who are able to rely on one another for mutual understanding and mutual aid and who can exchange diverse and conflicting opinions in a context of tolerance and cooperation.[46]

Now there can be no doubt about the importance of this model

43. Alexis de Tocqueville, *De la Démocratie en Amérique,* in *Oeuvres Complètes* (Paris: Gallimard, 1961 [1835]), vol. 1, p. 58.

44. Ibid., p. 63.

45. *De la Démocratie,* vol. 2, p. 116.

46. For a discussion of friendship in Tocqueville, see Roger Boesche, *The Strange Liberalism of Alexis de Tocqueville* (Ithaca: Cornell University Press, 1987), pp. 152–156.

for Tocqueville. His political thought emphasizes the peculiar and unprecedented perils inherent in modern democratic culture. These perils include, perhaps above all, a grave threat to genuine individual freedom. In Tocqueville's account, freedom is a matter of self-mastery, and this itself emerges only through a kind of communal process in which individuals come to understand, accommodate themselves to, and learn to utilize effectively the social and cultural contexts that in fact make them who they are. Unfortunately modern democratic culture proposes an alternative and seriously defective notion of freedom, one that views individuals as naturally discrete and separable entities related to one another only through conventional, artificial practices rooted largely in considerations of convenience. This is, for Tocqueville, a kind of conceptual error, but its consequences are tangible indeed.[47] Among other things, it conduces to a world where genuine freedom and self-mastery are gradually replaced by a kind of personal isolation in which individuals, socially and politically cut off from one another, stand defenseless in the face of society's great, central institutions.[48] In the premodern world, there could be no such threat, for there the individual was never alone; a person's identity and actions were utterly dependent upon and bound up with social/communal structures. In modernity, on the other hand, only something like the New England town can recreate that older sense of mutuality and interdependence, thereby preventing or at least delaying the seemingly inexorable deterioration of the social bond.[49]

47. Such a reading appears to stamp Tocqueville unequivocally as an idealist; a conceptual or intellectual error—an ideological error—causes serious, nonideological disruptions. But there is, of course, the further question of where that conceptual error came from in the first place, and I see no reason to think that Tocqueville's formulation would be inconsistent with a strongly materialist approach to that issue, of the sort offered by, say, C. B. Macpherson.

48. *De la Démocratie*, vol. 2, pp. 114ff. See also Pierre Manent, *Tocqueville et la Nature de la Démocratie* (Paris: Julliard, 1982), pp. 82–83; Jean-Claude Lamberti, *Tocqueville et les Deux Démocraties* (Paris: Presses Universitaires de France, 1983), pp. 195ff; Jean-Claude Lamberti, *La Notion d'Individualism Chez Tocqueville* (Paris: Presses Universitaires de France, 1970), pp. 40–41; Marvin Zetterbaum, *Tocqueville and the Problem of Democracy* (Stanford, Calif.: Stanford University Press, 1967), pp. 42, 59, 69, and 89; and Boesche, *The Strange Liberalism of Alexis de Tocqueville*, pp. 139ff.

49. For a discussion of free democratic association as a substitute for the

The political practices of the town empower individuals by bringing them together in contexts that encourage mutual recognition, cooperation, and interdependence. It is here that they learn to be citizens: "Town meetings (*Les institutions communales*) are to liberty what primary schools are to science; they teach men to enjoy the peaceful practice of it (*l'usage paisible*) and accustom them to make use of it."[50] Presumably Tocqueville's view is that the practice of deliberation instructs one in the art of deliberation; the skills of discussion, compromise, and consensus-building are acquired on the job, so to speak. We may well have our doubts about this; practice does not necessarily make perfect. It is nonetheless clear that Tocqueville saw in the New England town both a defense against the despotic, centralizing tendencies of modern democratic culture and also an instrumentality for encouraging and sustaining a kind of vital and self-directed citizenship.

At first blush, such a view seems not at all exceptional. It resonates with populist themes that have long been an established part of the modern political tradition. But there are also philosophical implications here that, upon analysis, prove to be rather less straightforward. In particular, the notion of politics as deliberation seems to presuppose a certain fundamental indeterminacy or intractability with respect to questions of a political nature. If there were clear answers to such questions, and if certain selected individuals had more-or-less direct access to those answers, then the utility and desirability of the deliberative process would be much more difficult to justify. Why discuss and debate a question when the answer has already been well established through logical or scientific demonstration? If the epistemological claims of the theoretical intellect—as variously outlined by, say, Plato, or St. Thomas, or Condorcet—are in fact applicable to matters of public consequence, then the importance of democratic deliberation as an approach to such matters becomes uncertain indeed.

Thus, there are and can be in the New England town no philosopher-kings, no divinely endowed social patriarchs, no members of

---

medieval commune, see Hans Arnold Rau, *Demokratie und Republic: Tocquevilles Theorie des Politischen Handelns* (Würzburg: Königshausen and Neumann, 1981), pp. 63ff. See also, Zetterbaum, *Tocqueville and the Problem of Democracy*, pp. 39, 91ff.

50. Tocqueville, *De la Démocratie*, vol. 1, p. 59.

an elite, universal class of political experts—no one, in short, whose knowledge of public affairs is in any obvious way privileged or superior. Were there to be such a person, someone who had the answers, then it is hard to see how the town meeting would serve any but a purely legitimating function, and since such a function could only be accomplished if it were not widely recognized as such, the result would be to rob citizen deliberation of much of its dignity. This cannot have been Tocqueville's intention. As a man of aristocratic background and sensibility, he surely recognized that humans differ substantially in their capacity for the intelligent pursuit of civic ends. But he must have believed also that the *demos* has, at least in principle, something of value to contribute to the public discussion. And this, again, seems to suggest that questions of public import do not admit of demonstrable, scientific solutions; there is no *rational knowledge* of them in the strict sense.

We may suggest, then, a fundamental, if also quite limited, kinship between Tocqueville and Machiavelli. For each, the activity of politics cannot properly be reduced or assimilated to that of the abstract theoretical or rational intellect. Politics is an autonomous enterprise that involves something quite different from the knowledge to be gained from philosophical or scientific investigation, traditionally understood. As we have seen, Machiavelli's view is that political wisdom is attendant to heroic *virtu* and the quest for glory, and manifests itself ultimately as a kind of indefinable knack. Such ideas are not at all foreign to Tocqueville, who wrote often and admiringly of "great nations" and their "love of glory."[51] But his larger emphasis is on deliberation and, presumably, on a particular and distinctive kind of wisdom that emerges out of citizen interaction. We may well wonder what kind of wisdom that is, and Tocqueville does not provide a very clear answer. But presumably individuals engaged in such deliberation bring to their enterprise a special sort of awareness—unscientific, nonlogical, atheoretical—regarding political or social matters. That awareness involves a certain sensibility, insight, or vision about the social world and a certain tangible, albeit ill-defined, intuition concerning what conduces to the public interest. More briefly, we may say that democratic citizens, properly so conceived, have common sense. This is what

51. For example, ibid., p. 164. See Zetterbaum, *Tocqueville and the Problem of Democracy*, p. 29.

enables them to interact productively with one another and allows a certain measure of plausibility and reliability in their deliberations and judgments. The "commonness" of common sense offers a basis for discussion and agreement, and the "sensibility" of it provides a capacity to see and to understand what it is that should be agreed to, what is the prudent thing to do. In the absence of scientific proof and logical demonstration, the town meeting must presuppose something like common sense; without it, the deliberations of the citizens would be aimless, uninformed, and utterly devoid of any claim to political wisdom.

We know that early in the second volume of *Democracy in America* Tocqueville does talk about the kind of "philosophy" practiced by the Americans. But this philosophy does not amount to very much *qua* philosophy. It is inchoate, inexplicit, largely tacit, and a far cry from the kinds of systematic inquiries envisioned and undertaken by Plato, Descartes, Newton, and the like. It is hardly philosophy at all but, rather, a set of unreflected dispositions based on a kind of homespun pragmatism. It is, again, a matter of common sense and is thought to be a requisite, and also a characteristic feature, of American deliberative politics.

Thus, Tocqueville's citizen, like Machiavelli's man of *virtu,* has a certain insight, a knack or faculty—a certain political wisdom—that is quite unrelated to the abstract, theoretical intellect. And like Machiavellian *virtu,* this idea of a common sense raises as many questions as it answers. From where does such a faculty arise, and how can it be cultivated in individuals? Assuming that some people have it in abundance and others do not, how do we ascribe it reliably to this or that person? What is the nature of the wisdom that common sense offers, and exactly how does this wisdom differ from the kind of knowledge produced by systematic theoretical speculation? How are the claims of common sense to be justified; what is it that takes the place of logical proof and scientific demonstration? How are disagreements resolved? Indeed, what precisely is the nature of the deliberations and discussions that occur between people purported to have common sense? How do they persuade one another? How do they prove their claims when the very notion of proof is under suspicion?

I believe that one looks in vain for Tocqueville's answers to such questions. Certain alternatives do suggest themselves, but none are very attractive. As we have seen, Tocqueville argues that the activity of deliberation itself develops and nurtures deliberative skills; one acquires common sense in the act, as it were. But of course, this can hardly count as an independent analysis of common sense, nor does it provide any reason to believe that common sense or political wisdom—whatever it may be—is in fact acquired this way. Does Tocqueville think that *anyone* who tries to have common sense will therefore have it, and in more-or-less equal measure? And does he believe that all those who try to have it will therefore come to agree about matters of public consequence? Our intuitions tell us that individuals differ substantially in the capacity for good judgment and that they are also likely to disagree seriously with one another from time to time. Such intuitions presuppose independent criteria regarding right and wrong, correct and incorrect, such that we can indicate with some justification whose views are prudent or wise and whose are not. No such formulation can be found in Tocqueville's writing.

One response is to suggest that democratic deliberation, properly understood, is praiseworthy and authoritative on what might be called moral/procedural grounds, and that no further, substantive justification is required. Thus, decisions made in a town meeting will be legitimate if citizens bring to their deliberations an equal measure of patriotism and good intentions. This seems to be part of what Rousseau had in mind, at least in the *Social Contract,* where he claims that "the general will is always right and tends to the public advantage; but it does not follow that the deliberations of the people are always equally correct. Our will is always for our own good, but we do not always see what that is; the people is never corrupted, but it is often deceived" (*Social Contract,* Book 2, Chapter 3). Presumably, Rousseau is saying that the decisions of the democratic sovereign, properly constituted, may indeed be incorrect, inaccurate, and uninformed, and may as a result have unfortunate consequences; the general will can be in error with respect to the facts of a case. But insofar as it is formulated out of the best of motives—out of a genuine concern for the common good—its decisions will always be morally legitimate.

This may well be Tocqueville's view, but if so, it fails to do justice to the question of judgment and common sense. For that question presumes not simply—perhaps not at all—an elevated moral position. Rather, it presupposes a special and privileged *epistemological* status such that the citizens truly have political wisdom and hence can indeed see what is the prudent course of action. In Rousseau, the good judgment and insight that sovereign citizens lack is provided in part by the Legislator: "a great and powerful genius" who has "a superior intelligence beholding all the passions of men without experiencing any of them" (*Social Contract,* Book 2, Chapter 7). Rousseau's solution is thus, in a certain sense, Machiavellian, relying as it does on the exceptional *virtu* or wisdom of a single individual.[52] No similar solution is found in Tocqueville's America. Prudence, good judgment, and political wisdom are attributed to the citizenry through an unargued leap of faith, and this attribution is made without providing a very clear account of what good judgment actually is.

I believe that Tocqueville's instincts on the question of political judgment are extraordinarily sound. His image of prudence as being somehow dialogic in nature, as emerging out of and yet, at the same time, providing a certain critical purchase on a common sensibility, as embodying a capacity for mutual insight rooted in linguistic communication and exercised by a republican "aristocracy" of the whole—all of this describes with perhaps unrivaled accuracy the outward appearance of political judgment. What is almost entirely missing, however, is its inner articulation: its ontology, its rationale, its underlying nature. The full account of this articulation presupposes a great deal that is quite foreign to Tocqueville, and must await a more comprehensive and satisfactory approach to political judgment, as proposed in Chapter 4 below.

III

As we have seen, the notion of politics as deliberation presupposes a certain skepticism with respect to standard forms of rational/theoretical analysis. Political issues cannot accommodate philosophical or scientific scrutiny; the hopes of the Western rationalist tradition, broadly defined, do not translate into the public realm. In the face of this,

---

52. Rousseau's explicit focus is, to be sure, on the legislator as founder, rather than as ruler: "The legislator is the engineer who invents the machine, the prince merely the mechanic who sets it up and makes it go" (*Social Contract,* Book 2, Chapter 7). Elsewhere in the *Social Contract,* of course, leadership and practical wisdom are provided by the government—as distinguished from the sovereign—and Rousseau is, in the end, rather indifferent as among democratic, aristocratic, and monarchical forms of government (e.g., Book 3, Chapter 9).

the republican, fearing a truly radical skepticism or nihilism, turns to common sense. Democratic citizens, devoid of philosophical or scientific skills and dispositions, nonetheless bring to the world of deliberation a kind of shared insight or intuition that permits a relatively clear if unsystematic picture of what conduces to the public interest.

Again, Tocqueville provides little reason to believe that the individual citizen in fact has such a common sense, and he certainly offers no account of what it is such that we could identify it when we see it. Still, the idea of a common sense is extremely attractive, and we can easily see why. Although most of us have our doubts about the degree to which abstract theoretical speculation can provide answers to political questions, we also tend to resist the kind of intellectual and, indeed, political anarchy that a truly radical skepticism might imply. We believe that in politics some answers *are* better than others, even if those answers cannot be proven in the traditional manner. One way to sustain this belief, then, is to posit the existence of a common sense, attribute it to the citizens of a republic, and find in it the more-or-less reliable and objective roots of political wisdom and good judgment.

An alternative approach, which we have already encountered briefly in our Machiavelli studies, is to focus on the so-called "art" of politics. According to this approach, politics is essentially an aesthetic enterprise, and political wisdom is a matter of creativity and taste. Like artistic judgment in general (at least on some influential understandings), judgment in politics is unscientific, yet involves standards and criteria that permit, nonetheless, a certain kind of clear justification. This saves us from nihilism. Just as we know that some art is good and some is bad, even if we cannot quite prove it, so we are entitled to believe that there are genuine truths to be found in the art of politics.

The most substantial formulation of such a view emerges out of a critique not simply of the abstract rational intellect but also of Western bourgeois culture in general, including the political culture of liberal democracy. According to this critique, rationalism is an ideology that serves to cut us off from that which is truly substantial and worthwhile in human existence. It does this by privileging otherworldly things—Platonic forms, for example—far above mere mortal existence, giving them a special kind of substantiality and truthfulness and denigrating thereby the significance of our earthly, empirical lives. The "tyranny of reason" is a sign of human decadence, a "pathologically conditioned" prejudice that amounts to a rejection of life itself, and establishes in its place a torpid and enervating existence, lived in a mausoleum filled with "conceptual mummies." The ideology of reason is, therefore, morally decadent. But it is also epistemologically corrupt, for it seriously distorts, rather than contributes to, our understanding of the world itself. "[O]ur prejudice in favor of reason compels us to posit unity, identity, continuity (*Dauer*), substance, cause, tangibility (*Dinglichkeit*), being"—when in fact all of those things are chimerical in a world hopelessly and inevitably beset, or perhaps set free, by contradiction and chaos.[53] Indeed, rationalism mixes up the most fundamental epistemological categories—cause and effect—perversely and persistently substituting the one for the other, thereby undermining entirely any effort to understand what the world really is about.[54]

Nietzschean philosophy thus "turns out to be an attack on the very foundations of logic and rational thinking."[55] Whereas antifoundationalism is an implicit theme in, say, Machiavelli's writing, in Nietzsche it is an explicit, fundamental, and defining presupposition. Ultimately, his work stands as "an unequivocal condemnation of everything that is 'fixed, canonical, and binding.' . . . Words make no sense unless they are arranged in a way that makes them 'fixed, canonical, and binding,' yet once they are so arranged, they cease to communicate with 'life.' "[56]

An important consequence of the cult of reason is the inevitable political, social, and intellectual mediocrity of modern life. "*La science* belongs to democracy," Nietzsche tells us, and democracy necessarily entails a mass society that enshrines the "right to stupidity," promotes a kind of "instinct-atrophy of the spirit" (*Instinkt-Verkümmerung des Geistes*), destroys community by setting individuals in opposition to one another, and "devours all seriousness for really spiritual things."[57] This applies both to liberal democracy, which is nothing but a "reduction [of

53. *Götzen-Dämmerung*, in Friedrich Nietzsche, *Werke: Fünfter Band* (Leipzig: A. Kröner Verlag, 1930), pp. 92–97, passim.

54. Ibid., pp. 107–112.

55. Richard Lowell Howey, *Heidegger and Jaspers on Nietzsche* (The Hague: Martinus Nijhoff, 1973), p. 68.

56. J. P. Stern, *A Study of Nietzsche* (Cambridge: Cambridge University Press, 1979), pp. 189–190.

57. Nietzsche, *Götzen-Dämmerung*, pp. 130, 149, 124, and 122, respectively. With respect to science, Nietzsche did have his so-called "positivistic" tendencies, for example, in *The Will to Power* (especially Book 3), but the relationship of his views on science to those on art remains very unclear. See Howey, *Heidegger and Jaspers on Nietzsche*, pp. 34ff.

the human individual] to the herd animal," and to socialist democracy, which is merely an undignified and slavish philosophy of envy.[58] It is true that, in *Ecce Homo*, Nietzsche identified himself as the "last antipolitical German," and one certainly finds nothing like a systematic political philosophy in his work. Indeed, it has long been common to think of his writings as having no important connection with politics whatsoever. Such a view, adopted by Heidegger but also reflected in the efforts of Walter Kaufmann and others to separate Nietzschean philosophy from the practice of Nazism, seems to overlook a great deal. For Nietzsche's work contains not only numerous political dicta (for example, in Section 8 of *Human, All Too Human* and Sections 8 and 9 of *Beyond Good and Evil*), but also profound implications of a political nature. And among these are a quite radical rejection of the constitutional/egalitarian tradition that emerges out of Enlightenment rationalism and a call, however vague, for what Nietzsche himself referred to as "a great politics."[59]

There is obviously a sense in which Nietzsche might well ridicule everything that Tocqueville stands for—local democracy, careful and prudent deliberation, dutiful citizenship. But, as in the case of Machiavelli and Tocqueville, I believe that there is here a certain limited kinship. Nietzsche seeks a "noble culture" free from the mediocrity of modern mass society; Tocqueville too regretted the demise of aristocratic brilliance and achievement, which had involved "a certain elevation of the human mind," and lamented the inevitable and prosaic blandness of a democratic world that would "divert the moral and intellectual activity of man to the production of comfort."[60] Like Tocqueville, Nietzsche prizes freedom highly, understands it as fundamentally a matter of self-mastery, and sees it threatened above all by the insidious, seemingly benign tendency toward equality or social

58. Nietzsche, *Götzen-Dämmerung*, pp. 159, 152.

59. See Tracy Strong, *Friedrich Nietzsche and the Politics of Transfiguration* (Berkeley: University of California Press, 1975), pp. 186–217. For a discussion of Nietzsche's politics, see Peter Bergmann, *Nietzsche: The Last Antipolitical German* (Bloomington: Indiana University Press, 1987), especially pp. 119–123 on liberalism and socialism. On Nietzsche's critique of "the modern democratic spirit," see Thomas L. Pangle, "The Roots of Contemporary Nihilism and Its Political Consequences According to Nietzsche," *Review of Politics* 45 (January 1983), pp. 45–70.

60. Nietzsche, *Götzen-Dämmerung*, p. 128; Tocqueville, *De la Démocratie*, vol. 1, pp. 255–256.

leveling.[61] Both agree that an older world, perhaps preferable, is nonetheless no longer retrievable, that to be a reactionary is to fight a losing battle: "[N]o one is free to be a crab. There is no helping it: one has to go forward."[62] And both see the role of the political thinker as essentially didactic and evocative, rather than argumentative or analytical; neither wrote systematic philosophy, though in Nietzsche's case the results are often more aphoristic and allegorical, and in Tocqueville's, more descriptive and historical.

But where Tocqueville chooses to go forward in the company of prudent and patriotic citizens, Nietzsche's choice is to rely on those individuals—in all likelihood but a few—whose tastes, sensibilities, and energies are quite different from those of the ordinary burger. In Nietzsche's writings, one encounters many metaphors and models for this kind of individual, but at least one important formulation is the image of the creative, artistic genius. Art is, above all, the "need to transform [things] into perfection"; its goal is to remake the world, or rather our understanding and vision of it, into something free from flaws. Such an endeavor requires, on Nietzsche's account, a deep knowledge of the world itself: the artist "possesses to the highest degree the instinct for understanding and divining . . . " Of course, this knowledge is hardly a matter of propositions and proof. To the contrary, it is explicitly and exclusively the result of the greatest unreason: "Intoxication (*der Rausch*) must first have intensified the excitability of the entire machine: no art comes before that happens." The artist, in the act of creation and understanding, must enjoy a "feeling of great power and fullness." His senses heightened, his desires swollen, "overladen with strength," he comes to see what nobody else sees, observes the world with a penetration and degree of comprehension that no one else can match. It is not the abstract detachment of philosophy and science but, rather, the excessive, intoxicated desire of art that leads initially to the truth.[63]

61. Nietzsche, *Götzen-Dämmerung*, p. 159; Tocqueville, *De la Démocratie*, vol. 2, pp. 324ff.

62. Nietzsche, *Götzen-Dämmerung*, p. 165.

63. Ibid., pp. 71–74, passim. For a useful qualification of this kind of interpretation, see Mark Warren, "Nietzsche and Political Philosophy," *Political Theory* 13 (May 1985), pp. 193–195. Warren argues that Nietzsche "condemned liberalism, democracy, equality, and the rights tradition. He glorified heroic leaders and looked forward to a future aristocracy in which

What kind of truth is this? In Nietzsche's view, our purchase on the world is always shaped and constrained by the horizon—the social and intellectual context—in which we find ourselves: "Nietzsche is saying that all knowledge is knowledge by a certain form of life and must then correspond to the particular 'horizons,' distortions, and simplifications that are made necessary by and define that form of life."[64] The "realm of theoretical reason" manifests, but fails to reflect upon, its own unquestioned, culturally based presuppositions. When it finds itself unable to deal with a recondite world that thoroughly resists systemization, it dissolves into nihilism and despair. The artist, on the other hand, is able to examine those unquestioned presuppositions, subjecting them to a kind of "genealogical" analysis that reveals them for what they are and that allows us to acknowledge and accept the partiality and cultural specificity of all truth claims. This is a liberating moment. It permits us to embrace the world more or less as it is, and hence to see that our illusions, however necessary and unavoidable they may be, are illusions nonetheless.

Among these illusions is the notion of the univocal, united self. Nietzsche's perspectivism is of a very radical nature. It claims not simply that the world can be approached in a multiplicity of ways, but that the self that knows the world is equally multiple, hence equally unfixed. The subject is a "container of multitudes."[65] It resonates with the inevitably rich variety of perspectives that compose, in part, its own genealogy, and that establish both the parameters and opportunities for knowledge of the world. The artist, peculiarly free from the prejudices of the "metaphysical self," has a unique and self-conscious insight into this condition, a unique capacity to embrace it not simply with equanimity but with enthusiasm.

Particularly useful in this respect is literary art, the tragic and the

---

the majority would be economic, political, and cultural slaves ruled by a caste of philosopher-legislators. He held that political arrangements should be judged only in terms of the spiritual and aesthetic achievements of their 'highest' types" (p. 185). But he denies that Nietzsche is an irrationalist, and emphasizes only Nietzsche's rejection of "traditional epistemological concerns."

64. Tracy Strong, *Friedrich Nietzsche and the Politics of Transfiguration,* p. 44.

65. Tracy Strong, "Texts and Pretexts: Reflections on Perspectivism in Nietzsche," *Political Theory* 13 (May 1985), p. 177. This is a typically intelligent essay that warns against the kind of epistemological approach to Nietzsche that I have taken.

poetic. Thus, "words are said to be the distant and distorted 'echoes of nervous impulses.' These 'echoes' or rudimentary elements are po-eticized and given coherence according to rules which are entirely invented by man. Thus, the relationship that obtains between words and the 'real world' is a metaphorical or aesthetic one."[66] The "truth" of the world is a human construct, composed of metaphorical interpre-tations: "what makes the world a world is that human beings take the metaphors and build. . . . The elaboration of metaphors into a framework—a working of art—gives us a world together."[67] Tragedy is perhaps uniquely effective in representing our metaphorical world to ourselves. It affords the tragedian an opportunity to mirror faith-fully that world in the metaphorical structure of the drama itself; and it affords the audience—a collectivity—the opportunity to understand the metaphorical world as a kind of collective undertaking.

Art is thus the way to knowledge, for the individual and for the community; all knowledge claims, properly understood, are essentially aesthetic and eventually manifest themselves in figurative language. Thus, Nietzsche disparages, partly on epistemological grounds, the idea of what he himself calls "theoretical man," as exemplified above all by Socrates. Socrates is "the archetype of the theoretical optimist," who insisted on the possibility of arriving at the truth of the world through rational methods and who claimed such an effort to be the most exalted of all human activities. For Nietzsche, the effort is doomed to fail. The scientist or logician who pushes his inquiry to its limits "sees to his horror how logic . . . curls around itself and bites its own tail—there comes then a new kind of knowledge, a tragic percep-tion that requires, to make it bearable, the refuge and remedy of art."[68]

Artistic endeavor also has powerful moral claims. The artist "en-riches everything out of [his] own abundance." What previously seemed prosaic and stale comes to life through the genius of the artist

66. Stern, *A Study of Nietzsche*, p. 184.

67. Tracy Strong, "Nietzsche's Political Aesthetics," in *Nietzsche's New Seas: Explorations in Philosophy, Aesthetics, and Politics,* ed. Michael A. Gillespie and Tracy Strong (Chicago: University of Chicago Press, 1988), p. 159. I ignore here the development over time of Nietzsche's views on these questions, which Strong treats briefly but very persuasively.

68. Nietzsche, *Die Geburt Der Tragödie,* in *Werke: Erster Band,* p. 130 [Section 15]. For an important treatment of Nietzsche and Socrates, see Werner J. Dannhauser, *Nietzsche's View of Socrates* (Ithaca: Cornell University Press, 1974).

and takes on a new-found dignity, even glory. This includes humanity itself. "In art, man takes delight in himself as perfection." The artist delineates, and also represents, the sublime, creative possibilities inherent in the human spirit. Perhaps above all, the artist exhibits the greatest moral courage and strength precisely in the act of depicting such courage and strength:

> What does the tragic artist communicate of himself? Does he not display precisely the condition of fearlessness in the face of the fearsome and questionable? This condition itself is a high desideratum: he who knows it bestows on it the highest honors. He communicates it, he has to communicate it if he is an artist, a genius of communication. Courage and composure in the face of a powerful enemy, great hardship, a problem that arouses dread (*Grauen*)—it is this triumphant condition that the tragic artist singles out, that he glorifies.[69]

We should note that Nietzsche's language, here and elsewhere, is martial. The virtue of the artist is the virtue of heroism, and of course it is in heroism—in war—that one attains true self-mastery, true freedom.[70]

The political relevance of artistic endeavor is often merely implicit in Nietzsche's writing. Again, his primary interests lie elsewhere, and his political thought, if that is even the right phrase, must be pieced together from rather disparate materials. But aesthetic experience is in fact central to the entire Nietzschean project, and this surely includes the realm of politics and society:

> [T]he activity of artists—traditionally seen as the makers of metaphors—and the aesthetic activity in general assume an entirely central position in the world. Art is in no sense esoteric or marginal, but becomes the human activity par excellence: it is creative existence. The "justification" of the world through "the aesthetic activity" is identical with the "justification" or meaning imprinted on the world through man the maker of linguistic conventions, that is, of a system of "metaphors."[71]

69. Nietzsche, *Götzen-Dämmerung*, p. 147.
70. Ibid., p. 159.
71. Stern, *A Study of Nietzsche*, p. 189.

In Heidegger's interpretation, Nietzsche sees the world as "a self-generating work of art" and understands "aesthetic existence" (*Künstlersein*) to be not simply a way of life but "the most revealing (*durchsichtigste*) way of life."[72] For this reason, according to Nietzsche, art is the only possible response or "counter-movement" (*Gegenbewegung*) to the "decadence" of modern religion, morality, and philosophy.[73]

It is but a short step to transport the image of the artist—energetic, penetrating, possessed both of deep understanding and great courage—from the purely aesthetic realm to the world of politics and society. Who better than a master of the "political art" to lead the struggle against the torpid, enervating vapidity of modern bourgeois life? What could be a more apt image for evoking the kind of insight and self-mastery required of the public realm? How could one better capture the peculiar features of political wisdom, namely, its irreducibility to traditional reason and method together with a unique appreciation of the vicissitudes of a deeply unstable world?

One upshot of all this is Nietzsche's notion of the "political genius," as manifested in his admiration for Caesar and other world-historical figures, and as applied, for a time, to Bismarck himself.[74] The political genius has a certain "nobility of style," and this in turn can be understood explicitly as an aesthetic quality:

> [T]he artist enclosed in the politician . . . is once more recognized for what he is: the posthumous brother of Dante and Michelangelo: and in truth, in view of the firm contours of his vision, the intensity, coherence, and inner logic of his dream, the depth of his meditation, the superhuman grandeur (*übermenschliche Grösse*) of his conception, he is like them and is their equal.[75]

Above all, the politician as artist has the capacity to understand the meaning of the collective metaphorical world that the community has created, and to transform that world into the realm of affairs. It is in this sense that Nietzsche comes to accept "aesthetics as the basis for

72. Martin Heidegger, *Nietzsche: Erster Band* (Pfullingen: Verlag Neske, 1961), pp. 82–85, passim.

73. Nietzsche, *Der Wille Zur Macht*, in *Werke: Sechster Band*, p. 533 [Section 794].

74. See Bergmann, *Nietzsche: The Last Antipolitical German*, pp. 33–34 and 181–184.

75. Nietzsche, *Wille Zur Macht*, p. 667 [Section 1018].

the political realm."[76] The peculiar intuition of the political genius is to perceive somehow the underlying figurative structure of the community's collective identity, and thereby to understand both the foundation of the collectivity and the nature of the truths that it presupposes.

Nietzsche would not, of course, be the first to conceive of social and political action in aesthetic terms. Numerous formulations in German Idealism, in the work of Schelling and Schopenauer, for example, prefigure such a move. But there is a sense in which Nietzsche's account, however inchoate, is also the most vivid. He proposes, with particular urgency, the characteristic claim that the sources of genuine political wisdom and leadership lie not in rationality as generally understood, but in a kind of insight into our unquestioned political presuppositions. There is, again, no possibility of proving the veracity of such insight, of demonstrating its truth through argument; like aesthetic truth, it involves nothing that could familiarly be called *foundational*. Political wisdom resists standard appeals to rational discourse and criticism; its claims are, in a manner of speaking, independent, autonomous, and self-sustaining.

Indeed, one might say that the truths of politics, like those of art, are both hopelessly obscure and entirely self-evident. They are obscure in that very few could ever have access to them; they are self-evident in that they are known by the privileged few, not on the basis of systematic discourse and analysis, but only and exclusively through a kind of immediate inspection. Of course, such an account presents a by now familiar problem. If we are ourselves among the few, then the truth of Nietzsche's formulation will be obvious to us; but in that case, we will also see the futility and absurdity of any attempt to demonstrate that truth rationally; hence we will make no effort to do so. If on the other hand, we do make such an effort, then this itself is a sure indication that we are not among the few; in that case, our effort is certainly doomed.

IV

The notions that we have been considering—*virtu*, deliberation, the aesthetic—may be said to compose a Second Iteration of our initial thesis regarding political wisdom. This Second Iteration has, I think,

76. Strong, "Nietzsche's Political Aesthetics," p. 162.

quite obvious advantages over the first. The First Iteration, even when suitably elaborated, merely asserted, without much clarification, the distinction between rationality, theory, and abstract speculation on the one hand, and good judgment, common sense, and political wisdom on the other. The Second Iteration provides, over and above this, a set of images and concepts in virtue of which the peculiar and distinctive character of political wisdom can be more keenly felt.

Political wisdom is either likened to or described as an instance of one or another kind of nonpolitical enterprise—glory-seeking, deliberation, or art. Each such enterprise is broadly familiar to us, and each is understood as having special and identifiable features. A rough awareness of these features provides us with a sense of, a feel for, the nature of the enterprise itself. To the degree that political wisdom is like one or more of these endeavors, it shares their features or qualities. Thus, to have a feel for *virtu*, deliberation, or aesthetic activity is to have a feel for what is involved in political judgment. This is not provided by the First Iteration, at least not to any great extent. The Second Iteration is, therefore, a considerable improvement. While it does not provide anything like a systematic, philosophical analysis, it does offer for our consideration a rather rich set of images, and these presumably allow for a much more vivid evocation of what it might mean to be a person of political wisdom.

The Second Iteration also provides a somewhat better reason for thinking that there is in fact a distinct faculty called good judgment or common sense. Machiavelli offers numerous putative instances of *virtu* in action; Tocqueville describes in some detail the actual operation of town government; Nietzsche adverts to the great aesthetic tradition of the West. In each case, practical ability is described in the context of real events and persons. These are said to exemplify a form of intelligence that is quite different from what we ordinarily associate with rational philosophy and science, but that seems to provide, nonetheless, a certain reliability and objectivity. It does so without invoking the kinds of "foundations" usually thought to be necessary for us to have knowledge. The prince, the virtuous citizen, the artist-hero—all seem somehow to know what they are doing, and this encourages us to accept the existence of a practical, judging faculty—modeled in terms of *virtu*, deliberation, or art—that differs from the rational intellect but is nonetheless able reliably to generate claims that are true.

These are powerful and extremely influential ideas. There are, nonetheless, ample reasons not to be satisfied. For the Second Iteration actually leaves us not much better off than we were before; if anything, our perplexities have multiplied. To begin with, the complex imagery of the Second Iteration presents a rather confused picture of what it means to have political wisdom. Our intuitions tell us that glory-seeking, deliberation, and aesthetics are quite different from one another in any number of ways. To say, then, that good judgment emerges out of democratic deliberation is very different from likening it to the actions either of princely *virtu* or creative genius; to identify political wisdom with the common sense of the citizenry is not the same as describing it in terms of the special talents of great and exceptional individuals. Upon inspection, it may turn out that these things are not so different after all, but to establish this would require an argument far more explicit and compelling than anything we have encountered thus far. The Second Iteration thus presents an interesting and influential but underspecified, quite diverse, and perhaps internally contradictory set of images; it fails, thereby, to provide a fully persuasive account of the nature of political wisdom.

Of course, it may be objected that this iteration is really an arbitrary and artificial construct entirely lacking in historical warrant, and that its deficiencies reflect not the works in question but the careless and unprincipled Frankenstein who created such a monster out of them. Now there can be no doubt that the interpretations offered thus far have been selective, and that my account of the connections and similarities between the writings of Machiavelli, Tocqueville, and Nietzsche do full justice neither to the works in question nor to their authors. I would note, however, that these connections and similarities are not wholly original with me and are by no means incompatible with the historical and textual evidence. Commentators have long noted affinities between Machiavelli and Tocqueville, and between Machiavelli and Nietzsche, and it is clear that both Tocqueville and Nietzsche greatly admired and were in some sense influenced by Machiavelli. Moreover, all three were certainly what Hannah Arendt called "political writers" rather than "political philosophers" (though each was also much more than that) who shared the project of depicting political wisdom as something different from, even opposed to, philosophical speculation. Our real question is whether this project has been, or can ever be, successfully completed.

But there is a much more serious difficulty with the Second Iteration. For I believe it can be shown that any effort to provide a mere "feel" for political wisdom is fundamentally misguided. Clearly, there are those who would argue that the notion of political wisdom can *only* be intuited, can only be "felt," since it defies any kind of systematic analysis. Political wisdom is, in this sense, rather like the concept *yellow:* it is known immediately and apart from any account of constitutive properties, functions, structures, and the like. I take it that to give someone who has not yet seen yellow a feel for yellow presumably involves presenting an array of examples (lemons, daffodils, school buses) that can be described reliably as yellow and distinguished from other examples (cherries, roses, fire engines) that happen not to be yellow. This presupposes that different people see the colors of these various objects—intuit or feel them—in roughly the same way. If this were not so, then yellow could not become a meaningful part of our conceptual and communicative apparatus.

The argument, then, is that this is also how one learns about judgment, common sense, and political wisdom. The political writer, unable to give a systematic account of that which defies description, presents pictures or images—historical, metaphorical, and the like—that stand as illustrations of the virtue in question. Upon encountering these images, readers, sharing certain basic intuitions, come to have a feel for what is involved, and hence come to know it even if they cannot then systematically give an account of it. The process requires of the political writer a special talent for the artful depiction of political wisdom, and this is a talent presumably possessed by Machiavelli, Tocqueville, and Nietzsche in great abundance.

As we shall shortly see, such a position has been taken up by various twentieth-century writers on political wisdom. I believe, however, that it is deeply problematic. The difficulty, in part, is that the political world is often characterized by serious conflicts precisely over what common sense is, who has wisdom, which decisions reflect good judgment, and the like. Such conflicts seem to be quite different from conflicts about, for example, the color yellow. There is no doubt that we do disagree about yellow. We disagree about various shades of yellow, about whether something is (say) closer to yellow than to orange, about which color is "more yellow" than another, and the like. But such disagreements actually presuppose those basic and widely shared intuitions that give us a feel for yellow in the first place; without those intuitions, disputes about marginal or difficult cases would be virtually unintelligible. If I say the object before us is yellow, and you say it is orange, we are not communicating intelligibly unless we agree in general about yellow and orange.

This kind of basic, immediate, intuitive agreement seems to be far less likely with respect to good judgment, common sense, and political wisdom. To my knowledge, no one has yet succeeded in pointing to a range of phenomena that unmistakably and self-evidently embody such virtues against which more marginal cases can be evaluated. There are, in the realm of political judgment, few if any lemons, daffodils, or school buses. Machiavelli, Tocqueville, and Nietzsche may think they have provided examples of this kind, but we can hardly accept their examples as self-evident and unarguable. People can and do disagree, for instance, about the abilities and merits of Francesco Sforza. When we think about more familiar cases, we discover that our disagreements are often deep and abiding. I think Harry Truman was the soul of good judgment; you find him a buffoon. Common sense tells me that vigorous tariffs are required to protect domestic industries; from your perspective, this is manifest folly. I regard the Supreme Court's decision in Baker v. Carr as wise indeed; you see it as deeply imprudent. Disagreements of this kind are the rule rather than the exception; they are recurrent, constitutive features of public life.

If this is correct, if there are few if any shared intuitions regarding the important features of such cases, then it is doubtful that a mere depiction of cases, however skillful and evocative, could reliably provide us with a feel for good judgment, common sense, and political wisdom. Our differing intuitions would very likely impel us to see or interpret individual cases in quite different ways. As a result, we would be apt to disagree sharply about which cases reflect political wisdom and which do not.

Yet, and this is a key point, we continue to have meaningful discourse about good judgment, common sense, and practical wisdom. The evident absence of immediate, intuitive agreement regarding such notions does not render conversation about them unintelligible. I think this suggests that they are actually quite different kinds of concepts from, for example, *yellow*. When I claim that the object before me is yellow, no one ordinarily asks me how I know that, what is it that makes it yellow, in what ways yellow differs from nonyellow, what are the constituent elements of yellowness, and the like. But with respect to matters of political wisdom, these are not only plausible questions; they are precisely the kinds of questions one expects. If I say that X is a person of political wisdom, then I must be prepared to answer such questions, and hence to defend or justify my claim about X with explicit arguments and evidence.

The Second Iteration offers very little in the way of systematic analysis. Indeed, it provides a conceptual muddle that calls for serious housecleaning. We have encountered notions of *virtu,* deliberation, and art that remain, beyond a certain point, inchoate and elusive, and that allegedly stand for a kind of political intelligence or knowledge the precise features of which continue to be a mystery. We have examined these various notions in order to clarify if possible our own conceptual apparatus, but the results have not been happy. We have relied heavily on such phrases as "good judgment," "common sense," and "political wisdom," but our purchase on these terms is hardly more secure than when we began. We may think we know what we are talking about when we employ such terms. But like Cephalus and Polemarchus, it is doubtful that our understanding of them would withstand an elenctic inquiry such that we could continue to use them with justifiable confidence and conviction. In the end, the Second Iteration is perhaps most useful in demonstrating, through its failures, just what it is that we require: explicit and direct efforts to establish the relevant distinctions, not through pictures and images, but through some kind of systematic conceptual account.

V

Students of contemporary political thought will know that such efforts have now been made and are available for our consideration. Perhaps the two most notable attempts of this nature emerge from what may be called, respectively, the theory of *politics as action* and the theory of *politics as conversation.* Each of these theories (to use that word somewhat loosely) is rooted in a direct and explicit effort to identify the characteristic and distinctive features of the political world as opposed to all of those other worlds that we inhabit—the social, the economic, the scientific. Each conceives of politics as a particular kind of endeavor that imposes upon us a more-or-less unique set of exigencies and opportunities. And each proposes to describe more directly than hitherto the features of a distinctive type of wisdom, knowledge, or intelligence uniquely suited to the requirements of political life.

These two theories are seriously disparate in many ways, and nothing could be more in error than to conflate them uncritically. But at least at the outset, and with respect to our own particular interests, we may identify in them certain basic shared dispositions.

To begin with, each is deeply committed to the view that rational philosophy, traditionally and broadly conceived, has little positive contribution to make to politics. In the theory of politics as action, this view manifests itself as a quite strict separation of the *vita activa* and the *vita contemplativa*.[77] A model of the purely contemplative life is said to have been established by Plato, who, in the sixth and seventh books of the *Republic*, described a philosophical existence devoid of anything that would distract the philosopher's attention from the pursuit of ideas. The concerns of the body, of the polity, of physical and social life—the concerns of the world itself—are, to the degree possible, kept radically separate from what is, as a result, an ascetic, sanitized, totally absorbing life of pure contemplation. If it seems unlikely that Plato was the first to conceive of such an existence, it is rather more probable that he delineated it with unprecedented clarity and power; and it is more likely yet that he, along with Socrates himself, was fundamentally responsible for the argument that a life of pure contemplation is not only different from but also superior to all other possible forms of mortal existence.

According to Arendt, this argument has been an important part of the Western intellectual and political tradition, both in its Greek and its Christian moods. It holds that a life of contemplation promises an encounter with truth rather than illusion, with eternity rather than transience, with knowledge rather opinion. Such a life provides both freedom from the feverish, unhealthy activity of the apparent world—"an almost breathless abstention from external physical movement"—and the kind of placid felicity that comes from constant communion with the "ancient truth of Being," a truth that "can reveal itself only in complete human stillness."[78] The intimate connection between abstract contemplation and truth means that those who wallow, so to speak, in the *vita activa* are doomed to a life of ignorance and error, of finitude and mortality, and hence of meaninglessness and dread.

This tendency to privilege contemplation over action amounts to a reversal of the prephilosophic or Homeric hierarchy that glorified a world of great deeds and words.[79] As such, it regards the realm of

77. Hannah Arendt, *The Human Condition* (Garden City, New York: Doubleday, 1959), p. 14–18.

78. Ibid., pp. 15–16. Also Hannah Arendt, *The Life of the Mind* (New York: Harcourt Brace Jovanovich, 1978), vol. 1, pp. 6–7.

79. Arendt, *Human Condition,* pp. 175–177.

human action itself as being properly subject to the demonstrated conclusions of detached, rational speculation. In Arendt's account, such a view manifests itself most notoriously in the great Platonic formula: "[W]hen kings become philosophers, and philosophers kings . . . " This formula understands the public realm to be simply one of the infinite regions of a universe that is, above all, rational and intelligible, through and through. Politics is part of the world, just like physics, or mathematics, or psychology. Since we come to know the world through rational contemplation, political knowledge must be acquired in the same way, through systematic philosophical analysis. There is, then, a rational, demonstrable truth to politics, as to everything else, and that truth is acquired by embracing, and living under the influence of, the principles and practices of rational philosophy.

According to Arendt, all of this amounts to a rather colossal category mistake, for it systematically and perversely ignores those considerations that make political life distinctive and that render it fundamentally opaque to the scrutiny of rational philosophy. In particular, the facts of political life are characteristically "haphazard." They are, as a result, ill suited to any intellectual discipline that requires and presupposes an orderly and coherent subject matter.[80] Let us consider these views more closely.

Arendt's work is based on central distinctions among the "private," the "social," and the "political" and, relatedly, among "work," "labor," and (political) "action." These formulations are outlined with extraordinary power in her writing; any effort to rehearse them here would be entirely superfluous.[81] For our purposes, we can be satisfied with noting that the concept of the political necessarily includes a sense of the volatility, incompleteness, and impermanence of public affairs. Among other things, the political realm is fundamentally "boundless":

> [A]ction, though it may proceed from nowhere, so to speak, acts into a medium where every reaction becomes a chain reaction and where every process is the cause of new processes. Since action acts upon beings who are capable of their own actions, reaction, apart from being a response, is always a new action that

80. Hannah Arendt, "Truth and Politics," in *Between Past and Future* (New York: Viking Press, 1968), p. 242–243.

81. On the concept of *society,* see Arendt, *Human Condition,* pp. 35–64; on "labor", pp. 72–94; on "work", pp. 119–138.

strikes out on its own and affects others. Thus action and reaction among men never move in a closed circle and can never be reliably confined to two partners.[82]

This boundlessness means that political action never occurs in an entirely manageable or reliable framework; as a result, it is most unlikely that any kind of political permanence or stability can be established with confidence. Boundlessness is also involved with what Arendt calls the "inherent unpredictability" of action. The consequences of a political act can never be foretold with precision: "its full meaning can reveal itself only when it has ended." Indeed,

> the strength of the action process is never exhausted in a single deed but, on the contrary, can grow while its consequences multiply. . . . The reason why we are never able to foretell with certainty the outcome and end of any action is simply that action has no end. The process of a single deed can quite literally endure throughout time until mankind itself comes to an end.[83]

Boundlessness and unpredictability are, for Arendt, constitutive features of political life, at least as we conceptualize it and distinguish it from other kinds of endeavor. According to Arendt, this implies further that politics is by definition a realm of novelty, freedom, and plurality. Novelty means that political action creates something new, something unexpected; without this, action would not be action at all but merely another predictable event in the single, ongoing, natural process of cause and effect. Freedom means that action is always undertaken by an autonomous actor or agent; without this, action would be indistinguishable from, say, animal behavior. Plurality means that humans are importantly different from one another in their dispositions, judgments, and ideals; without this, action would be unnecessary and unthinkable, since "signs and sounds to communicate immediate, identical needs and wants would be enough."[84] To the degree that we have a concept of politics as a distinctive, isolable kind of human endeavor, it must have these features; they are precisely what make it what it is. Without them, politics would simply dissolve into some other type of endeavor, for example, what Arendt calls "work" or "labor."

82. Ibid., p. 169.
83. Ibid., p. 209.
84. Ibid., pp. 156ff.

Of course, it may be that novelty, freedom, and plurality are all illusory, and that we humans are merely higher-order animals trapped in a hermetic web of stimulus and response. This would mean only that there is no such thing as politics. But if there *is* such a thing as politics, then by definition it must have the kinds of characteristics that we have just described.

The upshot is that, for Arendt, the procedures of philosophical speculation, the quest for what she calls "rational truth," are deeply inimical to politics.[85] Among other things, rational truth is inherently coercive, hence incompatible with the freedom of political action. Logical or mathematical proofs, for example, cannot be the results of debate and consensus; they do not emerge out of free agreement.[86] Rather, they are true in and of themselves, and when we encounter such a truth, we are uniformly *forced,* upon pain of incoherence, to acknowledge and accept it. Plurality, of course, is unthinkable for all philosophical realists, since rational truths must be true for everyone. Nor can such truths be said ever to be really new, unexpected, and unanticipated. A new truth of reason, properly speaking, is merely a further delineation or extrapolation of established truths, something thought to be implicit in them, to be already contained in them and hence every bit as old as they are. The novelty of the new truth is merely apparent, a result of contingent factors that prevented people from observing it; it cannot really be novel, however surprised we are to observe it.

Rationalism in politics, therefore, is incoherent in one of two ways:

1. If it does indeed succeed in establishing the universality of a rational truth, then it extirpates the possibility of politics. Politics will have been eliminated if humans decide to think of the world as entirely subject to intelligible, natural laws that can be discovered and proved. For in such a world, the defining characteristics of political life— novelty, freedom, and plurality—can have no place. I take it that Arendt's aim in this respect is not to demonstrate from a God's-eye point of view whether or not the world really is rational, through and through; any such question is inherently irresolvable, since none of us can take a God's-eye point of view. Her aim, rather, is to ask what are the consequences of our *believing* that everything is reducible to such

85. Arendt, "Truth and Politics," pp. 232ff.
86. Ibid., p. 240.

a rational truth; and at least one consequence is that we would have to give up our commitment to and interest in politics, properly understood.

2. If, on the other hand, political rationalism fails to cleanse the world, as we understand it, of its boundlessness, unpredictability, and freedom, then it is doomed to misconstrue the facts of politics, such as they may be. For if we cling to our intuitions regarding the inevitable disorder of the public realm, then we will always at some point be disappointed with a rationalistic analysis that understands the world in terms of boundaries, predictability, and order.

There is much in this account that is paralleled by what I have identified as the theory of politics as conversation. This theory is similarly rooted in a quite insistent and systematic separation of political practice and philosophical inquiry. It emphasizes

> the necessity of keeping philosophy unencumbered with the mood and postulates of practical experience, and the necessity of a world of practical experience without the interference of philosophy. . . . From the standpoint of practical experience there can be no more dangerous disease than the love and pursuit of truth in those who do not understand, or have forgotten, that a man's first business is to live.[87]

Indeed, the consequences for political endeavor are stated here with perhaps unequaled candor: "It is not the clearsighted, not those who are fashioned for thought and the ardours of thought, who can lead the world. Great achievements are accomplished in the mental fog of practical experience. What is farthest from our needs is that kings should be philosophers."[88]

As before, the argument derives from an understanding of the putatively distinctive features of political life. In *Experience and Its Modes,* a book of astonishing brilliance, Oakeshott claims that political or practical experience is concerned with a peculiar and unique kind

87. Michael Oakeshott, *Experience and Its Modes* (Cambridge: Cambridge University Press, 1985), p. 320. See Benjamin R. Barber, "Conserving Politics: Michael Oakeshott and Political Theory," *Government and Opposition* 11 (Autumn 1976), p. 448.

88. Oakeshott, *Experience and Its Modes,* pp. 320–321.

of fact, practical fact.[89] Practical facts are, above all, unstable. The facts of science, to pick a contrasting case, are necessarily thought of as fixed and unchanging; without this, science would be impossible. Practical facts, on the other hand, are by definition fluid and elusive: "practical activity assumes a world of facts which is not merely susceptible of alteration, but which has change and instability as the very principle of its existence." If there were no such facts, if everything could be known with a kind of permanent and universal certainty, then practice would not be practice. It is in the very nature of the practical or political, then, that it operates in a realm the particulars of which are understood to be perpetually shifting, evasive, and ephemeral. Oakeshott elsewhere writes: "In political activity . . . men sail a boundless and bottomless sea; there is neither harbour for shelter nor floor for anchorage, neither starting-place nor appointed destination." Or again, the world of politics "is neither fixed nor finished; it has no changeless centre to which understanding can anchor itself. . . . Everything is temporary."[90]

As with Arendt, it is doubtful that Oakeshott is interested in making claims about how the world really is. If he is frequently thought of as a latter-day Burke, and if his political views actually owe more to Hobbes, his general approach to philosophy is rooted in a kind of

89. Oakeshott's terminology changes substantially in his later writings. In particular, the word "practice" comes to have a much wider application. But while the new terminology may be rather clearer and more cogent than the old, there is—at least for our purposes—a basic doctrinal constancy in his work. See, Josiah Lee Auspitz, "Individuality, Civility, and Theory: The Philosophical Imagination of Michael Oakeshott," *Political Theory* 4 (August 1976), pp. 269ff.; and Jeremy Rayner, "The Legend of Oakeshott's Conservatism: Sceptical Philosophy and Limited Politics," *Canadian Journal of Political Science* 18 (June 1985), pp. 316–323. I have chosen to emphasize without argument the continuity of Oakeshott's positions at the risk of making certain exegetical errors regarding particular terms.

90. Michael Oakeshott, "Political Education," in *Rationalism in Politics* (London: Methuen, 1981), pp. 127–128. See also Michael Oakeshott, *On Human Conduct* (Oxford: Oxford University Press, 1975), pp. 81ff. For a lengthy controversy surrounding the issue of philosophy and politics in Oakeshott, see Dale Hall and Tariq Modood, "Oakeshott and the Impossibility of Philosophical Politics," *Political Studies* 30 (June 1982), pp. 158–76 and the accompanying exchange with John Liddington.

Hegelian idealism.[91] This means, roughly, that the metaphysical claims he does make are largely claims about the various ways in which humans, as intelligent creatures, experience and construct their various worlds. In Oakeshott's version, "reality is experience and is nothing but experience. And since experience is always a world of ideas, reality is a world of ideas."[92] This is not a Berkeleyan view, since Berkeley's proposals are, in effect, metaphysical claims about a transcendent reality. Nor is it a solipsistic view, as Oakeshott is at pains to emphasize; reality is not something that I, as an individual, make up arbitrarily in my own head. Rather, our "world" is composed of the gamut of experiences that we have had, all of which depend upon—can only be experienced in virtue of—the range of ideas that we have inherited from those social or cultural traditions that make us who we are in the first place.

In other words, we construct our worlds out of the "intellectual capital which composes our civilization."[93] We do this not willy-nilly but in terms of the habits, rules, and practices inherent in that civilization. The result is what Oakeshott, following Hegel, calls a "concrete" reality. Such a reality, as a world of ideas, is concrete in (at least) two senses: the various and complex ideas that we have about the world fit together without contradiction, and those ideas in turn similarly comport with the ideas of other individuals who share our traditions, our civilization, and our experience.

More specifically, the notion that such a reality is concrete means in part that its various components exist and are understood in terms of their constitutive connections with one another; each is what it is in virtue of its relation to all of the others. The concept *red* cannot meaningfully exist in isolation. It requires other concepts—*blue* and *yellow*, for example—if it is to be an intelligible part of any experience. For Oakeshott, as for Hegel, a world is experienced concretely when

91. Oakeshott, *Experience and Its Modes*, p. 6. On Oakeshott's idealism, see Bhikhu Parekh, "The Political Philosophy of Michael Oakeshott," *British Journal of Political Science* 9 (October 1979), pp. 481–485; and W. H. Greenleaf, "Idealism, Modern Philosophy, and Politics," in *Politics and Experience*, ed. P. King and B. Parekh (Cambridge: Cambridge University Press, 1968).

92. Oakeshott, *Experience and Its Modes*, p. 54.

93. Oakeshott, "The Study of 'Politics' in a University," in *Rationalism in Politics*, pp. 310ff. See J. R. Archer, "Oakeshott on Politics," *Journal of Politics* 41 (February 1979), pp. 157–159; and J. G. Blumler, "Politics, Poetry, and Practice," *Political Studies* 12 (October 1964), p. 356.

all of the ideas of which it is composed are, to the extent possible, understood in terms of their mutual similarities, differences, interdependencies, and the like. To conceive of anything in isolation, apart from its necessary connections, is to conceive of it "abstractly," and hence radically to misunderstand it.[94]

Similarly, since reality is constructed out of inherited intellectual capital, an individual's ideas must also be connected to those of other individuals who share that inheritance. This is not automatic, for a tradition is an ongoing and mutable thing. It is a "flow of sympathy," and while its main currents generally tumble forth in a constant, regular, and recurrent manner, there are always at the margins considerable opportunities for unanticipated ebb and flow, and these in turn, when multiplied many times over, can cause the tradition to meander in surprising ways. The individual is thus bound by his or her intellectual capital, but not rigidly, tyrannically so; there is considerable freedom to strike out on one's own. To venture too far is to risk losing touch with the tradition, thereby arriving at formulations that are likely to make sense to no one, perhaps not even to oneself. Such formulations would be abstract, unintelligible, and irrelevant (though, unfortunately, not necessarily inconsequential.) The independent or free thinker thus needs constantly to test opinions against his or her intellectual inheritance; but further, such opinions must also be tested against the views of others who are doing the same. For in this way, those who think seemingly "new" thoughts may do so collectively, in conversation with one another, and thereby subtly alter the path of, without at all abandoning, the tradition of which they are a part.

Reality is thus concrete when it is rooted in and sustained by an interconnected system of social/intellectual communication. The key notion in all of this appears to be the integrity or connectedness of a world. And since for Oakeshott the components of a world are ideas, the explicit criterion of connectedness must be coherence. We are having an experience truly, and hence can be said truly to "know" the world, when our various ideas about it cohere.[95]

94. For a discussion of the notions *concrete* and *abstract*, see Peter J. Steinberger, *Logic and Politics: Hegel's Philosophy of Right* (New Haven: Yale University Press, 1988), pp. 65–66; see also, J. Glenn Gray, "Hegel's Logic: The Philosophy of the Concrete," *Virginia Quarterly Review* (Spring 1971), pp. 175–189.

95. Oakeshott, *Experience and Its Modes*, p. 37. We should note that, for Oakeshott, practical experience, and scientific and historical experience as

This is certainly a "constructivist" perspective: a world of experience "is itself the arbiter of fact, for to be a fact means to have a
necessary place within it. . . . In experience, as I see it, fact is what is
achieved."[96] We create reality and hence the facts that compose it.
But again, we do so under the influence or sway of the intellectual
capital—traditions, presuppositions, prejudices, tacit understandings,
and so forth—that endows us with the capacity to think at all. That
capital both limits us and empowers us to create for ourselves meaningful worlds. As Oakeshott says, "what we have, and all we have, is a
world of 'meanings.'"[97] Or again,

> Images are made. . . . Further, these images are not made out
> of some other, less-defined material (impressions, or *sensa*), for
> no such material is available. . . . [W]hat we call a "thing" is
> merely a certain sort of image recognized as such because it be-
> haves in a certain manner and responds to our questioning ap-
> propriately. . . . [A]n image is never isolated and alone; it belongs
> to the world or field of images which on any occasion constitutes
> the not-self.[98]

In sum, when Oakeshott describes the realm of practical or political
experience, he is describing not a reality that exists "out there" and
apart from our experience, but an important feature of the world as
we have been taught to construct it.[99]

To say that practical facts are unfixed and elusive—one might as
well say "boundless" and "unpredictable"—is simply to argue that
we have a conception of a mode of experience that presupposes, for
it to make sense as a mode of experience, facts of that nature. Should

---

well, fall short of complete or absolute concreteness. Each is partial and hence
abstract (pp. 305–311). But this is so only in comparison to the "totality of
experience"; what Oakeshott calls practical experience is concrete indeed
when compared to other, defective accounts of political or practical life (e.g.,
ideological or behavioral accounts). See "Political Education," pp. 114–123.

96. Oakeshott, *Experience and Its Modes,* pp. 34 and 42.

97. Ibid., p. 61.

98. Oakeshott, "The Voice of Poetry in the Conversation of Mankind," in
Rationalism in Politics, p. 205.

99. The notion that this is something to be learned, that it is a matter of
education, is crucial for Oakeshott. See, for example, "The Study of 'Politics'
in a University," pp. 310ff; see also, *On Human Conduct,* p. 23, 24, 55–60.

we decide for some reason that there are no such facts, that all facts are in principle capable of strict scientific demonstration, explanation, and prediction, this would simply render practical or political experience incoherent and impossible. There would, perhaps, be nothing particularly wrong with that. But Oakeshott would wonder how such a choice itself could be possible, at least given our current beliefs and premises. For all decisions and experiences that make sense must be consistent with the intellectual capital that we necessarily carry with us; and for now, that capital seems very much to presuppose the notion that practical or political life is indeed an important part of our experience. Those who talk of a science of politics are certainly involved in a straightforward contradiction, since science and politics—insofar as they deal with different kinds of facts—are mutually incompatible. But those who more plausibly would *replace* politics with science are involved in a deeper contradiction; what they propose would contradict the traditions, presuppositions, prejudices, and tacit understandings that provide the opportunity for them to think at all.

The theories of politics as action and politics as conversation share, then, certain dispositions regarding what might be called the preconditions of politics. These preconditions, in turn, resonate with the kinds of themes encountered in Machiavelli, Tocqueville, and Nietzsche, themes involving *fortuna,* the variable, open-ended nature of the public realm, and the political irrelevance of philosophical or scientific rationality.[100]

When it comes to characterizing political endeavor itself, of course, the theories in question diverge quite sharply. According to the theory of politics as action, the novelty inherent in political endeavor is quite

---

100. Thus, for example, the regard that Arendt and Oakeshott have for Machiavelli is quite explicit. See Arendt, *Human Condition* (pp. 33, 68–69), where Machiavelli is described as the only postclassical theorist who understands something of the nature of the public realm; and Oakeshott, *On Human Conduct* (p. 244), where he is identified as an important theorist of *societas*. Tocqueville is also esteemed by both; the case of Nietzsche is far less clear. For an excellent treatment of Oakeshott's work prior to the publication of *On Human Conduct* that links Oakeshott to Arendt, and to Machiavelli and Tocqueville as well, see Hanna Fenichel Pitkin, "The Roots of Conservatism: Michael Oakeshott and the Denial of Politics," *Dissent* (Fall 1973), for example at p. 515. For a brief discussion of Arendt's connection with both Tocqueville and Nietzsche, see Sheldon Wolin, "Democracy and the Political," *Salmagundi* 60 (Spring–Summer 1983), pp. 4–5.

radical. Action produces genuine surprises—deeds, speeches, ideas, and structures that not only could not have been predicted but that, when they occur, strike us as utterly inexplicable, even miraculous. In the notion of politics as conversation, on the other hand, what happens properly in public life is rooted in, and emerges directly out of, established traditions or manners of acting. There is, strictly speaking, nothing that is entirely, radically new. The political actor is engaged merely in the "pursuit of intimations," in examining existing practices with a view not toward creating something new, but toward seeking revisions or improvements already implicit in the practices themselves. Again, the criterion is coherence: How can established arrangements be rendered more coherent on their own terms? It is true that such an inquiry is not a matter of deduction or logical entailment; rather, it involves what Oakeshott calls "conversation." But while its conclusions are certainly not predictable in the strong sense, neither can they be said to be truly novel or miraculous.[101]

This point of divergence is, in turn, related to what might be called an important dispositional difference. For Arendt, action is fundamentally heroic. It involves a plunge into the mysterious unknown; as such, it may expose the individual to great personal risk and thus requires unusual and extraordinary courage. If action is successful, it may for this reason provide the political actor with what no one else has, namely, the kind of immortality that comes from having achieved glory. To participate in the conversation of politics, on the other hand, appears to be a far more staid enterprise. Politics is a matter of "attending to arrangements"; it requires not so much courage as a sober, benign, clear-headed interest in making sense and achieving plausible accommodations. Oakeshott does describe conversation as "an unrehearsed intellectual adventure."[102] The adventure seems rather tame, though, compared to what Arendt has in mind. (This, of course, is not necessarily a bad thing.)

But there is, certainly, an even more fundamental divergence of a conceptual or analytic nature. In the theory of politics as action, political endeavor is explicitly and pointedly distinguished from the other regions of the *vita activa*, namely, work and labor. Indeed, it may be Arendt's greatest achievement to have provided an account of politics that differentiates it not just from contemplative or philosophi-

---

101. Oakeshott, "Political Education," pp. 123–127.
102. Oakeshott, "The Voice of Poetry," p. 198.

cal life but from alternative ways of acting in the world. In the theory of politics as conversation, on the other hand, these latter differences are, at best, submerged. While I have thus far identified Oakeshott's notion of the political with what he calls the "practical," his idea of the practical includes much more than just politics. For example, Oakeshott thinks of religion and art as practical matters.[103] Political endeavor is quite different from historical or scientific experience, but its fundamental traits—involving conversation and the pursuit of intimations—are shared with many other activities that similarly seek to move from an established "what is" to an as yet unrealized "to be."[104] Oakeshott is certainly aware of the kinds of distinctions that Arendt has drawn, but he appears to regard them as secondary, at least with respect to his own theoretical purposes.[105]

These divergences are, in my view, quite decisive.[106] We have before us two deeply different understandings of political endeavor. Yet even here there are important shared features that do suggest a certain kinship such that the two theories, though importantly discrepant, can nonetheless be said jointly to represent a particular kind of thinking about political questions. For each, political endeavor is fundamentally and by definition a free activity, uncoerced by the tyranny of scientific or rational truth, the vicissitudes of physical desire, the laws of sociological or psychological behavior, and the like. For each, such endeavor has a crucial dialogical aspect, evidenced in the very notion of conversation itself and, equally, in Arendt's view that "debate constitutes the very essence of political life."[107] For each, politics is primarily concerned not with particular goals or gratifications, not with the "sub-

103. *Experience and Its Modes,* pp. 292–296. But see footnote 111 below on the relationship between practice and art.

104. Ibid., p. 257.

105. See Oakeshott's discussion of fabrication in *On Human Conduct,* pp. 35–36.

106. Readers may point to an even more basic divergence. Whereas Arendt places political action at the center of what it means to be a human being, Oakeshott sometimes thinks of politics as "a second-rate form of human activity at once corrupting to the soul and fatiguing to the mind." Insofar as Oakeshott nonetheless conceives of political action, properly understood, to be a form of conversation having all of the features and benefits of conversation in general, this divergence is actually—at least with respect to our particular interests—rather secondary.

107. Arendt, "Truth and Politics," p. 241.

stance" of human affairs, but rather with the structures and conditions that relate individuals to one another as they pursue those goals. In Arendt, this is the public realm itself, the "common world" that establishes a "web of relationships" among individuals.[108] In Oakeshott, it is a "civil condition," rooted in a "system of *lex* which prescribes, not satisfactions to be sought or actions to be performed, but moral conditions to be subscribed to in seeking self-chosen satisfactions and in performing self-chosen actions."[109] For each, politics has an important aesthetic dimension, though for Arendt art is more the servant of politics,[110] while for Oakeshott it ultimately emerges as a distinctive voice in the conversation of mankind.[111] And for each, political endeavor is to be valued not primarily as an instrumentality but for its own sake, as something intrinsically, inherently worthy.

Perhaps most important, however, each views politics as invoking a particular kind of thinking, sharply differentiated from the standard

108. Arendt, *Human Condition*, pp. 45–53 and pp. 161–163.

109. Oakeshott, *On Human Conduct*, p. 158. This point of view has elicited a great deal of criticism of both Arendt and Oakeshott. On Arendt, see for example, Hanna Fenichel Pitkin, "Justice: On Relating Public and Private," *Political Theory* 9 (August 1981), pp. 327–352; and George Kateb, *Hannah Arendt: Politics, Conscience, Evil* (Totowa, N.J.: Rowman and Allanheld, 1984), pp. 117ff. On Oakeshott, see Barber, "Conserving Politics," pp. 457ff.; Parekh, "The Political Philosophy of Michael Oakeshott," p. 492; R. N. Berki, "Oakeshott's Concept of Civil Association: Notes for a Critical Analysis," *Political Studies* 29 (December 1981), pp. 574ff.; and Hanna Fenichel Pitkin, "Inhuman Conduct and Unpolitical Theory: Michael Oakeshott's *On Human Conduct*," *Political Theory* 4 (August 1976), pp. 303ff.

110. For a useful discussion of the "poetic" in Arendt's political thought, see David Luban, "Explaining Dark Times: Hannah Arendt's Theory of Theory," *Social Research* 50 (Spring 1983), pp. 238ff.

111. It seems that Oakeshott's views changed substantially in this respect. In *Experience and Its Modes*, art is thought to be an archetypical example of the practical life (pp. 296–297); in "The Voice of Poetry," the two are rather sharply distinguished. With respect to politics, the latter work describes the modern tendency to define politics in terms of the practical voice and contrasts this with the classical view of politics as fundamentally poetic, a view attributed also to Machiavelli (p. 202n). Oakeshott's own position here is not entirely clear, but at least one commentator attributes to him an aesthetic account of politics: see Blumler, "Politics, Poetry, and Practice," pp. 358ff. What is clear, in any case, is that Oakeshott views conversation as the "appropriate image of human intercourse" per se (p. 199), and that this pertains at least as much to the activity of politics as to any other.

account of rational inquiry and analysis, and embracing, among other things, a distinctive type of knowledge and intellectual discipline. This in turn involves each in an attempt to categorize and distinguish our various intellectual faculties with a view toward describing those that are most closely connected to political wisdom.

VI

It is generally presupposed that whereas *The Human Condition* and related writings such as *On Revolution* deal with the *vita activa*, Arendt's later writings—including *The Life of the Mind*, her last, unfinished, and posthumously published work—represent a dramatic shift of attention to the *vita contemplativa*.[112] This seems plausible enough, since the threefold typology of mental life (thinking, willing, and judging) appears to parallel the threefold typology of the active life (labor, work, and action). Indeed, it has even been suggested that such a shift amounts to a perhaps despairing rejection of the active life altogether, with its ever-present risks and uncertainties, in favor of the presumably more modest risks and uncertainties of contemplation.[113] This view seems most unlikely insofar as Arendt's goal is, in part, to criticize philosophical thinking for its hostility to the world of action and appearance.[114] In any event, *The Life of the Mind* is now widely thought to provide a more-or-less systematic account of the *vita contemplativa*.

This may well have been Arendt's intention.[115] Even so, it results in an interpretation the coherence of which is difficult to sustain. To begin with, the three faculties of *The Life of the Mind* can hardly be

112. See, for example, Hans Jonas, "Acting, Knowing, Thinking: Hannah Arendt's Philosophical Work," *Social Research* 44 (Spring 1977), pp. 28; and Seyla Benhabib, "Judgment and the Moral Foundations of Politics in Arendt's Thought," *Political Theory* 16 (February 1988), pp. 29–30.

113. John S. Nelson, "Politics and Truth: Arendt's Problematic," *American Journal of Political Science* 22 (May 1978), p. 292.

114. For an excellent treatment, see Kateb, *Hannah Arendt: Politics, Conscience, Evil*, pp. 189ff. See also J. Glenn Gray, "The Abyss of Freedom—and Hannah Arendt," in *Hannah Arendt: The Recovery of the Public World*, ed. Melvyn A. Hill (New York: St. Martin's Press, 1979), p. 226.

115. There are people who would certainly know a great deal more about this than I do, for example, Hans Jonas. See Arendt, *Life of the Mind*, vol. 1, pp. 7–8. See also, Elisabeth Young-Bruehl, *Hannah Arendt: For Love of the World* (New Haven: Yale University Press, 1982), p. 449.

relegated entirely and exclusively to the *vita contemplativa;* each plays a crucial role in the *vita activa* as well. To deny this would be, in effect, to deprive action of any mental component, to turn political actors into mindless zombies. It is, of course, absurd to believe that Arendt imagined the *vita activa* to be conducted unconsciously; for her, as for us, actors are people who think, will, and judge—or at least should. Thus, an account of those faculties cannot be simply and solely an account of the *vita contemplativa* since they are necessarily a part of the *vita activa* as well.[116]

Further, it is hard to see how much of *The Life of the Mind* is even relevant to a description of the contemplative life. The importance of willing and judging, in particular, with respect to a life of pure contemplation is rather dubious. The case of willing is, in this regard, quite complicated. But it seems that, at the end, Arendt did come to view the will as essentially related to action, not contemplation;[117] she herself remarks that contemplation, at least in some important formulations, entails "a delight that puts the will to rest."[118] The case of judgment is clearer; as will be discussed below, Arendt seems to view judging as being so intimately related to political action that it is difficult to discover just what role it could possibly play in a contemplative existence.[119] Thus, when Arendt describes willing and judging, she cannot in fact be describing the *vita contemplativa* at all. The case of thinking is, of course, quite different, but then thinking is hardly the whole of *The Life of the Mind.*

Finally, it seems quite certain that thinking, willing, and judging do not in fact correspond respectively to labor, work, and action. For example, in Arendt's account much of labor is largely thoughtless, unwilled, and without judgment; political action, on the other hand, may well require all three faculties in some measure. There is, I sug-

116. The three varieties of action, on the other hand, pertain only to the *vita activa* and have nothing to do with the contemplative life. This further undermines any presumed parallel between the theory of action and the theory of mental life.

117. Gray, "The Abyss of Freedom—and Hannah Arendt," pp. 227ff; also Suzanne Jacobitti, "Hannah Arendt and the Will," *Political Theory* 16 (February 1988), pp. 53–76.

118. Arendt, *Life of the Mind,* vol. 2, p. 124.

119. See, for example, Michael Denneny, "The Privilege of Ourselves: Hannah Arendt on Judgment," in *Hannah Arendt: The Recovery of the Public World,* ed. Hill, p. 253.

gest, no real parallel between the threefold structures of action and of mental life. As will be discussed shortly, I do think that there are mental/intellectual counterparts to labor, work, and action, but we must look for them elsewhere.

Thus, it seems awkward at best to read *The Life of the Mind* as a description of contemplative existence. It would be better to understand it more simply as an account of mental faculties per se, and therefore as relevant to both action and contemplation, perhaps equally so. As such, I believe that it continues and extends certain discussions that are already present in Arendt's earlier writings on the *vita activa*.

Those writings propose a deep distinction between thought, cognition, and logical reasoning.[120] Logical reasoning is described as a kind of intellectual "labor power." It involves the application of the so-called laws of thought (notably the principle of noncontradiction) to particular problems of the *vita activa*. Such problems are quite independent of logical reasoning itself; they emerge solely from the exigencies and requirements of action, work, and especially labor. Moreover, their peculiarities do not in any way influence the nature of the intellectual processes to which they are subjected. Logical reasoning can thus be thought of as a kind of neutral tool, entirely separate from and indifferent to the raw material it is made to analyze.

According to Arendt, the rules and methods of logical reasoning are rooted in human physiology. She presents little evidence in support of this extraordinary (though hardly original) claim. Nonetheless, its force momentarily shifts our attention from the nonmaterial mind to the physical brain, and leads us to conceive of the brain as nothing more than a computation machine.[121] In this sense, then, logical reasoning manifests itself as an automatic, unreflective, repetitive kind of endeavor characterized by preestablished programs, algorithms, or routines.

Cognition, on the other hand, is understood as a fundamentally

---

120. Arendt, *Human Condition*, pp. 150ff.

121. "The laws of logic can be discovered like other laws of nature because they are ultimately rooted in the structure of the human brain. . . . It is in the structure of the human brain to be compelled to admit that two and two equal four." Arendt, *Human Condition*, p. 151. From this, Arendt concludes that computers are generally better than humans at logical reasoning. See also, Hannah Arendt, *On Revolution* (New York: Viking Press, 1965), p. 194.

instrumental, goal-oriented faculty. It always has a particular substantive end, typically involving the discovery or construction of some useful or "relevant" fact, often in the service of science or fabrication. As a result, cognition is constrained by, and tends to take on the character of, the activities it is made to serve. Unlike logical reasoning, it cannot be indifferent to its substantive concerns, but is, in fact, decisively influenced by them. Cognition in, say, engineering is different from cognition in psychology. Each aims at constructing or otherwise establishing some kind of useful truth, but in doing so each employs a distinctive set of concepts, theories, and analytic protocols appropriate to its subject matter. Form and content are thus inextricably bound up with one another. Indeed, whereas logical reasoning denotes a purely formal and abstract set of mental operations, cognition is always inherently teleological. In Arendtian terms, if logical reasoning is, roughly, the intellectual equivalent of labor, then cognition is similarly identified with work.

Thought is evocative of neither labor nor work but of (political) action.[122] Like action, it is not primarily an instrumentality but something to be valued and enjoyed on its own account.[123] It does not seek to attain some goal external to itself; it is not limited or constrained by preestablished methods or purposes. It is importantly free, and its results—the results of free, unconstrained thinking—can be neither predicted nor retroactively reduced to systematic rules or procedures. Moreover, whereas logical reasoning aims at formal truth, and cognition aims at factual truth, the goal of thought is not truth at all but, rather, meaning.[124] One thinks not in order to discover a fact or prove a theorem but merely to attach a concept to an experience in order to render that experience meaningful and intelligible, so that it may give rise to further thoughts, some of which can, perhaps, be shared with other individuals. Just as political action creates a web of ongoing

122. Bhikhu Parekh, *Hannah Arendt and the Search for a New Political Philosophy* (Atlantic Highlands, N.J.: Humanities Press, 1981), pp. 121–123.

123. Arendt, *The Life of the Mind,* vol. 1, p. 64.

124. Ibid., pp. 59–65. See Jean Yarborough and Peter Stern, "Vita Activa and Vita Contemplativa: Reflections on Hannah Arendt's Political Thought in *The Life of the Mind,*" *Review of Politics* 43 (July 1981), pp. 331–332; Jonas, "Acting, Knowing, Thinking: Hannah Arendt's Philosophical Work," pp. 36ff.; Kateb, *Hannah Arendt: Politics, Conscience, Evil,* pp. 193ff.; and Parekh, *Hannah Arendt and the Search for a New Political Philosophy,* pp. 60ff.

public relationships between otherwise unconnected individuals, so does thinking serve to establish or sustain a tissue of meaning on the basis of which disparate persons can conduct with one another a coherent intellectual life.

Arendt is at pains to emphasize that thought is not the same as contemplation.[125] Contemplation is a way of life or a manner of being; thought is merely an intellectual faculty. The latter can serve the former, and indeed historically that has been its most important role, that is, as the "handmaiden" of the *vita contemplativa*.[126] But it can also become the handmaiden of those various kinds of endeavor that comprise the *vita activa*. This is not always a happy circumstance. As the servant of work and labor, thought becomes enslaved, so to speak, in an alien enterprise, its natural freedom and radical impulses domesticated by the requirements and vicissitudes of physical, biological, and technical necessity. Eventually, it loses its distinctive character and dissolves into either logical reasoning or cognition. As the servant of political action, on the other hand, it regains its natural freedom and identity, emerging finally as the definitive intellectual faculty of political life, the only kind of mental faculty appropriate to the public realm.

In Arendt's terms, thought in the service of political action comes to be identified as judgment. In her famous lecture on "Thinking and Moral Considerations," she appears to distinguish the two: thinking deals with "invisibles," judging with particular things that are "close at hand." But she also insists that they are profoundly "interrelated," that judging is "the by-product of the liberating effect of thinking," and that it "realizes thinking [and] makes it manifest in the world of appearances."[127] It seems not too much to suggest, then, that judging is in fact a particular species of thinking, the form that thinking takes in the political world.[128]

As such, judgment, like thought in general, is not oriented to the discovery of truth: in politics, "it is not knowledge or truth which is at

125. Arendt, *Human Condition*, pp. 264ff.

126. Ibid., p. 265; see also *Life of the Mind*, vol. 1, p. 7.

127. Hannah Arendt, "Thinking and Moral Considerations: A Lecture," *Social Research* 38 (Autumn 1971), p. 446. The passage is repeated nearly verbatim in *Life of the Mind*, vol. 1, p. 193.

128. Yarborough and Stern, "Hannah Arendt's Political Thought in *The Life of the Mind*," p. 337.

stake, but rather judgment and decision."[129] Indeed, to judge is not to
assert a truth claim at all but, rather, to make a meaningful assertion
that asks only for the assent of others. Just as the aim of thought in
general is to create structures of meaning, so the aim of judgment is
to establish for any society a common conceptual apparatus on the
basis of which social actors can come to share the kinds of understandings and discriminations that allow for intelligent collective action.

This means that the aim of judgment is not universal certainty or
rational truth but only "general communicability" and agreement.[130]
For Arendt,

> [t]he power of judgment rests on potential agreement with oth-
> ers, and the thinking process which is active in judging something
> is not, like the thought process of pure [logical] reasoning, a
> dialogue between me and myself, but finds itself always and pri-
> marily, even if I am quite alone in making up my mind, in an
> anticipated communication with others with whom I know I must
> finally come to some agreement.[131]

Logical or factual truths can, in principle, be discovered by the single
individual in isolation; logical reasoning and cognition do not presuppose a social world. But agreement obviously does. Hence, the faculty
of judgment, insofar as its aim is to secure agreement, "cannot function in strict isolation or solitude; it needs the presence of others."
Judgment is necessarily social or political.[132]

This implies, further, that the validity of judgment is quite different from that of logic or cognition. Logical or cognitive validity means

---

129. Hannah Arendt, "The Crisis in Culture: Its Social and Its Political Significance," in *Between Past and Future*, p. 223. Also, Hannah Arendt,
Lectures on Kant's Political Philosophy (Chicago: University of Chicago Press,
1982), p. 15.

130. Arendt, *Lectures on Kant's Political Philosophy*, p. 40.

131. Arendt, "Crisis in Culture", p. 220.

132. Denneny, "The Privilege of Ourselves," pp. 251–252. There is a further complexity here involving the putative distinction between the actor's
judgment and the spectator's judgment. Such a distinction would, I think,
in no way undermine the account thus far presented. See, Ronald Beiner,
"Hannah Arendt on Judging," in Arendt, *Lectures on Kant's Political Philosophy*,
pp. 117ff; and Richard J. Bernstein, "Judging—The Actor and the Spectator,"
in Bernstein, *Philosophical Profiles* (Philadelphia: University of Pennsylvania
Press, 1986), pp. 221–238.

truth, and that in turn involves notions of proof and universality. To have established a truth is to have provided an ironclad demonstration of it such that it can be thought of as always and undeniably true. This is obviously the case with mathematical propositions, but it is equally characteristic of, say, historical, sociological, and psychological propositions. If it is true that Germany invaded Belgium in 1914, then it is eternally and universally true that Germany invaded Belgium in 1914.[133]

But as we have seen, judgment is not primarily concerned with truth at all. The validity of judgment thus involves not proof or demonstration but, rather, the possible and actual assent of others. My judgment is valid if I can persuade others to subscribe to it. For Arendt, this means also that the validity of judgment is necessarily specific and particular, rather than universal. The particularity of judgment is twofold. First, judgment is always of a single thing—an object, event, or person—and implies nothing about any other single thing. Since we are outside the realm of proof and demonstration, to judge something is not to employ a universal theory or principle nor to provide a basis for such a theory or principle; it is merely to make a particular claim about a particular object. Second, as a persuasive rather than demonstrative endeavor, judgment operates exclusively and explicitly in light of the particular views and dispositions of those who would be persuaded. A valid judgment is not valid for everyone everywhere; it is "true" (so to speak) only for us.[134]

Arendt concludes from this that judgment inherently requires "common sense"—a set of shared intuitions, assumptions, concepts, and understandings on the basis of which persuasion might be possible. Common sense is a "sixth sense" that "fits the sensations of my strictly private five senses—so private that sensations in their mere sensational quality and intensity are incommunicable—into a common world shared by others. The subjectivity of the it-seems-to-me is remedied by the fact that the same object also appears to others though its mode of appearance may be different."[135] Without such a sixth sense,

133. For a criticism of Arendt on this general question, see Nelson, "Politics and Truth: Arendt's Problematic," pp. 282–284.

134. See Robert Grafstein, "Political Freedom and Political Action," *Western Political Quarterly* 39 (September 1986), pp. 471–473.

135. Arendt, *Life of the Mind*, p. 50; see also, *Lectures on Kant's Political Philosophy*, p. 27. For a discussion, see Ernst Vollrath, "Hannah Arendt and

judgment would be impossible. For insofar as judgment necessarily eschews universal proof, its power to persuade depends upon the presumption that different people will "see" certain things in the same way. This similarity or commonness of vision allows the person who judges to point to and describe what he or she senses in the hope that others will sense it as well. Perhaps I cannot prove that the United States Constitution includes a tacit right to privacy, or that *Lord Jim* is a great novel, or that building the B-1 bomber is a good idea; but if I can identify certain important shared observations and assumptions about the world and give an account of their relevance to the question at hand, I can perhaps convince others that my judgments are sound.

In Arendt's notion, the commonness of common sense is generally limited by particular social and historical contexts. Only individuals who share a culture can share the kinds of understandings that compose a common sense. The epistemological ambitions of such a sense must therefore be modest; knowledge-in-judgment is always attached to and dependent upon particular situations. Arendt wants to claim, nonetheless, that this specifies but does not at all undermine the very notion of good (i.e., knowledgeable) judgment. To judge something well is simply to know it in the light of a particular context. This is the only kind of political knowledge that we have, but it is not thereby insubstantial. It is a knowledge rooted in our common sense, and this does indeed provide us with a kind of "truth" or wisdom that is eminently, even exclusively, suitable for acting in the public realm.

We may summarize by suggesting that the real parallel in Arendt's work is between "activity" and "action" on the one hand and "thinking" and "thought" on the other. In the first pair, activity is the more general category (to be distinguished from contemplation), whereas action is—like labor and work—merely a subcategory, a particular species of activity. Similarly, thinking as described in *The Life of the Mind* is the

---

the Method of Political Thinking," *Social Research* 44 (Spring 1977), pp. 174–177. The role of commonness and community is already evident in Arendt's early thinking about action and existence: "Existenz can develop only in the togetherness of men in the common given world. In the concept of communication there lies embedded, though not fully developed, a new concept of humanity as the condition for man's Existence": Hannah Arendt, "What is Existenz Philosophy?" *Partisan Review* 13 (Winter 1946), pp. 55–56. Arendt links this position to the modern separation of thought and Being, in which project she gives Nietzsche a prominent place.

general category (to be distinguished from willing), of which there are three subcategories, namely, logical reasoning, cognition, and thought; and thought *qua* subcategory can properly serve either the contemplative life or the life of action. In the latter instance, thought is judgment—the intellectual process on the basis of which one seeks to establish for some society a common set of meanings or concepts.

To my knowledge, such a parallel is never made explicit by Arendt, and its terminology—especially the distinction between "thinking" and "thought"—may not comport fully with hers. Nonetheless, it seems to be the clearest way to explicate her approach to the mental faculties. As such, it helps to provide what is, I believe, a quite substantial and influential theory of judgment in politics.

The notion of politics as conversation embraces, in a strikingly similar way, an emphasis on the embeddedness of the political intellect. Indeed, for Oakeshott the cardinal vice of political life is the attempt to make judgments without relying on, perhaps even in opposition to, the established practices and understandings—the common sense—of a political or cultural tradition. Any such attempt is "ideological" in the worst sense. It proposes that "practical life should be governed by a set of ready-made and absolute principles or rules" that emerge not from the exertions and accommodations of actual political endeavor but from disembodied, disconnected speculation.[136] According to Oakeshott, an ideology is an "abstract principle, or set of related abstract principles, which has been independently premeditated."[137] It offers, at best, an abridgment of genuine political experience that is liable to distort or oversimplify that experience. At worst, it seeks to understand political life by invoking a truncated version of some entirely unrelated, wholly nonpolitical kind of activity (e.g., war, religion, or commerce).[138] In this latter circumstance, ideology makes a twofold error: it misunderstands the nonpolitical activity through oversimplification, and it misunderstands political activity by utilizing an inappropriate analogy. We should note that by refusing to conceive of politics nonpolitically, Oakeshott, along with Arendt, departs

136. Oakeshott, *Experience and Its Modes,* p. 301.

137. Oakeshott, "Political Education," p. 116.

138. Ibid., pp. 122–124. Historically, the most important case of this for Oakeshott is the age-old notion that political society is really a kind of "enterprise association." See *On Human Conduct,* pp. 117ff.; see also, Parekh, "The Political Philosophy of Michael Oakeshott," pp. 493ff.

from the strategy and language of the Second Iteration and thereby strengthens considerably its underlying thesis.

The upshot is that for Oakeshott, as for Arendt, political wisdom is a matter of absorbing and being faithful to whatever counts in a given society as common sense. In a famous passage, he considers the activity of following a cookbook recipe:

> It might be supposed that an ignorant man, some edible materials, and a cookery book compose together the necessities of a self-moved (or concrete) activity called cooking. But nothing is further from the truth. The cookery book is not an independently generated beginning from which cooking can spring; it is nothing more than an abstract of somebody's knowledge of how to cook: it is the stepchild, not the parent of the activity. The book . . . speaks only to those who know already the kind of thing to expect from it and consequently how to interpret it.[139]

Thinking about politics similarly presupposes an understanding, however tacit, of what political activity is all about. Such an understanding is likely to be local, circumscribed, and context-specific; it embodies the common sense of a culture. But as we have seen, while this certainly limits the scope of plausible political ideas, it is also an unavoidable and, indeed, salutary source of stability; it is that which makes coherence and intelligibility possible and which undermines, or at least permits us clearly to identify, notions that are irrelevant, unreliable, or dangerous. As a result, political thinking, like all thinking properly understood, "is a process of recognition in which we reconsider judgments already in some degree affirmed."[140]

I believe that all of this commits Oakeshott to a notion of what we have been calling "judgment," although he uses the word rather more broadly. Political wisdom is a matter of having good judgment, and this, again, involves the capacity to identify and make faithful use of the common sense of a culture. Such a capacity emerges out of conversations that we have with other individuals similarly engaged, and these conversations essentially involve the pursuit of intimations, that is, the search for what our common sense would say about this

139. Oakeshott, "Political Education," p. 119. See also Wendell John Coats, Jr., "Michael Oakeshott as Liberal Theorist," *Canadian Journal of Political Science* 18 (December 1985), pp. 780–783.

140. Oakeshott, *Experience and Its Modes,* p. 19.

or that particular problem. Oakeshott acknowledges that there is no foolproof method for pursuing such intimations; like Arendt, he points to the practice of aesthetic judgment as an example of thinking that is nonalgorithmic and unsystematic but that nonetheless results in something that may be called "knowledge" or "wisdom." He asks, "How does a critic arrive at the judgment that a picture is incoherent, that the artist's treatment of some passages is inconsistent with his treatment of others?" Oakeshott assumes that we do not know how the critic does it, but also that we are in no doubt about the fact that he does it indeed.[141]

Oakeshott acknowledges that the pursuit of intimations is not a matter of deduction or logical entailment, not a matter of adducing necessary consequences. Again, "there is no piece of mistake-proof apparatus by means of which we can elicit the intimation most worthwhile pursuing."[142] However, he rejects out of hand the notion that the process he is describing is somehow irrational and arbitrary. When Mr. N. A. Swanson suggests that the bowler in cricket should not be allowed to throw the ball, and when Mr. G. H. Fender demurs, Mr. M. Oakeshott insists that each is making an argument of some kind, based on evidence of some kind; each is appealing to an existing and accessible body of common sense about cricket; and each is making, therefore, a plausible and legitimate claim to have knowledge with respect to the practice in question.

Such claims are conversational claims. Like Arendt's concept of thought, conversation is something to be engaged in not for external purposes but on its own account, as something inherently worthwhile. It is with conversation as with friendship: the moment ulterior motives appear, it is ruined.[143] Conversation aims not at truth but at reiterating, clarifying, and revivifying understandings already established, however tacitly. Those understandings are part of a culture, a tradition of thought, and we may view conversation as the primary means by which a tradition keeps itself alive. The tradition talks to itself, as it

141. Oakeshott, "Political Education," p. 136.

142. Ibid., p. 124. For a criticism, see John C. Rees, "Professor Oakeshott on Political Education," *Mind* 62 (January 1953), pp. 68–74.

143. See Michael Oakeshott, "On Being Conservative," in *Rationalism in Politics,* p. 177. Compare this to Oakeshott's analogy between conversation and gambling in "The Voice of Poetry," pp. 198.

were; particular individuals engaged in particular conversations are merely its vehicles.

Crucial to conversation is the notion of *persuasion*. As with Arendt's account of judgment, the validity of a conversational utterance is largely a matter of its persuasive power. A claim is valid to the extent that it is convincing to other experienced conversationalists who, upon hearing it in the light of their knowledge of the tradition, are able to nod their heads, thereby acknowledging it to be an intelligible and plausible contribution.

Again, Oakeshott insists that none of this can be reduced to the fact that we sometimes have unreflective and unsubstantiated hunches.[144] Judgments are rooted in and make constant reference to the traditions and intellectual capital that give rise to and sustain our common sense. Their claims are defensible precisely in terms of the degree to which those claims comport with common sense. Coherence of this kind is what knowledge is all about. The absence of a foolproof, logical method does not render practical judgment noncognitive, in the Kantian sense. Rather, "the world of practical experience is a world of knowledge, and its character and criteria are those common to all worlds of knowledge; the principle of this world, as of every other, is one of coherence."[145]

VII

The two theories that we have been examining may be thought jointly to provide a Third Iteration of our thesis about judgment, common sense, and political wisdom. Whereas the First Iteration was merely assertoric, and the second largely metaphorical, this third version involves direct, explicit, and detailed efforts to distinguish rational thought, traditionally conceived, from a kind of thinking peculiarly suited to the needs and vicissitudes of the political world. Such efforts are rooted in an analysis of the special features of that world, features that render its problems by definition ineligible for orthodox philosophical analysis. In each case, the result is an account of those mental faculties that allow for something like political knowledge or political wisdom. And in each case, the account describes a kind of thought

144. Oakeshott, *Experience and Its Modes*, p. 253.
145. Ibid., p. 256. Cf. pp. 283–285.

process that is unconstrained by predetermined methods and rules, that pursues in a more-or-less unsystematic manner the implications of already established practices, theories, or common presuppositions, and that is undertaken not primarily for ulterior motives but because it is an intrinsically valuable and rewarding enterprise.

It has been said that Hannah Arendt's writings have given rise to no school of thought, and it seems equally unlikely that one would encounter in the community of political theorists Oakeshottians in the same way that one encounters, say, Marxists or Straussians.[146] Still, the question of influence is often murky. I would hazard the perhaps controversial view that the ideas of Arendt and Oakeshott have had, if only indirectly, an unrivaled impact upon political theorists in the academy. At the least, it seems to me that a number of the views expressed in the Third Iteration have become something of an orthodoxy for many intellectuals whose training and work occur primarily in departments of political science. One might mention in this connection a variety of contemporary themes, motifs, or tendencies:

The view of politics as always emanating from one or another kind of "vision" and a concomitant worry about the modern "sublimation" of politics.[147]

A more straightforwardly democratic or populistic perspective based in part on an energetic critique of the alleged epistemological foundations of standard liberalism.[148]

An interpretive, or hermeneutic, account of what it means to be a citizen.[149]

146. On Arendt, see Hill, *Hannah Arendt: The Recovery of the Public World*, p. ix; on Oakeshott, see Auspitz, "Individuality, Civility, and Theory," p. 261.

147. Wolin, *Politics and Vision;* also by Wolin, "Political Theory as a Vocation," *American Political Science Review* 63 (December 1969), pp. 1062–1082. For Wolin's debt to Arendt, see his "Hannah Arendt and the Ordinance of Time," *Social Research* 44 (Spring 1977), pp. 91ff.

148. Benjamin R. Barber, *Strong Democracy: Participatory Politics for a New Age* (Berkeley: University of California Press, 1984).

149. Charles Taylor, *Human Language and Agency* (Cambridge: Cambridge University Press, 1985); see, for example, the superb essay entitled "Atomism." See also, Ronald Beiner, *Political Judgment* (Chicago: University of Chicago Press, 1983); and John Dunn, *Political Obligation in Its Historical Context* (Cambridge: Cambridge University Press, 1980), especially Chapter 10.

A critique of political rationalism on either aesthetic or erotic grounds.[150]

A variety of skeptical, antirationalist approaches to political thinking which advert, variously, to Quine's doubts about analyticity, Sellars's doubts about the empirically given, and Kuhn's doubts about the rationality of science.[151]

A linguistic kind of skepticism based on the notion that political concepts are "essentially contested."[152]

A somewhat related approach to questions of judgment, action, and explanation rooted in certain traditions of ordinary language analysis.[153]

A general distrust of epistemological and foundationalist speculation per se.[154]

Efforts to reestablish the virtue of rhetoric in politics.[155]

A broad tendency—sometimes systematic, sometimes not—to read all manner of political writings in essentially literary terms.

These are strange bedfellows, no doubt. They hardly make up a "school" of thought, for their mutual antipathies are often deep and acrimonious. But it may be that their frequent and strenuous disputes are really family arguments. In fact, the Third Iteration reflects, I would suggest, a rather widespread mood among political theorists. It is a mood that embraces the notion of politics as a distinctive and inherently valuable kind of enterprise having intellectual properties

150. Herbert Marcuse, *The Aesthetic Dimension: Toward a Critique of Marxist Aesthetics* (Boston: Beacon Press, 1978); and *Eros and Civilization* (Boston: Beacon Press, 1955). Of course, Marcuse was not a political scientist, but his influence on certain individuals who are political scientists is hardly negligible.

151. For example, John G. Gunnell, *Between Philosophy and Politics: The Alienation of Political Theory* (Amherst: University of Massachusetts Press, 1986).

152. William Connolly, *The Terms of Political Discourse* (Princeton: Princeton University Press, 1983).

153. Hanna Fenichel Pitkin, *Wittgenstein and Justice* (Berkeley: University of California Press, 1972).

154. Don Herzog, *Without Foundations: Justification in Political Theory* (Ithaca: Cornell University Press, 1985); and Paul F. Kress, "Against Epistemology: Apostate Musings," *Journal of Politics* 41 (May 1979), pp. 526–542.

155. Ira L. Strauber, "The Rhetoric of an Ordinary Political Argument: Liberalism and Zionism," *Western Political Quarterly* 39 (December 1986), pp. 603–622.

peculiar to it and irreducible, as such, to the rules and principles of logic, systematic metaphysics, or the natural and technical sciences. It is, moreover, a mood sharply different from the more traditional, rationalistic disposition of those philosophers who have chosen to pursue, for example, questions of justice by seeking to generate logically sound deductions from presumably uncontroversial and widely held premises. If Hannah Arendt and Michael Oakeshott cannot be held responsible for this mood, they have almost certainly been its most compelling representatives.

But while the Third Iteration is, for our purposes, a substantial advance over the first two, it still leaves many of the most basic and serious questions untouched. As we have seen, Arendt and Oakeshott have provided us with a conceptual analysis of politics considered as a more-or-less distinctive type of human endeavor, and each has, in turn, described a kind of mental activity, hence a kind of knowledge or wisdom, peculiarly appropriate to such an endeavor. At least three problems persist, though, and these are sufficiently serious that the cogency of the Third Iteration must remain seriously in doubt.

1. To begin with, it is unclear in what precise sense we should understand and accept the claim that judgment (for Arendt) or conversation (for Oakeshott) can provide a basis for anything like knowledge or wisdom. Each case has its special difficulties. With respect to judgment, we know now that Arendt repudiates the notion that it is directly involved with truth or knowledge, conventionally conceived. Yet there is absolutely no doubt that she would distinguish between good judgments and bad, and that she would relate political action, properly understood, only to judgments having some kind of validity. We have seen further that, for Arendt, the validity of judgment involves its capacity to persuade and hence to elicit agreement and consensus. Yet it also seems clear that this requirement cannot be satisfied simply in plebiscitary terms; Arendt was more aware than most that the tyranny of the majority is tyranny indeed, and that the arts of persuasion are often most effectively employed in the service of that which is least wise, least valid.

We have an account, therefore, of the particular requirements and opportunities of political life and of the general kinds of intellectual endeavor best suited to that life. But we remain without a discussion of just why we should agree that those kinds of endeavor can be a source of knowledge or wisdom of whatever variety; we continue to lack anything approaching a criterion on the basis of which we might reliably distinguish good from bad judgment; we seem to have no very explicit idea of how the faculty of judgment might be cultivated and nurtured; we have no clear reason to believe that such a faculty is, in fact, a feature of human intellectual life; and ultimately, we have no straightforward account of what it might mean to have knowledge in the political, action-relevant, nonrationalist sense. The case of rational inquiry is, I think, quite different. There we have an established intellectual tradition that describes in some detail the very idea of knowledge, the criteria for deciding about truth claims, the rules and principles of rational thought, the habits and dispositions conducive to learning and internalizing those rules, and the like. While this tradition is by no means uniform, it offers nonetheless materials on the basis of which we can hope to understand the nature of rational knowledge. What is required, then, is an equivalent conceptual account of judgment such that its properties and principles can be understood with considerably more confidence and clarity than is now the case.

As for conversation, the ellipses here are equally troubling. Oakeshott insists that conversation does issue in knowledge of some kind. Again, he denies strenuously that this knowledge could be a matter of logical entailment; but then, exactly what is it a matter of? He provides what might be called an empirical account of conversation. We are all familiar with the experience of having conversations, of seeming to discuss without achieving—indeed, without striving for—proofs or logical demonstrations, of arriving at accommodations or other agreements simply by being persuaded to nod our heads. Indeed, the apparent familiarity of this experience is, I believe, the basic tool with which Oakeshott seeks to convince us about the nature and importance of conversation. We may well wonder, though, if such experience is precisely as Oakeshott describes it. Perhaps every conversation is really a moment in a larger, ongoing effort to arrive at logical and provable truths, an effort perhaps likely to fail but nonetheless motivated and guided necessarily by the goals and principles of rational inquiry. Perhaps conversational utterances are in fact nothing more than halting, incomplete, and unsatisfying attempts at systematic analysis and are, as a result, corrigible in precisely those terms. Perhaps the accommodations arrived at in conversation are best understood as stopgap measures, required for pragmatic reasons but ultimately subject to the standard tests of philosophical adequacy.

All of these possibilities seem to comport well enough with our ordinary conversational experiences, and they raise, in turn, further problems. Sometimes in conversation we are not persuaded, and it is difficult to find in Oakeshott an account of why persuasion is and is not successful. More important, sometimes we are persuaded when we shouldn't be. Oakeshott, like Arendt, cannot be thought to accept as the legitimate fruit of conversation just any kind of agreement regarding just any kind of proposition, but it is unclear what criteria he could invoke to make the relevant discriminations. Finally, when Oakeshott insists on coherence as the ultimate standard of experiential validity and concreteness, we may well wonder why this is not reducible to the kinds of methodical, algorithmic processes that he regards as foreign to conversation; after all, coherence is typically understood to be a matter of logical consistency.

In illustrating his views, Oakeshott writes as follows:

> [C]onsider how, in fact, a barrister in a Court of Appeal argues the inadequacy of the damages awarded to his client. Does he say, "This is a glaring injustice," and leave it at that? Or may he be expected to say that the damages awarded are "out of line with the general level of damages currently being awarded in libel actions"?[156]

Of course, the barrister does the latter, and Oakeshott claims, absolutely correctly, that this means that the barrister is indeed invoking "standards" and "criteria" of some sort. Why then should these not be the standards and criteria of logical and philosophical entailment? Perhaps, that is, the barrister is involved not in pursuing intimations but in deducing strictly the implications of recent judicial practices; if so, the soundness of his deductions would be subject to the usual philosophical tests. Oakeshott insists, again obviously correctly, that the barrister is engaged in "argument" of some kind; yet only pages earlier he had described any similar effort to pursue intimations as "a conversation, not an argument."[157] Such an apparent contradiction may represent little more than a terminological slip; on the other hand, it may suggest a more serious conceptual unclarity that would raise important doubts about the very distinctions that are the basis of Oakeshott's entire theory of conversation.

156. Oakeshott, "Political Education," p. 134.
157. Ibid., p. 125.

2. As we have seen, the Third Iteration, in either of its incarnations, is based on a particular understanding of the nature of political life. The facts of politics are, in some sense, boundless, unpredictable, haphazard; they lack the kind of fixity and reliability that would be necessary if one were sensibly to pursue a science of political action or a logic of political ideas. Traditional modes of rational analysis—empirical or speculative—are intolerant of the unexpected, the ambiguous, the random, the ineffable. For this reason, political knowledge or wisdom must be of a rather different nature.

All of this initially seems straightforward enough, but in fact it harbors some serious perplexities. As we have seen, Arendt and Oakeshott (like Machiavelli, Tocqueville, and Nietzsche before them) cling to the notion that there is such a thing as political wisdom, and that those mental faculties peculiarly suited to the public realm do produce a kind of truth or knowledge, however unconventional. Again, judgment may be good or bad; conversation and experience may be coherent or incoherent. If, however, the political world were in fact thoroughly and radically unpredictable—if a sense of randomness and complete instability were truly at its core—then it would surely be impossible to find any kind of warrant for any kind of claim to wisdom or knowledge. The argument is, roughly, Kantian. Kant claims that cognition presupposes, among other things, the fact of synthesis and combination, including the transcendental unity of apperception, in order that the so-called manifold of intuitions can be rendered intelligible. Without this, experience (if that is even the right word) would be totally chaotic, and there could be no question of anything resembling thought or cognition in the normal sense. In a similar way, then, if the political world were utterly lacking in structures, patterns, uniformities, and regularities, then the very notion of political wisdom or judgment—indeed, the very idea of coherent action itself—would be absurd.

Of course, this cannot be what Arendt and Oakeshott have in mind. They must view the world of politics as being somewhat *less* stable, somewhat *less* orderly than, say, the world of physics but as having, nonetheless, certain features that are regular, recurrent, and fixed. The sea may be boundless, but it is also navigable; one can learn about and predict the currents and the tides; one can identify in advance and avoid with some confidence dangerous obstacles; one is never simply and solely lost. But if this is true, we must wonder why public life is not—at least to some significant degree—available for standard kinds of rational analysis. For it seems unlikely that rationality requires a perfectly hermetic, completely transparent, and fully explicable field of inquiry in order to do its work. Mathematics proceeds in spite of Gödel's theorem; physics does not collapse in the face of the seemingly random motions of certain subatomic particles. Stated otherwise, the habits and dispositions associated with proof and rational demonstration are appropriate insofar as there is order in the world. Arendt and Oakeshott must presume that the political thinker or actor does not face total chaos, since that would render thought and action—judgment and conversation—virtually impossible; they must presume, therefore, that there is in the public realm a degree of rhyme and reason. If that is true, it remains unclear why that realm would not be, at least to that degree, available for scientific/rational scrutiny.

3. There is, finally and relatedly, the question of nihilism. In part, the entire perspective we have been considering—from Anthony Lewis and Nicholas Katzenbach, to Machiavelli, Tocqueville, and Nietzsche, to Arendt, Oakeshott, and the others—may be considered an attempt to define a middle ground somewhere between the lofty ambitions of Western rationalism and the prospect of a complete and unleavened skepticism. The focus, however, has been less on defending judgment, conversation, and the like against skepticism than on criticizing the putatively unrealistic pretensions of the rationalist tradition. This is, for historical reasons, quite understandable. Since the classical age, it has been rationalism, not skepticism, that has established the fundamental theses about political knowledge and wisdom against which any alternative account would have to struggle; the predominant concern, therefore, has been to raise serious questions about rationalism in politics. But in the process, it may be that political theorists have been insufficiently concerned to show just why nonrationalist alternatives do not dissolve ultimately into a kind of complete, perpetual, and unabashed assault on all intellectual standards per se.

Indeed, the Third Iteration has given rise to a literature that not only asserts but actually celebrates the elusiveness, the mystery, the irremediable ineffability of political affairs. We now have, for example, a political theory written in praise of ambiguity. It calls for, among other things, "an ontology of discordance" that would leave perpetually open the possibilities inherent in democratic liberty and would provide uniquely "a place for the pursuit of personal and common identity."[158] A politics of ambiguity would serve to undermine the stifling and confining structures of thought and action that emerge from the rationalist desire for certainty and coherence. It would provide, therefore, "a medium through which . . . voices of otherness can find expression in the self and the public world."[159]

Central to such an account is the view that the conventional quest for knowledge and certainty—and the concomitant emphasis on political order and stability—is rife with serious and undesirable social consequences. In brief, the categories of the rationalist tradition in their political aspects tend to foster institutions "whose primary purpose is to observe, control, correct, confine, cure, or regulate other people." The rationalist's goal is harmony, but the result is oppression. For a political theory of discordance would understand "harmonization to be normalization" and would see that "normalization, while unavoidable and desirable to some degree, also inflicts wounds on life."[160]

This is a most singular kind of perspective. The vicissitudes of fortune, which for a writer like Machiavelli are taken to be inconvenient and ineliminable features of a recondite world, features that present political actors and thinkers with difficult and unpleasant obstacles, are now thought of as virtues. The constitutive goal of all political life—order—is suddenly conceived of as a threat to, rather than a requisite for, the achievement of human good.

It must be noted that the argument toward this conclusion is not especially compelling. On the one hand, the notion that "harmonization" inflicts wounds is hardly controversial. The effects of law—or of efforts to establish new laws, sometimes revolutionary, sometimes not—are often personally painful, as any reader of *The Prince*, the Criminal Code, or the daily newspaper will know. Who would have thought otherwise? Moreover, the notion that establishing some "slack in the order"[161] can often be a beneficial political strategy is, of course, widely recognized by political thinkers including many (e.g., Hobbes and Hegel) who are rationalists primarily interested in order and har-

158. William Connolly, *Politics and Ambiguity* (Madison, Wisconsin: University of Wisconsin Press, 1987), p. 11. See also Connolly's "Taylor, Foucault, and Otherness," *Political Theory* 13 (August 1985), pp. 365–376.

159. Connolly, *Politics and Ambiguity*, p. 15.

160. Ibid., p. 8.

161. Ibid., p. 96.

mony. None of this leads to the conclusion that disorder, disharmony, and discordance are virtues; such a conclusion seems to require other grounds, and those grounds are not readily apparent.

Connolly adverts to certain "tribal festivals" which explicitly introduce discordant, inconsistent, or otherwise uncongenial elements into a culture:

> Seasonal festivals were enacted in which that which was forbidden was allowed and those who were normally subordinated (because their order necessitated it) were temporarily placed in a superior position. In these festivals, that which was officially circumscribed or denied was temporarily allowed and affirmed. The participants were able to glimpse the injustices implicit in their own necessities; they were encouraged to live these necessities with more humanity during the normal periods of the year. They acknowledged that some features of their own order, some of the dirt they produced, was mysterious to them. The reins of social coordination were not so tightly drawn that they had to pretend that they possessed sufficient categories to comprehend and eliminate the dirt in their order.[162]

I think it doubtful that this kind of evidence, in and of itself, can support a philosophy of discordance. The practices described might be plausibly interpreted as efforts to improve and make more secure the harmonious features of a culture. One would guess, for example, that the practice of publicizing the plight of subordinated members—presumably in safe, well-controlled situations—is done for the purpose not of fomenting genuine discord but for precisely the opposite reason, namely, to allow the culture to run more smoothly. This might be taken in a cynical, functionalist sense; these rituals operate as pressure valves, allowing society's discontented elements to blow off steam, thereby actually serving the long-term interests of those in power. But a more benign reading is certainly every bit as plausible; the rituals help produce an order that is truly and genuinely more humane and just. Similarly, the fact that participants are forced to confront "mysterious" features of their culture again seems quite unexceptional. There are undoubtedly limits to all human cognition; such limits may or may not be rooted in socially generated habits and categories of thought; but in either case, it is perfectly reasonable, indeed logical, that mem-

162. Ibid., p. 95.

bers should recognize those features of their culture that have the status of, so to speak, unproved premises.

Of course, it may be that Connolly's gloss is in fact correct, and that the rituals described do indeed provide evidence for an ontology of discordance. How we would actually come to know this is unclear. But, in another sense, the importance of *that* question—the question of knowledge—may well be what is at stake. For Connolly talks about the "contestable faith in the sufficiency of the knowing enterprise," thereby seeming to raise doubts about, among other things, the need for human thought and action to be coherent.[163] At this point, a range of old and not very interesting questions inevitably arises; for example, are Connolly's doubts about the importance of coherence themselves coherent? And this in turn raises, I think, the question of nihilism. If a theory of discordance is in fact an extension of the notions of judgment, common sense, and political wisdom that we have been considering, and if such a theory calls into account the very categories of coherence and knowledge that are generally thought of as basic to our idea of what it means to make sense, then perhaps the work of Arendt, Oakeshott and the others leads ultimately to a kind of intellectual chaos or anarchy that such authors themselves would vigorously disavow.[164]

The fundamental question thus remains: Is there in fact a coherent concept of political wisdom that would allow for a nonrationalistic account of knowledge or truth peculiarly suited to the world of public affairs? Our three iterations have illuminated, often in rich detail, some of the parameters of this question, but they have failed to answer it in a way that could be called truly rigorous and satisfying. I believe that all of this suggests a need to explore notions of judgment, common sense, and wisdom in a more general philosophical setting, unencumbered for the time being by considerations of a political nature, and focusing instead on the conceptual materials that we utilize in coming to grips with our own intellectual resources.

163. Ibid., p. 12.

164. Again, Arendt and Oakeshott can hardly be thought of as partisans of incoherence and discord. But Oakeshott's talk of the "mental fog" in which political decisions are made and Arendt's occasional references to things like the "clouded consciousness" and "ambiguity" that point to "a permanent way out" (in her *Rahel Varnhagen: The Life of a Jewish Woman* [New York: Harcourt, Brace, Jovanovich, 1974], p. 143) may be thought to encourage such tendencies in others.

Excursus: Political Judgment and the Individual

According to Benjamin Barber, the kinds of argument we have considered thus far misconstrue entirely the problem of political judgment, for they hold that political judgment is merely "a species of the underlying genus judgment . . . " and that it is, therefore, "little more than a particular kind of mental faculty."[1] Because of this, they fail to see that political judgment "is in essence political and not cognitive." Indeed, "what is missing [from such an account] is quite precisely politics. . . . The civic community engaged in public thinking is displaced by the rational individual engaged in private thinking as the source of judgment, so that cognition rather than common activity necessarily becomes the target of inquiry."[2] For Barber, the problem of political judgment has nothing to do with issues of cognition or "epistemology" but is, rather, bound up with the particular exigencies of political life. He sketches political life in passages such as the following:

> [T]he citizen must put her private views to a test that is anything but epistemological: she must debate them with her fellow citizens, run them through the courts, offer them as a program for a political party, try them out in the press, reformulate them as a legislative initiative, experiment with them in local, state, and federal forums, and, in every other way possible, subject them to the civic scrutiny and public activity of the community to which she belongs.[3]

All of this is said to be somehow "political" rather than "cognitive," "sociable" rather than "solitary," "communal" rather than "individual," "public" rather than "private." And since politics is what political judgment is all about, such judgment must similarly be political, sociable, communal, and public, rather than cognitive, solitary, individual, and private. Indeed, political judgment is not at all a feature of the individual human being in his or her cognitive isolation, but of "the multitude deliberating, the multitude in action."[4] Thus, in analyzing the concept

1. Benjamin R. Barber, *The Conquest of Politics: Liberal Philosophy in Democratic Times* (Princeton: Princeton University Press, 1988), p. 194.
2. Ibid., pp. 199–200.
3. Ibid., p. 199.
4. Ibid., p. 210.

of political judgment, the emphasis should be less on "judgment" than on "the political."

We might well recognize and warrant the sketch of political life that Barber provides. But in and of itself, it begs the question of political judgment altogether. According to the passage quoted above, the citizen is required to "debate," "run through," "offer," "try out," "reformulate," "experiment," and "subject to civic scrutiny." Do these verbs pertain to the actions of individuals or of collectivities? It seems plausible enough to suggest that Barber's citizen would have to do these various things in the light of, in interaction with, even in cooperation with other citizens. But that is hardly enough to refute the hypothesis that, in some important sense, it is the individual *qua* individual who is involved in these doings and who brings to bear on them cognitions and judgments that are in some ultimate sense his or hers alone. In other words, to say that politics is a matter of joint action is hardly surprising and in no way controverts the view that such action is rooted in the political judgments and cognitions of individuals. This certainly does not show that Barber's view of judgment is wrong, but simply that his sketch of the political is utterly indifferent to the question of whether or not political judgment is best understood as an individual mental faculty. Thus, his claim that "political judgment is the multitude deliberating" casts not the slightest doubt on the enterprise of examining above all the mental faculties of those individuals who happen to compose the multitude.

Barber's own account of political life shows that he himself cannot avoid the metaphysics of political judgment as a property of individuals:

1. According to Barber, political judgment "is defined by activity in common rather than by thinking alone."[5] This certainly sounds right. But we must ask, further, what it might mean to "think alone." Such a question could involve us in the most difficult issues in the philosophy of mind and cognitive science, and those are best avoided. We can suggest, nonetheless, that in many contemporary accounts, inspired roughly by Wittgenstein, there can be strictly speaking no such thing as "thinking alone"—if that phrase is understood to mean a process of individual cognition unconnected with and uninfluenced by considerations of a social nature. There is (arguably) no such thing as a private language, and this suggests in turn that we can make no

5. Ibid., p. 199.

sense of an individual using concepts unless we recognize that those concepts emerge out of some collective form of life of which that individual is a part. Barber's image of the solitary critic "in the dark" who judges what he sees in complete and utter isolation—"the rational individual engaged in private thinking"—describes no person that we know or can imagine.[6]

The account of political judgment that will be developed in the present book fully acknowledges and understands this. It accepts the view of Kant and Wittgenstein, Gadamer and Oakeshott, Arendt and Habermas that the radically isolated thinker simply cannot exist, and that the faculty of judgment is explicitly bound up with the idea of a "common sense"—a set of socially generated norms, intuitions, or premises without which judgment would be impossible. Judgment aims not at absolute truth but at "agreement," and this is explicitly and necessarily understood to be an interactive and political endeavor.

If, then, Barber opposes political judgment to thinking alone, and if by thinking alone he means a purely private state of individual cognition abstracted from and completely independent of social and political activity, then he is surely arguing against a straw man.

2. But perhaps Barber's point is rather different. It is one thing to recognize the social contexts of individual thought; it is something quite different to claim that political judgment is not really an individual endeavor at all. At times this seems to be Barber's position. He explicitly denies that such judgment is a matter of "intersubjectivity": "Where intersubjectivity suggests individuals in agreement, citizenship suggests individuals transformed by membership in a political association into common seers who produce a common judgment."[7] Political judgment is a feature of collectivities or multitudes, not of individuals. Presumably one should not say of an individual that he or she is a person of good (political) judgment; rather, we should only say that the committee or the majority or the board or the legislature showed good judgment in making this or that decision. Political judgment, as *political*, refers only and exclusively to "the integrity of a single whole judgment" produced by some kind of social entity: again, it is "the multitude deliberating, the multitude in action."[8]

---

6. One wonders about the philosophical (as opposed to rhetorical) usefulness of Barber's image here. After all, what could the critic see in the dark?

7. Barber, *The Conquest of Politics*, p. 203.

8. Ibid., p. 210.

As a purely linguistic matter, there seems to be nothing wrong with attributing good political judgment to collectivities (e.g., "the American people showed good judgment in electing Ronald Reagan"). But attributing such judgment to individuals is certainly equally acceptable usage and, I would say, conceptually preferable. Consider Barber's own account of what political judgment consists of. It results from "citizens interacting with one another in the context of mutual deliberation and decision." It occurs when "the wise citizen" recognizes his or her "duty to offer general principles for the application of policy." It depends upon the citizens coming "to acquire the kind of civic competence we associate with wise political judgment." It requires citizens to be "as insightful and prudent as congressmen or presidents."[9] I would suggest that it is virtually impossible to entertain such claims without deciding that they refer to the traits—the cognitive/intellectual traits—of individuals, albeit individuals embedded in social contexts. Collectivities are not "citizens" who "interact with one another" but products of such individual civic interactions; the "duty" of the citizen is certainly the duty of an individual—"the wise citizen"—for which he or she, *qua* individual, can be held responsible. One might talk about the "civic competence" and the "insight and prudence" of the American people, but even so one is almost certainly speaking euphemistically about the aggregated competence of the individuals who compose "the people."

Barber presents as a model of political judgment "the wise president" whose job is to "initiate policies and make decisions . . . [based upon] his political judgment."[10] If political judgment is necessarily a matter of collective or "common judgment," it is hard to see how one could predicate political judgment of "the wise president." Indeed, Barber's account of the civic or political process, properly understood, emphasizes an analogy between the individual traits of such a president and those of the citizen. Thus, for example, "the wise citizen, like the wise politician or the wise president, need not master fully the technical details of every issue up for decision." This "wise citizen" can hardly be other than an individual; as a result, here and elsewhere we can only conclude that in Barber's own description the wisdom of the

9. Ibid., pp. 200–202, passim.

10. Ibid., p. 201. When referring to the citizen, Barber often uses "she"; when referring to presidents, he uses "he."

collectivity is a direct function of the wisdom—the political judgment—of the individual citizens of which it is composed.

3. Now it would be possible to claim that political judgment or wisdom truly is a feature of the multitude that does not necessarily correlate with the cognitive features of individuals. Aristotle might be thought to contemplate some such view when he suggests that the aggregated opinions of democratic citizens may well contain a good deal of wisdom even though the individual opinions of each citizen, taken in isolation, are not likely to be very impressive. For Barber to endorse such a position would, I think, require that he jettison virtually everything that he says about effective citizen interaction, "the wise citizen," "civic competence," "insight and prudence," and the like, all of which seems to be central to his own political views. Nonetheless, there are indications that he might indeed incline in this direction, especially when he cites Rousseau's notion of the general will as a case of political judgment:

> This line of argument would seem to ally political judgment closely with the Rousseauian concept of the general will. . . . The general will depends on particular citizens practicing the craft of citizenship in a particular time and place. . . . It arises out of the intersection of interests but is disclosed by their collision. For in Rousseau's conception it is only when individual interests collide and sectarian biases cancel one another out that citizens can eventually discover in the residue of their combative interaction what they share in common—that which unites them as citizens and permits them to call themselves a community. . . . [The general will] depended neither on reason nor on good will but . . . asked only that men interact in a civic community in accordance with their interests as they saw them. Wise political judgment demanded no special cognitive faculty, no virtuous altruist, no universal imperative.[11]

Barber explicitly contrasts his interpretation of Rousseau to Kant's, and we may certainly find his reading to be arguable. But even accepting it, the claims of commonness here are belied by the seemingly inevitable language of individuality. Is it not true that the general will ceases to exist when individual citizens fail to "practice the craft of

11. Ibid., pp. 203–204.

citizenship"? Does not such a practice somehow depend on the capacities and inclinations of citizens *qua* individuals, even as they interact with one another? If each citizen brings to the deliberations not wisdom and civic competence but venality, selfishness, and obtuseness, do we not then have simply the will of all?

There is, however, a further problem with Barber's account of Rousseau. For in at least one plausible (admittedly Kantian) reading of the *Social Contract,* the general will is hardly the embodiment of political judgment. As noted earlier, Rousseau tells us that "the general will is always right," but "it does not follow that the deliberations of the people always have the same correctness. . . . One can never corrupt the people, but the people can often be misinformed (*trompé*)."[12] This seems to suggest rather the opposite of what Barber intends. The general will is, by definition, morally upright; its intentions are always "general," always good, and therefore it is never corrupted. But it often makes mistakes, often fails to apprehend what will really serve the general interest, and hence often displays bad judgment or a lack of prudence. The fact that it frequently "fails to see" what is the best course of action is hardly an indication of practical wisdom.

There is, to be sure, an element of political judgment in the *Social Contract.* But this is to be found, we have seen, not in the general will but in the Legislator—an individual whose knowledge is not scientific or rationalistic but who nonetheless understands and is able accurately to judge the abilities, passions, and needs of a people. Legislators are, for Rousseau, the truly "wise men" (*les sages*) who bring to the social world those ineffable but undeniable insights and skills that we associate with, among others, Plato's statesman and Machiavelli's founder.[13]

12. Jean-Jacques Rousseau, *Du Contrat Social,* 2:iii.
13. Ibid., 2:vii.

The Dichotomy of Judgment

OLLOWING KANT, WE MAY DEFINE judgment as the mental process by which universals and particulars are somehow brought together.[1] When we ask if Robert Bork has good judgment, we are asking if he is good at predicating certain universals of certain particulars. I use the word "universals" to refer to concepts— ideas or abstractions that do not necessarily apply to any particular thing but that may, in principle, apply to any number of such things. I use the word "particulars" to refer to individual things either actually or possibly existing in the world. This usage is intended to be nontechnical. While I believe that it is broadly consistent with most versions of the major philosophical approaches to the subject (e.g., realism, conceptualism, nominalism, resemblance theories), my aim is to avoid altogether controversies in metaphysics.

As for the phrase "somehow brought together," this speaks to the very heart of the philosophical problem of judgment.

I

In pursuing this problem, it will be useful to specify somewhat further the nature of what we are calling judgments. Consider the act by which we judge that *Churchill is a statesman*. In formulating such a judgment, we use a concept—*statesman*—that applies not just to Churchill but to any and all particular statesmen; the number of cases to which it refers is potentially unlimited. "Churchill," on the other hand, refers entirely and exclusively to a particular individual existing at a particular time

---

1. Immanuel Kant, *Kritik der Urteilskraft* (Hamburg: Felix Meiner, 1968 [1790]), Introduction 4:26.

and place. Further, the concept *statesman* would continue to be what it is—would continue to mean the same thing—regardless of whether or not Churchill in fact is a statesman. If we were to discover that Churchill is actually a bus driver, we would not then say that the concept statesman had changed. Rather, we would change our judgment: *Churchill is not a statesman.* Indeed, the concept *statesman* would remain unchanged even if all particular statesmen were suddenly to vanish from the face of the earth. In that case, we would likely offer yet a different judgment: *There are, at the present time, no statesmen.*

Such conclusions would seem to hold for many theories that treat universals as essentially linguistic expressions. For example, in certain meaning-is-use accounts, the meaning of the word "statesman" would stay the same whether or not particular statesmen continued to exist, since the rules for correctly using that word would not be affected by either circumstance; presumably, only our beliefs about the truth of certain sentences containing the word would change. Similarly, in some verificationist theories of meaning, the absence of all particular statesmen would not change the criteria of verification for the concept *statesman,* and hence would not change the meaning of the word; again, only specific claims involving statesmen would change.

Now to say that judgment is a matter of somehow bringing together universals and particulars is to imply that judgments are often expressed by sentences having the form "X (a particular) is Y (a universal)." But it should be clear that judgments need not involve only one particular and one universal. We may predicate a single universal of multiple particulars (e.g., *Churchill and Eden are statesmen*), multiple universals of a single particular (*Churchill is an aging, elitist statesman*), and multiple universals of multiple particulars (*Churchill and Eden are aging, elitist statesmen*). Moreover, judgments can bring together universals and particulars under different modalities: we can judge not simply that *Churchill is a statesman* but also that *Churchill is probably a statesman* or *always a statesman,* or that *Churchill is necessarily a statesman* or *contingently a statesman,* or that *Churchill ought to be [or ought not to be] a statesman,* and the like. But we should also be clear that not all statements of the form "X is Y" express judgments. For example, the sentence "Red is a color" does not at all bring together a universal and a particular. In that sentence there is no particular; both "red" and "color" denote universals. Such a sentence does not express a judgment, as here defined. The same is true of the sentence "$E = mc^2$." There is, indeed, a very large class of mental operations, typically resulting in meaningful expressions, that do not involve bringing together universals and particulars and hence are not matters of judgment. Judgment denotes a specific kind of mental activity, though obviously a common and important one.

Any judgment—as the bringing together somehow of a universal and particular—would seem to require at least three things: (1) the universal *qua* concept must be identified, and this means being able to specify at least some of the conceptual features that make it what it is; (2) the particular must be identified, and this means being able to specify at least some of the characteristics that individuate it;[2] and (3) there must be a mental faculty that allows us to establish some kind of demonstrable and explicable connection between the universal's features and the particular's characteristics such that we can say with some justification that "X is (or is not) Y." Together these three presuppositions may be thought to compose the basis of a *tripartite model of judgment.* The first involves (at a minimum) a logical or linguistic premise about what it means to have a concept; the second involves a premise about some of the things that make up the world; and the third has serious implications for the nature and possibility of rational knowledge. Each involves enormous practical and philosophical problems: What does it mean for a conceptual feature to be specified? What sorts of things function as individuating characteristics of particulars? What kind of relationship could there be between a conceptual feature on the one hand and (say) an empirical characteristic on the other? Do the cognitive sciences give us any reason to believe that we actually have, and could learn about, a capacity to establish relationships between universals and particulars?

Theories of judgment generally differ at least in part in terms of the way in which such questions are answered. But these are all questions about the specifics of the tripartite model; to treat the issue of judgment by addressing such questions is, by implication, to accept the general outlines of that model. Moreover, to accept the model is, we shall see, typically to endorse in one form or another a rationalistic account of judgment. For the tripartite model involves conceptual features, characteristics of particular things, and a mental faculty for link-

2. As Kripke has suggested, definite descriptions may not be necessary for identification per se. But identification for the purposes of judgment does seem to require such descriptions. See Saul Kripke, *Naming and Necessity* (Cambridge: Harvard University Press, 1980).

ing up those features and characteristics. The model is often thought to imply, further, that there are rules and procedures of inference according to which the features of various concepts and the characteristics of various particular things are juxtaposed to one another so that certain features can be said to correspond to certain characteristics and not to others. Any judgment is authorized and constrained by those inferential rules and procedures, and anyone who cares to justify a judgment must do so, therefore, by showing in terms of a rational argument how it is faithful to them.

Judgment is thus a matter of subsumption. Our conceptual apparatus may be pictured as a series of cubbyholes, each concept/cubbyhole distinguished from the others in terms of its peculiar conceptual features. Particular objects are to be placed in the various cubbyholes according to whether their characteristics correspond to the conceptual features of those cubbyholes. The process cannot make sense unless there are rules and procedures for determining such correspondence, and insofar as there are such rules, any placement of an object in a cubbyhole is subject to review according to whether or not the rules were faithfully and correctly followed. Particular objects are thus subsumed under—classified or categorized in terms of—various concepts. This is what it means to judge objects, and any such judgment may be evaluated in light of the rules of subsumption.

Such a picture is often understood to be rationalistic for two reasons. First, to follow a rule is generally thought to require rationality insofar as the rule-follower must be able logically to relate his or her choice to the dictates of the rule. That is, one must be able to understand how one's choice conforms to or is consistent with the rule, and that, in turn, presupposes that one can and does invoke the principles of logic or rationality. Of course, such an account pertains only to self-conscious and autonomous rule-followers; it does not apply to cases of mindless, reflexive obedience. As such, the account is not necessarily correct or useful; Wittgenstein, among others, raised serious questions about the degree to which rule-following can be understood in this way.[3] But such questions can be put aside for the time

3. Ludwig Wittgenstein, *Philosophical Investigations* (New York: Macmillan, 1968), for example, nos. 199–206. See also, Saul A. Kripke, *Wittgenstein on Rules and Private Language* (Cambridge: Harvard University Press, 1982). Wittgenstein's approach is discussed in Chapter 3 below.

being. At this point, I am offering only the empirical hypothesis that most of those who endorse our tripartite model of judgment proceed as though rule-following were a rational activity, and that they understand rationality, at least in part, in terms of the standard principles of argument and inference.

Second, the tripartite model usually involves a rationalistic interpretation of judgment insofar as the rules of subsumption are thought to be nonarbitrary. Specifically, they are generally understood as making rational sense—and are, hence, authoritative—only to the degree that they respond to "true" or at least justifiable connections between the features of concepts and the characteristics of things. The nature of such connections is, of course, a matter of fundamental philosophical disagreement. A Platonist and a nominalist can both accept the tripartite model and still have dramatically different views about what it means to judge truly. But insofar as they endorse that model, they are, I believe, equally committed to the view that the rules of subsumption must possess some kind of reasoned justification and that there is, or in principle ought to be, a way of making that justification clear and explicit.[4]

In sum, the tripartite model usually requires not simply a faculty for connecting conceptual features to characteristics of particulars but also a set of inferential procedures that both operate according to and can be defended in terms of the principles of reason. Such a rationalist account of judgment is of classical origin. One finds an especially forceful defense of it, for example, in Plato's *Gorgias,* and it will be useful to consider briefly the arguments to be found there and the issues that they raise. For the *Gorgias,* perhaps more than any other Platonic dialogue, confronts directly the question of reason and rationality in judgment. In doing so, it presents with particular clarity a central tenet of the rationalistic viewpoint: Any purported effort truly to connect universals and particulars that operates in violation of the tripartite model is in fact not a case of judgment at all; and since judgment is that which reliably and accurately connects universals to particulars, failing to judge necessarily means failing to make such a connection.

4. Here and throughout, I ignore serious disagreements about the precise nature of rational argument, inference, justification, and the like. For a useful recent discussion, see Douglas N. Walton, "What Is Reasoning? What Is an Argument?" *Journal of Philosophy* 87 (August 1990), pp. 399–419.

II

Gorgias is an inquiry into the nature of rhetoric and the business of teaching rhetoric. The inquiry posits and develops the implications of an extremely important and influential distinction between two kinds of human endeavor: those that are a matter of craft (*technē*) and those that are a matter of experience (*empeiria*).[5] To say of an activity that it is a matter of craft is to say that it necessarily involves what may be called "craft knowledge." Conversely, to say of an activity that it is a matter of experience is, for Plato, directly to deny that it necessarily involves craft knowledge.

Plato views rhetoric as an archetypical example of experience-activity and writes of it as follows:

> Pandering (*kolakeian*) is what I call it, and I assert that such a thing is shameful, Polus—I am addressing this directly to you—because it aims at pleasure rather than at what is best. I assert that it is not a craft-activity (*technēn*) but an experience-activity (*empeirian*), for it can give no rational account (*logon*) of the nature of its applications (*prostherei*), hence cannot explain the foundation (*aitian*) of each. I do not give the name craft to any activity that is nonrational (*alogon*). (*Gorgias,* 465a)

According to Plato, craft knowledge involves explicit principles and rules for achieving some specified end. Those principles and rules can be identified, articulated, and learned, and they can be used as criteria for deciding in a particular case whether or not a craft is being properly executed. Each craft is, in some sense, constituted by its own particular principles and rules.[6] These latter, therefore, are the standards according to which one determines whether or not the craft has been performed correctly. Anyone who attempts a craft may be held responsible for showing that his or her actions comport with the principles of that craft. Of course, such a demonstration requires knowledge

5. On the meaning and history of these terms, see the "Commentary" by E. R. Dodds in his edition of the *Gorgias* (Oxford: Clarendon Press,1959), pp. 228–229. Dodds suggests that the sharp distinction between *technē* and *empeiria* is characteristically, and perhaps originally, Plato's. Irwin is more equivocal: see Terence Irwin, "Notes" to his addition of the *Gorgias* (Oxford: Clarendon Press, 1979), p. 130.

6. On the uniqueness of individual crafts, see John Gould, *The Development of Plato's Ethics* (Cambridge: Cambridge University Press, 1955), p. 32.

of those principles; and to know the principles is to know the craft, that is, to have craft knowledge.

In addition, any craft, as a rational endeavor, must have principles or rules that make sense in that they demonstrably lead to the desired end. Not just any principles and rules will do. This, in part, is what permits a craft-activity to give "an account of the nature of its applications" and to "explain the foundation [or rationale] of each." It can explain and justify itself, in other words, by showing how it produces that which it wishes to produce.[7]

It is for this reason, moreover, that a craft-activity aims not at pleasure but at what is best.[8] In Plato's view, there is no rational accounting for what does and does not provide pleasure. Some of the things that give me pleasure—certain kinds of music or food, for example—may be repulsive and unpleasant to you and, of course, vice versa. This is an empirical fact, but Plato seems to think that it reflects a necessary truth: there is no principle for determining what is pleasurable. Indeed, pleasure itself is not only purely private and subjective but, as far as we can tell, entirely random, inexplicable, and beyond—or beneath—rational explanation. There is no accounting for taste. Of course, it may be that a certain individual should not indulge in certain things that he finds pleasurable because they are in some respect demonstrably harmful. But this in no way denies that those things are pleasurable to him, and it in no way compromises the view that their pleasurability defies any kind of rational analysis.

I take it that such a position presupposes a strong distinction between feeling pleasure and being happy (*Gorgias*, 465a, 472c–473d). Whereas pleasure (*hēdonē*) is an entirely subjective, nonrational feeling for which there is, apparently, no rhyme or reason, happiness (*eudaimonia*) on the other hand is not a feeling at all but an objective fact that presumably involves the degree to which one is living in accordance with one's nature.[9] The two are distinct and separate in that

7. C. D. C. Reeve, *Socrates in the "Apology"* (Indianapolis: Hackett, 1989), pp. 39–45; and Gould, *The Development of Plato's Ethics*, p. 34.

8. But compare the discussion in *Gorgias* with those of the *Laches* (195b), *Charmides* (171c), and *Republic* (333e–335a).

9. As should be apparent, I incline to the rather old and widely criticized account of *eudaimonia* offered by J. D Mabbott, "Is Plato's *Republic* Utilitarian?" in *Plato II: Ethics, Politics and Philosophy of Art and Religion*, ed. Gregory Vlastos (South Bend, Indiana: University of Notre Dame Press, 1971), pp. 62–63. According to Mabbott, *eudaimonia* is not pleasure derived from living a good

pleasure does not necessarily make one happy, and happiness is not by definition pleasurable. Such a formulation can help make sense of Socrates's claim that "to commit injustice is worse than to suffer it" (*Gorgias,* 473a) and that a just man who has been "arrested and tortured on the rack (*streblōtai*) and castrated . . . and forced to watch his wife and children being tortured . . . and crucified or tarred and burned alive" will nonetheless be happier than the unjust man who leads a life of opulence and physical gratification.

It is certainly true, as commentators have noted, that Plato elsewhere contemplates a hierarchy of pleasures, and that happiness involves, or is related to, a capacity to enjoy the higher or greater pleasures (e.g., *Republic,* 580d–583b; *Laws,* 653b). But happiness is not synonymous with the maximization of pleasure. Plato is, in this sense, no hedonist. To seek pleasure is to pursue a will-o'-the-wisp, to engage in an undertaking that is likely to fail. To seek happiness, on the other hand, is a rational endeavor having a clear and discoverable goal. That goal is to live a certain kind of life and be a certain kind of person. The achievement of this goal may well lead to the greatest or purest pleasure; but this is, for Plato, a fortuitous by-product, rather than a definition, of *eudaimonia. Eudaimonia* is the preeminent moral category and, in Irwin's words, "our hedonic judgments offer no independent standard of good and evil."[10]

Against this kind of interpretation, Gosling and Taylor suggest that Plato, in the *Gorgias,* is in fact an enlightened hedonist who privileges intellectual pleasure while disparaging bodily pleasure. According to their account, the *Gorgias* does reject the cruder hedonism of Callicles (*Gorgias,* 495a) and of Socrates (as expressed in *Protagoras,* 335c–336c), but it nonetheless holds that certain pleasures, suitably defined, are constitutive of happiness.[11] Gosling and Taylor agree that

---

life; rather, it is identified as the good life, and this means that it is nothing other than a correct relationship between the parts of the soul.

10. Terence Irwin, *Plato's Moral Theory: The Early and Middle Dialogues* (Oxford: Oxford University Press, 1977), p. 122. For rather different views, see Gould, *The Development of Plato's Ethics,* pp. 74–87 and C. D. C. Reeve, *Philosopher-Kings: The Argument of Plato's Republic* (Princeton: Princeton University Press, 1988), pp. 144–159.

11. J. C. B. Gosling and C. C. W. Taylor, *The Greeks on Pleasure* (Oxford: Oxford University Press, 1982), pp. 98–122. For a discussion, see Roslyn Weiss, "The Hedonic Calculus in the Protagoras and Phaedo," *Journal of the History of Philosophy* 27 (October 1989), pp. 511–529.

Plato in the *Republic* begins to give up hedonism altogether, a process developed further in the *Philebus;* but even in the *Republic* he continues to maintain that the higher pleasures, though not constitutive of happiness, have a certain special relationship to happiness and are, as a consequence, rationally and objectively demonstrable.

This is a controversial reading, and one may wonder in particular about the very idea of intellectual pleasure. Can something that is not at all a matter of perception, hence not sensed or felt in any way, be pleasurable? These are murky waters, and to pursue them in depth would take us far afield. My own intuition is that what Gosling and Taylor call intellectual pleasure is quite close to what I am calling *eudaimonia.* Each is an objective state of being that is attainable through rational procedure. Each is thus different from "aesthetic pleasure," which is a matter of feeling and perception (*aisthēsis*) and is, for that reason, unaccountable.[12]

Since any craft-activity must be able to give an account of itself that explains how it leads to its desired end, and since there is no accounting for (aesthetic) pleasure, and hence no possibility of determining reliably what will and will not be gratifying, there can by definition be no craft-activity that aims at pleasure.[13] Since happiness, unlike pleasure, is capable of objective determination, and since this seems to be a minimum condition for knowing how happiness is to be obtained, craft-activities can and should aim at "what is best" or happiest. Only by aiming at what is best rather than at what is pleasurable can an activity hope to give a rational justification and explanation of itself.[14]

---

12. An ingenious and powerful approach to the problem of Platonic hedonism is provided by Reeve, who argues that happiness and pleasure are, respectively, the form and content of the good. Reeve, *Philosopher-Kings,* p. 144.

13. Irwin seems to doubt that Plato has shown this: "[Plato] apparently thinks that the concern of rhetoric with pleasure disqualifies it from being a craft. But why is that?" Irwin, "Notes," p. 135.

14. My account implies that Plato endorses an analogy between craft-knowledge and virtue. I think that this is clearly true of the *Gorgias.* But the degree to which the craft-analogy persists in Plato's later writings, especially the *Republic,* is a matter of considerable debate. For arguments in favor of a craft-analogy interpretation of the *Republic,* see Julia Annas, *An Introduction to Plato's Republic* (Oxford: Oxford University Press, 1981), p. 261; J. R. Bambrough, "Plato's Political Analogies," in *Philosophy, Politics and Society,* 1st series, ed. Peter Laslett (Oxford: Blackwell, 1956); J. R. Bambrough, "Plato's Modern

Plato provides as examples such alternatives as cookery versus nutrition and cosmetics versus medicine. In each case, the first is an experience-activity that aims, literally, at appearances, at merely sensuous experiences the pleasurableness of which cannot be rationally proved, whereas the second is a craft-activity that aims at an objective good. Cookery seeks to make things taste good, but of course there is no accounting for taste; nutrition seeks to provide a sound diet and this, presumably, is amenable to strict scientific analysis and proof. Similarly, the goal of cosmetics is to make you appear to be healthy, whereas the goal of medicine is to make you healthy in fact, and only the latter can give a rational account of how it works. Obviously, to be a good nutritionist requires one to know nutritional science; to be a good doctor is to know medicine.

Now it seems clear that all types of craft-activity, insofar as they necessarily rely on craft knowledge, involve judgment as described in our tripartite model. Each is a matter of bringing together a universal and a particular; each necessarily presupposes knowledge of conceptual features and particular characteristics; and each presupposes a capacity and a method for relating the one to the other. In the case of medicine, for example, doctors know what it means to be physically healthy and, thus, know (at least some of) the various features of the concept *healthy body;* further, they have observed and hence know certain distinguishing characteristics of this or that particular body; and finally, they have a method for relating characteristics to features such that they can decide to what extent a particular body can be classified as a healthy body. Moreover, they have a concept of how the body works such that they know that certain kinds of practices will make it healthier and others not; they are able to observe or understand the characteristics of particular acts that have been, or might be, performed on bodies; and finally, they are able to assess those particular

Friends and Enemies," *Philosophy* 37 (1962), pp. 97–113; M. B. Foster, *The Political Philosophies of Plato and Hegel* (London: Russell and Russell, 1965), pp. 18–19; Hans-Georg Gadamer, *Truth and Method* (New York: Crossroad, 1986), pp. 281–289; G. M. A. Grube, *Plato's Thought* (Boston: Beacon, 1958), p. 265; and Leo Strauss, *The City and Man* (Chicago: University of Chicago Press, 1964), pp. 71–79. For demurrals, see R. C. Cross and A. D. Woozley, *Plato's Republic: A Philosophical Commentary* (London: Macmillan 1964), pp. 12–16; Gould, *The Development of Plato's Ethics,* p. 31; and Irwin, *Plato's Moral Theory,* pp. 177–185, 201–204.

acts in order to determine whether or not they can be classified as healthful.

Experience-activities, on the other hand, do not comport with the tripartite model, and hence in Plato's account do not involve judgment at all. There are, it seems, at least three ways in which an activity can fail to meet the requirements of the tripartite model: either there is no knowledge of conceptual features, or there is no knowledge of particular characteristics, or there is no faculty or method for relating the one to the other. It will be useful to consider each of these tests in more detail, though not *seriatim.*

1. Plato's cases of experience-activity seem generally to fail the *first* test—knowledge of conceptual features. Cookery, for example, aims at making things that are delicious. But since there is no accounting for taste—since taste is random and inexplicable—there is, strictly speaking, no concept of delicious. We could not know the features of a concept of delicious; hence we could not know the concept itself, and if we don't know the concept, strictly speaking we don't have such a concept at all.[15] Of course, it appears that we utilize a concept of delicious all the time. But, by implication, Plato wants to claim that when we use the word "delicious" we are really expressing not a concept of *delicious* but the concept of *personal gratification with respect to food;* for the sake of clarity, we really should be saying something like "This pleases my palate" or "I am enjoying this." Further, Plato wants to claim that such a concept of personal gratification pertains not at all to what is being eaten (nor, perhaps, even to my actual sensations themselves, since those are utterly private, nonconceptual, and inexpressible),[16] but to certain behavioral consequences of my having eaten it. I smile, I smack my lips, I say that I want to eat more of the same thing, I ask for the recipe—these all are evidence of, or represent features of, the concept of my being gratified. They are thus features of a concept that does not in any direct way apply to the thing that has somehow caused my gratification.

Since there is no concept of delicious, there can be, according to the tripartite model, no judgment about what is delicious; that is, there

15. In Kantian terms, delicious is, like beauty, an indeterminate concept (*unbestimmten Begriffe*); see *Kritik der Urteilskraft* 57: 237.

16. For a relevant discussion of Frege's approach to these issues, see W. P. Mendonca and P. Stekeler-Weithofer, "Was Frege a Platonist?" *Ratio* 29 (December 1987).

is no cubbyhole marked "delicious" into which this or that particular food could be placed. And since Plato understands craft knowledge to be importantly a matter of judgment, there can be, in fact, no craft of cookery. Cookery can only be an experience-activity that fails the first test of the tripartite model of judgment: it involves no knowledge of the concepts that would have to be known for it to be a craft-activity.

2. We may wish, nonetheless, to press Plato on this. Since we do have a concept of personal gratification, could there not be a craft of cookery that focuses precisely on that? This suggestion, of course, would entail a change in our definition of cookery: cookery aims not at making things that are delicious but, rather, at making things that produce evidence of personal gratification. This seems plausible enough. Are there not observable empirical regularities such that certain kinds of foods are widely thought to be personally gratifying and others not? Not everyone likes *boeuf à la mode,* but most people do. Perhaps a good cook is one who knows from experience which preparations will please most people. Could that not be the basis of a craft-activity?

The empirical premise of this suggestion is open to some question. It may be that "most people" having certain sociohistorical characteristics are gratified by *boeuf à la mode,* but it is unclear to what extent those preferences can be generalized to include "most people" regardless of when and where they live. Would Spartan helots or Mongol warriors or Hindus of a specific caste or Africans belonging to a certain tribe or, indeed, vegetarians of a particular county in California be equally gratified by a serving of *boeuf à la mode?* Further, even if we limit our area of activity to a fairly specific sociohistorical setting, the question of gratification remains unclear. After all, preferences change; tastes vary inexplicably, perhaps randomly. And this, in turn, raises doubts about the possibility of a craft-activity that aims at personal gratification, since any craft is, by definition, an activity that can give an account of itself, that can explain how its procedures work.

There are, however, stronger reasons to doubt that there could be a craft of cookery that aims at personal gratification. If it is anything, cookery involves a knowledge of the particular characteristics of particular foods. But there seems to be no way of drawing a theoretical connection between such characteristics and the features of the concept of personal gratification sufficient for us to make a judgment, as here defined. Perhaps we could (*pace* Plato) discover certain observable regularities that would allow us to predict the popularity of *boeuf à la mode* with some accuracy. But in a Platonic account, regularities of this kind would provide, at best, only statistical summaries of contingent, possibly accidental relationships, and these would not provide sufficient information for a craft of personal gratification. Again, any such craft presupposes the ability to offer a systematic account of *why* certain particulars correlate with one another. The lack of any discernable internal connection between the characteristics of particular foods and the features of personal gratification makes it unlikely that we could explain those correlations that we did happen to observe.

Here, then, we are describing an activity that fails the *third* test of the tripartite model—the capacity to relate particulars and universals. This activity involves knowledge of certain conceptual features (pertaining to personal gratification) and also knowledge of the characteristics of certain particulars (pertaining to food), but it has no way of establishing any kind of justifiable connection between those features and characteristics. Thus, it can only be an experience-activity in which no judgments are possible.

3. Imagine, finally, a fictional world in which the characteristics of particular foods and food preparations are radically unstable. In such a world, for example, the traits of one piece of beef would differ dramatically from those of other pieces of beef and, moreover, would themselves change inexplicably and unpredictably from moment to moment. To my own taste, this piece might be salty one moment, sweet another; it might seem soft for a while, then suddenly turn to leather. Roasting it for a certain length of time and at a certain temperature might make it tender and juicy or might make it hard and dry or might make it disappear altogether; the results of any particular cooking method might be completely unpredictable. In such a Kantian nightmare, any effort at cookery would fail the *second* test of our tripartite model—reliable knowledge of particulars. Even if there were established concepts such as *sweet* and *salty,* one would not be able justifiably to apply these concepts to individual foods, since the characteristics of those foods would be so unstable. In short, there would not be sufficient knowledge of particulars to allow for reliable and defensible judgments; hence, cookery could not be a craft-activity.

The unlikeliness of cases such as this does not prevent Plato from taking them most seriously. In the *Theaetetus,* for example, he explicitly confronts the doctrine of radical flux according to which everything in the world is "always in motion" (*Theaetetus,* 179e). Such a view— attributed by Plato to Homer, Heraclitus, and Protagoras—holds precisely that we can have no reliable purchase on particular things or their properties because they are so unstable. For example, "since not even white continues to flow white, and whiteness itself is a flux or change which is passing into another color, and is never to be caught standing still, can the name of any color be rightly used at all" (182c)? The result is that the very idea of judgment becomes absurd: "But if nothing is at rest, then every answer upon whatever subject is equally right" (183a).

While Plato vigorously rejects this theory as an account of the world in general,[17] he does believe that it describes accurately the particular facts of personal gratification. The fact that I like raw clams, whereas you find them repulsive, or that I am a sadist, while you are a masochist, or that Schoenberg's music sounds sweet to me upon one hearing and offensive the next—all of this suggests a kind of radical instability not with respect to clams or torture or Schoenberg (though that surely would be possible) but with respect to the characteristics of individual cases of personal gratification. The private, variable, and inexplicable nature of sensation itself means that, from the perspective of judgment, the world of personal gratification is as unreliable and irrational as our fictional world of ever-changing foods. And this, in turn, means that any effort at judgment regarding personal gratification would necessarily fail the second test of the tripartite model, namely, insufficient knowledge of relevant particulars.

Plato is thus committed to a fundamental dichotomy between craft-activity and experience-activity. With respect to the body, medicine and nutrition are craft-activities, cookery and cosmetics are experience-activities. With respect to the polis, politics properly understood is a craft-activity, and this primarily involves legislation and administration; politics improperly understood is an experience-activity, and this primarily involves rhetoric. Among the other experience-activities mentioned by Plato are varieties of what we today would call the "fine arts," for example, flute-playing, poetry, and drama (*Gorgias*, 501c–503a). According to Plato's account, none of them is a matter of judgment; unlike medicine, nutrition, and politics, all fail at least one of the three tests of our tripartite model; none of them invokes anything that can plausibly be called knowledge; hence, none of them is engaged in anything rational.

17. However, see footnote 19, below.

III

This Platonic dichotomy informs the entire debate about the concept of judgment. Its burden is to argue that judgment can only be rational, and this is a position that will surely sound plausible to a civilization that views science and logic, traditionally conceived, as models of what it means to think clearly and to have knowledge. There are, however, reasons to wonder if the Platonic dichotomy can be drawn with much precision or, indeed, if it can be coherently maintained at all. At the very least, it seems that certain crucial features of what Plato calls craft-activities may also be features of experience-activities and vice versa, and that the tripartite model discriminates between them less strictly than one might think.

Empeiria, which we have rendered as "experience-activity," is most often translated as "knack." This translation successfully evokes the kind of ineffable, haphazard, unspecifiable endeavor that Plato has in mind. But it misses altogether the etymological significance of *empeiria*. For Plato, a knack, or experience-activity, is based precisely on an ongoing empirical acquaintance with the relevant particulars; the more such acquaintance one has, the more one is an "experienced" practitioner of the activity in question. The cook's knack is thus rooted in, and is a product of, a familiarity with culinary things—with ingredients, preparations, the apparent likes and dislikes of diners, and so on. This kind of familiarity, acquaintance, or experience is quite different from and inferior to the systematic, discursive knowledge associated with craft-activity; nonetheless, it is what makes experience-activity possible in the first place.

Now as we have seen, Plato argues that all experience-activities fail at least one of the three tests of the tripartite model. Yet he himself concedes that *empeiria* does work. There are indeed individuals who can engage successfully in experience-activity, who have "the knack," whatever that might be. He agrees, for example, that the accomplished rhetoritician has "a bold (*andreias*) and skillful (*stochastikēs*) soul which is naturally clever (*deinēs*) in conversation with men" and which enables him to persuade his listeners (*Gorgias*, 463b). The experienced cook is similarly able to make better meals, to gratify the palate; and so too with the skillful poet, the tragedian, and the other "clever" practitioners of experience-activities. Few of us would deny that such individuals exist; many successful human endeavors certainly seem to be the products of knacks rather than of rational, discursive knowledge.[18]

For Plato to concede this, however, is to raise serious questions about the very distinction that he proposes between craft-activity and experience-activity. If the experienced practitioner is able to accomplish specific goals with some considerable success, then this suggests that the endeavor is not as random and unpredictable as we may have thought, and that experience does provide a genuine kind of knowledge. Indeed, our belief in the reality of such knowledge implies the further belief that experience-activities must in fact pass all three tests of the tripartite model of judgment. To begin with the second test, knowledge of particulars, how could one be a successful cook (i.e., a reliable maker of meals that gratify the palate) unless one had knowledge of those particulars involved in the culinary arts? Surely to concede that cookery can be successful is to concede that the experienced chef can distinguish good beef from bad, proper braising techniques from improper ones, and the like. This itself implies, further, a substantial acquaintance with or knowledge of universals. To distinguish qualitatively between one piece of beef and another requires that one has some purchase on such concepts as good beef and bad beef; and this means that cookery must also pass the first test of the tripartite model, knowledge of relevant universals. Finally, if all of this knowledge is ultimately to result in successful cookery, we must of course presuppose the existence of some capacity, however unreflective and inchoate, for bringing together particulars and universals. How else could the expert cook produce good meals with regularity? Thus, experience-activities necessarily pass the third test of the tripartite model as well. The price that Plato pays for conceding the existence of clever or skillful practitioners of *empeirian*—for conceding that some people really do have "the knack"—is to concede that such individuals can and do make reliable judgments, as defined by the tripartite model.

Of course, this is precisely what Plato intends to deny, and the result is, I think, an extremely serious problem. His account of the irrational, seemingly random nature of all physical gratification serves to undermine the coherence, or what Kant might have called the cognitive status, of experience-activities; as a result, such activities cannot be matters of judgment. But if we agree that cooks, orators, tragedians,

18. Irwin, "Notes," p. 135.

and the like, do somehow "know" what they're doing, then it seems that we must attribute to them the capacity to make judgments, at least as defined by the tripartite model. As far as I can tell, Plato never resolves this apparent inconsistency.

Such a contradiction emerges not simply from an exegesis, however faithful, of the *Gorgias,* but also from an analysis of our ordinary views of judgment and rationality in general. For both of the intuitions expressed in the *Gorgias* appear to be eminently plausible. Only craft-activities operating under the aegis of logic and science can claim to involve reliable, rational judgments; and yet, who would deny that many people do indeed have "the knack," such as it may be? To have the knack seems to presuppose the capacity for judgment, but how can this be, given the apparent exigencies of the tripartite model?

If Plato's notion of experience-activity seems problematic, so too does his account of craft. We have seen that Plato rejects the doctrine of radical flux as attributed, rightly or wrongly, to Homer, Heraclitus, and Protagoras. But the full development of his own metaphysical system contemplates the empirical world as, indeed, profoundly unstable, so much so that empirical knowledge seems to be not really knowledge at all.[19] This suggests, then, that craft knowledge, insofar as it presupposes empirical knowledge of the characteristics of particulars, is impossible. It may be that Plato comes to view philosophy as the

19. For a concise statement of the standard view, see Nicholas White, *Plato on Knowledge and Reality* (Indianapolis: Hackett, 1976), pp. 91–93. But some commentators deny that Plato regarded universals as the only objects of knowledge. See, for example, Annas, *An Introduction to Plato's Republic,* pp. 203–215, and Reeve, *Philosopher-Kings,* pp. 91–92. Both Annas and Reeve acknowledge that theirs is the minority view.

We may restate the problem as follows: Plato's general metaphysical views would ascribe true stability and knowability only to ideas or forms; the empirical world is, for him, in perpetual motion and hence elusive and insubstantial. Of course, this creates serious interpretive difficulties. How can Plato deny the doctrine of radical flux, and do so by relying on examples of sense perception, yet maintain that the world of appearances is constantly moving? One approach would be to say that, for Plato, the motion of empirical things is, ontologically, a matter of "becoming" and is, as a result, constrained by the rock-solid facts of "being." The shadow world is a reflection of reality. As such, it is controlled by that reality, at least to some significant degree. A shadow is a shadow of something; and the something of which it is a shadow has a crucial influence upon how that shadow will appear to us. Thus, the motion of the empirical world is not at all the aimless, unconstrained motion of radical flux.

only genuine craft-activity.[20] But since philosophy per se is concerned entirely and exclusively with the contemplation of forms or universals, it cannot involve bringing together universals and particulars; hence it is not a matter of judgment as we have defined it. Plato clearly believes that there are reliable ways of making judgments; the philosopher-kings are induced or compelled to return to the cave where their abilities can have some practical consequences. But exactly what justifies this belief, and what warrants the practical judgments of philosopher-kings, is not entirely clear.

One way of resolving these dilemmas would be to specify two different methods for making judgments successfully, one rational/scientific, the other "experiential," both of which conform to the spirit of the tripartite model of judgment, though in quite radically different ways. Such an effort, I believe, can be traced directly to the sixth book of the *Nicomachean Ethics*.

IV

Aristotle's argument is based on a distinction between *sophia* (theoretical or scientific wisdom), *technē* (craft wisdom), and *phronēsis* (practical wisdom). His discussion of them is rooted in a complex and idiosyncratic technical vocabulary that raises, in and of itself, serious questions in the philosophy of mind about the relationships among mental states, mental capacities, and mental activities. It is not clear to me that Aristotle's answers to such questions are entirely persuasive.

It is certain, nonetheless, that he chooses to treat *sophia, technē,* and *phronēsis* as parallel, in the sense that they may be compared and contrasted in terms of several common dimensions (see, for example, *Nicomachean Ethics,* 1140b1–5 and 1141b1–10). I believe that his inten-

20. Those who believe that Plato regarded philosophy as a craft include Ernest Barker, *Greek Political Theory: Plato and his Predecessors* (London: Methuen, 1961), pp. 218–219; Dale Hall, "The Philosopher and the Cave," *Greece and Rome* 25 (1978), pp. 169–173; Kenneth Henwood, "Of Philosophers, Kings, and Technocrats," *Canadian Journal of Philosophy* 9 (1979), pp. 310–312; and J. E. Tiles, "Techne and Moral Experience," *Philosophy* 59 (1984), pp. 49–66. For criticisms of this view, see Annas, *An Introduction to Plato's Republic,* pp. 262–271; Blair Campbell, "Intellect and the Political Order in Plato's Republic," *History of Political Thought* 1 (1980), pp. 365–367; and Peter J. Steinberger, "Ruling: Guardians and Philosopher-Kings," *American Political Science Review* 83 (December 1989), pp. 1207–1209.

tions in this respect are evident enough. *Sophia, technē,* and *phronēsis* describe distinctive ways of thinking, associated with particular intellectual virtues and states of mind, and presupposing certain characteristic mental capacities and mental actions. Thus, *sophia,* as the state of having scientific wisdom, is bound up with the capacity for and activity of doing science properly; similarly with *technē* and *phronēsis.*[21]

Special problems arise with *technē,* however. To begin with, Aristotle denies that *technē* is itself an intellectual virtue, as are *sophia* and *phronēsis* (*Nicomachean Ethics,* 1140b25). He explains this by saying that there is "virtue in the use of *technē* but not in the use of *phronēsis.*" Presumably, there can be no virtue in the use of *phronēsis,* since *phronēsis* is itself a virtue and hence something that, when done, is by definition done only well. *Technē,* on the other hand, is not itself a virtue, since it can be done either well or badly (see *Nicomachean Ethics,* 1141a9–14). While the terminological distinction is clear enough, one may wonder if it really does any philosophical work. For insofar as *technē* can be done well or badly, it seems that there must be a particular virtue involved in doing it well, a virtue perhaps peculiar to—or at least necessarily linked with—craft-activity. We might not want to call such a virtue *technē,* but we ought to call it something.

More importantly, Aristotle distinguishes *technē* from *sophia* on the grounds that *technē* operates in the realm of "freedom" rather than that of "necessity." The scientist or mathematician is forced, so to speak, by the true and ineluctable features of the world to believe this or that particular proposition; the craftsman, on the other hand, has a choice regarding what to construct and how to construct it. In this respect, *technē* is rather like *phronēsis*—a matter of freedom—except that whereas *technē* is concerned with producing things (*poiēsis*) external to itself, *phronēsis* is concerned entirely with the intrinsic merits of action (*praxis*) (*Nicomachean Ethics,* 1140b3). These distinctions raise all sorts of difficulties. Kant, for example, argued rather persuasively that technical endeavor is really assimilable to scientific activity, since the craftsman or technician is essentially engaged in the prescribed and "unfree" application of technical rules to particular and specifiable

---

21. This account comports with Terence Irwin's view. According to Irwin, an intellectual virtue is, indeed, a mental state (*hexis*), and this is in turn both a "first" activity (*energeia*) and a capacity (*dunamis*). See the terminological discussions in Irwin's translation of the *Nicomachean Ethics* (Indianapolis: Hackett, 1985), pp. 385, 388, 426, 430.

problems. Such a view, in turn, seems akin to the Platonic account of *technē* as described above, especially insofar as craft-activity, as opposed to experience-activity, is thought to be rationally explicable. On the other hand, if we reject the Kantian view and accept Aristotle's position on the freedom of the craftsman, then this raises serious questions about the difference between *technē* and *phronēsis;* for again, the latter difference presupposes the further distinction between "production" and "action," and the implications of *that* distinction, which are hardly self-evident, are also not very well specified by Aristotle (*Nicomachean Ethics,* 1140a1–20; cf. *Metaphysics,* 1048b18–33). Consider, for example, Aristotle's explicit claim that *phronēsis* is "productive" of happiness (*Nicomachean Ethics,* 1144a1–10).

For our purposes, these controversies can best be put to one side. Wherever we choose to place *technē,* whether with *sophia* or *phronēsis* or in some conceptually unspecified third area, the basic Platonic dichotomy outlined in the previous section of this chapter is, I believe, largely preserved in Aristotle. As we have seen, Plato proposes a central distinction between craft-activities and experience-activities. He thinks that craft-activities, and craft knowledge as well, are rational— as defined by our tripartite model of judgment—whereas experience-activities are irrational and inexplicable and involve nothing that plausibly could be called knowledge. We have provided some reasons to doubt the persuasiveness of this distinction. Nonetheless, the fundamental dichotomy substantially recurs—*mutatis mutandis*—in Aristotle's distinction between *sophia* and *phronēsis.* Aristotelian *sophia* is similar to Plato's craft-activity; it is discursive, scientific, and inferential, a matter of argument and rational justification, and hence fully consistent with our tripartite model of judgment. Aristotelian *phronēsis,* on the other hand, is similar to Plato's experience-activity insofar as it explicitly and necessarily defies any kind of systematic accounting; we encounter in the practical world no possibility of demonstration or argument, traditionally conceived.[22]

There is, however, one all-important difference between the Platonic and Aristotelian positions: whereas Plato regards experience-activity as irrational, unreliable, and incoherent, Aristotle insists that *phronēsis* is "necessarily a matter of attaining rational truth and is concerned with actions involving what is good for man" (*Nicomachean Eth-*

22. See John M. Cooper, *Reason and Human Good in Aristotle* (Cambridge: Harvard University Press, 1975), pp. 24, 32–33, 46, 51.

ics, 1140b5). *Phronēsis* is not haphazard, noncognitive, and foundation-less; it is, rather, a coherent, truth-producing mode of thought in its own right.[23] Indeed, Aristotle is quite direct in rejecting Plato's view. Whereas Plato had referred to experience-activities as matters of *eustochia* or "shrewd guessing" (*Gorgias* 464c), Aristotle says that *eustochia*, is precisely and explicitly what deliberation and practical judgment are not (*Nicomachean Ethics*, 1142a35–1142b5). In effect, then, Aristotle's goal is to describe how it is that things like experience-activities or knacks, though failing our usual tests of rationality, can nonetheless provide knowledge reliably. His task, in short, is to show how *phronēsis* can and must describe a kind of knowledge that is utterly distinct from, yet as reliable as, the knowledge associated with *sophia*. The Aristotelian approach to this endeavor raises several very serious problems.

1. *Sophia* is concerned with the realm of necessary truths. This means, among other things, that the conclusion of any philosophical or scientific argument is strictly determined by the unchanging facts of logic or of the world. Things are as they are and cannot be other-wise. The task of the logician or the scientist is, as Hegel might have said, simply to uncover what is already necessarily there. The truth, once discovered, forces itself upon us.

Phronēsis, on the other hand, is a matter of choice. It is involved in rendering judgments, making decisions, and performing actions that, as Aristotle puts it, "could have been other than they are" (*Nicomachean Ethics*, 1140a1 and1140a33–1140b5). This means that the re-sults of *phronēsis* are not foreordained; there is no necessity with re-spect to questions of practice, whether moral, political, or aesthetic.

Aristotle's argument for this conclusion is roughly as follows. The various types of inquiry that we engage in are distinguished from one another, in part, by the degree of accuracy (*akribeia*) that they can achieve. The more accurate the inquiry, the more scientific it is; the more scientific, the more its conclusions are necessary and unchang-ing. Accuracy itself is a function of the degree to which the object of

23. Troels Engberg-Pedersen, *Aristotle's Theory of Moral Insight* (Oxford: Oxford University Press, 1983), pp. 189–191; also, Cooper, *Reason and Human Good in Aristotle*, p. 9. For a discussion of *phronēsis*, see C. D. C. Reeve, *Practices of Reason: Central Themes in Aristotle's Nicomachean Ethics* (Oxford: Oxford University Press, 1992), Chapter 2. My account differs from Reeve's in many important respects, but I have learned a great deal from him, and have learned to disagree with him only with the greatest trepidation.

study is enmattered. For "matter resists form to varying degrees. . . . We can have exact, unconditional scientific-knowledge of an essentially matterless universal, or its definition, but when we turn to necessarily enmattered universals, exactness is lost."[24] Thus, according to Aristotle, the most accurate and scientific of inquiries are theology and mathematics, since they are concerned with purely abstract things. Biology and the other physical sciences, though true sciences, are somewhat less accurate, since they deal with universals that are necessarily connected in some way to material things. Least accurate of all is practical inquiry. For such inquiry always focuses primarily on particular, individual judgments and actions involving particular, unique circumstances. *Phronēsis,* in other words, is concerned above all with enmattered particulars, and these are the most unstable and unreliable parts of reality. For this reason, practical questions do not allow for knowledge based on deduction (*syllogismos*) and demonstration (*apodeixis*). To decide about particulars—to arrive at practical judgments—involves, instead, making choices that are always, to a significant degree, independent of and unsupported by rational proof.

This is not to say that practical reasoning is entirely without a scientific basis. Imagine, for example, that we have to decide whether or not to annihilate the city of Mytilene, killing many of its inhabitants and enslaving the rest. To a significant degree, such a decision will necessarily be informed by a variety of objective, scientific determinations. Ethical science will tell us that certain kinds of individuals deserve mercy in certain kinds of situations; military science will describe the best strategy for invading Aegean islands; biological science will tell us that people who are attacked may bleed, suffer, and die. All of this and more will constitute part of the demonstrated background for our decision about Mytilene and will, as a consequence, have a considerable influence. But the decision itself must depend ultimately on our understanding and assessment of certain enmattered particulars—the character of the Mytilenians themselves, the nature of their past actions, the actual and specific political consequences of a slaughter, and the like. There is no science for deciding about such particulars and hence no clear and precise way of proving that one policy is better than the other. In the face of this, in the absence of a complete and compelling scientific answer, we must simply listen to Cleon and Diodotus, and then choose.

24. Reeve, *Practices of Reason,* p. 16

The upshot is that questions of morality, politics, aesthetics, and the like absolutely require that we engage in a process of deliberation and decision (*bouleusis* or *prohairesis,* depending upon whether the emphasis is on the protocols by which one prepares to choose or the act of choosing itself).[25] For the impossibility of proof and demonstration means that we have to make a choice, and choosing is either an exercise of the arbitrary, isolated will, in which case it is merely an irrational and unreflective impulse, or else it emerges from a careful and thoughtful weighing of the possible virtues and defects of alternative courses of action (i.e., deliberation) in which case it is an intelligent enterprise worthy of being considered a part of *phronēsis.* Deliberation of this kind has no place in the realm of necessary truths. We have, for example, no choice as to whether two plus two equals four. In mathematics, and in science more generally, one simply deduces and demonstrates; there is no room for discussion; there is nothing to discuss, nothing to deliberate. Only in the practical realm, where the facts of the world do not strictly and straightforwardly determine our conclusions, does deliberation make any sense.

These general ideas, to which we have hardly done justice, play an important role in Aristotle's philosophical system. In the light of our present interests, however, they are deeply perplexing. Indeed, an exploration of some of these ideas raises, I believe, serious questions about the very distinction that we are considering, namely, the distinction between theoretical and practical wisdom.

According to Aristotle, *phronēsis,* unlike *sophia,* is importantly a matter of deliberation and choice. But if by "choice" one simply means the opportunity to select well or badly an answer to a question, then this is surely as characteristic of logic and science as it is of morals, politics, and aesthetics. In pursuing a mathematical problem, for example, one either follows or fails to follow the traditional, orthodox rules and procedures of mathematics, and the result will be a judgment that is correct or incorrect according to those rules and procedures. Failure to follow the standard rules may, of course, betoken simply a lack of understanding, and that is not necessarily a matter of choice (though it might reflect certain subsidiary choices). But it may also betoken a decision, based on deliberation, to pursue an unconventional approach, to "do it one's own way," or "try a shortcut," or "strike

---

25. The distinction between the act of choosing and the process by which one prepares to choose is itself hardly self-evident.

out on a new path." This perhaps rarely occurs in mathematics; people usually follow or try to follow the rules as taught. But even that may reflect a deliberate choice, namely, the decision *not* to pursue an unconventional approach. Thus, deliberation and decision is, at least potentially, an important part of mathematics, and of the sciences in general. And if this is so, then it is not at all clear how *sophia* and *phronēsis* might differ with respect to necessity and choice.

It may be objected that to choose badly in mathematics or science is to be incoherent—to make no sense—and that this is not really a viable choice at all. According to the objection, we should perhaps view choice less as a *psychological* phenomenon than as a *metaphysical* fact. In psychological terms, we can always decide to be incoherent and say that two plus two equals five. We can, that is, choose to be wrong. Metaphysical choice, on the other hand, implies the availability of two or more mutually inconsistent but equally "correct" answers to a single problem, and this is something that science does not seem to allow. It is absolutely required, for example, that two plus two equal four, and the rules for obtaining that result are not merely conventional; they are objectively valid. Thus, mathematics in particular and *sophia* in general cannot be a matter of metaphysical choice. *Phronēsis,* on the other hand, since it deals with enmattered particulars, must somehow involve both kinds of choice, psychological and metaphysical. This, then, is what it really means to say that practical judgments may be other than they are; hence it distinguishes *phronēsis* from *sophia.*

My own view is that the very notion of metaphysical choice—two or more mutually inconsistent but equally correct answers—is troubling; it seems potentially to violate, for example, the law of the excluded middle and the principle of contradiction upon which we base our very idea of making sense. But even putting this problem aside, the hypothesis we are considering—that *sophia,* unlike *phronēsis,* is a matter of psychological but not metaphysical choice—merely shifts the burden from logic and science to practice without really addressing the problem. For if there are in logic/science no metaphysical choices, only psychological ones, why should we assume that politics, morality, and aesthetics are any different? If, for example, we are convinced that some practical judgments are right, could we not agree that those judgments are themselves governed by more-or-less strict rules and inferential procedures for discovering answers—procedures that allow for psychological, but not metaphysical, choice?

2. As we have seen, Aristotle claims to have an answer to such questions. His argument is that practical judgments are concerned above all with enmattered particulars which, because of their unreliability, do not allow for the kind of accuracy and necessity characteristic of science. As a result, metaphysical choice is a constitutive feature of the practical realm. But at this point, two questions arise. First, why should we believe that enmattered particulars are so unstable as to prevent us from making objective, scientific claims about them? Pursuing this question in any detail would take us far indeed from the concerns of the present study. Suffice it to say that, according to many influential accounts, the data of sense perception are in fact the most reliable, indubitable data that we have, and that objective proof and demonstration is often precisely a matter of observing, classifying, and systematizing empirical particulars and their interactions. While such views are not necessarily correct, they do suggest that the truth of Aristotle's position is hardly self-evident.

Second, and more importantly, even if we accept his view of enmattered particulars, it is not entirely clear why practical questions cannot be the objects of (Aristotelian) science. As indicated above, Aristotle regards biology as less accurate than theology and mathematics, since it deals with universals that necessarily manifest themselves in material things. Nonetheless, it does remain a true science, the conclusions of which emerge from a process not of deliberation and decision but of objective proof and demonstration. This is because biology is, in large part, concerned with analyzing universals that are embodied in particular things, rather than analyzing the particular things themselves. Like theology and mathematics, its aim is to understand necessary relationships between universals.

It is perhaps easy to see why practical reasoning might not be as accurate as theology and mathematics, as understood by Aristotle. But why couldn't it be at least as accurate—at least as scientific—as biology? Just as biology deals with universal principles that are embedded in material things, could we not also develop and analyze objective principles of practical life that emerge from and are applied in terms of rational deductions and demonstrations? Such principles could be formulated without relying on processes of deliberation and decision; they would involve, therefore, nothing that could plausibly be called choice. They would be concerned with relations between universals—albeit necessarily enmattered universals—and hence could form the basis of a science every bit as rigorous and nondeliberative as any of the physical sciences.

Aristotle believes that ethical inquiry of this kind is both possible and important. In his view, however, such inquiry is a matter of ethical science, not *phronēsis*. He certainly agrees that *phronēsis* presupposes scientifically demonstrated principles of ethics. Such principles lend moral direction and legitimacy to the decisions of the practical person, and indicate that practical wisdom is not wholly unconnected with scientific wisdom. In our case of the Mytilenian debate, for example, we suggested that any decision would necessarily be informed by the conclusions of ethical science about what kinds of persons deserve mercy. The decision itself, however, would not be a matter of discovering and legislating such principles but of considering them in the light of the particular and peculiar facts before us. *Phronēsis*, then, is not primarily concerned with universals; it is concerned, rather, with *applying* universals to particular things, and this, according to Aristotle, cannot in and of itself be scientific.

There are, I believe, reasons to doubt this conclusion. Again, biology provides a useful analogy. We know that some biologists are empirically oriented. They are engaged in predicating biological universals of particular things according to specified and justifiable rules and procedures, as contemplated by the tripartite model of judgment. In so doing, they do not rely on deliberation and decision. The taxonomist does not make a free and uncoerced choice. Particular organisms are classified through the application of fixed methods and protocols that have themselves been justified in terms of demonstrated theories. Such a process is scientific, insofar as its conclusions can be explained and evaluated in the light of strict and recognized rules of inference, the utility of which has been established on solid, theoretical grounds.

It would seem that the process of applying ethical principles to particular cases could be quite similar. The ethical scientist formulates universal moral laws. The person of practical wisdom straightforwardly applies those laws to individual situations, utilizing accepted procedures that do not require, do not even permit, deliberation. Again, the results are controlled by, and evaluated in terms of, specific and justified inferential rules. In this sense, the conclusions of practical wisdom would be every bit as accurate and necessary—every bit as scientific—as those of biology.

One might insist, nonetheless, that any such procedure for predicating universals of particulars can never be entirely automatic and straightforward, and must therefore involve some deliberation and decision. Again, the argument would be that enmattered particulars, by their very nature, resist pure scientific analysis. But there is no reason to believe that this would not be equally true of biological science, insofar as its orientation is empirical. The enmattered particulars of biology are, after all, every bit as enmattered and particular as those of practice. The question thus remains: Why should choice be any more characteristic of practical inquiry than of scientific inquiry?

Stated perhaps more simply, it is not clear that Aristotle provides compelling reasons for believing that the tripartite model of judgment, with its emphasis on rational procedure and proof, does not apply to practical judgments. Hence, it is not clear why deliberation should be a peculiar and defining characteristic of *phronēsis*.

3. Perhaps, though, the difference between *sophia* and *phronēsis* pertains to the *nature* of their interest in enmattered particulars. While empirically oriented biologists must be concerned about such particulars, their interests are fundamentally theoretical. They seek to formulate covering laws, inductive generalizations, causal theories, and the like. These often take the form of empirical proofs whose goal is to account for (some aspect of) the structure of the world. Practical knowledge, on the other hand, is exclusively knowledge of the characteristics of individual things (*ekasta*).[26] It does not generalize, and it has no theoretical ambitions; its function is not to understand how the world works but simply to provide accurate characterizations of particular things taken in their isolation. According to Aristotle, this is a kind of knowledge that many scientific persons lack. Thus, for example, "people say that Anaxagoras or Thales or that sort of person is scientifically but not practically wise because they see that he is ignorant of what benefits himself. And so they say that what he knows is extraordinary, wondrous, difficult, and divine, but useless." (*Nicomachean Ethics*, 1141b5). Perhaps, then, empirically oriented science is a matter of bringing together universals and particulars for the purpose of generating sound theories, while *phronēsis* is interested only in par-

---

26. Aristotle also uses the term *eschata* (*NE* 1142a24). This is variously translated as "ultimate particulars" or "last things." But it seems that Aristotle must have in mind here simply the most extreme or purest particulars—"bare particulars," perhaps. They are pure or bare in that one perceives and grasps them without relying on any kind of conceptual, discursive, or analytic process. Such a rendering is, I believe, authorized by Liddell/Scott.

ticulars and, for this reason, need not concern itself with universals at all.

Aristotle offers the following example: "Someone who knows that light meats are digestible and healthy, but not which sorts of meats are light, will not produce health; whereas someone who knows that poultry is light and healthy will be better at producing health" (*Nicomachean Ethics*, 1141b16–21). Presumably the first individual has scientific knowledge. This means that he or she understands the structure of certain aspects of the world, pertaining to the proper function of the human body as it digests various kinds of meat, and therefore can account systematically for the health consequences of various diets. But by focusing on such general theoretical issues, the scientist *qua* scientist is unable to discern which particular food is a case of light meat and hence—like Anaxagoras or Thales—is unable to act prudently and wisely. The person of practical wisdom, on the other hand, can look at this or that particular morsel and, in virtue of the faculty of *nous*, determine accurately whether or not it is an example of light meat.[27]

Now it seems clear that in order to discover that light meats are healthy, one must have knowledge, not necessarily of poultry, but at least of some particulars. One requires, for example, knowledge of the human body, and this presupposes an acquaintance with at least some particular human bodies. Without such an acquaintance, how could one obtain sufficient knowledge of the nature of human bodies to understand how they function? And in the absence of this kind of understanding, how could one possibly conclude that the human body is in principle benefited by light meats? Indeed, how could one produce plausible and accurate principles of nutrition without understanding at least some particular cases to which those principles apply? To have *sophia* thus requires abilities and habits of the sort described in our tripartite model of judgment—a knowledge of particulars, a knowledge of universals, and a set of subsumptive rules and principles.

But in this respect, *phronēsis* seems to be no different, for despite its practical focus, it too requires knowledge of both universals and particulars. To say that poultry is light and healthy presupposes not only knowledge of particular pieces of meat, but also an understanding of certain universals. The sentence "This is a piece of poultry and it is, therefore, healthy" invokes the tripartite model of judgment at least

27. Cooper, *Reason and Human Good in Aristotle*, pp. 57–58.

twice, subsuming the particular morsel under the category "poultry" and, again, under the category "healthy." Judgments made by the person of practical wisdom, therefore, seem to be every bit as scientific, inferential, and subsumptive as those made by the person of *sophia*.

None of this necessarily undermines Aristotle's claim that certain individuals have theoretical but not practical ability, for it is not at all necessary, or even very persuasive, to formulate such differences in epistemological terms. Perhaps Anaxagoras and Thales were genuinely inept when it came to their own practical welfare, but this would almost certainly reflect psychological or moral features having to do only with the kinds of things Anaxagoras and Thales chose to think about. For contingent reasons, they presumably tended to focus on universals and particulars that were not especially germane to their own welfare. As a result, it appeared that they had their heads up in the clouds. But there is no good reason to doubt that their scientific abilities could have been applied as assiduously and effectively in the world of affairs, and that such an application would have reflected not a profound and structural intellectual change but merely a change of focus.[28]

Ultimately, then, Aristotle's example of light meat and health does not show that the processes of scientific and practical judgment are importantly different from one another, at least with respect to knowledge of universals and particulars. And if this is so, then we have, indeed, no reason to believe that *phronēsis* describes a distinctive and unique kind of knowledge.

4. It might be argued that the foregoing misconstrues Aristotle's notion of scientific wisdom. Perhaps he views *sophia* as being so nonempirical that it need not or should not deal with particulars at all. Science is a matter of conceptual analysis, the analysis of universals and their implications, and this does not require any familiarity with individual cases. Thus, to know that light meat is healthy simply requires knowing the concept of the human body and the concept of light meat and being able to deduce the implications of the one for the other. In such an account, knowledge of particulars—empirical knowledge—is strictly a practical activity; hence, all attempts to bring together universals and particulars would be examples of *phronēsis*.

---

28. Indeed, Herodotus (*Histories,* Book 1, 74–77) reports a famous story about Thales's practical abilities in helping the Lydian king Croesus cross the river Halys.

This view seems not to comport with science as Aristotle prescribed it or as he actually practiced it, though there is some substantial controversy about this.[29] Moreover, it would result in the bizarre conclusion that all claims about particular things, since they cannot be matters of *sophia,* must be matters of *phronēsis.*[30] Such a conclusion would undermine the kind of distinction that Aristotle clearly has in mind. Sentences such as "This creature is a basset hound," or "That is a molecule of water," or "Martin Luther lived in the sixteenth century," do not express Aristotelian practical judgments. To believe otherwise is to make a mockery of the very idea of practical wisdom.

But even were we to accept this kind of account, it would obviate altogether the notion that practical wisdom involves an epistemologically distinctive and peculiar kind of intellectual activity. For in such a circumstance, *sophia* would not be a matter of judgment at all, since it would not involve the subsumption of particular cases under universals, and *phronēsis* would, in most instances, be a straightforward example of rational judgment according to the tripartite model since, ac-

29. See G. E. L. Owen, *"Tithenai Ta Phainomena,"* in *Logic, Science, and Dialectic* (Ithaca: Cornell University Press, 1986), pp. 239–241. The view presented here is held also by J. O. Urmson, *Aristotle's Ethics* (Oxford: Basil Blackwell, 1988), p. 80. At this point, we should also note that our rather laconic assimilation of rational philosophy to science is, in Aristotelian terms, quite problematic. Irwin, for example, emphasizes that the distinction between them is importantly and deeply methodological. Aristotelian philosophy is "dialectical"—in the Socratic sense—and aims at coherence; the sciences are "demonstrative" and aim instead at truth. See Terence Irwin, *Aristotle's First Principles* (Oxford: Oxford University Press, 1988, pp. 14–15, 137–138). Without at all doubting this distinction, we can nonetheless suggest that both dialectic and demonstration may well involve familiar notions of rational proof and justification, roughly of a syllogistic nature. The issue between them has to do with whether "first principles" or foundations of knowledge admit of objective demonstration, and not necessarily with the question of nonrational knowledge or alternative forms of rationality. Thus, to argue, as some do (Cooper, *Reason and Human Good in Aristotle,* pp. 67–70), that Aristotle views practical deliberation as dialectical is, in and of itself, to beg the question of *sophia* and *phronēsis.* On the other hand, the dialectical account (or something rather like it) has been used effectively to connect Aristotelian ethics to processes and formulations that may be loosely termed "hermeneutical." The now-standard work here is Nussbaum, *The Fragility of Goodness: Luck and Ethics in Greek Tragedy and Philosophy* (Cambridge: Cambridge University Press, 1986), for example, pp. 245–258.

30. Admittedly, one might equally conclude that they could be matters of *technē,* but this conclusion is hardly more plausible.

cording to Aristotle, that is what bringing together universals and particulars usually involves. There might be situations (e.g., moral or political situations) in which such a bringing together would have to be done quite differently, but this would merely commit Aristotle to the notion that there are two kinds of *phronēsis*, one for certain types of practical questions, another for others. I know of no textual evidence to suggest that Aristotle had any such distinction in mind. But if he did, it would only revive once again all of the difficulties that we have raised thus far, only this time with respect not to the *phronēsis-sophia* distinction but to the putative distinction between two varieties of *phronēsis*. And, of course, our conclusion would remain unchanged: one can find in Aristotle no clear epistemological distinction between practical/moral judgment and rational/subsumptive judgment.

5. Perhaps, then, the distinction needs to be formulated in different terms. According to Aristotle, *sophia* is composed of *nous* and *epistēmē* (*Nicomachean Ethics*, 1141a18–21 and 1141b3–5). *Nous*—generally translated as "intelligence," "understanding," or "intellect"—in this context refers to a kind of immediate intuition or insight. Logic and science cannot be undertaken unless one accepts certain very basic, necessary, and presumably self-evident principles that are themselves incapable of any kind of proof or demonstration and that, therefore, can only be known through immediate intuition. For example, the various rules and procedures of logical inference presuppose the principle, of contradiction. But that principle is itself resistant to logical proof. Any attempt to prove it would necessarily presuppose the notion of logical proof, and since that notion necessarily presupposes the principle of contradiction, the attempted proof would merely assume that which one is trying to demonstrate. Doing logic thus requires that we simply "see" or "understand" the necessity of the principle of contradiction, and this can only be a matter of immediate insight or intuition. So too in empirical science, where certain foundational principles (e.g., the notion that causes are temporally prior to effects) are themselves incapable of empirical verification and can only be simply and immediately intuited.

Nous is a necessary condition of *sophia*. But so too is *epistēmē* or scientific knowledge. *Epistēmē* is a matter of systematic, rationally justified doctrines or truths.[31] It depends on the basic principles uncovered

---

31. See the terminological discussion in Irwin's translation of the *Nicomachean Ethics*, p. 424.

by *nous,* but builds on those principles through methods of rational inference, however characterized, in order to produce justified beliefs about the world. Thus, to have scientific wisdom is to have insight into basic, self-evident principles along with the fruits of rational logical/ scientific inquiry and discourse that build upon such insight.

Phronēsis, on other other hand, is described as *nous* plus *aretē* (*Nicomachean Ethics,* 1144a28–37 and 1144b15–21). While it is often believed that Aristotle is here using *nous* in a very different way, in fact it seems that the *nous* of *phronēsis* is quite similar to the *nous* of *sophia.*[32] Aristotle's view is that practical judgment is importantly a matter of knowing particulars (i.e., being able to discern the character- istics of individual things) and that this again requires a kind of imme- diate insight or intuition. To be sure, in this case it is intuition not of basic logical or scientific principles but, rather, of the identifying and individuating traits of particular things. In both cases, though, the intuition or insight defies analysis and discourse. Like *sophia,* then, *phronēsis* presupposes a type of noninferential knowledge that resists any kind of systematic explication, knowledge that is produced by *nous.*[33] As for *aretē,* or the virtue of character, Aristotle claims that practical wisdom absolutely requires it, that the goodness or badness of any practical judgment is importantly a matter of selecting the right end or goal, and that such a selection can be made only in terms of those learned habits or dispositions that constitute moral virtue.[34] *Nous* and *aretē* are together necessary and sufficient for *phronēsis;* hence, to have practical wisdom is to be a person of virtue who also has insight into the true character of particular things.

As we have seen, *sophia* is said to operate in the realm of necessary truth, where things cannot be other than they are, whereas *phronēsis* operates in a realm of comparative instability, where things might indeed be other than they are. The logician or scientist is forced by the facts of the world to accept those propositions that are true; the person of practical wisdom, on the other hand, is subject to no compa- rable coercion and must therefore make choices based on a process of deliberation and decision. Presumably, then, the concepts of *sophia*

---

32. This is Cooper's view as well: see *Reason and Human Good in Aristotle,* pp. 65–68. See also Martha Nussbaum, *The Fragility of Goodness,* p. 305.

33. Engberg-Pedersen, *Aristotle's Theory of Moral Insight,* p. 213.

34. Cooper, *Reason and Human Good in Aristotle,* pp. 61–62.

and *phronēsis* ought to be such that we are able conceptually to account for this difference. As we have seen, however, the concept of *sophia* can be described by the formula *nous* plus *epistēmē*, while the concept of *phronēsis* can be described by the formula *nous* plus *aretē*. Again, *nous* appears to be a common factor, a kind of immediate, indubitable, self-evident knowledge that is not subject to discourse and analysis and hence presumably not open to refutation. It is highly unlikely, therefore, that the difference between *sophia* and *phronēsis* with respect to necessity and choice can be accounted for by the faculty of *nous*. The difference must be traceable, rather, to the distinction between *epistēmē* (as a constituent of *sophia*) and *aretē* (as a constituent of *phronēsis*.)

Indeed, this seems to be precisely what Aristotle has in mind. When describing the sense in which practical things can be other than they are, he writes as follows:

> The pleasant and the painful do not destroy and pervert every view [*hypolēpsin*] we hold—not, for example, our view that a triangle does or does not have two right angles—but only the view we hold concerning how one should act. For the underlying principle [*archai*] of an action is the end [*eneka*] for the sake of which the action is performed. And if pleasure or pain has corrupted someone, it follows immediately that the principle will no longer be discernable to him. Hence it will not be apparent that this must be the end (or final cause) of his choice and action, for vice tends to corrupt the principle. (*Nicomachean Ethics,* 1140b12–16).

To say that things can be other than they are means, in part, that the actor conceivably and coherently may do one thing or the other, and that the determining factor is the presence or absence of *aretē*. If the actor is virtuous, then he will choose and act one way; if not, he will choose and act differently. Judgments of a logical or scientific nature, on the other hand, are not like this. They are in no way influenced by virtue but are, again, imposed on us by the ineluctable facts of the world. A virtuous mathematician and an unvirtuous one are both forced to agree that two plus two equals four, provided of course that each has the knowledge—*epistēmē*—that two plus two in fact equals four. Judgments of this nature, unlike practical judgments, cannot be other than they are.

The problem with this formulation is that it distinguishes *sophia* from *phronēsis* in moral but not in cognitive terms.[35] The non-necessity of *phronēsis* reflects the fact that an individual may or may not be virtuous. One's practical choices will vary depending entirely upon one's moral character; an immoderate person will decide one way, and a temperate person another, even though their knowledge of the situation may be identical. Thus, the element of variability in no way reflects the knowledge—derived from *nous*—upon which practical decisions are based. Given a certain knowledge of the situation, our moral character simply determines whether or not we are able and inclined to choose in a manner that comports with the implications of that knowledge.

For this reason, moreover, it is hard to see why knowledge of practical matters should be any different from knowledge of logical or scientific matters. In each case, judgment is importantly informed by the fruits of having exercised *nous*. And in each case, it seems that *nous* should reveal to us the true facts of the world, facts that, as true, cannot be other than they are. *Sophia* and *phronēsis* do indeed differ with respect to necessity, but again this difference arises not at all from epistemological or cognitive considerations but from the moral exigencies involved in actually acting upon our judgments.

Stated otherwise, we would presume with Aristotle that *phronēsis* must involve some kind of knowledge. To make intelligent practical choices requires that one know the facts involved in such choices. But insofar as *phronēsis* is explicitly defined as *nous* plus *aretē*, and insofar as *aretē* is, in this context, largely a matter of moderation and self-control, it seems that the knowledge required to make practical choices is basically a product of *nous*. And since, as we have seen, the *nous* of *phronēsis* is substantially similar to the *nous* of *sophia*, it seems further that there is nothing peculiar or distinctive about the kind of knowledge involved in practical judgment. At the very least, such knowledge or wisdom has nothing to do with the notion that practical things can be other than they are, since that notion is entirely rooted not in the facts to be known, nor in the faculty of *nous* with which we come to know them, but in the presence or absence of moral virtue. Presumably, *aretē* leaves the facts untouched. It tells us nothing about the

---

35. Throughout the ensuing discussion, my use of "epistemological" may strike some readers as etymologically inapt. Suffice it to say that, in my view, our word "epistemological" embraces not just Aristotelian *epistēmē* but Aristotelian *nous* as well.

truth of the world. It simply determines whether or not, given that truth, we are able to act with moderation.[36]

In epistemological terms, then, the uniqueness of practical wisdom remains most unclear. *Phronēsis* and *sophia* both presuppose the faculty of *nous,* and in each case this can only mean a kind of immediate, intuitive knowledge of things that cannot be other than they are. An obvious objection arises here: *sophia,* unlike *phronēsis,* includes *epistēmē* as well as *nous;* perhaps, then, *phronēsis* differs from *sophia* simply in not having *epistēmē.* But as we have seen, Aristotle often acknowledges that practical judgments are, indeed, more sound if they are informed not simply by an immediate, intuitive knowledge of particular facts but by a sustained, systematic, and scientific understanding of the world. *Phronēsis* benefits from ethical science. Thus, to say that *sophia* does not require *aretē* appears to be quite true; but to conclude that *phronēsis* has no need of *epistēmē* is both philosophically and exegetically implausible.[37]

6. It will be argued nonetheless that *aretē,* as Aristotle understands it, does have important epistemological implications, that the virtuous person has a type of knowledge that the unvirtuous one lacks, and that—as the passage quoted above indicates—pleasure and pain do blind the individual, making it difficult or impossible to "discern" the truth. To say, then, that *aretē* leaves the facts untouched is mistaken. Whereas Socrates may have thought that knowledge is a sufficient condition of virtue, Aristotle in fact thinks that virtue is a necessary (though not sufficient) condition for a certain kind of knowledge, namely, practical knowledge.

36. It will be argued that the foregoing distorts Aristotle's views, insofar as it overlooks the crucial role played by the intellect in *phronēsis.* See Richard Sorabji, "Aristotle on the Role of Intellect in Virtue," in *Essays on Aristotle's Ethics,* ed. A. O. Rorty (Berkeley: University of California Press, 1980), especially pp. 203–210. But even if Sorabji's account is correct, its consequence again is to call into question the epistemological distinctiveness of *phronēsis.*

37. One might argue here that *epistēmē* is excluded from *phronēsis* simply on conceptual or definitional grounds; *phronēsis* simply *is* unsystematic, nonscientific knowledge. But the effect is the same. For to say that *phronēsis* is that intellectual virtue peculiar to the realm of practical affairs and decision making, and to claim further that it is nonscientific, is to imply ultimately that scientific knowledge cannot be an important feature of practical judgment. Again, this seems to be a most unusual conclusion. We should add, though, that Aristotle is not always unequivocal on this point. See, for example, 1141b14–24.

But it seems that this objection runs largely counter to the main thrust of what Aristotle actually says, especially with reference to the problem of incontinence (*akrasia*). Much here depends upon exactly what it means to "have" knowledge. According to Aristotle, there is a difference between someone who is knowledgeable but does not use knowledge and someone who is knowledgeable and who uses knowledge as well (*Nicomachean Ethics*, 1147a15–35). A person who is drunk, mad, or asleep may know the truth but, because of his or her situation, be unable or unwilling to act upon that knowledge; the same person when sober, sane, or awake can put knowledge into action. Similarly, a person who lacks virtue and moderation may have either true belief or genuine knowledge but nonetheless be dispositionally or circumstantially ill equipped to put that knowledge to use; the virtuous person operates under no such handicap.[38]

As a result, we might want to decide that continent and incontinent individuals "have" knowledge in different ways.[39] But from this I doubt that we would conclude that incontinent individuals are less knowledgeable. Indeed, from any orthodox epistemological stand-

38. It will be objected that I am uncritically conflating continence with moderation (and incontinence with immoderation), whereas Aristotle explicitly distinguishes them (e.g., *Nicomachean Ethics,* 1150a10–30 and 1152a1–5). Principally, continent persons can, and incontinent persons cannot, control their base desires, while neither moderate nor immoderate persons have such desires. Moderation is explicitly described as the state of having no base appetites, and immoderation is a matter of behaving badly not because one is overcome by appetite but, rather, because one has simply chosen to be evil or perverse. As a result, Aristotle says that moderation (*sōphrosunē*) is a virtue, but continence is not; and immoderation (*akalosia*), but not incontinence, is a vice. These formulations, however, seem not to comport very well with Aristotle's much earlier discussion of immoderation, where he claims, for example, that "the immoderate person has an appetite for all pleasurable things" (*Nicomachean Ethics,* 1119a1). Nor does it jibe well with his further claim that "the continent person's state is excellent (*spoudaia*)" (*Nicomachean Ethics,* 1151a28); as both Liddell/Scott and Irwin note, *spoudaios* often refers to virtue of character and is regularly used by Aristotle as the adjective corresponding to *aretē*. Perhaps then the clearest account is to suggest either that continence is a kind of virtue, even though it is not mentioned in the formal list of virtues, or else that it reflects at least a substantial degree of some virtue such that the continent person can be said to have more *aretē* than the incontinent person. In either case, our argument about knowledge and virtue is unaffected.

39. Plato's distinction between "having" and "possessing" would seem to be relevant here. *Theaetetus,* 198c–199c.

point, there seems to be no real difference at all between what continent and incontinent people actually know. The continent person would, for example, know what ought to be done, but so would the incontinent person, and to the same degree. Indeed, the entire controversy surrounding *akrasia* presupposes precisely the idea that the incontinent person knows very well what is right and wrong—knows exactly what the continent person knows—but is nonetheless unable to act correctly. The difference is a matter of character, not knowledge.[40]

In this sense, one can perhaps imagine constructing a test of some kind, say the epistemological equivalent of a Turing test (but with features that would take into account controversial matters such as intensionality) on the basis of which we would decide whether or not an individual really does have knowledge. As far as I can tell, such a test would not be able to discriminate the virtuous from the unvirtuous individual as Aristotle describes them. Both would be equally able to answer factual questions, provide explanations, exhibit comprehension, and the like. As Aristotle explicitly puts it, both would "utter the same words," and their answers would be every bit as likely to reflect not simply right opinion or true belief but genuine knowledge (*Nicomachean Ethics*, 1147a19–25).

We can perhaps best make sense out of Aristotle's discussion here by saying that *aretē* does indeed influence decisively the consequences or practical effects of having knowledge. The virtuous person is able properly to put knowledge to good use, and that may mean that he or she "has" knowledge in a different way. The person's possession of it is, perhaps, more immediate, more germane, more secure, and better integrated with the rest of his or her life. But this does not turn *aretē* itself into a knowledge-generating faculty. From a purely epistemological perspective, virtue is irrelevant. Hence, if the distinguishing feature of *phronēsis* is the presence of *aretē*, this is not sufficient to show that *phronēsis* entails a distinctive kind of knowledge or wisdom.

7. We have stated above that the *nous* of *phronēsis* is fundamentally

---

40. I have here greatly oversimplified, and dogmatically "resolved," what is in fact an extremely difficult and controversial question, namely, what does the incontinent person know? For an excellent recent discussion, see William Charlton, *Weakness of Will* (Oxford: Basil Blackwell, 1988), pp. 41–59. Ultimately, Charlton concludes, against the view presented here, that Aristotle does not believe in "clear-eyed" *akrasia*.

similar to the *nous* of *sophia*. Without in any way rejecting this claim, we might also suggest that the differences between them may nonetheless account for an epistemological distinction between scientific and practical wisdom. In each case, *nous* describes a kind of immediate intuition or insight that is, therefore, unamenable to systematic rational proof or demonstration. But each also involves insight into a different part of the world, and hence perhaps a different kind of insight. The *nous* of *sophia* involves insight into the logical or empirical presuppositions of rational analysis; the *nous* of *phronēsis* involves insight into the particular character of individual things. Perhaps, then, this difference implies a deep epistemological difference, one more substantial than what we have thus far been able to construct.

In fact, I believe that this is very much what Aristotle must have had in mind. Ultimately, insight seems to be a very good translation of *nous*, since *nous* is, like sense perception, both indubitable and undemonstrable. One sees and knows that the fire engine is red without being able to explain or account for that knowledge; in the same way, one sees and knows the truth of logical principles or of the character of certain particulars without any kind of discursive elaboration. Moreover, just as our senses of sight and hearing are similar in being self-evident and undemonstrable, yet different in being of different aspects of the world, so too with the *nous* of *sophia* and the *nous* of *phronēsis*.

This analogy between sense perception and *nous* is made explicitly by Aristotle. He calls the *nous* of *phronēsis* the "eye of the soul" (*Nicomachean Ethics*, 1144a30; also 1143b10–15) and claims that, unlike theoretical or scientific wisdom, people seem to acquire such insight not through training and education but unreflectively and instinctively. Like sense perception, it is a purely natural endowment (*deinotēs*). And just as some people have better eyesight than others, so does insight into the character of particular things vary from person to person (*Nicomachean Ethics*, 1143b5–8).[41]

For Aristotle, then, *phronēsis* describes an epistemologically distinct faculty that is rooted in a quite special and unique kind of perception or *aisthēsis* (1141b14–22). I will argue in subsequent chapters that such a notion is, indeed, a conceptually necessary part of our idea of what it means to make a judgment. But at this point, its epistemological significance is unclear. For while Aristotle asserts the distinction be-

---

41. Sorabji, "Aristotle on the Role of Intellect in Virtue," p. 206; Nussbaum, *The Fragility of Goodness*, p. 305.

tween scientific insight and practical insight, hence between different kinds of perception, it is not clear that he provides an adequate account of the nature of that difference or its epistemological importance. Why should perception of logical principles and perception of the character of particular things be so different as to provide two quite distinct and essentially unrelated kinds of knowledge? How is it, moreover, that perception of particulars can provide us with knowledge that is rational and reliable without being scientific? Indeed, if the foundations of practical judgment are entirely resistant to discursive analysis, on what basis can we assert with confidence that a particular judgment is good or bad, useful or useless, correct or incorrect?[42]

While I believe that Aristotle's discussion has the virtue of bringing such questions into particularly bold relief, I doubt that his answers to them are entirely persuasive. Indeed, he ultimately leaves us wondering just what kind of distinct work *phronēsis* is able to perform. One is tempted to say "practical work." But in the end, Aristotle does not make it clear why practical work cannot be accomplished perfectly well by *sophia* and *technē* in some combination. We are thus inclined to raise questions about the usefulness of *phronēsis* or, indeed, about whether there is any such concept at all. If *phronēsis* has no distinct work to do, can it really be anything?

Our basic problem remains quite clear: Can we identify a concept of practical judgment that is distinct from—but not epistemologically inferior to—the notion of rational/scientific judgment as presented, for example, in our tripartite model? Aristotle's account of *phronēsis* seems to leave the question largely intact. (For further discusion, see the Appendix to this chapter.)

V

This question, rooted in the most basic divergences between Platonic and Aristotelian philosophy, recurs once again in modernity, where it

42. For a very different and challenging account of Aristotle's views on these questions, see C. D. C. Reeve, *Practices of Reason*. On the one hand, Reeve believes that *phronēsis* has a much more strongly argumentative or justificatory cast than I do. On the other hand, he seems to recognize that Aristotle has great difficulty describing just what the rationality of *phronēsis* might be and concludes that the Aristotelian project is not at all to account for the nature of practical reasoning but to describe the kind of person that is most likely to make sound practical decisions.

provides the fundamental problem for what we may call the modern theory of judgment. That theory, in its characteristic form, is concerned immediately with the nature of aesthetic experience and, above all, with the issue of whether such experience is a matter of reason or of feeling. As such, it asks whether reliable judgment must in all respects be of an inferential nature, or whether there are certain modes of intellection which, while violating the standard rules of systematic rational inquiry, nonetheless carry substantial epistemological weight.[43]

As we have seen, Plato and Aristotle differ rather decisively with one another in their treatment of this dichotomy. For Plato, truth is essentially of a piece, and any intellectual process that violates the rules of reason can provide us with nothing that could be called knowledge; thus, in Plato's hands the dichotomy is between knowledge and ignorance, rationality and irrationality, sense and nonsense. For Aristotle, on the other hand, there are indeed two kinds of real knowledge; one inferential or scientific, the other not. Hence, in Aristotle's hands the dichotomy is between systematic knowledge and practical knowledge, theoretical rationality and practical rationality, the wisdom of inference and demonstration and the wisdom of insight and experience.

The modern theory of judgment, with its focus on aesthetic matters, is in this respect fundamentally Aristotelian. Its implicit goal is to vindicate the Aristotelian defense of nonlogical, nonscientific thought. Writers such as Addison and Pope (despite their sharp differences), Shaftesbury and Hutcheson, Burke and Hume saw clearly enough that neither the production of beautiful objects nor their identification and appreciation could be understood plausibly as cases of logical or scientific endeavor. Emblematic here is Shaftesbury's claim that although the poet's "intention be to please the world, he must nevertheless be, in a manner, above it, and fix his eye upon that consummate

43. In fact, I believe that most modern philosophers of politics—Hobbesians, utilitarians, many Marxists—implicitly reject what I am calling the "modern theory of judgment." Such theorists hold to one or another rationalistic model, as embodied in the tripartite model. But with respect to judgment itself, they tend to do so only tacitly. The problem of judgment is not really an explicit problem for them. So it is those who have questioned the standard view, like Kant, who have tended to dominate the discussion about judgment and hence have produced the most important explicit statements of what judgment is.

grace, that beauty of Nature, and that perfection of numbers which the rest of mankind, feeling only by the effect whilst ignorant of the cause, term the *je ne sçay quoy*, the unintelligible or the I know not what, and suppose to be a kind of charm or enchantment of which the artist himself can give no account."[44] Similarly, Hutcheson argues with respect to the aesthetic criterion of "uniformity" that "the constitution of our sense so as to approve uniformity is merely arbitrary in the Author of our nature, and . . . there are an infinity of tastes or relishes of beauty possible, so that it would be impossible to throw together fifty or a hundred pebbles which should not make an agreeable habitation for some animal or other, and appear beautiful to it."[45] Presumably, neither the "unintelligible"—the *"je ne sçay quoy"*—nor the "infinity of tastes and relishes" can provide any basis for objective, demonstrable knowledge of the kind contemplated by logical or scientific endeavor and embodied in the tripartite model of judgment.

Yet both Shaftesbury and Hutcheson—along with Addison, Hume, and the others—would insist that aesthetic judgment is real, that it invokes standards having some grounding, that the beautiful and the merely ordinary can indeed be distinguished from one another with a degree of confidence, regularity, and validity. In Shaftesbury, such judgment is rooted in a certain aesthetic sensibility that ultimately manifests itself in the notion of "good taste."[46] For Hutcheson, the criterion of "uniformity amidst variety" presupposes some intuition according to which one can objectively rank objects in terms of aesthetic value.[47] Even Hume proposed an "ideal observer" theory on the basis of which one might preserve a genuine sense of aesthetic rationality.[48] Such writers thus embrace the Aristotelian view that knowledge and rationality are of (at least) two sorts, and that realms

44. Anthony, Earl of Shaftesbury, "Advice to an Author," in *Characteristics of Men, Manners, Opinions, Times* (Indianapolis: Bobbs-Merrill, 1964 [1711]), Treatise 1, p. 214.

45. Francis Hutcheson, *An Inquiry Concerning Beauty, Order, Harmony*, Design (The Hague: Martinus Nijhoff, 1973 [1725]), 5: 1.

46. Shaftesbury, "Advice to an Author," pp. 220ff.

47. Hutcheson, *An Inquiry Concerning Beauty*, 2: 3.

48. David Hume, "Of the Standard of Taste," in *Philosophical Works*, ed. Thomas Hill Green and Thomas Hodge Grose (Darmstadt: Scientia Verlag Aalen, 1964). For a treatment of Hume along these lines, see Steven Sverdlak, "Hume's Key and Aesthetic Rationality," *Journal of Aesthetics and Art Criticism* 45 (Fall 1986), pp. 69–76.

of experience that are unamenable to logical or scientific inquiry may nonetheless allow for a coherent and potentially fruitful search for truth.

The modern theory of judgment culminates in Kant's Third Critique,[49] and it is there that we find for the first time a systematic attempt to provide a satisfactory philosophical account of the faculty of judgment. Among the other writers, the notion of good judgment or taste is presented largely without analysis, as though its features were self-evident, and the fact of its existence is merely asserted. In this sense, their work provides a restatement of, but hardly an improvement on, Aristotle's formulation. Kant's effort, on the other hand, is to describe the logic of aesthetic judgment, and to provide a "transcendental proof" of its existence. As such, his work provides by a good measure the most important and powerful account of judgment that the West has yet produced.

This account, moreover, has the virtue of being part of a larger and comprehensive philosophical system wherein the role of aesthetic judgment vis-à-vis other intellectual faculties can be identified with some precision. Indeed, Kant's claim is that the arguments of the Third Critique are absolutely required in order to make full sense of the first two Critiques.[50]

The *Critique of Pure Reason* seeks to describe the necessary conditions for humans to have (scientific) knowledge. This entails an account of the difference between, say, "raw feels" on the one hand and "experience" on the other. Presumably amoebae and other lower life forms have raw feels—their organs of sense perception allow them to respond to external stimuli. Of course, humans are physiologically able to have raw feels as well. But unlike amoebae, humans also have

---

49. On the continuity of what I am calling the modern theory of judgment, from the English writers of the Augustan period to Kant, see Dabney Townsend, "From Shaftesbury to Kant: The Development of the Concept of Aesthetic Experience," *Journal of the History of Ideas* 48 (April/June 1987), pp. 287–305. See also, Werner Strube, "Burkes und Kants Theorie des Schönen," *Kantstudien* 73 (1982), pp. 55–62, for a brief and extremely clear comparison.

50. Peter Heintel, *Die Bedeutung der Kritik der ästhetischen Urteilskraft für die transzendentale Systematik* (Bonn: Bouvier 1970); Wolfgang Bartuschat, *Zum systematischen Ort von Kants Kritik der Urteilskraft* (Frankfurt: Klostermann, 1972), pp. 23–91; and Richard E. Aquila, "A New Look at Kant's Aesthetic Judgments," in *Essays in Kant's Aesthetics* ed. Ted Cohen and Paul Guyer (Chicago: University of Chicago Press, 1982).

the capacity to organize those feels into a coherent and systematic pattern of some kind, and it is this capacity that translates mere feels into experience. Such a capacity is essentially cognitive and involves, as is well known, both intuitions of space and time and the various categories of thought grouped under the rubrics quality, quantity, relation, and modality. These features of the mind (along with the transcendental unity of apperception, the schematism, and the like) are what enable humans to take the otherwise chaotic and undifferentiated manifold of events that compose our world and render it orderly and cognizable. Since Kant believes that human experience would be unthinkable without attributing to the mind the intuitions and categories of thought, he regards the latter as being transcendentally proven. Specifically, if we have experience, then we have necessarily those intuitions and categories. Moreover, we must believe that we have experience, since to deny that would make no sense; thus, the existence of the intuitions and categories cannot itself be coherently denied.

All of this is said to provide a foundation not simply for ordinary experience but for scientific experience as well, since science seems clearly to involve the ability to construct laws describing a world that is orderly and cognizable. The *Critique of Pure Reason* leaves us, so to speak, with the capacity to generate empirical principles. But this is still far short of what science demands. For Kant writes as follows:

> The task, which lies *a priori* in our understanding, is to make a coherent (*zusammenhängende*) experience out of given perceptions of a nature containing, quite possibly, an infinite variety of empirical laws. The understanding is, of course, in possession *a priori* of universal laws of nature, without which nature could not be an object of experience at all; but it needs in addition a certain order of nature in its particular rules, which can only be empirically known and which are, as regards the understanding, contingent.[51]

In other words, the capacity to generate empirical laws or principles is consistent with the possibility that we might nonetheless construct an infinite and mutually contradictory panoply of such laws and principles. The potential chaos of raw feels has been overcome by the or-

---

51. Immanuel Kant, *Kritik der Urteilskraft* (Felix Meiner: Hamburg, 1968 [1790]), Introduction 5: 35.

ganizing features of our intuitions and categories, but the potential chaos of an infinity of scientific theories is every bit as threatening to the possibility of systematic knowledge. What is needed, then, is some further organizing principle, analogous to the transcendental principles of the First Critique, on the basis of which scientific endeavor can itself be rendered systematic and coherent.

This organizing principle is the principle of purposiveness (*Zweckmässigkeit*). According to Kant, we can hope to discern a common thread in the various empirical laws we have discovered only if we presuppose that those laws do indeed fit together so as to reflect some kind of overall end or purpose in nature, a purpose that presumably has been legislated by an unknown and unknowable intelligence. There is, Kant claims, no other way to account for the (potential) unity of scientific knowledge or to explain how "a cognizable order of nature is possible."[52] And since we necessarily believe, on pain of incoherence, that there is such a unity and order, the notion that the world of experience is suffused with purposiveness is transcendentally proved. As with all of Kant's transcendental proofs, what has been demonstrated is not the absolute truth of a proposition from a "God's-eye" point of view but, rather, the simple fact that we humans must necessarily and universally believe in that proposition.[53]

Purposiveness is also transcendentally necessary for the coherence of Kantian ethics. In the *Critique of Practical Reason*, Kant seeks to establish grounds on the basis of which an act can be deemed ethical or not. Of course, those grounds have to do with the universalizability of a self-legislated maxim of action and are rooted in the concept of a rational will that is free from the demands of irrational impulse and desire. But as such, they also presuppose the prospect that individuals can, at least in principle, put their self-legislated maxims into effect, so that their actions may have, at least to some extent, predictable consequences. Without this, it is hard to see how one could attempt to invoke the categorical imperative in any meaningful way. For example, my effort to treat you as an intrinsically valuable being, as part of the "kingdom of ends," requires that I understand the world to be

52. Ibid.

53. The role of purposiveness in completing Kant's epistemology is discussed intelligently in Mary-Barbara Zeldin, "Formal Purposiveness and the Continuity of Kant's Argument in the Critique of Judgment," *Kantstudien* 74 (1983), pp. 45–55.

coherent, so that my actions can be logically related to the role you play in that rational kingdom. The ethical actor, as an intelligent and purposive being, needs to believe that deeds will make sense in terms of—will mesh with—a world that is itself the product of an intelligent and purposive being. Ethics, like science, thus absolutely presupposes our capacity to discover in the world this sense of purposiveness.[54]

But purposiveness, as the requirement of both science and ethics, cannot itself be the product of science or ethics. As a presupposition, it is, so to speak, prior to both of them, and this means that neither science nor ethics—neither the understanding (*Verstand*) nor reason (*Vernunft*)—can be the faculty in terms of which purposiveness in the world comes to be observed and recognized. To discover purposiveness thus requires some third faculty, and that is the faculty of aesthetic judgment or taste (*Geschmack*). In this sense, Kant's notion of aesthetic judgment is, roughly, the modern equivalent of Aristotelian *phronēsis*. It involves a kind of intellectual enterprise that differs substantially from logical and scientific inquiry, that violates the tripartite model of judgment, but that seems nonetheless to embrace an important part of what it means to have genuine knowledge.

Again, Kant's aim is not merely to assert the fact and value of such an enterprise, but to provide both a transcendental proof of its existence and a reconstruction of its peculiar and distinctive logic.

VI

We have stipulated that judgment itself is a matter of bringing together a universal and a particular. This means predicating a concept of some individual thing. In the case of aesthetic judgment, the concept in question is beauty (*Schönheit*). Thus, aesthetic judgment is simply a matter of calling something beautiful.

Now Kant insists time and again that such an endeavor in fact involves no concepts: "The judgment of taste is not a cognitive judgment (neither theoretical nor practical) and thus is neither based on nor is purposefully directed toward concepts."[55] If aesthetic judgment

54. On the systematic importance of the aesthetic idea internal to the Third Critique, see Rudolf Lüthe, "Kants Lehre von Aesthetischen Ideen," *Kant-studien* 75 (1984), pp. 65–73.

55. Kant, *Kritik der Urteilskraft*, 4:13. See also, for example, 6:18 ("This universality cannot arise out of concepts") and 39:156 ("He who judges with

were a matter of subsuming particulars under concepts, then it would be no different from, but merely a special variety of, scientific judgment. Kant believes that it is no such thing; he regards aesthetic judgment as a quite distinctive enterprise. This is puzzling, since calling something beautiful certainly appears to involve using a concept, namely, the concept of beauty. Moreover, to insist that aesthetic judgment is entirely nonconceptual seems tantamount to saying that it is utterly irrational, private, random, and unreliable, and hence merely a matter of arbitrary preference and caprice—and, of course, Kant wants to say that it is rather more than that.

He identifies this problem as part of "the antinomy of taste,"[56] and his solution to it is, up to a point, clear enough. Beauty is indeed a concept, but it is an indeterminate concept (*unbestimmten Begriffe*).[57] It is "a concept that cannot be determined or established through intuition, a concept through which nothing can be known and which does not allow for any proof of the judgment of taste."[58] This means, among other things, that aesthetic claims must violate our tripartite model of judgment. According to that model, the universal *qua* concept must be identified, and that means being able to specify at least some of the conceptual features that make it what it is. This kind of specification is, in part, what allows us to demonstrate a connection between a concept and the characteristics of an individual thing such that the latter can be subsumed reliably under the former. But the concept of beauty contains or implies no such determinate features and hence provides no basis for demonstrating or proving that "X (some particular thing) is or is not Y (beautiful)". Thus, aesthetic judgment can never be a matter of following a rule, and can never involve a demonstrable, explicable connection between the universal and the particular.

For Kant, the process of bringing together a universal and a particular when an indeterminate concept is involved is always a matter of "reflective judgment," as distinguished from "determinate judgment."[59] In determinate judgment, the universal comes first, so to

taste . . . may impute subjective purposiveness—i.e., his satisfaction in the object—to everyone else, and may assume that his feeling is universally communicable, and all this without the mediation of concepts."

56. Ibid., 56: 234.

57. Ibid., 57: 237.

58. Ibid., 57: 236.

59. Ibid., 4: 26. Such a notion of reflective judgment is already to be found in the *Nicomachean Ethics* at, for example, 1143b4–5.

speak. It is what is "given." A knowledge of it and of its various features is available antecedent to our encounter with the particular. As a result, the particular can be subsumed under the concept according to rules or principles already implicit in the latter. Determinate judgment thus exemplifies straightforwardly our tripartite model. In reflective judgment, on the other hand, only the particular is "given." One must judge it without having a determined, rule-laden concept in hand; there is no already existing cubbyhole into which it can be placed. Judgment here is still a matter of bringing together a particular and a universal, but in this case the universal is an indeterminate concept that emerges out of, rather than guides, the encounter with the particular. As Kant puts it, reflective judgment is "obliged to ascend from the particular in nature to the universal."

The concept of beauty is thus a product of, and can only result from, our encounter with beautiful things in the world. We have, however, no a priori basis for reliably calling those beautiful things beautiful, since there is no determinate concept of beauty with which we could make such a claim. Again, the only concept of beauty that we do have comes, as it were, after the fact. Moreover, such a concept, although it presumably speaks to that which all beautiful objects have in common, nonetheless can have no determinate content and hence can never be the basis of a determinate judgment. That is, it does not describe those characteristics of beautiful things that make them beautiful, for if it did that it would be a determinate concept, and Kant insists that it is no such thing. Nor does the concept of beauty summarize the beauty-relevant characteristics of beautiful objects, since that would require an independent account of what those characteristics are. It would require, in other words, having a concept of beauty prior to encountering particular beautiful things, for how else could one determine certain characteristics to be beauty-relevant? Such an a priori concept would be determinate and, again, we know that beauty is not that. Indeed, the concept of beauty is such that some brand-new, hitherto unknown and unanticipated object with characteristics never previously encountered nonetheless could be considered beautiful. No determinate concept can accommodate that kind of novelty.

Given all of this, how do we know that something is beautiful? The brief answer is that we do not. Aesthetic judgment is, in Kant's terms, noncognitive. It involves no knowledge, no rules of inference, no objectively justified procedures. One can never demonstrate or prove, or provide any kind of account for, the correctness of an aesthetic claim, and thus the faculty of taste is radically subjective: "[T]he judgment of taste is in no way a cognitive judgment, and is thus not logical but, rather, aesthetical, by which one understands something whose specific foundation (*Bestimmungsgrund*) can be nothing other than subjective."[60]

Despite this, however, aesthetic judgment has a certain definite structure that differentiates it quite decisively from matters of purely private impulse, inclination, and caprice. This structure is captured more or less adequately by three central Kantian notions: *purposiveness without purpose, subjective universality,* and *disinterestedness.* These together provide the basis for Kant's claim that there is such a thing as being a person of good judgment, and that taste and inclination do not always, and need never, coincide.

1. We have seen above that purposiveness is the organizing principle in terms of which nature's apparent diversity may be thought ultimately to be coherent. This sense of coherence is rooted simply in our intuition that nature has a structure that can plausibly be attributed only to a rational, purposive intelligence of some kind. We observe a world that seems to work; its various parts fit together in such a way that it is reasonable to use a singular noun—"nature"—to refer to it. More generally, the possibility of objective scientific knowledge requires, as a transcendental principle, that we assume such a unified and ordered world. But it would be both highly implausible and intellectually objectionable to suggest that this unity could be merely an accident. It would be implausible because it would presuppose the astonishing and fortuitous coming together of nature's seemingly infinite and manifold processes, a kind of cosmic luck that would defy our own intuitive sense of what probability allows. It would be intellectually objectionable because it would raise the prospect that our luck might at any time run out, thereby throwing the world and our putative knowledge of it into a state of complete and utter chaos. We are thus inclined to see the world, in its orderliness, as a reflection of some higher purpose.

As mere mortals, however, we can have no notion of what that purpose might be. Kantian epistemology, rooted in the distinction between phenomena that can be known and things-in-themselves that are beyond our ken, precludes any access to the details of the cosmic

60. Kant, *Kritik der Urteilskraft,* 1: 4.

design. All we can have is the intimation of purposiveness in nature without any knowledge of the purpose itself:

> An object, a mental state, or an action is called purposive even if its possibility does not necessarily presuppose the representation (*Vorstellung*) of a purpose; this is merely because its possibility can be clarified and grasped by us only insofar as we assume for its ground a causality according to purposes—i.e., a will—that has ordered it in accordance with the representation of a certain rule. There can be, then, purposiveness without a purpose, insofar as we do not locate the causes of this form in a will, but yet can make the explanation of its possibility intelligible to ourselves only by deriving it from a will.[61]

We see a flower. We examine it and we find it impossible to imagine that such a complex and highly integrated thing could have occurred merely through chance. We see it, in other words, as an extraordinary and intricate structure, and we intuit that it must be the handiwork of a purposive intelligence of some kind. We may be wrong about this. But if we are, if the flower is (along with the rest of the world) pure accident, then we forfeit any pretensions we might have about knowledge, science, or even coherence. Since we cannot know for sure how the flower came to be, whether accidentally or otherwise, and since we are strongly, perhaps necessarily, inclined to think of ourselves as cognitive, knowledge-oriented creatures, we are both permitted, and virtually forced, to accept our intuition. The flower is no accident; it is suffused with purposiveness.

But exactly what purpose does the flower serve? To know this would require having a knowledge of the will that created it, and there is no reason to believe that such a knowledge is possible for humans. Thus, we have a sense that it does indeed serve some purpose, that its possibility presupposes a creative and rational intelligence, but the precise purpose that it serves necessarily remains opaque to us.

This is *purposiveness without purpose*. For Kant, it is the basis of our concept of beauty. To call something beautiful is to feel, to have the intuition, precisely that it is a purposive entity, that its diverse elements do reveal a structure or, rather, a structuredness—an order, a harmony, a character of organization reflective of some unknown, and unknowable, creative agency. There is nothing scientific or "cognitive"

---

61. Ibid., 10: 33.

about this. We do not deduce or otherwise rationally infer the purpose that a beautiful thing serves; nor, again, can we be sure that our intuition of structuredness is not an illusion of some kind. Nonetheless, this is our intuition, and it is the basis of all aesthetic judgments.

In Kant's formulation, such judgments are characterized by a certain element of surprise. Upon encountering the flower, we are startled, so to speak, by this sense of orderliness, for it is not something we expect. While we may be inclined to think of the world as purposive, we can never know where or when this trait will reveal itself to us. Moreover, the particular way in which the various parts of the flower seem to hang together has a sudden, revelatory aspect to it. It is this, perhaps more than anything else, that explains our sense of satisfaction—our intellectual or contemplative enjoyment—upon encountering beauty. We know ourselves to be willful, purposive creatures. Thus, to stumble upon a beautiful object in nature—an embodiment of willfulness and purposiveness—is unexpectedly to see something oddly familiar, something like us, and to feel surprisingly at one with nature, to discover or rediscover the sense that the world is somehow not at all alien but is, in fact, continuous with our own selves. The result is a feeling not of physical pleasure but of mental or spiritual delight.[62]

2. To call something beautiful is thus to claim that it is an embodiment of purposiveness. This means, further, that purposiveness, like beauty itself, is an indeterminate concept. Again, the result is that aesthetic judgment can only be a kind of reflective judgment: "[T]here can be no science of the beautiful, but only a critique of it; and no beautiful science, but only beautiful art."

All of this suggests, and Kant strenuously affirms, that aesthetic judgment is necessarily subjective. Objective knowledge always rests upon rules and principles of inference that can be established with some confidence and applied to particular cases with some reliability. Again, the tripartite model embodies this notion. That model rests crucially on the availability of determinate concepts. Such concepts

---

62. Given that nature is presumed to be purposive through and through, one might then attribute to Kant the view that everything must be beautiful. This does not mean, however, that all individuals must perceive all of its beauty all of the time. For a discussion, see Theodore A. Gracyk, "Sublimity, Ugliness, and Formlessness in Kant's Aesthetic Theory," *Journal of Aesthetics and Art Criticism* 45 (Fall 1986), pp. 49–56.

make it possible to specify rules of subsumption such that one can objectively decide whether or not a particular judgment has proceeded according to the rules and is, therefore, correct. In aesthetic judgment, on the other hand, where determinate concepts are unavailable, an objective evaluation of this kind is impossible. From indeterminate concepts, one can infer no rules of subsumption, and in the absence of such rules, one cannot demonstrate the validity of bringing together a universal and a particular. There is, in short, absolutely nothing that I can do or say to prove or justify my claim that the flower is beautiful.[63]

Kant nonetheless insists that there is the greatest difference between aesthetic judgments and judgments based on sensual pleasure, or between the taste of reflection (*Reflexionsgeschmack*) and the taste of sense (*Sinnesgeschmack*).[64] Sensuality is subjective, but also purely private; what *you* find pleasurable need not have any relationship to what gratifies *my* senses. As a result, the logic of sensual claims is such that they pertain strictly to the person doing the judging. To say that *boeuf à la mode* tastes good is really to assert only that *boeuf à la mode* gives me pleasure and to imply absolutely nothing about whether it does, or should, give you pleasure too.

On the other hand, aesthetic judgments necessarily involve claims of universal validity.[65] When I say that the flower—or the Monet painting or the fashion model—is beautiful, I am implicitly claiming that this is a fact that everyone should acknowledge as true. In Kant's words, it is nonsense to say of something that it is beautiful *for me:* "for if it is he alone that favors it (*es bloss ihm gefällt*), he must not call it beautiful."[66] Stated otherwise, to make a purely private judgment is, by definition, to make a judgment of the taste of sense; similarly, to

63. Kant, *Kritik der Urteilskraft*, 8:25.

64. Ibid., 8:22. See also Eva Schaper, *Studies in Kant's Aesthetics* (Edinburgh: Edinburgh University Press, 1979), Chapter 2.

65. These might be thought of as factual claims or claims of rational expectation: Paul Guyer, *Kant and the Claims of Taste* (Cambridge: Harvard University Press, 1979), pp. 256, 354; and Donald Crawford, *Kant's Aesthetic Theory* (Madison: University of Wisconsin Press, 1974), pp. 125–131. Alternatively, they might be thought of as imperatives or "oughts." See Kenneth F. Rogerson, "The Meaning of Universal Validity in Kant's Aesthetics," *Journal of Aesthetics and Art Criticism* 40 (Spring 1982), pp. 315–326.

66. Kant, *Kritik der Urteilskraft*, 7:19.

make an aesthetic judgment is, by definition, to assert a putatively universal truth.

Consider the flower. I might decide that it smells good, but that would be perfectly consistent with recognizing that your sense of smell is different from mine and that what smells good to me may smell putrid to you. I might discover that its yellow color gratifies me, realizing without contradiction that yellow may have bad connotations for you so that you find all yellow things to be offensive. If, however, I decide that the flower is beautiful—that it is an example of purposiveness without purpose then I am saying nothing about the way it affects my private sensual apparatus, nothing about the pleasure or pain it gives me. Rather, I am making a claim about a certain aspect of what the flower really is in itself, a claim that all who observe it should agree with. Again, it is a claim that I cannot demonstrate or even argue for. There is no rule that I can point to in order to justify the truth of my assertion; the tripartite model of judgment does not obtain. The claim is thus a subjective one. But insofar as it demands the assent of others, it also purports to assert a universal truth. If scientific or determinate judgment is a matter of "objective universality," if sensual taste and physical gratification are matters of "subjective particularity," then aesthetic judgment is a matter of "subjective universal validity" (*subjectiven Allgemeingültigkeit*).[67]

3. Kant further clarifies these distinctions by listing three different kinds of approbation. In the moral sphere, the object of approbation is called "good" (*gut*), and we say of it that it is esteemed (*geschätzt*) or approved (*gebilligt*). In the realm of sensuality, the object of approbation is called "pleasant" (*angenehm*), and we say that it elicits in us pleasure (*Vergnügen*). In the area of aesthetics, the object of approbation is called "beautiful" (*schön*), and we say that it is what we "favor" (*gefällt*) and that it is, in that sense, the "favored" (*Gunst*).[68]

This classification is rooted in the primary distinguishing feature of aesthetic judgment, namely, that it is disinterested.[69] Human interests necessarily play a role in both moral and sensual life. To call

67. Ibid., 8: 24.

68. Ibid., 5: 15.

69. For a rather different view, which sees disinterestedness as far less central, see Karl Ameriks, "Kant and the Objectivity of Taste," *British Journal of Aesthetics* 23 (Winter 1983), 3–17. As the ensuing discussion implies, I think Ameriks's view is untenable.

something morally good is not simply to approve it but to assert also a stake in it; as a matter of logic, we are committed to nurturing and enhancing the presence of the good wherever we are able to find it or create it. As rational creatures, we cannot be indifferent to, but must be vitally interested in and dependent upon, its continued existence. Our very being is bound up with the possibility of actually living in a "kingdom of ends." Similarly, in the sensuous realm, pleasure is necessarily a matter of great concern to us, and to call something pleasurable is to state an interest in being able to enjoy it. We are not only rational but also sensuous creatures, and we cannot be indifferent to those things that gratify our senses. A desperately thirsty individual necessarily craves a glass of water. This person may, in certain circumstances, refuse the water if proffered; perhaps moral considerations require that someone else—a thirstier person—be allowed to drink it. But even so, the individual's stance vis-à-vis the water and the physical pleasure it would provide cannot be one of indifference.

We have, however, no need and no desire for beautiful things.[70] If we "esteem" something beautiful, then we are regarding it not for its beauty but for its ethical value. If we take "pleasure" in it, then again we are responding not to the beauty of it but to its sensuous rewards. Only if we "favor" it on purely aesthetic grounds—only if we see it and appreciate it solely as an embodiment of pure purposiveness without purpose—are we paying attention to its beauty, and in Kant's account we can have no interest in it as such. That is to say, neither our rational/moral nor our physical/sensuous well-being is any way affected by its beauty; hence, we have no stake at all in its continued existence.

One clear implication of this is that Kantian aesthetics are strictly formalistic.[71] What we admire as beautiful is simply the evocation of purposiveness, the sense of structural or formal integrity that we suddenly, unexpectedly discover in the midst of the apparent diversity of the world. To dwell upon the sweet tones produced by a pianist as he

70. Guyer, *Kant and the Claims of Taste*, pp. 195ff.

71. For a discussion of at least some of Kant's influence in this respect, see Deane W. Curtin, "Varieties of Aesthetic Formalism," *Journal of Aesthetics and Art Criticism* 40 (Spring 1982), pp. 315–326. A rather different kind of summary, examining such post-Kantian aestheticians as Heidegger, Gadamer, Adorno, and Benjamin, is found in Rudiger Bübner, "Über Einige Bedingungen Gegenwärtiger Ästhetik," *Neue Hefte für Philosophie* 5 (1973), pp. 38–73.

performs a Chopin *Nocturne* is to operate in sensual rather than aesthetic terms; to be moved or beguiled by the gorgeous colors of a Monet canvas is to attend to the painting's pleasures but not its beauty. If the *Nocturne* is beautiful, it can be so only in virtue of its compositional qualities, that is, the patterns or structural relationships that we intuitively attribute to it; similarly, the beauty of the Monet can only be a matter of form, composition, structuredness.[72] Again, none of this provides us with pleasure; rather, it provides us with intellectual delight. Our satisfaction in the beautiful is purely, pristinely contemplative. For Kant, aesthetic judgment is debased and perverted when it is influenced to any degree by feelings of pleasure: "Taste is always barbaric where satisfaction relies upon a mixing in of charms and emotions, and still more if it makes these the criteria of its approval."[73]

Of course, one might come physically to crave some beautiful thing, and Kant would not necessarily disapprove of this. Beautiful things need not be only that. Kant would merely point out that the thing craved would have ceased to exist for the craving person as an aesthetic object. It would have become, to speak perhaps anachronistically, a commodity, and the commodification of beauty is, for Kant, its death *qua* beauty. It may also be that humans cannot live by bread alone, that aesthetic experience is morally and politically uplifting and hence socially useful. Again, Kant could well agree. But he would insist that any putative aesthetic judgment based on such considerations would be hopelessly perverted by nonaesthetic interests, however noble, and that the result would be the fatal contamination of aesthetic experience itself.

This is a highly intellectualistic notion of beauty, to be sure.[74] But Kant's claim is not that he is inventing or prescribing a particular kind of aesthetic experience; rather, he is simply reconstructing and tracing out the logic of aesthetic judgment as it already exists, albeit only implicitly, as a distinctive kind of human endeavor. If that logic is all too rarely pursued, if its purely contemplative quality is regularly overwhelmed by emotional and moral considerations, then this only shows that aesthetic experience is often misunderstood. Moreover, to call such experience intellectualistic is not at all to reduce it to a sci-

72. Kant, *Kritik der Urteilskraft*, 14: 42.

73. Ibid., 13: 38.

74. A rather different account is to be found in Aquila, "A New Look at Kant's Aesthetics."

ence. For it cannot be overemphasized that, in Kant's view, aesthetic judgment is utterly noncognitive. It involves no knowledge, no determinate concepts, no rules or inferential methods. It relies solely on the undemonstrable but nonetheless putatively universalizable intuition of purposiveness, and this does not require that we *know* the beautiful object. Indeed, we may call something beautiful—a found object, an abstract figure, an inexplicable design—without having the slightest idea of what it actually is.[75]

What, then, is the intellectual faculty that allows us to gain purchase on the beautiful? It is amply clear from the foregoing that Kant has in mind a certain kind of intuition. Of course, in the Kantian system, "intuition" is a rather broad term, insofar as all empirical knowledge is rooted in intuitions of one kind or another. Is there some special type of mental activity, distinguishable from scientific "understanding" and ethical/logical "reasoning," on the basis of which peculiarly aesthetic intuitions are possible?

Kant provides a partial answer in the "General Remark on the First Section of the Analytic." There he introduces the notion that beauty is detected through the free play of the imagination. This is said to be a matter of "free lawfulness." The imagination is a faculty for postulating or inventing patterns or structures in the world—past, present, or future—that resist scientific demonstration. It operates entirely without restriction, perhaps even randomly, yet must presuppose that its endeavors have a universalizable quality that makes them lawlike. Kant fully acknowledges, but does not systematically explore, the seeming contradictoriness of such a formulation.[76] His discussion focuses rather on the virtues, from an aesthetic standpoint, of nature's "prodigal variety," and on the tedious, unaesthetic repugnance of everything that is stiff and regular. He implies that the imagination is a faculty somehow adept at rummaging through the richness, the near anarchy of the world as it presents itself, and discovering or imputing, here and there, embodiments of purposiveness.

Kant provides no systematic account of how this actually occurs. He does insist, however, that the notion of aesthetic judgment presupposes, as a matter of transcendental principle, the existence of com-

75. Kant, *Kritik der Urteilskraft,* 4: 11.

76. In Guyer's view, this problem simply highlights a fundamental dialectical strain in Kant's aesthetics. See Paul Guyer, "Autonomy and Integrity in Kant's Aesthetics," *Monist* 66 (April 1983), pp. 167–188.

mon sense. As we have seen, to call something beautiful is necessarily to claim that everyone should agree that it is beautiful; the logic of aesthetic judgments is that they are subjective but also universal. Of course, the truth of such judgments cannot be demonstrated or justified. Rather, their universality presupposes of you and I the possibility that our various intuitions, rooted in the free play of our respective individual imaginations, will coincide. I cannot prove to you that the flower is beautiful. But when I judge it to be so, I necessarily assume that you must also be able to see—to sense somehow—the purposiveness that I claim to detect. I presuppose, therefore, that we share a common sense.

This notion of common sense is functionally similar to Aristotle's claim that practical wisdom is rooted in a kind of insight, in *nous* as the "eye of the soul." In each formulation, the analogy with sense perception is fundamental, and Kant is careful to distinguish common sense from "common understanding," which would, presumably, be analogous to Aristotelian *sophia*. But the differences between the two views should also be clear. Aristotle appears to claim as a matter of absolute fact that *nous* is a human intellectual faculty; Kant's claim, rather, is that common sense must be presupposed as an attribute of human beings if aesthetic judgment is to be possible and coherent. Again, Kant is providing a transcendental proof. Moreover, in Kant the commonness of the aesthetic faculty is rather more explicit than in Aristotle. While the distribution of Aristotelian *nous* is unclear and seemingly irrelevant from the standpoint of its existence and function, Kantian aesthetic judgment absolutely requires the imputation of common sense to, in principle, everyone. For Aristotle, it would be possible to imagine that only one person had practical wisdom, or even the capacity for practical wisdom, and it would be further possible for that one person to understand, accept, and act in terms of that fact. Kant, of course, would agree that some people may have good taste while others may not. But he would attribute this to historical contingencies, not to basic capacities, and he would insist that the person making an aesthetic claim must be committed to the view that, in principle, everyone could be taught somehow to observe the beauty—the purposiveness without purpose—that allows for aesthetic satisfaction.

VII

I have argued that the modern theory of judgment culminates in Kant's Third Critique. In at least one important sense, though, his formulation deviates substantially from the main line of development in aesthetic theory. Specifically, Kant insists on sharply distinguishing aesthetic judgment not just from scientific judgment but from moral judgment as well. Whereas scientific claims are rooted in the understanding and moral claims in reason, aesthetic claims are rooted in reflective judgment. And while understanding and reason are themselves dramatically different, they nonetheless share the characteristic that each is a matter of truth involving some kind of rational justification. This is a feature that aesthetic judgment utterly lacks.

Knowledge in science is empirical, and knowledge in ethics is logical, but in both cases it is rational and objective. The phrase "knowledge in aesthetics," on the other hand, is virtually incoherent, since aesthetic judgment is not a matter of knowledge at all. It is universal in intention but only subjective in substance. And while its element of universality does distinguish it from judgments of sense (e.g., judgments about what feels good) its subjectivity radically separates it from moral as well as scientific endeavor. For Kant, it is not just that the good and the beautiful are different; it is, further, that the good and the beautiful are apprehended in entirely different ways.

For most of Kant's predecessors in the modern theory of judgment, the relationship of aesthetics and ethics is far closer, to the point that the faculty of aesthetic judgment is widely thought to be analogous to, or perhaps even identical with, the faculty of moral and political judgment. Shaftesbury, for example, affirms that his goal is "to assert the reality of a beauty and charm in moral as well as natural objects, and to demonstrate the reasonableness of a proportionate taste and determinate choice in life and manners."[77] Hume links both morality and aesthetics to "some internal sense or feeling, which nature has made universal in the whole species."[78] For Adam Smith, "the same regard to the beauty of order, of art and contrivance, frequently serves to recommend those institutions which tend to promote the public welfare."[79] Throughout the eighteenth century, British moral

---

77. Shaftesbury, *Characteristics of Men, Manners, Opinions, Times,* Treatise 2, p. 344.

78. David Hume, "Concerning the Principles of Morals," in *Essays: Moral, Political, and Literary* (London: Longmans, Green, and Co/. 1907), vol. 2, p. 172. See also, "Of the Standard of Taste," in vol. 1, pp. 266–267 and 282–284.

79. Adam Smith, *The Theory of Moral Sentiments* (Oxford: Oxford University Press, 1976 [1759]), p. 185. See also, pp. 19–20, 26.

theorists, despite their many differences, insisted that morality, like aesthetics, was rooted in a kind of noninferential sense or sentiment and that our faculties for judging both beauty and the good were somehow connected to one another.

Kant's rejection of this position in no way refutes the fact that his work constitutes the perfection of the modern theory of judgment. Indeed, one needs only to put aside his ethical theory to arrive at the conclusion that his account of aesthetic judgment may serve very well as a theory of reflective judgment in general, authoritative not simply for questions of beauty but for moral and political questions as well. That is, the modern theory of judgment, though immediately concerned with aesthetic matters, is also equally a theory of moral and political consequence; to the degree that Kant's Third Critique is the culmination and leading achievement of that theory, it may be thought to represent a basic modern approach to political and moral judgment, albeit one that Kant himself did not adopt.

This extension of Kantian aesthetics to the world of politics has been pursued most explicitly by Hannah Arendt. Arendt's theory of judgment, as outlined in Chapter 1, is fundamentally Kantian. Her claim is that the *Critique of Judgment,* suitably revised, can be best interpreted as the political philosophy that Kant himself never wrote, and she regards her own work on judgment as an effort to translate the insights of Kantian aesthetics into the political realm.[80] Many of the other materials presented in Chapter 1 also demonstrate, albeit less directly, that what we have called the modern theory of judgment is connected to—and can help us provide a systematic account of—a quite venerable tradition of political thought. This tradition views moral and political questions as being, beyond a certain point, unamenable to rational analysis and hence dependent upon modes of intellection of a quite different sort. Notions of *virtu,* deliberation, the aestheticization of politics, the conversational pursuit of intimations, and the like all reflect an underlying dichotomy: Logical/scientific thinking is somehow different from moral/political thinking. Our goal in Chapter 2 has been precisely to search for the details of this distinction, and thus to provide an account of just what moral/political thinking might be.

80. Hannah Arendt, *Lectures on Kant's Political Philosophy* (Chicago: University of Chicago Press, 1982), pp. 7–27.

The pursuit of this goal has, I believe, produced significant results. If we agree that Kant's work is the capstone of the modern theory of judgment, and if we agree that such a theory is the most systematic effort to describe the nature of human thinking that is noninferential, nonscientific, yet oriented toward generalization of some kind, then we arrive at the following philosophical conclusion: Moral/political thinking, as distinct from logical/scientific thinking, is a matter of "subjective universality." As such, it is noncognitive and involves no element of knowledge, proof, or rational justification. It invokes no concepts, no rules or principles of inference, and hence is entirely nonobjective. It violates, in short, the tripartite model of judgment. It does presuppose a certain disinterestedness, a rejection of mere caprice and private satisfaction, and hence a quest for, and presumption of, universality. It presupposes further the existence of a peculiar and distinctive human faculty—a kind of intuition, common sense, *nous*, perception, or insight—that is widely shared. It traces all moral and political, as well as aesthetic, judgments to this faculty. The belief in such a faculty is what allows us to say in aesthetics that this is beautiful, in morals that this is good, and in politics that this is prudent. But none of those claims can ever be demonstrated or rationally justified.

The implications of this position for the differences between Plato and Aristotle are quite complex. On the one hand, it endorses Plato's view that all knowledge is a matter of rational science and logic, and that any endeavor, or experience-activity, that resists scientific/logical analysis is for that reason irrational, noncognitive, and merely subjective. Of course, it also rejects Plato's claim that moral and political questions are fully amenable to scientific or logical analysis. There can be no science of politics, just as there can be no science of flute playing; hence the Platonic connection between virtue, knowledge, and political leadership is an error. The conclusion thus agrees with Aristotle's view that political and moral questions can only be matters for practical wisdom, and that there are (at least) two kinds of legitimate human thinking. It agrees further with Aristotle that noninferential thinking does involve, or at least must presuppose, a type of sixth sense, a peculiar and inexplicable faculty of perception or insight on the basis of which reliable practical judgments are possible. But as finally formulated by Kant, it also strenuously denies Aristotle's claim that practical wisdom is a kind of knowledge involving objective, rational, and somehow demonstrable truth. Thus, the ultimate Aristotelian goal, to show how practical judgments can be clearly and objectively demonstrated on other than scientific/logical grounds, is systematically frustrated. The faculty of judgment remains something of a mystery.

It is here, then, that we can locate both the triumph and the utter failure of Kantian aesthetics. As we have seen, Aristotle postulated a notion of *phronēsis* but seemed unable to provide a satisfying positive account of it. In particular, he failed to describe just what kind of work *phronēsis* does that cannot be done by *sophia* and *technē* in some combination. Without specifying such a distinctive field of endeavor, he thus gave us little reason to believe that *phronēsis* is anything at all. Kant solves this problem with the notion of reflective judgment. *Sophia* and *technē* are matters of determinate judgment, wherein the particulars that we encounter are classified and understood in terms of an already given scheme of universals. But human mental life is also sometimes a matter of encountering particulars without already given universals. This requires that we generate concepts out of such an encounter—after the fact. Such a task clearly cannot be performed by *sophia* or *technē* as exemplars of determinate judgment. It is precisely here, then, that we have the distinctive, peculiar, and important kind of work that only *phronēsis/Urteilskraft* can undertake.

I believe this insight is one of the great achievements of Kantian philosophy, perhaps comparable to the idea of the synthetic a priori. But from our perspective, the failure of Kant's project lies precisely in his insistence that *phronēsis/Urteilskraft* is noncognitive and hence not at all a source of knowledge. His conclusion may be absolutely correct. But if so, then our belief that good judgment is an identifiable property involving some kind of rational justification remains unsupported. Kantian aesthetics systematically undermines our search for a knowledge-relevant faculty different from traditional rationality and suited to the peculiar problems of reflective judgment.

We are left with the dichotomy of judgment quite intact. Knowledge-in-judgment is a matter of science and logic, the principles and procedures of which can be elaborated with comparative clarity and precision. Political and moral judgment, on the other hand, rest upon an elusive and ineffable faculty of sense, the existence of which cannot be demonstrated, and the procedures of which, even if they do exist, must remain for us utterly opaque. The tripartite model of judgment simply does not apply, and this means, among other things, that the correctness or incorrectness of a particular moral or political judgment must necessarily remain moot.

In the end, such a conclusion does not comport with our residual intuition that moral and political judgments (and aesthetic ones, as well) are somehow more than this, that knowledge and justification in the practical realm are both possible and necessary. It may be that this intuition simply cannot be sustained. But it may be that we have not yet pursued its claims with sufficient thoroughness. I believe that the dichotomy we have drawn presents a reasonably faithful reconstruction of the theory of judgment as it has evolved up to and including Kant's Third Critique. But I believe that the dichotomy itself is miscast, and that an elaboration of its errors can put a much clearer light on the problems and prospects of practical judgment.

Excursus: A Neo-Aristotelian Theory of Practical Reason

David Wiggins, a contemporary philosopher of note, has proposed a "neo-Aristotelian theory of practical reason."[1] Given the extraordinary development of philosophy since the time of Descartes and the substantial contributions that Wiggins himself has made to a number of philosophical discussions, one would expect him to have shed considerable light on the perplexities that we have discovered in Aristotle's account of *phronēsis*. But as it turns out, his formulation only underlines the illusive and ultimately unsatisfying nature of the Aristotelian approach.

Wiggins correctly distinguishes Aristotle's theory of practical reason from theories that conceive of judgment as a matter of purely instrumental rationality. Such theories offer a distinctly modern and technically oriented version of the tripartite model. They argue that practical questions—including, presumably, questions of a political nature—can be resolved by relying on algorithmic calculations of expected utility. They assume that such calculations can be made with some reliability and objectivity, that practical reason is fundamentally concerned with means rather than ends, that the outcomes of various decisions are mutually commensurable, and that problems of a practical nature can be abstracted from particular and local settings and decided on the basis of a universal method of judgment.

Wiggins believes all of these assumptions to be false. He proposes, instead, a theory of practical judgment that is, he claims, fully respon-

---

1. David Wiggins, "Deliberation and Practical Reason," in *Essays on Aristotle's Ethics,* ed. Amélie Oksenberg Rorty (Berkeley: University of California Press, 1980), pp. 221–240.

sive to the actual circumstances of practical reasoning. Unfortunately, at nearly every point his exposition is beset by the same ambiguity, imprecision, and question-begging that we encountered in Book 6 of the *Nicomachean Ethics*.

1. Wiggins begins by claiming that "there is nothing which a man is under antecedent sentence to maximize."[2] The crude utilitarian and instrumentalist reliance on scientific methods for achieving predetermined ends thus ignores the crucial practical problem of ends themselves. This criticism is, I think, not entirely faithful to Aristotelian doctrine, for according to Aristotle, we are in fact required to pursue excellence and, as a by-product, happiness or *eudaimonia*. The end or goal of our actions is thus very much predetermined, and the function of *phronēsis* is largely to discover just how that end is best attained. Wiggins would perhaps respond by saying that discovering exactly what constitutes excellence and happiness is not at all self-evident, but that is very different from claiming that the determination of ends is always and invariably an open question. Indeed, Aristotle seems to believe that the excellence and hence the *telos* of anything can be discovered through systematic rational analysis. The important implication is that we can determine with some objectivity the ends that we should be pursuing, and that practical reasoning, as a result, should be concerned with methods for achieving those ends. Nothing Wiggins says would refute such an interpretation.

2. Wiggins also claims that "a man usually asks himself 'What shall I do?' not with a view to maximizing anything but only in response to a particular context." This is a peculiar claim in at least two respects. First, there is nothing problematic about asking "What shall I do?" *both* within a particular context *and* with a view toward maximization. Wiggins's implied disjunction is not a disjunction at all. Second, if I make decisions not with a view to maximizing, then how do I make them? What criteria do I employ? Someone might suggest that I "satisfice" rather than "maximize." But this would be a mere word game; for satisficing is really nothing other than maximizing in conditions of bounded rationality, limited information, time pressure, and the like. Alternatively, one might say that we don't really maximize in real life, since we're generally too lazy, distracted, or imperceptive. But a description of bad practical judgment can hardly count as a theory of practical judgment itself. Wiggins gives us no reason to believe that

2. All explicit claims are to be found in Ibid., pp. 232–234.

maximization is not the implicit goal of all practical judgment, and provides no hint as to what an alternative goal might be.

3. Wiggins argues further that the technical/utilitarian approach must be wrong since all decisions are made within a particular situation and "the relevant features of the situation may not all jump to the eye." It is hard to see what force this claim has, since even the most narrow-minded advocate of instrumental rationality would cheerfully concede the point. The maximization of expected utility by definition occurs within a particular situation; this is precisely what calls for calculations of probability, on the basis of which utility is "expected" rather than assured. Moreover, the fact that such calculations will inevitably be imperfect simply suggests that we are human; we cannot know everything, but this in no way undermines the claim that our job is to determine, as best we can, which of a range of alternative actions best serves our true interests.

4. Wiggins objects, though, that we inevitably face a "plurality of ends," that these are generally not "hierarchically ordered," and that they often make "competing and inconsistent claims." If he simply means that practical life is complex and that it is difficult to know what maximization entails, then this shows only that calculating expected utilities is a challenging endeavor. It in no way refutes the claim that maximization is the aim of practical judgment, however difficult it may be to achieve. If on the other hand he means that the various considerations we face are truly and deeply incommensurable with one another, then it is hard to see how one could act at all, except randomly. If there is simply no basis at all on which even to compare two alternative courses of action, then the choice of them certainly cannot be a matter of practical *reason*.

Ultimately, when Wiggins asserts that "the unfinished or indeterminate character of our ideals and value structure is constitutive of both human freedom and, for finite creatures who face an indefinite or infinite range of contingencies with only finite powers of prediction and imagination, of practical rationality itself," he is saying nothing that advocates of technical, instrumental rationality would deny.

5. Wiggins himself cannot articulate a theory of practical reason without lapsing into the language of utility maximization. He says that "the man of highest practical wisdom is the man who brings to bear upon a situation the greatest number of genuinely pertinent concerns and genuinely relevant considerations commensurate with the importance of the deliberative context." Such a man is thus able to identify,

presumably with some precision, the "greatest number" from some lesser number, is able to evaluate concerns according to "genuine pertinence" and "genuine relevance," and is able, therefore, to weigh the various implications of various courses of action. Such a calculation may only be rough, imprecise, and imperfect; but it is a calculation nonetheless. Indeed, to determine that a potential course of action has a greater number of genuinely pertinent and relevant considerations in its favor is precisely what any utility maximizer attempts to do.

Wiggins concludes that in practical reasoning the imagination is prompted "to play upon" the question at hand and let it "activate in reflection and thought-experiment whatever concerns and passions it should activate." This seems to beg almost all of the relevant questions. What constitutes a "concern," and how are "pertinent and relevant" concerns to be distinguished from others? What does it mean to "play upon" a question? How does one know whether one's "playing upon" is fruitful and productive? How should we characterize a successful "thought experiment"? What does it mean to "activate" a concern, and how does such activation lead to judgment and decision? The failure to answer such questions means, I think, that the most interesting and important issues about practical reason and judgment remain not only unresolved but unacknowledged. For this reason, Wiggins's version of Aristotelian theory does not substantially improve upon the original formulation.

THREE

Insight and Interpretation

THE DICHOTOMY OF JUDGMENT is inextricably bound up with the characteristic rationalism of the Western philosophical tradition. According to the canon, principles of rational argument and inference of the sort contemplated by our tripartite model stand as indispensable criteria for assessing the truth value of particular judgments.[1] To the degree that certain kinds of judgments (e.g., aesthetic or religious judgments) fail to pass the test, they are epistemologically suspect. To the degree that a culture embraces and embodies such judgments, it is similarly suspect. Of course, it may be that most of our judgments, and most Western cultures, fall into this suspect category. But that is only to suggest that there is a great difference between the Western tradition and the Western philosophical tradition: what philosophers have prized is not always what governments, priests, artists, and the larger number of people have prized.

If this is even roughly correct, then it seems that any effort to provide a warrant for judgments that fail to satisfy the requirements of our tripartite model is likely to be an uphill battle. Aristotle's account of *phronēsis*, for example, may be thought of as a bold, heterodox challenge designed to assert the value of certain noninferential endeavors against the apparently inexorable and imperial claims of reason. This challenge may indeed have been made in the interest of the larger culture and community, and hence might well have the appearance of something quite orthodox, commonsensical, and con-

1. To be sure, the presently accepted canon may in fact provide only a distorted picture of the history of philosophy and may underestimate the degree to which serious philosophers in the past have arrived at skeptical or antirationalist conclusions.

servative. Within the philosophical community, however, the notion of a truth claim that cannot be justified in terms of standard inferential procedures is inherently problematic. Similarly, the modern theory of aesthetic judgment seeks to preserve somehow the integrity of taste and artistic sensibility in the face of a scientific leviathan that seems ultimately destined to be the sole arbiter of what is true and false, good and bad, beautiful and ugly. That this theory finally collapses into Kant's aesthetic noncognitivism is, I think, a measure of the degree to which the principles of rational argument have set the terms of the debate. Those who would defend unreason or "alternative rationalities" have done so reactively and selectively, seeking only to find some small, isolated niche safe from the hegemony of a rationalistic impulse, the essential principles of which are largely unquestioned.

One result is, as we have seen, the dichotomy of judgment, presented either as (for Plato) a distinction between reason and nonsense or as (for Aristotle) a distinction between two kinds of truth-relevant thought, one rational in the traditional sense, the other not. In either version, the problem is only to determine how far the principles of reason apply. The integrity of rational thought as an inferential, rule-governed endeavor involving notions of systematic argument and demonstration is not doubted; the sole issue is the extent of its purview and of its claims to exclusivity.

These generalizations are, I think, no less true for being crude, but they are also generalizations about the past. For it is plausible to suggest that much has changed, that the nineteenth-century witnessed, and the twentieth-century has prosecuted, a certain revolution in thought that has substantially refigured the debate about rationality and hence about the nature of judgment. In certain philosophical circles, at least, rationality itself now stands accused. The accusation takes many forms. The laws of thought are said to be merely convenient tools of a bloodless bourgeois culture that makes a virtue of comfortable complacency and a vice of spirited, passionate engagement. Truth is deeply perspectival and hence completely dependent on premises and presuppositions that defy rational analysis. The meaningfulness of the world inheres not in the world itself but in the mental activities of subjects who arbitrarily construct that world and whose thoughts are inextricably bound up with the transient, irrational demands of body and culture. Philosophy is no haven from rhetoric but, rather, a form of rhetoric itself, motivated solely by the need to communicate and persuade, and subject to the same processes of explication and demystification that we bring to bear upon works of literature.

The implications for the theory of judgment are, in principle, quite substantial, for it is now possible to imagine that the dichotomy of judgment, as outlined in Chapter 2, will collapse, but in a very special way. Formerly, we encountered the claims of a rational dominion purporting to hold sway not simply over matters of science and mathematics but over political, aesthetic, and religious matters as well. Those claims, rooted in Plato, culminated, one might suggest, in Hegel's account of absolute spirit. For Hegel, the state stands as the objective actualization of reason, art is judged according to whether it embodies and represents a rational idea, religion is shown to cohere in most important respects with philosophy, and the impulses and passions of individual humans are governed by, fully integrated with, and entirely in the service of rational thought. In such a formulation, the dichotomy of judgment collapses in the face of triumphant, hegemonic rationality.

But now we encounter the very different claims of a universal unreason. The ineffability of emotive, aesthetic, and impulsive life is not only irreducible; it is also all-encompassing. Science itself is necessarily rooted in structures of received belief, the truth of which "can never be unequivocally settled by logic and experiment alone."[2] Mathematics is fundamentally an aesthetic enterprise based on inexplicable insight and intuition and governed by a vague, undemonstrable sense of elegance. Logic is an art; its claims to objectivity and certainty are no more or less plausible than those of a poem or a play. Judgment, then, is invariably reflective rather than determinative, and *sophia* is really *phronēsis* in disguise. The tripartite model describes either nothing that can exist or, at best, nothing that has any special epistemological warrant.

The emergence of such views may seem paradoxical in light of the widely believed and extremely plausible Weberian hypothesis about modernity and rationalization. If the modern world is fundamentally "disenchanted," increasingly and characteristically absorbed by scientific, bureaucratic, and technical concerns, then how persuasive can the claims of unreason be? But of course, there is no paradox. For the emergence of a deep skepticism about the reason/unreason distinction

2. Thomas S. Kuhn, *The Structure of Scientific Revolutions* (Chicago: University of Chicago Press, 1970), p. 94.

is, in actual fact, bound up with the political view that science, bureaucracy, and technique have illicitly contaminated and undermined all forms of cultural life, turning the free play of imagination into dogmatic "truth," transforming a rich and pluralistic life-world into something shallow and one-dimensional, subverting the civilized and uplifting conversation of mankind into a deadly, unedifying monologue.

What is at stake, in part, is whether the dichotomy of judgment can be maintained, either in its Platonic or Aristotelian form. But given the apparent ineffability of *phronēsis*, taste, and reflective judgment (and of related political/social concepts such as *virtu*, deliberation, and conversation), the stakes are actually rather higher. For if we are to collapse the dichotomy of judgment on the grounds that rationality is an ideology having no special epistemological status, then we face the possibility that all human judgment is elusive in the sense of being inexplicable, mysterious, and ineligible for genuine systematic justification. Such a possibility would once and for all undermine the claim that judgment—aesthetic, moral, political, and the like—can be objectively valid; it would force us, therefore, to reconsider our strong intuition that good judgment, practical wisdom, and common sense can be identified with some reliability and confidence.[3]

A theory of judgment cannot, I think, be satisfied with the dichotomy of judgment as presented in Chapters 1 and 2. We are thus strongly motivated to see if the dichotomy is somehow false. But to collapse it in favor of unreason may be to give up the possibility of a theory of judgment altogether, and this is something we are also inclined to resist. Our task is therefore intricate: to pursue the arguments of those who would deny the dichotomy, but with a view toward clarifying rather than undermining the concept of judgment. This will inevitably require, in turn, an account of what in the contemporary philosophy of unreason is useful and what is not. In developing such an account, moreover, we shall not be interested in those who would merely assert the primacy or universality of unreason and would dogmatically deny to rationality any epistemological privilege. Simply to state such a thesis is of little interest, since anyone can do that. Our concern, rather, is with formulations that do indeed deny the dichotomy of judgment, that seek to question the orthodox claims of reason,

---

3. Jean-Francois Lyotard and Jean-Loup Thebaud, *Just Gaming* (Minneapolis: University of Minnesota Press, 1985). pp. 74–83.

but that do so immanently, so to speak, with arguments designed to show that rationality cannot *in its own terms* be what it appears to be.

We have seen in Chapters 1 and 2 that traditional approaches leave us unclear about the concept of judgment. In Chapter 1, we outlined some influential views about political wisdom without, however, arriving at a satisfying understanding of what that might be. Consequently, we explored in Chapter 2 the notion of judgment itself as it appears in certain philosophical literatures. That exploration was useful in clarifying, but not in resolving, the issue of judgment, for *phronēsis* remains ill-defined and elusive; aesthetic judgment continues to look like a will-o'-the-wisp. We have as yet no acceptable account of a kind of judgment that is at once noninferential and epistemologically compelling, and hence no certain philosophical basis for describing the nature of political wisdom.

To pursue now the "rational" side of the dichotomy of judgment in critical, even subversive, terms will, I think, be most enlightening. It will suggest strongly that certain putative distinctions, apparently central to the dichotomy of judgment, are in fact not distinctions at all. At the same time, new distinctions will arise that may improve our understanding of the concept of judgment and ultimately shed considerable light on the question of political wisdom itself.

I

The fact that humans are able to communicate linguistically with one another provides perhaps the clearest and most certain evidence that reliable and accurate judgment is possible. Such communication requires, for example, that I be able to interpret accurately the meaning of your utterances and hence to subsume correctly the particular words that you are using under conceptual categories that we share. It is impossible to claim that communication of this sort does not occur, for the meaningful expression of such a claim would itself presuppose precisely the possibility that is being denied. No discussion, no argument, no philosophical issue—indeed, no sentence that you are currently reading—makes any sense unless we stipulate the ability to judge correctly the meaning of what we say to each other, at least a good part of the time. This indubitability suggests that linguistic communication is virtually a paradigm case of correct and reliable judgment.

A traditional approach to linguistic usage explains our communicative capacities in terms of something like the tripartite model of judgment. To communicate linguistically is to manipulate and comprehend "symbols" that have specifiable meanings according to established conventions. These conventions imply or describe rules of inference that permit us to identify accurately the meaning of particular expressions. Such identification is a matter of subsuming expressions under shared conceptual categories, roughly as outlined by the tripartite mode. Using language thus involves a more or less straightforward application of rational, inferential thought.

Such a view has been strenuously criticized, however, by certain emergent and extremely influential trends in the philosophy of language that seek to specify and elaborate the evidently noninferential character of much successful discourse. As we will see, these emergent approaches do attempt to preserve for discourse an important, ineliminable substrate of logical inference. But they also believe that language must be more than this, and that logical inference, in and of itself, cannot account for linguistic communication. Such a conclusion is antirationalist, since it ultimately affirms the claim that a great deal of sensible human communication does not proceed according to the principles of rationality, standardly conceived. The implications are considerable. For if linguistic understanding is indeed a bedrock case of reliable and accurate judgment, and if such an understanding nonetheless has an importantly noninferential character, then the privileged claims of inferential rationality with respect to judgment are placed in some jeopardy.

Speech-act theory provides an important case in point. It rests decisively on the proposition that the full meaning of an utterance is by no means reducible to the meaning of its nouns and predicates. Consider the following utterances:

Will John leave the room?
John will leave the room.
John, leave the room!
Would that John left the room.
If John will leave the room, I will leave also.[4]

4. J. R. Searle, "What Is a Speech Act?" in *Philosophy in America*, ed. Max Black (London: Allen and Unwin, 1965), pp. 221–239.

According to Searle, each of these has both a "propositional content" and an "illocutionary force." The propositional content is identical in all of them; each expresses the proposition that John will leave the room. But each also constitutes a quite different act, for example, the act of asking a question, predicting the future, requesting or ordering someone to do something, and the like. This is a matter of illocutionary force. It seems to be the case, moreover, that both of these elements are essential in determining the meaning of an utterance. That is, the meaning of "Will John leave the room?" depends equally and entirely on its propositional content and its illocutionary force. To change the propositional content (e.g., "Will Jane leave the room?" or "Will John leave the car?") is to change what the utterance means. Similarly, the illocutionary difference between "John will leave the room" and "Will John leave the room?" also results in a substantial difference of meaning.

My use of the word "meaning" here may be technically controversial. Austin, in particular, was at pains to distinguish quite sharply the meaning of an utterance from its force, and to stress that the illocutionary properties of a speech act express or constitute only the latter.[5] Subsequent writers, though, have found that the relationship between meaning and force is not at all clear. Strawson, for example, suggests the possibility that utterances simply have different levels of meaning, one of which is indeed expressed primarily by its illocutionary properties.[6] Austin seems to concede that his use of the word "meaning" is highly technical and even arbitrary: "Admittedly we can use 'meaning' also with reference to illocutionary force—'He meant it as an order,' etc. But I want to distinguish *force* and meaning in the sense in which meaning is equivalent to sense and reference."[7] Similarly, Searle talks of "utterance meaning" or "speaker's meaning," as distinct from literal meaning, and indicates that "the illocutionary force of an utterance is as much a part of its meaning—i.e., of the rules of its use—as any

5. J. L. Austin, *How to Do Things with Words* (Oxford: Oxford University Press, 1962), Lecture 8.

6. P. F. Strawson, "Austin and 'Locutionary Meaning,'" in *Essays on J. L. Austin* ed. Isaiah Berlin et al. (Oxford: Oxford University Press, 1973), pp. 50–51. While Strawson ultimately comes to reject this interpretation, his reasons have more to do with Austin exegesis than with the strength of the argument.

7. Austin, *How to Do Things with Words*, p. 100.

other semantic component."[8] In the end, it appears that if a hearer is to *grasp* an utterance, he or she must grasp or *understand* its illocutionary force; if we assume further that grasping or understanding pertain somehow to meaning (e.g., "I grasp or understand your meaning"), then we may conclude that the illocutionary force of an utterance does indeed express a meaning not expressed solely by its propositional content.[9]

The distinction between propositional content and illocutionary meaning is crucial for understanding the implications of speech-act theory with respect to judgment. In Searle's influential account, propositional content is a matter of reference and predication.[10] The utterances "John will leave the room" and "Will John leave the room?" have the same propositional content insofar as they refer (presumably) to the same person and predicate of that person the same act of leaving the room. This suggests, further, that the propositional content of an utterance is analyzable in terms of Fregean sense and reference.[11] For as Searle says, "a referring expression must have a sense . . . must have a meaning," and this meaning is to be found in the "predicate expression" of which it is a part.[12] Now, from a (roughly) Fregean view the sense and reference of a proposition provides us with its literal meaning.[13] Thus, since the propositional content of an utterance is composed of reference and predication, and since this in turn is analyzable in terms of sense and reference, we may suppose that the literal meaning of an utterance is to be found precisely in its propositional

8. John R. Searle, Ferenc Kiefer, and Manfred Bierwisch, eds., *Speech Act Theory and Pragmatics* (Boston: D. Reidel, 1980), pp. ix–xi.

9. Levinson agrees: "illocutionary force is an aspect of meaning, broadly construed, that is quite irreducible to matters of truth and falsity. That is, illocutionary force constitutes an aspect of meaning that cannot be captured in a truth-conditional semantics." See Stephen C. Levinson, *Pragmatics* (Cambridge: Cambridge University Press, 1983), p. 246.

10. Searle. "What Is a Speech Act?" p. 43.

11. Austin seemed to believe this. See *How to Do Things with Words*, p. 100.

12. John R. Searle, *Speech Acts* (Cambridge: Cambridge University Press, 1969), pp. 92 and 125.

13. In fact, Frege's account of the relationship between sense and reference and what we are here calling literal meaning is rather more obscure than this, and the problem is not helped by difficulties of translation. "Sense and reference" is a translation of Frege's terms *Sinn* and *Bedeutung,* but perhaps a better translation would be "sense and meaning."

content, together with the syntactic structure in which that content is embedded.

If this is correct, then it would seem that propositional content can be determined and identified inferentially, that is, on the basis of certain clearly defined semantic/syntactic conventions or rules. For according to the view we are considering, the literal meaning of a proposition, rooted in sense and reference, expresses nothing other than the truth conditions of that proposition. To know the conditions under which the proposition would be true is to know what the proposition literally means, and this is itself a matter of knowing rules for determining the relevant criteria of truth. If we wish to understand the propositional content of "John will leave the room," we need only to look up the words in the dictionary and be familiar with the formal rules of grammar that determine in English the relationships between subject, object, and predicate. This will provide us with criteria for determining the truth of the proposition and hence with an understanding of its literal meaning.

Clearly, though, such a procedure—an example of the tripartite model of judgment—will not provide us with the illocutionary meaning of the utterance. For illocutionary meaning, being distinct from propositional content, is not reducible to reference and predication, not fully analyzable in terms of sense and reference, not expressive of literal meaning, and hence not rooted in truth conditions. As a result, the rational procedures used for apprehending truth conditions, based on the semantic and syntactic properties of propositions, do not in and of themselves provide access to the nonliteral meaning of utterances. Looking up words and applying syntactic principles are not sufficient for identifying illocutionary force.

In actual fact, the relationship between illocutionary force and semantics/syntax is quite complex. The difference between "John will leave the room" and "Will John leave the room?" is obviously rooted in a difference of syntactic mood. That is, the formal/syntactic properties of each utterance seem to be crucial in determining its illocutionary force. Similarly, the utterance "I, John, promise to leave the room" has the force of a promise partly in virtue of the formal/semantic properties of the phrase "I promise." That phrase is an example of what certain theorists call an "illocutionary force indicating device."[14]

14. Searle, *Speech Acts*, pp. 30ff.

Consider, however, the following utterance: "I'll be there before you."[15] Depending on the circumstances, this might be a promise, a prediction, or a warning. Thus, its illocutionary force can be quite variable, while its syntactic and semantic properties remain entirely unchanged. Even in cases where we do find illocutionary force-indicating devices or differences of syntactic mood, it is doubtful that these suffice to indicate illocutionary meaning. For example, in certain circumstances the utterances "John will leave the room" and "Will John leave the room?" though syntactically different, might nonetheless have precisely the same force, each intended and understood not as a prediction or as a question but as an order. It seems likely, then, that "syntactic mood does not determine the speech act. Rather, syntactic mood *participates* with all other linguistic properties of a given surface expression F in delimiting the set of use-conditions of F."[16]

How then do speech acts work? According to many versions of the theory, one must attend not simply to the surface structure of an utterance but to its "deep structure" as well. For example, the utterance "Be careful" is really an abbreviated version of "I implore [command, beg, advise, etc.] you to be careful." The added words simply make explicit the underlying structure of the original utterance. In such an account, then, there is a close connection indeed between illocutionary force and the formal semantic/syntactic properties of an utterance, once those properties are understood to be often only implicit. Every utterance contains, in effect, an illocutionary force-indicating device, however tacit.[17]

---

15. See Manfred Bierwisch, "Semantic Structure and Illocutionary Force," in *Speech Act Theory and Pragmatics,* ed. Searle, Kiefer, and Bierwisch.

16. Roland R. Hausser, "Surface Compositionality and the Semantics of Mood," in *Speech Act Theory and Pragmatics,* ed. Searle, Kiefer, and Bierwisch.

17. See, for example, J. M. Sadock, *Toward a Linguistic Theory of Speech Acts* (New York: Academic Press, 1974), and J. R. Ross, "On Declarative Sentences," in *Readings in English Transformational Grammar,* ed. R. A. Jacobs and P. S. Rosenbaum (Waltham, Mass.: Ginn, 1970), pp. 222–272. While the position is anticipated by Searle in *Speech Acts* (for example, at p. 64), he also sharply rejects its more extreme versions. See his review of Sadock in *Language* 52 (1976), pp. 966–971. For a rather different kind of approach, see Jerrold J. Katz, *Propositional Structure and Illocutionary Force* (New York: Thomas Y. Crowell, 1977). Katz emphasizes semantic (rather than syntactic or purely pragmatic) theory, and seeks to rehabilitate, among other things, the performative/constative distinction.

But the arguments against such an account seem to be very strong. Some philosophers of language have suggested cases where the truth conditions of an utterance as actually uttered are completely different from the truth conditions of the same utterance when its putative deep structure is made manifest. Other theorists have shown that certain common utterances resist being translated into straightforward performative syntax and hence do not in fact express an otherwise tacit force-indicating device. Perhaps most important, the emphasis on deep structures tells us little about how we know what the deep structure of a particular utterance is. There seems to be no semantic or syntactic rule for determining whether "Be careful" really means "I command you to be careful" or "I beg you to be careful." Ultimately, then, the notion that force is assimilable to standard theories of syntax and semantics "fails both on internal grounds, because it leads to semantic and syntactic incoherencies, and on external grounds because it fails to capture the basic intuitions that led to the theory of speech acts in the first place."[18]

Thus, there are good reasons to believe that the formal/inferential procedures for determining syntactic and semantic properties (e.g., parsing sentences, looking up words in the dictionary) are insufficient for determining the force or nonliteral meaning of speech acts. Yet no one would argue that nonliteral meaning is indecipherable. Successful linguistic communication occurs all the time; we are obviously very well equipped to judge correctly the meanings of linguistic utterances. Since those meanings generally involve illocutions, and since illocutions resist the kind of rule-based formalization presumably characteristic of syntax and semantics, we are compelled to conclude that reliable judgments occur regularly and routinely without the aid of rules or structures of inference. Austin, Searle, and others do seem to allow for a logical substrate in language involving propositional content, sentence structure, the literal meaning of words, and the like. But again, the force of utterances goes well beyond their propositional

18. Levinson, *Pragmatics*, p. 263. See also, Geoffrey N. Leech, *Principles of Pragmatics* (London: Longman, 1983), pp. 174ff, and Gerald Gazdar, "Speech Act Assignment," in *Elements of Discourse Understanding*, ed. Aravind K. Joshi, Bonnie L. Webber, and Ivan A. Sag (Cambridge: Cambridge University Press, 1981), pp. 74ff. I can hardly claim to have done more than scratch the surface here, since the literature on this subject is massive and replete with controversy.

content, is largely independent of standard linguistic formulas, yet poses no insurmountable obstacle to communication.

Thus, if you and I disagree about the propositional content of "I'll be there before you," it appears that there are available to us certain relatively unambiguous methods or procedures for resolving decisively that disagreement. If, however, we agree about its literal meaning but disagree about its force—you think it's a prediction, I a threat—it is not immediately clear how such a difference of judgments could be reliably and accurately adjudicated. But the fact is that such disagreements, though almost always possible, are also relatively rare, and where they do occur, they are usually easily resolved. Human intercourse confronts and conquers problems of this nature all the time. Given, then, that we *are* able successfully to engage in linguistic communication, and assuming further that speech-act theory has something correct to say about the distinction between literal meaning and illocutionary force, we are inclined to conclude that a great deal of reliable and objective human judgment about communication—about the intended meanings of utterances—appears not to depend upon the principles and practices of rational argumentation, and hence seems to violate the tripartite model.

Such a conclusion applies with equal force to the rather more systematic and compelling view of linguistic communication provided by the theory of conversational implicature. Like speech-act theory, the notion of *implicature* seeks to account for the fact that we often mean much more than we actually say, and that this is a normal, generally unproblematic feature of human communication. According to the term of art, many statements "conversationally implicate" meanings far different from those which they literally assert or even logically imply. Unlike speech-act theory, however, the idea of implicature seeks systematically to account for meanings that cannot plausibly be reduced even to the deepest structures of utterances.[19]

Consider the following exchange. *A:* "When is Aunt Rose's birthday?" *B:* "It is sometime in April." The literal meaning of *B*'s utterance

19. The basic text is H. P. Grice, *Studies in the Way of Words* (Cambridge: Harvard University Press, 1988), pp. 3–57. For a brief discussion of criticisms made against Grice, see Richard E. Grandy, "On Grice on Language," *Journal of Philosophy* 86 (October 1989), pp. 514–525. See also, Robert M. Harnish, "Logical Form and Implicature," in *An Integrated Theory of Linguistic Ability*, ed. Thomas G. Bever, Jerrold J. Katz, and D. Terence Langendoen (New York: Thomas Y. Crowell, 1976), pp. 338–364.

is entirely unambiguous. But in many contexts, that utterance also expresses an additional meaning, namely, that *B* does not know the exact date of Aunt Rose's birthday. If one knows the exact date, then one presumably gives it. In failing to do so, the speaker makes clear that he or she knows only the month, not the day. This is the implicature of the utterance. The implicature cannot be derived from the semantic/syntactic properties of the utterance, nor is it logically entailed by what is said. Rather, it operates only through certain principles of conversation, the elaboration of which is the main task of the theory of conversational implicature.

It seems that what speech-act theorists call illocutionary force is merely one case, and perhaps not the most interesting case, of implicature. As we have seen, to the degree that force is distinguished from literal meaning, it cannot confidently be derived from the literal meaning of words or their logical entailments. But this fits precisely the notion of conversational implicature insofar as implicature involves a meaning distinct from what is said. If we determine that, in a particular context, "John will leave the room" and "Will John leave the room?" have the same force, then this is to claim, in effect, that each has the same implicature. As far as I can tell, virtually everything that we find in speech-act theory can be subsumed under the theory of implicature.[20]

The converse, however, is not obviously true. For there appears to be an extremely wide range of implicature cases that are not very easily handled by speech-act theory. Consider the following exchange. *A:* "I want to have a serious discussion now about our relationship." *B:* "Hey, how about those Mets?" According to speech-act theory, *B*'s utterance would be an "indirect speech act," that is, an act that has two forces, one closely related to its literal meaning, the other not. But it is doubtful that the principles governing the analysis of speech acts are well suited to explaining the indirect force of such an utterance. In many contexts, "Hey, how about those Mets?" would really mean something like "I'd rather not talk about that now." Such a meaning cannot easily be derived from some putative deep structure of the utterance, much less from the literal meaning and logical implications of its words. Not only does *B*'s utterance lack an appropriate force-indicating device, it is difficult to see how we could adduce for it some such device, hitherto tacit, that would enable us to account for its

20. Levinson, *Pragmatics,* p. 270.

full conversational function. Similarly, the question of the utterance's syntax seems to be entirely beside the point, for as far as I can tell the meaning and function of the utterance would be in no way illuminated by a change of syntactic mood designed to illuminate some kind of deep structure. Indeed, the utterance itself appears to have no deep structure at all. It is what it is, no more and no less. If this is correct, then its meaning and function can only be apprehended elsewhere, namely, in the light of those principles that govern the conduct of conversation.

According to Grice, four general principles or maxims obtain: (1) an utterance should be true, (2) it should provide neither more nor less information than is appropriate, (3) it should be relevant, and (4) it should be perspicuous (e.g., free of ambiguity).[21] While it is easy enough to see that interlocutors who followed such principles would be able to communicate successfully, it is also clear that the maxims seem to be violated regularly and routinely. But Grice's point is precisely that these maxims are so intrinsic a part of conversation that when a speaker appears to violate them, the hearer nonetheless assumes, despite appearances, that they are being adhered to at some deeper level and that, therefore, it is his or her task to discover how this is so.[22] Thus, for example, the speaker who says "Hey, how about those Mets?" appears to be deliberately violating (at least) the maxim of relevance. The hearer assumes, however, that the speaker is making an apt response. The hearer therefore searches for the utterance's probable implicature, and concludes that the interlocutor really means something like "I'd rather not talk about that now." For Grice, such cases of deliberately and ostentatiously "flouting" the maxims are quite characteristic of implicature and quite typical of ordinary conversation.[23]

The entire analysis assumes, of course, that interlocutors are actually interested in and capable of communicating successfully with one another. In Grice's terms, conversation presupposes a Cooperative Principle: "Make your conversational contribution such as is required, at the stage at which it occurs, by the accepted purpose or direction

21. Grice, *Studies in the Way of Words,* pp. 26–29.

22. Levinson, *Pragmatics,* p. 102.

23. Indeed, it may be that Grice regarded implicatures as occurring only in cases where maxims are flouted. This strikes me, however, as too narrow a construal of his own central insights regarding conversation.

of the talk exchange in which you are engaged."[24] It is always possible that the utterance "Hey, how about those Mets?" is, in fact, the raving of a lunatic, a drug-induced non sequitur, mere sounds that have been memorized and iterated by someone who knows no English, and the like. In such cases, the utterance implicates nothing since, among other things, a conversation is not occurring at all. But whenever conversation does occur, the Cooperative Principle is in effect, and this forms the indispensable basis for applying to any exchange the four principles of conversation.

The theory of implicature thus makes explicit a feature that is also characteristic of speech-act theory: Linguistic understanding is rooted in extralinguistic communal processes. Conversation depends on typically unstated background assumptions, norms, prejudices, and the like, all of which may be said to compose the fabric of a common sense. This common sense is not the product of strict, explicit calculations; it is not arrived at by rational argument and inference; and it is not applied self-consciously to conversational situations as one often applies the rules and methods of semantic and syntactic analysis. Rather, the implicature of an utterance is rooted in ineffable and tacit communal dispositions irreducible to rational method. There is no rule for correctly interpreting "Hey, how about those Mets?" There are no semantic/syntactic formulas for deciding whether and to what extent the utterance is relevant, sufficiently detailed, perspicuous, and the like. The utterance succeeds only insofar as it emerges out of a complex array of practices, judgments, and implicit stipulations that provide answers to such questions and help to form, thereby, the intellectual bases of a community.

Again, it is impossible to deny that such implicatures are regularly and routinely understood. As a result, the theory of conversational implicature, building on speech-act theory, amounts to an important first step in collapsing the dichotomy of judgment. For if objectively correct judgment is possible without relying on standard inferential procedures, then at least one important version of the dichotomy of judgment—the Platonic version—will be shown to be overstated at best, untenable at worst. What Aristotle claimed and failed to prove for *phronēsis,* and what Shaftesbury et al. asserted for aesthetics, only to be refuted by Kant—namely, the reliability and accuracy of judg-

24. Grice, *Studies in the Way of Words,* p. 26.

ments that seem to violate the tripartite model—now appears to have a much stronger justification.

II

The theory of conversational implicature, like speech-act theory, retains a twofold account of language. Just as Austin, Searle, and others posit an inferential, rule-based substrate to all speech acts involving propositional content and literal meaning, so does Grice emphasize that every conversational utterance has, in addition to its implicature, a rationally analyzable core that he calls "what is said." This "what is said" is functionally similar to propositional content insofar as it denotes the truth-conditional content of an utterance.[25]

Following Leech, we may say that the "what is said" is a matter of *rules* (e.g., grammatical and semantic rules), while the implicature is a matter of *principles* (e.g., Grice's maxims of conversation). In the first case, "rules either apply or they do not apply. There is no question of rules being applied *to a certain extent,* of one rule *conflicting* with another, of one rule *overruling* another, etc., according to variable factors of context."[26] Principles, however, possess no such certainty. Their application is fraught with ambiguity and variability and, again, is bound up with the elusive and often indeterminate vicissitudes of the community. While the theory of implicature entails the notion that not all correct judgment is rational in the standard sense, it nonetheless clings to the idea of a rule-based linguistic substrate—the "what is said"—and thereby preserves the rational/nonrational distinction that is at the core of the dichotomy of judgment in its Aristotelian form.

Further inquiries into the philosophy of language, however, call even this elementary distinction into question. Much depends here on our notion of what it means to follow a rule, insofar as this manifests

25. Levinson, *Pragmatics,* p. 97n. Wilson and Sperber make a very strong case for rejecting Grice's narrow interpretation of "what is said." They show that to understand the literal meaning of an utterance itself requires reference to Gricean maxims and that the scope of his theory is thus even wider than he imagined. Deirdre Wilson and Dan Sperber, "On Grice's Theory of Conversation," in *Conversation and Discourse,* ed. Paul Werth (New York: St. Martin's, 1981), pp. 156–159.

26. Leech, *Principles of Pragmatics,* pp. 21–24.

itself both in language usage and elsewhere. The issue is absolutely central to the entire question of judgment, for as was argued in the previous chapter, the tripartite model of judgment seems almost certainly to presuppose the capacity to understand and obey rules. According to that model, judgment requires an ability to connect somehow the conceptual features of a universal with the characteristics of some particular thing, and this ability is typically bound up with rules and procedures on the basis of which the judgment is authorized. Anyone who cares to justify a judgment must do so by showing how it is faithful to the rules. This means at least two things. First, we must be able rationally to relate our judgment to the dictates of the rule. That is, we must be able to specify the rule and demonstrate somehow that we have indeed been faithful to it. Second, the rule itself must be thought of as making sense insofar as we have strong reasons to believe that it responds to true connections between the features of concepts and the characteristics of things (though, of course, our notion of what a true connection is may vary considerably). In other words, the tripartite model presupposes that there is some accurate theory about the world and that the rule according to which we judge is, at the least, consistent with that theory. For convenience sake, we may say that following a rule therefore requires both an *interpretation* of the rule, so that we can be faithful to it, and *reasons* for following the rule, so that we may be able to justify the judgment that is based upon it.

Since the capacity to use language effectively is a basic human trait, and since we are quite convinced that accurate communication and correct interpretation occur much of the time, a theory of linguistic practice that emphasizes rules promises to provide an unusually clear and unambiguous case of how it is that rule-following reliably takes place. We are, to be sure, inclined to have intuitions about this already. Rule-following is algorithmic. A rule specifies certain procedures or steps which, when implemented, will produce a result in accordance with the rule, that is, a correct inference. To interpret and follow the rule is to specify those procedures or steps, perhaps to see their rational connection with one another, and to understand how each step can be instantiated. Moreover, the rule follower also understands, however tacitly, at least some of the reasons behind those steps, that is, how it is that they make sense in light of our theory about the world. The algorithmic sequence of the rule is thought to produce a justifiable inference not fortuitously or haphazardly but as a matter of explicable necessity. It is, as a result, the very soul of rationality.[27] We would expect a theory of linguistic practice to illustrate and elaborate upon these intuitions, perhaps to describe necessary and sufficient conditions for understanding each step in a procedure, and finally to indicate which kinds of interpretations and reasons are suitable for correctly playing a language game.

It turns out that we get something quite different. The (arguably) most influential theory of linguistic practice insists, above all, that following a rule—in language or otherwise—involves neither interpretation nor reasons:

> [I]n the course of our argument, we give one interpretation after another; as if each one contented us at least for a moment, until we thought of yet another standing behind it. What this shews is that there is a way of grasping a rule which is *not* an *interpretation*, but which is exhibited in what we call "obeying the rule" and "going against it" in actual cases. Hence there is an inclination to say: every action according to the rule is an interpretation. But we ought to restrict the term "interpretation" to the substitution of one expression of the rule for another.[28]

This suggests that the very notion of providing an interpretation cannot explain how it is that we know how to follow, and actually do follow, rules. Such an activity is not attendant to, and does not depend upon, the ability to justify or give reasons. This is perhaps most clearly indicated in the process by which someone learns a rule, for example, a mathematical rule:

> How can he *know* how he is to continue a [mathematical] pattern by himself—whatever instruction you have given him? Well, how do I know?—If that means "Have I reasons?" the answer is: my

27. This is essentially Kant's account of rationality. See *Kritik der Urteilskraft*, 47:184. It is also broadly consistent with standard contemporary approaches. See, for example, Harold I. Brown, *Rationality* (London: Routledge, 1988), pp. 3–35, and Michael Scriven, *Reasoning* (New York: McGraw-Hill, 1976), pp. 29–100. I believe that it is even consistent with Toulmin's approach, appearances notwithstanding: See Stephen Edelston Toulmin, *The Uses of Argument* (Cambridge: Cambridge University Press, 1964), Chapters 3 and 4.

28. Ludwig Wittgenstein, *Philosophical Investigations* (Oxford: Basil Blackwell, 1953), §201. Hereafter cited as *PI*. See also, Ludwig Wittgenstein, *Remarks on the Foundations of Mathematics* (Cambridge: MIT Press, 1978), Pt. 1, Section 34; Pt. 2, Sec. 9; Pt. 4, Sec. 9; Pt. 6, Sec. 18. Hereafter cited as *RFM*.

reasons will soon give out. And then I shall act, without reasons. . . . When someone whom I am afraid of orders me to continue the series, I act quickly, with perfect certainty, and the lack of reasons does not trouble me.[29]

Passages such as these are designed to undermine our usual understanding of rule-following. We are not necessarily conscious of the various steps involved in a rule. We are not particularly clear about the nature of the connection between those steps or about the logic of the algorithm that we are engaged in. We certainly need not have in mind the rationale for the procedure we are following or its relationship to some truth about the world. Indeed, Wittgenstein's point is that rule-following is something natural, spontaneous, unreflective, immediate, and automatic. To understand the meaning of a word, for example, is to "grasp it in a flash."[30] This occurs without analysis or reasoned justification, tacit or otherwise, and in no way presupposes that any such analysis or justification has occurred in the past. "Following a rule," says Wittgenstein, "is analogous to obeying an order. We are trained to do so; we react to an order in a particular way."[31] We don't think about it, dissect it, or rationalize it: it is simply what we do.[32]

It may be suspected that such an account would see the rule-follower as less than completely free and self-conscious. In fact, Wittgenstein is rather explicit about this: "When I obey a rule, I do not choose. I obey the rule *blindly*."[33] To participate in a practice is to be "under the compulsion of a rule," and this kind of compulsion is itself rooted in the fact that the rule and the individual are together embedded in a social/historical situation of which the practice is a part. According to the famous formulation, rule-following is always internal to a "form of life."[34] Each of us is immersed in one or more such forms that define, in part, who we are and determine what kinds of thoughts we can have. Our particular being is thus deeply bound up with the

---

29. Wittgenstein, *PI*, §211–212. See also *RFM*, Pt. 6, Sec. 38.

30. Wittgenstein, *PI*, §138–9; *RFM*, Pt. 1, Secs. 123 and 130.

31. Wittgenstein, *PI*, § 206. See also *RFM*, Pt. 1, Sec. 10.

32. Wittgenstein, *PI*, § 217.

33. Wittgenstein, *PI*, § 219.

34. Thus, for example, "to imagine a language is to image a form of life." Wittgenstein, *PI*, § 19; *RFM*, Pt. 6, Sec. 34.

gamut of rule-governed practices that constitute our social and cultural existence. It may be that we can escape from the forms of life that currently establish our identity, but this would presuppose only that we enter into other forms of life and that these, in turn, would make us different kinds of persons thinking different kinds of thoughts. We will always be submerged in one form of life or another; hence, we will always be under a compulsion to obey the rules, whatever they might be.

Forms of life are various and diverse, but each determines for itself, so to speak, how particular words are to be used and what kinds of judgments we can make. In metaphysics, we may encounter energetic disputes about the words "simple" and "composite" and have great difficulty deciding how they should be applied. Are hydrogen and oxygen simples that make up the composite water, or are they themselves composites made up of simples which, upon inspection, can also be seen as composites made up of simples, and so on?[35] Wittgenstein has, I believe, little patience with such disputes. In some language games, "simple" and "composite" are used one way, in other games another; in each case, usage is likely to be intelligible, uncontroversial, and relatively unambiguous.[36] To be sure, there is always some fluidity in any practice; the rules of a language game are generally unfixed, inexact, and open. But this is very different from saying that they are hopelessly ambiguous and unusable.[37] Rules are always constitutive of a practice, however imprecise they may be, and their very vagueness and ineffability generally poses little problem since, again, rule-following is not a matter of critical self-reflection but of blind, instant, unhesitating behavior.[38]

Such behavior is learned. It is a matter of having internalized the practice through regular and repeated use: "I have been trained to react to this sign in a particular way, and now I do so react to it."[39]

35. Cf. G. W. F. Hegel, *Phänomenologie des Geistes* (Hamburg: Felix Meiner Verlag, 1952 [1807]), Section 113.

36. Wittgenstein, *PI*, § 47, 48, 51, 57.

37. Wittgenstein, *PI*, § 85, 88, 99, 100.

38. For discussions of this point, see Colin McGinn, *Wittgenstein on Meaning* (Oxford: Basil Blackwell, 1984), pp. 23 and 39, and Andrew Lewis, "Wittgenstein and Rule-Scepticism," *Philosophical Quarterly* 38 (July 1988), pp. 290 and 293.

39. Wittgenstein, *PI*, § 198; see also, § 206; and *RFM*, Pt. 6, Sec. 17–23.

Rule-following is thus habitual. It is a matter of "mastering a technique" through many replications.[40] One does not learn a rule by discovering its logic, interpreting it discursively, or analyzing the theory behind it; one learns it by rote. Moreover, this is absolutely all that is meant when we say that someone "knows" or "understands" a rule. In the case of language, for example, one understands the meaning of a word only insofar as one is able to use it correctly, that is, in accordance with the rules of the particular language game in question. For Wittgenstein, therefore, "understanding is not a mental process."[41]

The foundation and strength of this argument seems to be largely empirical. At many points, Wittgenstein invites us to consider just what it is that *we* do when we engage in a rule-governed practice, and he concludes quite plausibly that our behavior is indeed nonreflective and noninterpretive. Consider the case of reading a written word:

> I might say that the written word *intimates* the sound to me. Or again, that when one reads, letter and sound form a *unity*—as it were an alloy. . . . When I feel this unity, I might say, I see or hear the sound in the written word. But now just read a few sentences in print as you usually do when you are not thinking about the concept of reading; and ask yourself whether you had such experiences of unity, of being influenced and the rest, as you read. Don't say you had them unconsciously! Nor should we be misled by the picture which suggests that these phenomena came in sight "on closer inspection." If I am supposed to describe how an object looks from far off, I don't make the description more accurate by saying what can be noticed about the object on closer inspection.[42]

Wittgenstein provides similar examples from mathematics designed to show, again, that our participation in practices is generally perspicuous and accurate and yet, at the same time, automatic, immediate, and unself-conscious. Accurate and reliable judgment occurs in this way all the time. One reads, adds large numbers, obeys traffic laws, follows dinner table etiquette, and the like without specifying or being aware

---

40. Wittgenstein, *PI*, § 150, 199. See McGinn, *Wittgenstein on Meaning*, p. 31, and Robert J. Fogelin, *Wittgenstein* (London: Routledge and Kegan Paul, 1976), pp. 129, 143.

41. Wittgenstein, *PI*, § 154.

42. Wittgenstein, *PI*, § 171.

of the putative logic of what one is doing. Such examples are, I think, quite compelling. It seems to be a matter of clear fact that many human activities involving judgments are indeed practices in the sense of being rule-governed, but that we engage in them perfectly well without at all noting, identifying, or attending to—much less analyzing or justifying—the various steps involved or their various rationales.

The empirical argument is buttressed, however, by a quite serious conceptual argument. Wittgenstein explicitly considers the thesis that rule-following must be an interpretive endeavor, and he rejects this on the grounds that no interpretation can ever be complete, definitive, and satisfying. He asks what it could possibly mean to interpret a rule, and he concludes that interpretation is at best "the substitution of one expression of the rule for another."[43] For example, if I want to learn the meaning of a word so as to use it properly, I might look it up in the dictionary, but this would only provide me with another word or group of words—substitutes for the first—which, in principle, would also have to be looked up in the dictionary with, again, the same result. Thus, "if following a rule must always involve interpretation of the rule, then it must also involve interpreting the interpretation, and interpreting the interpretation of the interpretation, etc. And if this is so, one will never be able to arrive at knowledge of what the rule requires."[44] This seems to be very much what Wittgenstein has in mind when he says that "any interpretation still hangs in the air along with what it interprets, and cannot give it any support. Interpretations by themselves do not determine meaning."[45]

The upshot is that one can never show through rational argument alone that a particular action accords with a rule. As Wittgenstein says in the very first section of the *Philosophical Investigations*, "explanations come to an end somewhere."[46] When I interpret a word correctly (i.e., according to the rule that governs its use in a particular language game), I do so both in a flash and in a manner that is ultimately inexplicable. Similarly, when I add two numbers, I do so without reconstructing the rules of arithmetic and also without being able finally

43. Wittgenstein, *PI*, § 201.

44. Lewis, "Wittgenstein and Rule-Scepticism," p. 285.

45. Wittgenstein, *PI*, § 198.

46. Wittgenstein, *PI*, § 1; *RFM*, Pt. 6, Sec. 38; Ludwig Wittgenstein, *On Certainty* (New York: Harper, 1969), §34, 110.

and definitively to justify any such reconstruction. In all cases, the effort to explicate a rule merely amounts to the substitution of one expression of the rule for another; the resultant circularity means that interpretation can never determine the correct application of a rule. To be sure, successful and correct rule-following occurs all the time. But from this we can only conclude that rule-following is not necessarily attendant to, and does not depend upon, explication and interpretation.

III

There are, roughly, two quite different glosses on this theory of rules and rule-following. The most notorious is Kripke's, according to which Wittgenstein is a skeptic. Indeed, Kripke claims that "Wittgenstein has invented a new form of skepticism" which poses, moreover, "the most radical and original skeptical problem that philosophy has seen to date."[47] Kripke focuses, for illustrative purposes, on the rules for addition—and on the word "plus"—and attributes to Wittgenstein the view that I cannot possibly be sure that what I mean today by "plus" is at all consistent with what I meant yesterday. Yesterday I concluded that the correct answer to the problem "20 plus 10" is "30." Today I encounter the problem "68 plus 57," but I am not necessarily justified in concluding beyond a doubt that the correct answer is "125." For the word "plus," as I used it yesterday, might really have denoted something different, say "quus," according to which—to use Kripke's unabashedly bizarre example—any number "quus" any other number is always the sum of the two numbers unless that sum is greater than 57, in which case the correct answer is "5."[48] There is no reason to believe that such a rule would be impossible; board games sometimes feature such seemingly odd outcomes, designed to inject additional uncertainty and unexpectedness into the game. And there is, according to Kripke's Wittgenstein, no way to show that such a strange rule was not in fact what I had in mind when I added "20" and "10" yesterday; perhaps, that is, "when I used the term 'plus' in the *past*, I always meant quus: by hypothesis I never gave myself explicit direc-

47. Saul A. Kripke, *Wittgenstein on Rules and Private Language* (Cambridge: Harvard University Press, 1982), p. 60. See also Fogelin, *Wittgenstein*, pp. 138ff.

48. Kripke, *Wittgenstein on Rules*, p. 9.

tions that were incompatible with such a supposition."[49] As a result, the fact that "20 plus 10" yielded "30" yesterday is entirely consistent with either "125" or "5" being today the correct answer to "68 plus 57."

Kripke extrapolates from this seeming paradox to the case of rule-following in general, including in particular the problem of linguistic rules. He concludes that, for Wittgenstein, there can be no such rules in any meaningful sense, at least as traditionally understood. Indeed, "Wittgenstein's main problem is that it appears that he has shown *all* language, *all* concept formation, to be impossible, indeed unintelligible."[50] Any time we use a word we necessarily "make a leap in the dark; any present intention could be interpreted so as to accord with anything we may choose to do."[51]

Such a reading has been vigorously challenged by a second gloss according to which Wittgenstein was in no sense a skeptic. Colin McGinn writes as follows:

> To lack reasons is not to be in a predicament to which doubt is the proper response; for doubt can be removed (better preempted) by our natural and habitual reactions. This epistemological position would prompt Wittgenstein to dismiss Kripke's skeptic with the remark that of course our reasons come to an end but this does not mean we are in any sort of epistemological trouble; that I cannot *prove* to a determined skeptic that my present use of '+' is correct does not show that I do not know how to apply it correctly or that I have anything less than a perfect right to proceed as I feel inclined.[52]

McGinn does not at all deny the account that we have provided above: rule-following is unreflective and automatic, a matter of training and habit rather than interpretation and demonstration. He simply concludes that this is entirely consistent with the claim that we do indeed

49. Ibid., p. 13.
50. Ibid., p. 62.
51. Ibid., p. 55.
52. McGinn, *Wittgenstein on Meaning*, p. 72. See also, Lewis, "Wittgenstein and Rule-Scepticism," pp. 297–298; G. P. Baker and P. M. S. Hacker, *Scepticism, Rules and Language* (Oxford: Basil Blackwell, 1984), p. 19; G. P. Baker and P. M. S. Hacker, *Wittgenstein: Rules, Grammar, and Necessity* (London: Basil Blackwell, 1985), pp. 81ff; and Crispin Wright, "Critical Notice," *Mind* 98 (April 1989), p. 289.

know how to follow a rule, that we may indeed *understand* a rule correctly, and that a rule may therefore have the kind of fixity and stability that we expect of any object of knowledge and understanding.

Two very different issues arise here. The first is exegetical: Was Wittgenstein in fact a skeptic? I believe, at least preliminarily, that the weight of evidence is against Kripke. Wittgenstein strongly suggests a disdain for all skeptical arguments,[53] and Kripke himself is extremely hesitant about making exegetical claims (though certainly not consistently so.) Moreover, when Wittgenstein argues, for example, that we are generally able to follow an arithmetic rule "with perfect certainty," it seems highly unlikely that he is making a merely psychological claim.[54] The second issue, rather more important for our purposes, concerns whether Wittgenstein *should* have been a skeptic, given his views about rules. One can phrase the question in several ways. Lewis, for example, argues that there is in Wittgenstein a deep distinction between "interpreting" a rule and "understanding" a rule. Specifically, "understanding or grasping a rule . . . is an ability which is exhibited in one's application of the rule, an ability which may consist simply in being able to act in accord with the rule."[55] Understanding, unlike interpretation, need not be a matter of discourse, reflection, or rational thought. With respect to skepticism, then, we must ask if this strikes us as plausible or if, rather, such a view is inconsistent with our concepts of knowledge and understanding. Is it possible truly to understand unreflectively, blindly? Similarly, McGinn talks of Wittgenstein's "antifoundationalist epistemology," and insists that the absence of explanation and interpretation in no way compromises or undermines knowledge claims.[56] But since epistemological speculation ordinarily seems to presuppose some basis for knowledge claims, it is not immediately clear that there can be an epistemology that is truly, deeply antifoundational (though many believe that there can).[57] Perhaps, then,

53. See, for example, Baker and Hacker, *Scepticism, Rules and Language*, p. 5; also Crispin Wright, *Wittgenstein on the Foundations of Mathematics* (Cambridge: Harvard University Press, 1980), p. 27.

54. Wittgenstein, *PI*, § 212.

55. Lewis, "Wittgenstein and Rule-Scepticism," p. 285; cf. Wittgenstein, *PI*, § 146–155.

56. McGinn, *Wittgenstein on Meaning*, p. 28.

57. For a discussion of foundationalist and antifoundationalist epistemologies, see Laurence Bonjour, *The Structure of Empirical Knowledge* (Cambridge: Harvard University Press, 1985).

Wittgenstein's antifoundationalism does have skeptical consequences, even if these were not recognized or made explicit by Wittgenstein himself.

In Kripke's account, Wittgenstein never dispels the skeptical problem but provides only a "skeptical solution," that is, a solution that essentially concedes the skeptic's doubts. This solution involves, among other things, the replacement of a truth-conditional theory of rule-following with an assertion-conditions theory.[58] According to the former, following a rule presupposes an explanation or interpretation on the basis of which one can justify an action as being somehow correct or true according to the rule. Thus, when I say that the answer to "68 plus 57" is "125," I must be able to justify this answer by providing an account of what "plus" means. This, in turn, requires that I be able to explain, however crudely, the theory of addition. If, however, rule-following is not at all a matter of explanation or interpretation, then it is hard to see how one could actually know (or, at least, how one would have to know) whether or not a particular effort to comply with a rule is correct. Without explanation or interpretation, we would seem to have no independent criterion for making such a determination. Kripke's Wittgenstein accepts this skeptical criticism, but is nonetheless clearly committed to the seemingly paradoxical view that there is a firm and identifiable distinction between correctly and incorrectly following a rule. His solution is to base this latter distinction on assertion conditions, namely, those conditions which make it permissible or acceptable to follow a rule in a particular way. Such conditions, for Kripke, are essentially a matter of social convention and agreement. For example:

> Any individual who claims to have mastered the concept of addition will be judged by the community to have done so if his particular responses agree with those of the community in enough cases, especially the simple ones. . . . An individual who passes such tests is admitted into the community as an adder; an individual who passes such tests in enough other cases is admitted as a normal speaker of the language and member of the community.[59]

58. Baker and Hacker, *Scepticism, Rules and Language*, pp. 33ff.

59. Kripke, *Wittgenstein on Rules and Private Language*, p. 92. See also Fogelin, *Wittgenstein*, pp. 143–144.

In other words, one has the right answer simply if that answer accords with the community's expectations. Following a rule is not a matter of theory and interpretation but of emulation. You are entitled to think you have added two numbers correctly or used a word correctly (i.e., you have "understood" a rule) insofar as others agree with your answer.

Again, a host of objections have been raised to this "solution," both in terms of its faithfulness to Wittgenstein's text and its philosophical usefulness. Some have emphasized that Wittgenstein's discussion of assertion conditions pertains to meaning rather than truth (e.g., the meaning of "68 plus 57 equals 5" in a particular language, rather than the truth of that sentence), and that therefore it is not directly germane to the problem of skepticism. To say that the meaning of a word is conventional is not to say that truth is decided by mere human agreement.[60] Others have claimed that the notion of justifiably or legitimately using a rule necessarily presupposes some explanatory ability, since this is precisely what is implied by words like "justifiably" and "legitimately"; as a result, justifications based solely on community assent cannot really be justifications at all.[61] Further, the very idea of assent or agreement is problematic. Agreement presupposes that our answer to a particular question is the same as (nearly) everyone else's, but the identification of sameness is itself a rule-governed activity and hence subject to the (dare I say) same skeptical criticisms that allegedly undermine truth-conditional theories. To claim that my response is the same as yours depends upon an understanding of, among other things, the word "same." But since "same" is just another word in a language game, our understanding of it cannot be a matter of interpretation since, again, explanations must come to an end somewhere. The upshot is that agreement, as a criterion for following a rule, is subject to the same infinite regress that we found in rule-following generally; hence it cannot be the path that leads us out of that regress.[62]

But if the skeptical solution as formulated by Kripke is troubling, it is nonetheless unlikely that this has any real force against Wittgenstein. For while Wittgenstein does indeed seem to hold an asser-

60. McGinn, *Wittgenstein on Meaning*, pp. 54–55.

61. Baker and Hacker, *Scepticism, Rules and Language*, pp. 34ff.

62. Warren Goldfarb, "Kripke on Wittgenstein on Rules," *Journal of Philosophy* 22 (1985), pp. 483–485.

tion-conditions rather than truth-conditional view of rule-following, I doubt that Kripke's account of the former is altogether accurate or that it presents Wittgenstein's position in the strongest possible philosophical light. Two related elements in Wittgenstein's work are especially and immediately germane. First, it is clear that Wittgenstein does see rule-following as somehow social, but in a very special sense. He discusses, for example, the problem of teaching someone to play chess, and asks how it would be possible to learn the moves of the piece called the "king" without already knowing what it means to talk about "a piece in a game".[63] Just as Oakeshott argues that following a recipe presupposes a knowledge of how to cook, so does Wittgenstein insist that rule-following is embedded in ongoing and established practices or "customs" that involve deep and complex, if only tacit, understandings: "To obey a rule, to make a report, to give an order, to play a game of chess, are *customs* (uses, institutions)."[64] An important implication, found throughout the *Philosophical Investigations*, is that the automatic, unreflective nature of rule-following does indeed rest upon the typically inchoate and unarticulated suppositions of a community. But this, in turn, suggests an account of assertion conditions quite different from that provided by Kripke. Assertability is not plebiscitary; it is not a matter of empirical, behavioral agreement. Rather, it is rooted in background conditions that must obtain in order to say, or even think, something intelligible. If one must know about the culture of games (so to speak) in order to learn chess, then such knowledge—such acculturation—is a necessary condition for intelligibly talking or thinking about the moves of the king.[65]

Second, this kind of knowledge need not be discursive, interpretive, or explanatory. Much here depends upon the word "knowledge." There is at least some evidence that Wittgenstein would restrict its use rather substantially. For example, he claims that "it can't be said of me at all (except perhaps as a joke) that I *know* I am in pain. What is it supposed to mean—except perhaps that I *am* in pain?"[66] Knowledge evidently has something to do with defeasibility. We can accept this with equanimity and still insist that I can be quite *certain* about the judgment *I am in pain.* As Lewis argues, this kind of certainty involves

63. Wittgenstein, *PI*, § 31–33; see also, *RFM*, Pt. 6, Sec. 21.

64. Wittgenstein, *PI*, § 199; see also *On Certainty*, § 41.

65. Wittgenstein, *On Certainty*, § 94.

66. Wittgenstein, *PI*, § 246; see also *On Certainty*, § 30.

no interpretation or explanation—no knowledge, perhaps—but is no less certain for that.[67]

Wittgenstein's account of rule-following appears to involve certainty of this general variety. It is certainty based not on the immediacy of physical sensation but on the equivalent immediacy of a socialized and acculturated self deeply embedded in forms of life that determine what kinds of things make sense, and hence what kinds of things are intelligibly assertable. In this connection, it may be helpful to suggest a distinction between claims that are unintelligible and claims that are simply incorrect. Imagine that someone says "68 plus 57 equals 115." Those of us who believe in addition, and who agree about the meaning of "plus" and "equals," will say that the claim is incorrect. But we will also be inclined to say that the mistake is corrigible (perhaps simply a matter of failing to carry the 1); and this implies, I think, that the claim, though incorrect, is nonetheless perfectly intelligible. The person who utters it probably understands addition well enough. The mistake is most likely a technical error, or perhaps reflects an insufficient or incomplete mastery of the rules of arithmetic. In either case, we understand what the utterer is trying to do and are able to make an apposite and constructive response.

But imagine now a rather different utterance: "68 plus 57 equals sour-tasting." This claim is not so easily corrigible. One could perhaps say a great deal about how it fails to jibe with certain rules. But our stronger inclination is to suggest that the utterer (if sincere) really has no conception at all of what addition is and, indeed, might even be unable to understand our efforts to describe what is wrong. The claim, therefore, is not incorrect but unintelligible. We don't know what to make of it, and can find no clear basis for an appropriate conversational response. Indeed, the utterance is not really a violation of the rules at all but is, instead, unrelated to the rules—outside of their purview—and could have been made only by someone alien to, among other things, the practice of addition. The failure of such an utterance is not a matter of the community deciding that "sour-tasting" is the wrong answer to the problem; rather, the community simply does not understand what is being said. The utterance, as nonsense, thus violates the relevant conditions of assertability.[68]

This distinction between correctness and intelligibility/assertability

67. Lewis, "Wittgenstein and Rule-Scepticism," p. 300.

68. See Wittgenstein, *On Certainty*, § 54.

may not always be easy to apply. Imagine again that someone says "68 plus 57 equals 115." Imagine further that we explain to this person the nature of the error and that we teach him to be better at addition. Assume that our efforts are successful and that the individual eventually demonstrates an excellent ability to add all kinds of numbers, large and small. Now suppose that, despite all of this, he continues to insist that "68 plus 57 equals 115." After all of our efforts, what we took to be an incorrect response now begins to look unintelligible. We check again to see that the utterer really can add, and suffers from no psychological or physiological condition that would prompt one to overlook the properties of two and only two numbers, 68 and 57; we try to reconfirm that the utterance was made in complete sincerity, that the utterer is sober, and the like. Assuming that all of these tests are passed, our ultimate response will be that we do not know at all what to make of the utterance since it is, for us, nonsense. It violates our assertion conditions and hence is deeply unintelligible.[69]

For Wittgenstein, the immediate and unreflective nature of rule-following is, I think, bound up with this kind of criterion for what is assertable. The result is a decidedly nonskeptical view. To see this more clearly, consider the Kripkean utterance "68 plus 57 equals 5." This might be simply incorrect rather than unintelligible since, unlike the "sour-tasting" example, it at least offers a numerical answer to a problem of addition. On the other hand, the answer "5" is so far off that it seems most unlikely that anyone with even a rough sense of addition could make an error of such magnitude; the utterance might thus be unintelligible. Kripke's example, however, has a further twist, since the answer "5" turns out to be absolutely correct according to the rules of "quus." It seems to me that Wittgenstein's approach to such a case would be quite different from the "skeptical solution" as developed by Kripke. The Kripkean utterance is either incorrect or unintelligible. If we find it to be intelligible, then that is simply what it is. In an important sense, we have no choice about this. The intelligibility of an utterance is something like the reality of a pain; it is a brute fact about which there can be neither justification nor doubt, a fact rooted not in our physiology (as the pain would be) but in our form of life. The utterance either makes sense to us or it does not. To be sure, this does not necessarily rule out Kripke's skeptical objections. But for Wittgenstein, such objections, far from being central, seem to

69. Wittgenstein, *On Certainty*, § 67ff.

be in fact uninteresting. Some things clearly *are* intelligible, and this fact suffices to allow for successful communication.

Of course, the Kripkean utterance may be unintelligible rather than incorrect, that is, we may simply not understand it. It may violate the assertion conditions of our language; hence it is, for us, nonsensical. But again, no skeptical problem arises, since the general possibility of intelligibility is in no way called into question. The Kripkean utterance is little more than noise and does not qualify as a meaningful statement.

In Kripke's account, Wittgenstein's "skeptical solution" is closely analogous to Hume's treatment of induction.[70] In Hume's view, we can have indubitable empirical knowledge of brute facts (sense perceptions) but of nothing else; in particular, we can have no knowledge of the causal relationships between those facts. In the face of this, the best we can do is to construct, more or less arbitrarily, theoretical fictions thought to be useful in helping us to live our lives. We are entitled to retain such fictions as long as they fit the facts, but should be under no illusions that they in fact accurately describe some true feature of the world. Explanation is thus entirely a matter of what we choose to believe, and such a choice, since it is not imposed by the truth of the world, can only be conventional and arbitrary.

Kripke's Wittgenstein similarly "solves" the problem of skepticism in rule-following by relying on a community's arbitrary decision to regard this or that particular answer as legitimate. But in fact, Wittgenstein's position is not like this at all. One might do better to draw an analogy with Carnap's distinction between "internal" and "external" questions. For Carnap, all intelligible and meaningful questions are necessarily asked and answered within a particular language, theoretical framework or, in Wittgenstein's term, form of life; it is the existence of such a framework that allows for meaningfulness in the first place. But one consequence of this is that to move outside of frameworks altogether—to ask metaframework questions—is to forfeit the possibility of talking meaningfully at all. For example, to ask whether there is a real world "out there" independent of human consciousness is, from the standpoint of the accepted framework, quite literally nonsense. This formulation is, I believe, similar to what Wittgenstein has in mind when he argues that "It is what human beings *say* that is true

---

70. Kripke, *Wittgenstein on Rules and Private Language*, pp. 62–68, 97–98, 108. See also Fogelin, *Wittgenstein*, p. 143.

and false; and they agree in the *language* they use. That is not agreement in opinion but in form of life."[71] The community does not arbitrarily ratify answers as being true and false according to some artificially constructed fiction. Rather, it operates naturally and unreflectively in terms of the language or theoretical framework that makes it a community in the first place and that determines, therefore, what is and is not comprehensible. In such a circumstance, individuals act "blindly"; when they speak, they necessarily speak intelligibly since, for them, that's what speaking is. They do not "choose" to follow the rules, unless perhaps we consider it a choice simply not to be crazy.

Thus, when Wittgenstein talks of certainty in rule-following, he is talking about the automatic and unselfconscious invocation of assertion conditions that determine not what is correct and incorrect but what is intelligible. These are conditions for making sense. They are, again, rooted in and (at least partly) constitutive of forms of life. Each set of assertion conditions is part and parcel of and determinative of the very mode of thinking characteristic of a particular form of life. Of course, to be human is to participate in one or more such forms of life. Thus, to be human also means to have learned and internalized assertion conditions such that intelligibility can be recognized "in a flash" and with complete certainty. This, for Wittgenstein, is a necessary and irrefutable presupposition of human existence as we know it.

IV

As indicated in Section 1, the ability to use language is virtually a paradigm case of judgment. To interpret an utterance is to judge its meaning, to connect particular sounds (or symbols) to universal concepts. This kind of judgment in language is generalizable to many or even all cases of rule-following, and in each such case, the outcome is, again, a judgment (e.g., a judgment about the answer to a mathematical problem, the meaning of a stop sign, the proper way to behave at the dinner table, etc).

The language philosophies that we have outlined suggest above all that reliable and accurate judgment can occur in ways that are not self-evidently assimilable to rational thought standardly conceived. The more moderate position is that language has necessarily both an

71. Wittgenstein, *PI*, § 241. Fogelin seems to be sensitive to this: see *Wittgenstein*, p. 146.

inferential, rule-based element (roughly, semantics and syntax) and a noninferential one (illocutionary force or implicature). The more extreme view would tend to collapse this distinction by denying the inferential nature of even the most fundamental kinds of rule-following. In either case, we are provided with what I take to be quite substantial evidence that at least some judgments that are certainly true—since they involve undeniably successful communication—nonetheless violate the tripartite model, since they fail to operate in terms of clear and justifiable rules and procedures for subsuming particulars under universals.

These views share a further implication, however. Each seeks to account for successful judgment in terms of an ineluctable grounding in social or communal contexts. Illocutionary force operates on the basis of tacit conventions that interlocutors share by virtue of being part of the same linguistic community. Implicature similarly presupposes a world of common assumptions and preunderstandings that make it possible to comprehend nonliteral meanings, often without much evident difficulty. Or again, rule-following in linguistic activity involves reliance not on truth conditions but on assertion conditions that are embedded in the community—the form of life—that makes an intelligible speaker intelligible in the first place. All of this suggests that reliable and accurate judgment is often a matter of invoking, however automatically and unconsciously, the range of norms, assumptions, conceptual materials, and rhetorical tools that constitute the linguistic/intellectual community of which one is a part.

At this juncture, two questions emerge: Exactly how does the community-judgment relationship occur, and to what extent does it pertain to judgments that are not purely linguistic? These questions may appear to be sociological in nature, the first concerning the social foundations of knowledge, the second involving (roughly) the scope of communal life. But in fact, they also raise difficult philosophical issues about how judgment itself should be conceived. What kind of positive characterization can be given to noninferential thought processes? What are the criteria for deciding the truth or falsity of judgments that do not operate according to the tripartite model? How should assertion conditions be conceptualized? What are the implications of this conceptualization for our concept of judgment? To my knowledge, the traditions of language philosophy that we have been examining are largely silent on such questions. However, there are other philosophical traditions, of a quite different pedigree, that can be most helpful here, and that may serve to deepen and radicalize substantially our doubts about the dichotomy of judgment.

The so-called hermeneutic school, at least in its major contemporary iteration, has its roots in Herder, Hegel, and Heidegger, among others, and hence takes its bearings from themes and theses quite foreign to those of Austin, Wittgenstein, and Grice. But such themes and theses nonetheless resonate with the same general problem of how reliable judgments are possible in circumstances where standard rationality seems not to obtain. Indeed, the entire project of hermeneutics may be thought of as an effort to reconstruct an "alternative rationality" wherein one acquires truth and knowledge without recourse to the usual modes of rational inference. In a sense, then, the problem of illocution and implicature is simply taken up and pursued in new and broader directions by the hermeneutic tradition. It is analyzed with respect to the ways in which assertion conditions impose themselves on speakers; it is examined in the light of its implications for historical and aesthetic interpretation; and it is shown to be a fundamental feature not simply of verbal/linguistic communication but of human cognition itself.

According to the hermeneutic tradition, the problem of understanding the full meaning of an utterance is simply one case of a far more general problem: How do we understand anything? The peculiar feature of illocutionary force or implicature, namely, that one does not typically apprehend it on the basis of specifiable rules and procedures of inference, is equally characteristic of an entire range of human institutions and modes of expression. It is certainly as true of written texts as it is of oral texts: an utterance penned is as much in need of interpretation as an utterance uttered. But the very idea of textuality and textual interpretation must itself be conceived as generously as possible:

> [T]he hermeneutics that was merely ancillary to theology and philology was developed into a systematic teaching (*Ausbildung*) and made the basis of all the human sciences. It fundamentally transcended its original pragmatic purpose of making it possible, or easier, to understand literary texts. It is not only the literary tradition that is estranged and in need of new and more vital appropriation (*Aneignung*). Everything that is no longer immediately situated in a world—that is to say, all tradition, whether art or the other spiritual creations of the past, e.g., law, religion,

philosophy, and so forth—is estranged from its original sense and depends on the disclosing and mediating spirit that we, like the Greeks, name after Hermes, the messenger of the gods.[72]

To understand, and hence judge correctly, the meaning of a law, an historical event, a philosophical treatise—all of this presents problems similar to those involved in interpreting the force or implicature of a conversational utterance.

In some ways, the most extreme and also most informative cases of this general problem are to be found in aesthetics. As discussed in Chapter 2 above, our initial inclination is to assume that there are no inferential rules or procedures on the basis of which we might interpret and evaluate correctly a work of art. This presumption, central to the British aesthetic tradition of Shaftesbury, Hutcheson, and Hume, is pursued pitilessly by Kant who, as we have seen, concludes that aesthetic judgment is noncognitive, that claims about the meaning or value of a piece of art have nothing to do with knowledge, justification, or determinant concepts.

Despite this conclusion, however, art criticism continues apace, much of it informed by the (at least) implicit claim that some judgments about art do in fact have more validity than others and that aesthetic judgment does, therefore, involve a certain kind of genuine knowledge. The hermeneutic tradition seeks to vindicate this claim by criticizing both the "Kantian subjectivization of aesthetics" and also

---

72. Hans-Georg Gadamer, *Wahrheit und Methode* (Tübingen: J. C. B. Mohr, 1972), p. 157. In rendering passages from this book, I have relied heavily on the excellent translation by Joel Weinsheimer and Donald G. Marshall (*Truth and Method,* New York: Crossroad, 1989), although I have also made numerous emendations, largely in the interest of literalness.

By identifying the hermeneutic tradition with Gadamer, I do not intend to deny the deep differences between Gadamer and others in the hermeneutic tradition (e.g., Schleiermacher and Dilthey in the nineteenth-century, Betti and Ricoeur more recently). Gadamer's debt to and critique of his nineteenth-century predecessors is outlined in Part 2, Chapter 1 of *Truth and Method.* For general historical discussions, see Josef Bleicher, *Contemporary Hermeneutics* (London: Routledge & Kegan Paul, 1980); Roy Howard, *The Three Faces of Hermeneutics* (Berkeley: University of California Press, 1982); Michael Ermarth, "The Transformation of Hermeneutics: 19th Century Ancients and 20th Century Moderns," *Monist* 64 (April 1981), pp. 175–194; and Georgia Warnke, *Gadamer: Hermeneutics, Tradition, and Reason* (Stanford: Stanford University Press, 1987), pp. 5–41.

the Romantic "aesthetic consciousness" that extended and radicalized Kant's theory.

According to the notion of an aesthetic consciousness (as embodied variously in the views of Schelling and Schiller, among others), great art is the product of great individual genius and is, as such, something quite separable from the prosaic concerns and practices of the everyday social world. The artist is able to step outside of social contexts and create art through a kind of radical independence. As a result, "art becomes a standpoint of its own and establishes its own autonomous claim to supremacy."[73] Indeed, the artistic endeavor, rather than being an expression of the world out of which it emerges, becomes instead the negation of that world: "the poetry of aesthetic reconciliation must seek its particular self-consciousness against the prose of alienated reality."[74] This is the aesthetic consciousness—a consciousness divorced from and uncontaminated by the concerns and vicissitudes of the common world and hence purely, pristinely aesthetic.

Unencumbered by social norms and institutions, the nature and identity of the work of art can be approached only in terms of the eccentric, irreducible, and completely subjective standpoint of the artist. This, in turn, creates serious difficulties for the art critic. Since a work of autonomous genius is unconstrained by standard, socially located criteria of what is good and bad, appropriate and inappropriate, true and false, and the like, the critic can hardly be expected to employ such criteria when rendering an interpretation or judgment that purports to be accurate and faithful. To say, for example, that a poem has a particular meaning because it invokes images or tropes having specifiable connotations in ordinary language is, in fact, to undermine the work, to deny its very poetic quality by forcing it back into the undignified world of common discourse. Similarly, to say of a painting that it is aesthetically unsuccessful because it fails to perform properly a social or political function of some kind is to apply criteria that have nothing to do with art itself. Thus, in the absence of clear, identifiable standards, the critic must bring to the work his or her own imaginative and creative faculties. But this means that art criticism, lacking any objective basis for judgment, comes itself to be understood entirely in subjective terms: the unrestricted autonomy of the artist is paralleled

73. Gadamer, *Wahrheit und Methode*, p. 78.
74. Ibid., p. 79.

by the equally unrestricted autonomy of the critic. As a result, the entire aesthetic process—interpretation as well as creation—is deprived of a speculative rational grounding.

For Gadamer, all of this represents a substantial error: "the work of art cannot be understood in terms of 'aesthetic consciousness.'"[75] Artistic endeavor, like all human endeavor, is or ought to be connected to and preoccupied with the social and historical conditions out of which it arises.[76] Indeed, "the great ages in the history of art were those in which people without any aesthetic consciousness and without our concept of 'art' surrounded themselves with structures (*Gestaltungen*) whose function in religious or secular life could be understood by everyone and which gave no one solely aesthetic pleasure."[77] Properly understood, then, aesthetic endeavor is not at all autonomous but is inextricably bound up with the social organism: "The work of art cannot simply be isolated from the 'contingency' of the chance conditions in which it appears, and when this kind of isolation occurs, the result is an abstraction that reduces the actual being of the work. It itself belongs to the world to which it represents itself."[78] Gadamer is at pains to show that this applies to all art forms—for example, painting, architecture, and literature—and that certain kinds of art, especially "decorative" and "occasional" art, are wrongly denigrated by the aesthetic consciousness precisely for being "functional."[79]

It may seem that Gadamer is merely positing arbitrarily one conception of art against another. But in fact, his critique is rooted in a complex and powerful epistemological perspective that has extremely important consequences for the entire question of judgment.[80] As we

75. Ibid., p. 137.

76. There is a persistent question as to whether Gadamer is describing or prescribing. See Lawrence M. Hinman, "Quid Facti or Quid Juris? The Fundamental Ambiguity of Gadamer's Understanding of Hermeneutics," *Philosophy and Phenomenological Research* 40 (June 1980), p. 527.

77. Gadamer, *Wahrheit und Methode*, p. 77.

78. Ibid., p. 111.

79. Ibid., pp. 147–154, passim.

80. It is perfectly correct to say that Gadamer's hermeneutics, following Heidegger's, is "ontological" and therefore distinct from the methodological or "epistemological" hermeneutics of, inter alia, Schleiermacher and Dilthey. But this should not blind us to the fact that Gadamer's work has an important epistemological component. The claim that we are fundamentally interpretive beings has decisive implications for what we can know and how we can know it.

will see, the upshot is a twofold rejection of the aesthetic consciousness: first, art is not different from but fundamentally similar to other
cognitive activities; second, all such activities, including art, are by
definition embedded in and inseparable from traditional structures
of meaning and value that constitute, in part, the everyday world of
affairs.

Gadamer begins with what we already know: the artist, in representing the world, invariably heightens certain things and deempha-
sizes or ignores others. Aesthetic vision is selective. Even the most
photographic of paintings or the most realistic of novels will necessarily choose from the infinite range of images available, placing some in
the foreground and others off to the side, representing things from
certain angles and not from others, lending to the world a shape and
structure that is not self-evident in the world itself.[81] The task of art
is not to copy but to imitate, and mimesis always involves amplification,
perspective, and choice.[82]

By engaging in mimesis, however, the artist merely undertakes in
a particularly vivid manner a task that we all undertake when we engage the world. For the fact is that our ordinary prosaic attention is
equally selective. Specifically, Gadamer rejects what he calls the notion
of "pure perception." Such a notion would hold, roughly, that our
sensuous faculties are neutral instruments for observing and recording
an independent, external world, and that this neutrality allows for
objective, reliable and indubitable knowledge. Of course, the indubitability of our sensual intuitions is central to the modern positivist account of knowledge. As such, it has been subjected to a great deal of
criticism, but no criticism has been harsher than Gadamer's. In his
view, "perception is never just a mirror image of what is given to the
sense. . . . never a mere mirroring of what is there."[83] Rather, we
always approach the world in a particular way, from a particular standpoint, and this has an important influence on what we actually see.
Perception is invariably "articulated." We disregard much of what is

81. Gadamer, *Wahrheit und Methode,* pp. 109–110.

82. Ibid., pp. 130–134. See also, William Schweiker, "Beyond Imitation:
Mimetic Praxis in Gadamer, Ricoeur, and Derrida," *Journal of Religion* 68 (January 1988), pp. 24–27, and Warnke, *Gadamer,* pp. 56–64.

83. Gadamer, *Wahrheit und Methode,* pp. 85–86.

really there, and read in what is "not there at all."[84] Attending to the world is never pure but always informed by a point of view that lends shape, identity, and sense to the thing perceived.

Clearly the selectivity of aesthetic vision is not at all unique. The artist is simply one articulated perceiver among many, and the homely criteria by which we decide what is true and false are equally and identically applicable to artist and nonartist alike. Gadamer's rejection of the aesthetic consciousness is thus based in part on the claim that the essential features of aesthetic endeavor are characteristic of human thought in general. Art, as a cognitive enterprise, is continuous with thinking itself, performing specifiable social functions—involving our appropriation and understanding of the world—that are performed in different and complementary ways by a host of other social practices.

But the continuity of art with life is not simply a matter of its similarity to other forms of cognition, for aesthetic activity, like all cognitive activity, is also part and parcel of the everyday world out of which it emerges. Gadamer's basic views in this regard are too well known to merit more than a brief rehearsal.[85] His perspectivism assumes that our selective or articulated encounter with the environment is rooted in established traditions or communities of discourse. To be human is to be embedded in, and to owe one's identity to, some such community. The community, in turn, provides for us the conceptual, theoretical, and normative materials that guide and constrain our selective encounter with the world. In Gadamer's terms, the historical/traditional situation in which we happen to find ourselves is a "lifeworld" that constitutes our "horizon."[86] This horizon is a realm of ideas

---

84. Ibid., p. 86. Gadamer's formula of "reading in what is not there at all" is surely unfortunate. In one sense, what is read in *is*, in fact, there, simply *because* it is read in. Reality is always an interpreted reality, and the interpretation, as constitutive of what is real, could never be something that "is not there at all." On the other hand, Gadamer cannot be holding that we can read in just anything at all, for this would be to endorse a kind of "existentialist radicalization" of subjectivism that Gadamer explicitly rejects (pp. 94–95).

85. For good, brief introductory discussions, see Hinman, "Quid Facti or Quid Juris? The Fundamental Ambiguity of Gadamer's Understanding of Hermeneutics," pp. 516–521, and Brice R. Wachterhauser, "Prejudice, Reason, and Force," *Philosophy* 63 (April 1988), pp. 221–238.

86. Gadamer's debt to Husserl here is quite explicit. See *Wahrheit und Methode*, pp. 252–253.

composed essentially of prejudgments, or "prejudices," often tacit and implicit, that determine in advance how we are to make sense of the environment. Since we are all members of an historical/traditional community, and since all such communities are constituted, in part, by one or another set of prejudgments, our way of thinking and, indeed, our very identity are importantly determined by the prejudices we have inherited. Such prejudices "constitute the historical reality of [our] being."[87]

Our discussion of Oakeshott in Chapter 1, and again in this chapter, produced a particularly apt example, namely, that of using a cookbook. For Oakeshott, as we have seen, "a cookery book presupposes somebody who knows how to cook."[88] In Gadamer's terms, our prejudgments or preunderstandings regarding cooking are absolutely indispensable if we are to use the cookbook intelligently. Perhaps there is, or could be, a culture where cooking is unknown, where nourishment is obtained solely through pills produced in laboratories, and where the institution of cooking had never existed or, if it did exist, had been completely and totally forgotten. In such a world, the cookbook would be extremely difficult to interpret correctly. It would no doubt have the status of a strange, alien object, inherently meaningless and available for a potentially wide range of uses, none of them necessarily connected to its intended purpose. It would be like the (by now proverbial) Coca Cola bottle dropped accidentally from an airplane and found by members of a culture that has no knowledge of bottles or glass, much less soda pop. We might try to imagine a similar circumstance occurring in our own culture, but this would be very difficult for us to do since all of our imaginings would themselves be embedded in and entirely dependent on the structure of concepts and prejudices that compose our mode of cognition. Thinking is always bound up with a conceptual horizon; hence, it is impossible to think something that is truly, utterly alien.

Such a theory has important epistemological implications. Since

---

87. Ibid., pp. 260–261. Of course, the hermeneutic tradition is not alone in making this kind of claim. For example, Mead wrote of "the existence of a universe of discourse, as that system of common or social meanings which thinking presupposes as its context." See G. H. Mead, *Mind, Self, and Society* (Chicago: University of Chicago Press, 1962), p. 156.

88. Michael Oakeshott, "Political Education," in *Rationalism in Politics* (London: Methuen, 1981), p. 119.

our encounters with the world are fundamentally determined by our prejudgments, we may well wonder what it could mean to have knowledge and, in particular, how it is possible to add to our store of knowledge. If new knowledge is to be truly new, then it would seem to be in some sense alien to our old way of thinking; but if it is impossible to think that which is truly alien, it is hard to see how we could acquire new knowledge. This is an old problem, and Gadamer's treatment of it is, in a sense, equally old. For him, knowledge is a matter of bringing to light and recognizing explicitly something that we already "know," but only implicitly. Just as Meno's slave boy "recalls" a mathematical theorem that in another sense he could not have known at all, so does Gadamer see all knowledge as involving a kind of remembrance or *anamnēsis:* "The 'known' enters into its true being and manifests itself as what it is only when it is recognized."[89]

Gadamer certainly does not doubt that we can and do acquire genuinely new knowledge. We discover hitherto unknown facts about the world all the time, and this suggests that knowledge is hardly a figment of the human imagination. The world "out there" has an existence and an identity separate from the human mind, or so we must suppose, and to understand that world is, at least up to a point, not to invent it but to record faithfully its autonomous, self-subsistent reality. Even written texts are sufficiently independent that we are often "pulled up short" by what we read insofar as its meaning "is not compatible with what we had expected."[90]

In all such cases, however, the newly discovered datum is observed by a faculty that is predisposed to observe some such fact. It is a faculty informed and guided by concepts and prejudices that allow only certain kinds of information to be processed, and that seem actually to anticipate at least some features of things yet to be encountered. Unexpected data are never wholly unexpected. They are recognized and recorded on the basis of a mode of thought that permits, however tacitly and inchoately, only a certain range of observations, that is essentially blind to anything falling outside of that range, and that predetermines therefore the kinds of things that might be encountered. The discovery of a new element in chemistry may well come as a surprise. But such an event nonetheless presupposes an entire intellectual system—modern chemistry—that allows for and even con-

89. Gadamer, *Wahrheit und Methode,* p. 109.
90. Ibid., p. 252.

templates, at least as a logical possibility, the discovery of new elements. Such a system, rooted in established traditions of inquiry and characterized by a complex array of prejudgments or prejudices, guides and constrains our faculties of perception, determining what it is that we attend to and providing a basis for interpreting or making sense out of that which is observed.

On the topic of discovery, Mead wrote as follows:

> The social process, as involving communication, is in a sense responsible for the appearance of new objects in the field of experience of individual organisms implicated in that process. . . . [T]he social process in a sense constitutes the objects to which it responds, or to which it is an adjustment. That is to say, objects are constituted in terms of meanings with the social process of experience and behavior through the mutual adjustment to one another of the responses or actions of the various individual organisms involved in that process, an adjustment made possible by means of a communication which takes the form of a conversation of gestures in the earlier evolutionary stages of that process, and of language in its later stages.[91]

Shorn of its behavioristic language, such a view accords well with the hermeneutic account. It also helps to reveal an important discrepancy between Gadamer's approach to discovery and the contemporary theory of scientific revolutions.[92] While much of Kuhn's account of normal science comports nicely with hermeneutic epistemology, the notion of revolutionary science seems rather less compatible. For if scientific investigation and, indeed, cognition itself are necessarily tied to and dependent upon given modes of analysis and inquiry, then the very idea of a scientific revolution becomes difficult to sustain. Paradigms do not arise out of thin air. They emerge, rather, from a well-prepared soil—an established and ongoing tradition of inquiry—and hence necessarily make contact with and are understandable in

91. Mead, *Mind, Self, and Society*, p. 77.

92. Admittedly, I present here something of a caricature that is not fully responsive to either the subtleties or the ambivalences of Kuhn's own formulation. On the other hand, the comparison between Kuhn and Gadamer is hardly gratuitous, since Kuhn refers to his own work as hermeneutical; see Thomas S. Kuhn, *The Essential Tension* (Chicago: University of Chicago Press, 1977), p. xiii.

the light of earlier modes of analysis. Gadamer must be committed to the view that scientific revolutions are never truly revolutionary, and that the incommensurability of one paradigm with its predecessor is unimaginable.

All of these epistemological claims apply to aesthetic endeavor as much as to anything else. Rather than being isolated and unconnected, the artist, like the scientist and the moralist, is embedded in a community of discourse that provides the materials—the prejudices—on the basis of which the world is selectively interpreted and represented. Art is "a mode of knowledge" precisely because it can offer us "the joy of recognition . . . the joy of knowing *more* than is already familiar."[93] A novel about (say) connubial life provides us with truth and knowledge if it allows us to see with great clarity an aspect of marriage that we already knew but only vaguely and tacitly. *Madame Bovary* surely paints a distorted, exaggerated picture of domestic relations. But in so doing, it brings to the forefront elements of desire, disappointment, and deceit that are familiar to all of us, features that invariably affect every ordinary marriage no matter how deeply hidden or successfully managed they may be. Our tacit knowledge is thus brought to light by what we read, and the pleasure—or, indeed, the shock—of recognition improves our understanding of our world. For this to occur, however, we must presuppose that the artist is equally embedded in that same world of tacit prejudgments or preunderstandings out of which emerges our shared sense of knowledge and recognition.

Implicit here is a particular account of what it means to be in possession of truth, and this in turn helps to show that Gadamer's relationship to the aesthetic consciousness is rather more complex than one might think. In his "Epistemo-Critical Prologue" to *The Origins of German Tragic Drama,* Walter Benjamin describes truth as a "direct and essential attribute" that is "not open to question" and that is, in some sense, self-evident.[94] Possessing the truth is not a matter of argument, systematic discourse, or rational justification. Rather, truth simply presents or reveals itself to us, often in some kind of aesthetic form, and our appropriation of it requires only that we engage its presentation—

---

93. Gadamer, *Wahrheit und Methode,* p. 109. See also Joel C. Weinsheimer, *Gadamer's Hermeneutics: A Reading of Truth and Method* (New Haven: Yale University Press, 1985), pp. 108–109.

94. Walter Benjamin, *The Origin of German Tragic Drama* (London: New Left Books, 1977 [1928]), p. 30.

its artifact or embodiment—in a spirit of "total immersion and absorption." This is something like looking at a picture that has captured our fancy: truth is apprehended immediately and without analysis; its dimensions and contours, its integrity and meaning, are instantly, unreflectively recognized. (On the other hand, it differs quite sharply from simply observing a picture, in that what is apprehended is not primarily the image of a physical thing but, rather, a quite abstract idea.)

Benjamin's (early) work may be thought of as a twentieth-century manifestation of the aesthetic consciousness and hence quite at odds with anything we might find in Gadamer.[95] Nonetheless, his views on truth do comport in certain important ways with Gadamer's account of knowledge, which emphasizes a quite similar process of immediate presentation and recognition. For Gadamer, as for Benjamin, we acquire truth not through systematic methodical analysis and inference but, rather, through a kind of revelation. The truth of *Madame Bovary* is, in a sense, manifest: one reads, one recognizes, one is enlightened. In this respect, Gadamer differs from Benjamin only in emphasizing the historical/communal setting that allows for such recognition and that helps to demystify the knowing process.[96] But as we have seen, this difference is absolutely crucial since, again, it serves to distinguish quite decisively Gadamer's views from those of the aesthetic consciousness. The immediate, revelatory nature of truth-recognition does not necessarily lead to Romantic noncognitivism or mysticism. The rejection of systematic, inferential rationality as the only source of knowledge, which Gadamer shares fully with the aesthetic consciousness, need not imply Kantian subjectivism or a Schellingian leap of faith.[97]

95. On the affinity between Benjamin and such early Romantics as Schelling and Schiller, see Richard Wolin, *Walter Benjamin: An Aesthetic of Redemption* (New York: Columbia University Press, 1982), p. 49.

96. Benjamin seeks sharply to distinguish truth from knowledge: "the object of knowledge is not identical with the truth"(p.30). Gadamer, on the other hand, links knowledge and truth quite closely (as most of us do). I believe that the difference is merely terminological; Benjamin uses the word knowledge (*Erkenntnis*) in a quite narrow, technical sense.

97. For a useful introduction to Schelling's views and their rejection by Hegelian rationalism, see John Toewes, *Hegelianism: The Path Toward Dialectical Humanism, 1805-1841* (Cambridge: Cambridge University Press, 1980), pp. 42–44, 53–54, and 71–73. One might suggest a historical parallel here. Hegel's rejection of Schelling's aestheticism and of related movements, includ-

Rather, for Gadamer it forces us to attend precisely to those shared traditions of discourse—assertion conditions or, more broadly, conditions of judgment—that allow us to recognize anything at all. In the case of *Madame Bovary,* recognition is possible because our prejudices presumably comport, at least to some extent, with those of Flaubert—and this, in turn, because his life-world overlaps ours.

Aesthetic endeavor, no longer understood as the mysterious activity of an autonomous, unconnected genius, is thus endowed with an epistemological dimension that had been denied by the Kantian tradition. Indeed, art is, if anything, a paradigm case of knowledge and judgment, understood in terms of life-world and horizon, recognition and *anamnēsis.* For, as we have seen, the function of art is mimetic, and, according to Gadamer, the "cognitive import of imitation lies in recognition." This is of the greatest epistemological significance, since "in recognition what we know emerges, as if illuminated, from all the contingent and variable circumstances that condition it; it is grasped in its essence. It is known as something."[98]

It is important to note that Gadamer's cognitivist approach to art has its direct counterpart in what might be called the aestheticization of everyday experience. Just as art is assimilated to cognition in general, so are other cognitive practices—including practical, moral, and scientific activity—said to reflect features associated with art, properly understood. In particular, and as should now be evident, Gadamer affirms with Kant that aesthetic judgment is not at all a matter of standard, inferential rationality: "[I]t is clear that the validity of aesthetic judgment cannot be derived and proved from a universal principle. No one supposes that questions of taste can be decided by argument and proof."[99] Neither the artist who interprets the world nor the critic who interprets the interpretation is engaged primarily in a systematic, methodical, inferential enterprise. But, *pace* Kant, this is

---

ing Schleiermacher's reactionary conservatism, is perhaps reflected and repeated in Gadamer's clear and strong preference for Hegel over Schleiermacher (*Wahrheit und Methode,* pp. 166–168).

Of course, throughout these sections my reference is to Schelling's early transcendental idealism of around 1800, rather than to his later and rather more pessimistic views.

98. Gadamer, *Wahrheit und Methode,* p. 108–109. Cf. Jean Grondin, *Hermeneutische Wahrheit? Zum Wahrheitsbegriff Hans-Georg Gadamers* (Berlin: Forum Academicum, 1982).

99. Ibid., p. 39.

true not just of aesthetic endeavor; it applies equally to all other cognitive, knowledge-relevant activities. It is true of linguistic activity, wherein we interpret the force or implicature of conversational utterances; it is true of historical investigation, which is deeply interpretive and does not rest upon "procedure" or "method";[100] it is even true of scientific activity (though the argument here is rather less straightforward—see Section 5 of this chapter). In all such cases, the fundamental characteristic of aesthetic endeavor—that it is *both* noninferential or nonrational *and* a source of genuine knowledge—is in fact a feature of human judgment in general.[101]

We might restate this by saying that all human judgment is interpretive. Interpretation is, briefly, a noninferential source of objective knowledge. Just what this means and how it relates to Gadamer's notion of truth will be pursued below. For now, we may suggest that Gadamer has taken a radical step in attempting to dismantle the dichotomy of judgment. Aesthetics, often thought of as a paradigm case of irrationality, is now said to be of a piece with linguistic communication, historical understanding, and even scientific analysis, all standard examples of rational activity. Each of these is deeply interpretive. This means that each is a source of knowledge, yet each operates without relying fundamentally on rational argument and proof. As a result, the gulf that separates the cognitive from the noncognitive, the rational from the nonrational, the methodological from the intuitive is said to collapse in a sea of continuous and otherwise undifferentiated interpretive or hermeneutic activity that constitutes, for Gadamer, the essence of what it means to be a thinking human being.

V

How then should we characterize assertion conditions that allow for successful judgment? According to the hermeneutic approach, they are composed roughly of those prejudgments and conceptual presuppositions that constitute, in part, a community of interpretation. Such a community—born of tradition and perpetuated unselfconsciously as a form of life—determines for us the kinds of thoughts we can have and hence shapes and structures at the outset our engagement with and understanding of the world. Moreover, judgments are true and

100. Ibid., p. 279.
101. See Uwe Japp, *Hermeneutik* (Munich: Wilhelm Fink, 1977), pp. 46ff.

false at least in part according to whether they cohere with the interpretive presuppositions of our conceptual horizon. In this sense, understanding illocutions, implicatures, and rule-based imperatives simply involves the general cognitive process of subsuming particulars under universals and demonstrates that subsumption, in order to be successful, need not operate according to the tripartite model of judgment.

These views are hardly exclusive to or original with the modern hermeneutic tradition. In at least one influential account, a rather similar perspective can be found, for example, in Aristotle's ethics. Aristotle insists that "practical wisdom is not a type of rootless situational perception that rejects all guidance from ongoing commitments and values."[102] Rather, ethical judgments are necessarily made internal to a linguistic and conceptual community: "We take our evidence about *F*s only from communities where the relevant conditions of experience are similar to those that obtain in our own community, because the very meaning of *F* is given by an account couched in terms of laws and conditions of our actual community. Our ability to introduce *F*s into discourse arises from actual experience."[103] Such a view of ethical thinking in fact reflects a broader understanding of human cognition that is quite in conformity with the hermeneutic approach:

> Aristotle is promising to rehabilitate the discredited measure or standard of tragic and Protagorean anthropocentrism. He promises to do his philosophical work in a place from which Plato and Parmenides had spent their careers contriving an exit. He insists that he will find his truth *inside* what we say, see, and believe, rather than "far from the beaten path of human beings" (Plato's words) "out there."[104]

More contemporaneously, the notion that our thoughts and judgments are necessarily embedded in linguistic and conceptual forms of life is central to a rather diverse and seemingly unrelated array of intellectual viewpoints. We have seen, with Mead, that the idea of a "universe of discourse" as a context for all thinking is a central theme

102. Martha Nussbaum, *The Fragility of Goodness: Luck and Ethics in Greek Tragedy and Philosophy* (Cambridge: Cambridge University Press, 1986), p. 306.

103. Ibid., p. 249.

104. Ibid., p. 242–43. Given Gadamer's explicit reliance on Aristotle, these affinities should come as no surprise.

of the pragmatic tradition. This theme has been taken up by so-called neopragmatists who have, in turn, received considerable sustenance from the findings of certain logical/analytic philosophers concerning the theory-dependence of meaning.[105] One such account holds that

> unless pretty firmly and directly conditioned to sensory stimulation, a sentence S is meaningless except relative to its own theory; meaningless intertheoretically. . . . It is rather when we turn back into the midst of an actually present theory, at least hypothetically accepted, that we can and do speak sensibly of this and that sentence as true. Where it makes sense to apply "true" is to a sentence couched in the terms of a given theory and seen from within the theory, complete with its posited reality.[106]

If meaning somehow presupposes theory, then theory must in fact function rather like a universe of discourse, establishing assertion conditions for what can and cannot intelligibly be said. In fact, Quine's view seems to be even more radical than this: "[O]ur coming to understand what the objects are *is* for the most part just our mastery of what the theory says about them. We do not learn first what to talk about and then what to say about it."[107] Again, it appears that our very engagement with the world is shaped and structured by intellectual contexts that do not emerge out of but are the necessary preconditions of meaningful thought.

Similar formulations are to be found in the neo-Wittgensteinian philosophy of social science, with its emphasis on the constitutive role of "forms of life" and "common meanings";[108] in the sociological analysis of "background understandings" that help to explain the success of conversational implicatures;[109] in contemporary, nonliteralist theo-

105. Richard Rorty, *Philosophy and the Mirror of Nature* (Princeton: Princeton University Press, 1979), pp. 165–212.

106. Willard Van Orman Quine, *Word and Object* (Cambridge: MIT Press, 1960), p. 24.

107. Ibid., p. 16.

108. Peter Winch, *The Idea of a Social Science and Its Relationship to Philosophy* (London: Routledge & Kegan Paul, 1958), pp. 40ff, and Charles Taylor, "Interpretation and the Sciences of Man," *Review of Metaphysics* 25 (September 1971), pp. 3–51.

109. Harold Garfinkel, *Studies in Ethnomethodology* (Englewood Cliffs, N. J.: Prentice-Hall, 1967), pp. 38–75.

ries of jurisprudence;[110] and in the description of literary interpretive communities that "are responsible both for the shape of a reader's activities and for the texts those activities produce."[111] These similarities should not be overestimated. We have already touched on certain fundamental differences between Gadamer's view of interpretation and Kuhn's notion of revolutionary science. There are at least equally deep differences between, say, Quine's "theoretical holism" and the "practical holism" of Heidegger and Gadamer, or between Fish's radical constructivism and Dworkin's more modest interpretivism. Such differences are certainly of primary consequence. But this in no way refutes the claim that there is an underlying thesis common to a rather wide range of otherwise disparate views: Knowledge and judgment are importantly embedded in, constrained by, and dependent upon linguistic, conceptual, and other social-contextual factors that cannot themselves simply be matters of knowledge and judgment.

The degree to which this thesis applies to knowledge and judgment in the physical sciences is a matter of particular contention, and requires some brief attention here. Many writers highly sympathetic to the hermeneutic tradition nonetheless insist on a fundamental distinction between the human and the physical sciences, thereby exempting the latter from at least certain consequences of the hermeneutic account. According to one important version of this argument, the activity of social science is similar to, and even bound up with, the very activities that it seeks to understand.[112] We analyze social behavior at least in part in terms of the conceptual and linguistic contexts that help to make that behavior what it is. We are, that is, attentive to the hermeneutic dimension of the objects under study. But such a dimension is equally determinative of our own social scientific activity. Social science is, after all, just another social practice, hence very much shaped by the conceptual and linguistic contexts that help to make *it*

110. Ronald Dworkin, *A Matter of Principle* (Cambridge: Harvard University Press, 1985). See also Joachim Hruschka, *Das Verstehen von Rechtstexten* (Munich: C. H. Beck'sche Verlagsbuchhandlung, 1972).

111. Stanely Fish, *Is There a Text in This Class?* (Cambridge: Harvard University Press, 1980), pp. 322–337.

112. I uncritically conflate "human" and "social" science only for the sake of convenience, mindful that many studies of human behavior, especially psychological studies, pay little attention to the social dimensions of such behavior.

what it is. Moreover, our capacity to interpret correctly the object of study presupposes some overlap or connection between its hermeneutic context and ours. As a result, "in the human sciences, the background is internal to the science."[113] Natural science is quite different. Though it too necessarily emerges out of a rich hermeneutic context, the objects of its investigations are not themselves conceptualized in that way. The objects of natural science—atoms, elements, mechanical relations, and the like—do not operate in terms of intrinsically meaningful, linguistic interactions. The world of natural objects is not inherently hermeneutical. As a result, the human and natural sciences must involve substantially different kinds of understanding.[114]

Such an argument clearly agrees that judgments in natural science are importantly influenced by linguistic, conceptual, and other social-contextual factors. It is certain, moreover, that this is Gadamer's view.[115] However, the key question involves to what extent scientific claims are nonetheless guided and shaped by objective, external factors not at all reducible to categories of meaning or understanding. It seems that most parties would agree minimally that scientists must talk to one another, that their talking necessarily involves a conceptually and theoretically rich language, and that the ability to use this language presupposes contexts suitable for hermeneutic description and analysis. Science necessarily involves two relations: that between scientist and object and that between scientist and scientist. Even if the first relationship is different for natural scientists and social scientists (because of a difference in the nature of the objects under study), this in no way undermines the claim that for both kinds of science the

113. Hubert Dreyfus, "Holism and Hermeneutics," *Review of Metaphysics* 34 (September 1980), p. 20.

114. Charles Taylor, "Understanding in Human Science," *Review of Metaphysics* 34 (September 1980). Cf. Richard Rorty, "A Reply to Dreyfus and Taylor," Ibid., pp. 39–46. Also, Ronald Dworkin, *Law's Empire* (Cambridge: Harvard University Press, 1986), p. 422.

115. Hans-Georg Gadamer, "Was ist Wahrheit?" in *Gesammelte Werke:Band 2* (Tübingen: J. C. B. Mohr, 1986), pp. 44–57. Gadamer insists that "es kann keine Aussage geben, die schlechthin wahr ist" (p. 52). For discussions of Gadamer's approach to natural science, see Josef Bleicher, *Hermeneutic Imagination* (London: Routledge & Kegan Paul, 1982), p. 79; Susan J. Hekman, *Hermeneutics and the Sociology of Knowledge* (Notre Dame: University of Notre Dame Press, 1986), pp. 166–167; and Warnke, *Gadamer: Hermeneutics, Tradition and Reason*, pp. 3, 108, 145–146.

second relationship is fundamentally similar. Thus, natural scientists need to interpret meaningfully their colleagues, but not their objects of study; social scientists need to interpret both.

I suspect that such an account would be endorsed by Dreyfus and Taylor among others, that is, by hermeneuticians who nonetheless insist on the difference between natural and human science. However, it is not self-evident that this position is ultimately persuasive, for it assumes implicitly that the objects of natural science, being intrinsically meaningless, can at some level be recorded and systematized without reference to or reliance on structures of meaning. Our purchase on those objects might be simply a matter of indubitable perceptions of qualities imprinted on a blank tablet. If this is so, then the data are what they are—and are apprehended by us—apart from and independent of linguistic, conceptual, and other social-contextual factors. But this would seem to undermine the hermeneutical understanding of science altogether. For it is not immediately clear why such an account of perception would not allow for purely technical exchanges of information between scientists, exchanges that would be useful in progressively systematizing and concretizing our scientific knowledge of the world without at the same time plunging scientists themselves into a morass (so to speak) of meaningful, interpretively loaded communications. If the scientist-object relationship need not be hermeneutic, then perhaps the scientist-scientist relationship need not be as well.

Still, there seem to be very good reasons to insist both that natural science is deeply hermeneutic and substantially different from human science. A perhaps clearer account of how this can be the case would view the objects of natural science as neither independent and self-evident nor as having the meaningfulness characteristic of the objects of human science.[116] According to such an account, it is simply and straightforwardly impossible to articulate the idea of pure sense certainty of natural objects. For the moment we try to say something—anything—about a particular object, we find ourselves utterly dependent on a rich and complex conceptual scheme that is quite independent of the object and that itself demands interpretation. Most

116. G. W. F. Hegel, *Phänomenologie des Geistes*, §§95–100. For a discussion, see Charles Taylor, "The Opening Arguments of Hegel's Phenomenology," in *Hegel: A Collection of Critical Essays,* ed. Alasdair MacIntyre (Notre Dame, Indiana: University of Notre Dame Press, 1976).

primordially, we say of a thing that it is simply "this" and that it is "here" and "now." But even such primitive notions—identity, space, time—are universals that demand contextualization and interpretation. "Now" is relative to other "nows" and hence incomprehensible without searching for exactly which "now" one has in mind and in what ways it is thought to be conceptually distinct from other "nows." Similarly, "the 'here' that is pointed out, and which I cling to [*festhalte*], is a this 'here' which, in fact, is not this 'here,' but a 'before' and 'behind,' an 'above' and 'below,' a 'right' and 'left.' "[117] Thus, the moment we try to express our seemingly pure intuitions, even to ourselves, we find it impossible to avoid embedding those intuitions in a world of meaningful concepts. As a result,

> [i]t is clear that the dialectic of sense-certainty is nothing else but the simple history of its movement or of its experience, and sense certainty itself is nothing else but just this history. . . . It is therefore astonishing when, in the face of this experience, it is asserted as universal experience and put forward, too, as a philosophical proposition, even as the outcome of Skepticism, that the reality or being of external things taken as Thises or sense-objects has absolute truth for consciousness. To make such an assertion is not to know what one is saying.[118]

But if all objects of our experience are necessarily conceptualized, mediated, meaningful objects, this certainly does not imply that all such objects are conceptualized in the same way. Indeed, we explicitly conceptualize certain objects—"natural" objects—as being themselves incapable of conceptualizing, while human or "spiritual" objects are conceptualized quite differently, that is, as having themselves the capacity for thought. In each case, our concept of the thing in question certainly does call for some kind of interpretive accounting; as a result, natural science is every bit as hermeneutic as human science. But human science remains distinct in that the kinds of things that it is apt to say about its objects, and the specific kinds of analysis that it is apt to engage in, will be quite different.

Thus, to say of an object that it is "here" and "now" is to say something that requires understanding and interpretation. To say of an object that it "intended to do or say thus and so" is to say something

117. Hegel, *Phänomenologie des Geistes*, § 108.
118. Ibid., § 109.

quite different that nonetheless equally requires understanding and interpretation. The objects of natural and human science are deeply distinct; yet those sciences remain more or less equally embedded in contexts that call for hermeneutic description and analysis. In this way, we can retain our intuition that the natural and human sciences are fundamentally different while acknowledging that each is an unavoidably, irreducibly hermeneutical enterprise.

VI

We can now see that the hermeneutic school does indeed pose a quite radical challenge to the dichotomy of judgment. It suggests that all human judgment—even in natural science—rests importantly on interpretation. It conceives of interpretation as representing a generalized version of the nonrationalistic thought processes characteristic of linguistic communication. Hence, judgment operates at least in part on the basis of cognitive practices that cannot plausibly be thought of as inferential. But such a claim, however far-reaching it may be, does not quite bring us to the truly radical nature of hermeneutical theory.

It is something of a commonplace to say that hermeneutics comes into play when we need to bridge a gap in communication.[119] Typical cases would involve attempts to understand texts produced in different historical periods and efforts to translate texts from one language to another. As Gadamer might put it, discourse necessarily emerges out of horizons, and hermeneutics enters the scene when one seeks to "fuse horizons," that is, to establish some kind communicative connection between two otherwise separate and discrepant worlds. Plato's dialogues emanate from, are shaped by, and reflect a world evidently so different from our own that any straightforward and naive reading is likely to be seriously misleading. We cannot simply assume that Polus's discussion of rhetoric, or Glaucon's rendering of the Gyges story, or Socrates's musings on Simonides's ode meant the same to Plato and his readers as they do to us. Similarly, we can hardly be confident that an English translation of a poem by Baudelaire will be

119. See, for example, Charles Taylor, "Interpretation and the Sciences of Man," pp. 46–51, and Richard Rorty, *Philosophy and the Mirror of Nature* (Princeton: Princeton University Press, 1979), pp. 347–355. Of course, the modern hermeneutical enterprise, beginning roughly with Schleiermacher, arose largely in the light of historiographic concerns.

able to capture the "poetic truth" of the original. Or again, it is not at all certain that a European anthropologist can come to understand truly the nuances and full significance of an aboriginal ritual. In all such circumstances, it seems likely that there is no set of rules that would permit one rationally and justifiably to infer the correct interpretation or translation.

Searle's analysis of the "Chinese room" provides a quite powerful (though not uncontroversial) argument for why a purely formal procedure cannot account for successful interpretation and translation.[120] An English-speaking individual who knows no Chinese is given rules in English for "responding" to questions written in Chinese. The questions are, from the individual's viewpoint, simply configurations of characters labeled as questions. The rules indicate how those configurations are to be recognized, and specify procedures by which the individual can construct new configurations that stand as "answers." Assuming that the rules are adequate, the individual's answers to the questions will be apt and accurate. From this, however, we would not want to conclude that the individual knows how to speak Chinese, since he certainly does not know the meanings either of the questions he has answered or of the responses he has constructed.

I believe that this example can be generalized to typical cases of language use and language translation. For it suggests that the manipulation of symbols in response to some external stimulus, even if that stimulus is in fact related to the symbols, cannot in and of itself account for the meaningful use of language. Simply to point to some object in the world and relate it to a verbal or written expression (e.g., "dog") is not the same as having and understanding the concept *dog;* and to have and understand a concept is to participate in a form of life, to think from the perspective of a horizon that endows things with meaning. It is clear that animals can be taught to manipulate linguistic symbols in order to obtain things that they desire, but it has yet to be shown that they can really be involved in meaningful linguistic communication, properly understood.[121] This seems connected, moreover, to the notion that language must involve sense as well as reference and, further, to Wittgenstein's rejection of the "surrogate theory

120. John Searle, *Mind, Brains, and Science* (Cambridge: Harvard University Press, 1984), p. 32.

121. Peter J. Steinberger, *Logic and Politics: Hegel's Philosophy of Right* (New Haven: Yale University Press, 1988), pp. 170–172.

of meaning."[122] Such views suggest that interpreting or translating an utterance can never rely simply on a mechanical application of rules that ignore the sense or meaning of the utterance, a meaning that is, once again, embedded in and determined by complex sociocultural contexts.

Communication between seemingly "incommensurable discourses" therefore involves becoming acquainted with, and making constant reference to the horizon or form of life that makes a discourse what it is. For many nineteenth-century hermeneuticians, this meant that in order to be an interpreter one must abstract oneself from one's own contexts, place oneself in the shoes of some historically or culturally distant interlocutor, and render an interpretation in light of the interlocutor's horizon. For Gadamer, on the other hand, such a process of abstraction is in fact impossible; interpretation therefore must be rendered in the light of, and under the sway of, one's own prejudices. In either case, the result is an interpretation that emerges not through some process of systematic rational inference—and certainly not according to the tripartite model of judgment—but through the kinds of immediate, unsystematic, and intuitive experiences that result in what we have called "recognition."

If, however, interpretation comes into play with respect to discrepant horizons or "incommensurable discourses," it seems equally clear that those discourses cannot be entirely incommensurable. I take it that Davidson's claims in this respect stand up well to critical scrutiny: "The dominant metaphor of conceptual relativism, that of differing points of view, seems to betray an underlying paradox. Different points of view make sense, but only if there is a common co-ordinate system on which to plot them; yet the existence of a common system belies the claim of dramatic incomparability."[123] If someone's horizon were deeply and totally incommensurable with mine, most or all of what that person said would strike me as utterly absurd and unintelligible; indeed, I might not even be able to recognize that anything at all had been said. I must presuppose that the gap that separates me from

122. Wittgenstein, *PI*, § 1. See also Fogelin, *Wittgenstein*, pp. 98–105, and George Pitcher, *The Philosophy of Wittgenstein* (Englewood Cliffs, N.J.: Prentice-Hall, 1965), pp. 179–183.

123. Donald Davidson, "On the Very Idea of a Conceptual Scheme," in *Inquiries into Truth and Interpretation* (Oxford: Oxford University Press, 1984), p. 184.

Plato or from Baudelaire is not total, but that there is some substantial overlap in our points of view; otherwise, no interpretation would be possible. Of course, the evidence for such overlap is not hard to find. Plato's world led directly to other worlds that led directly to still other worlds culminating, ultimately, in my world; my world is, thus, deeply rooted in Plato's, albeit only indirectly. Baudelaire and I similarly share numerous and substantial points of cultural connectedness.

Hermeneutics thus presupposes both a discrepancy and a connection between disparate horizons. This seems to suggest that the fusion of horizons is always a matter of degree. The sociohistorical distance between me and Plato is greater than that between me and, say, J. L. Austin. One supposes that the hermeneutical task of understanding Austin would therefore be easier. Since understanding is a matter of invoking the materials of my own horizon in order to bestow meaning on an otherwise alien text, the similarity of Austin's and my points of view means that I am likely to "recognize" the meaning of his work with greater speed and clarity. Similarly, Baudelaire's language is closer to mine than is that of Huang Tsun-hsien. Baudelaire and I share an alphabet, certain etymologies, numerous principles of syntax, and the like, all of which would make the problem of translation and interpretation somewhat less daunting.

However, I believe that the "gap-overlap" account of hermeneutics, though accurate as far as it goes, in fact misconstrues certain features of the hermeneutic enterprise. For proximity of horizons does not rule out, and perhaps does not even limit, the necessity for hermeneutic endeavor, and this for at least two reasons. First, even where a horizon is substantially shared, understanding still requires invoking the materials of that horizon in order to perceive—intuitively, immediately, and unreflectively—the truth and meaning of a text or utterance. Virtually all of the language philosophies that we have encountered suggest that successful communication, even within a form of life, involves interpretation rather than rational, systematic inference. It is a matter of immediate recognition emerging out of shared sociocultural contexts. The clear implication is that hermeneutics is as important for discourse internal to a horizon as it is for the fusion of horizons. It is, indeed, the very soul of meaningful communication.

But further, and relatedly, it is unlikely that there could ever be a true identity of horizons. Even if you and I share a form of life in most significant respects, your life experiences will certainly be importantly different from mine. Our points of view can never be entirely congruent, and as a result it is always possible that I will misinterpret what you say. The task of understanding Polus's discussion of rhetoric is mirrored precisely in the task of my grasping your conversational gesture. Again, it may be that the latter task is easier. The large overlap in horizons perhaps reduces the possibilities for misinterpretation, and our face-to-face encounter increases the possibility that I can verify my interpretation, for example, by asking you specific questions about what you have said. But these advantages should not be overstated. It is simply wrong to think that I have no basis for confirming my understanding of Polus; philological and historiographic research can provide substantial and compelling evidence. It is equally wrong to think that my evidence for understanding your conversational implicature is necessarily ironclad. Misunderstandings in ordinary intercourse do occur and are sometimes extremely difficult to correct.

The upshot is that hermeneutics necessarily comes into play wherever meaningful communication takes place. The problem of understanding illocutions, implicatures, or rules is always a problem of interpretation. Interpretation, in turn, is always embedded in a form of life or horizon—a world of conceptual materials and prejudgments—that allows us to recognize the truth of a text or utterance and thereby endow it with meaning. We interpret in order to bridge historical and linguistic gaps. But we also interpret one another in ordinary communication, and this is, indeed, an important part of what it means to have a conversation.

How can we be sure that our interpretation is accurate, that we have indeed recognized the truth of a text or an utterance? It seems to me that, from the standpoint of hermeneutical theory, we can never be sure, and this strikes me, further, as a quite reasonable and unproblematic conclusion. I can never be finally and completely certain that I understand your conversational implicature, just as I can never prove beyond any doubt that my interpretation of Polus or Baudelaire is correct. There is always a possibility that you are lying to me, playacting, deeply insane, or cunningly ironic, and that your "real" meaning will be lost to me. Hermeneutics provides no guarantee, no scientific protection against such possibilities. The consequences of this are not too serious, however. We cannot deny that successful communication occurs with great regularity; to deny this would be to contradict the very possibility of articulating the denial itself. We must assume, therefore, that interpretations do not need to be absolutely proven, that the evidence of philology and historiography or the evidence of everyday communicative interaction (e.g., the nodding of heads in apparent agreement) is enough to justify interpretive outcomes.

We may conclude, then, that the hermeneutic perspective implies a quite powerful challenge to the dichotomy of judgment in general and the tripartite model in particular. By presenting a compelling account of the noninferential foundations of interpretation and communication, it suggests that an enormously wide range of judgments—connecting particulars to universals—rest on intellectual foundations that have nothing to do with systematic and methodical processes of rational inference. This, in turn, raises questions about the accuracy and adequacy of the orthodox notion of rationality itself.

If the story were to end here, one might be inclined to conclude—with some widely read and astonishingly influential writers—that the very idea of rational inference is suspect. Naturally, and happily, we are not likely to accept such an outcome. For the notion of noninferential thought itself suggests what we already know, namely, that we do indeed have a quite firm, though perhaps only tacit, concept of rational inference. Without such a concept, the notion of noninferential thought would be unavailable to us, just as the concept of white presupposes the concept of black. Rationality is inevitably a part of our conceptual apparatus. This suggests, further, that we do and will continue to believe that at least some people at least some of the time can prove theorems, test hypotheses, engage in deductive and inductive reasoning, and the like. The concept of rationality would make no sense if we could never imagine an approximation of it in our world.

But more importantly, to claim that all judgment—even judgment in natural science—has an ineluctable hermeneutical dimension is not necessarily to claim that inferential thought plays no role at all in connecting particulars and universals. Our strong intuition is that rational inference is hardly an idea to be dispensed with lightly. And this suggests, in turn, that we would be wise to pursue a perhaps deeper and more complex account of judgment, one which gives both the hermeneutical and rational perspectives their due while sublating their opposition, annulling yet preserving them in a new, more comprehensive concept, and situating them, finally, in a theory of judgment that responds persuasively to the genuine insights of each.

Judgment as Intelligent Performance

TO DEMONSTRATE OF AN ACTIVITY that certain features of it do not rely upon standard methods of rational inference is not to show that the activity, taken as a whole, is or can be free from such methods. Oakeshott says that experience in general

> stands for the concrete whole which analysis divides into "experiencing" and "what is experienced." Experiencing and what is experienced are, taken separately, meaningless abstractions; they cannot, in fact, be separated. Perceiving, for example, involves a something perceived, willing a something willed. The one side does not determine the other; the relationship is not that of cause and consequent. The character of what is experienced is, in the strictest sense, correlative to the manner in which it is experienced. These two abstractions stand to one another in the most complete interdependence; they compose a single whole.[1]

It is, I think, much the same with art, with politics, and even with conversation and judgment per se. These are concrete manners of acting, each of which presupposes a variety of seemingly discrete but necessarily connected elements without which the activity would not in fact be what is. The activity of art presupposes, among other things, not simply an artist but also a viewer (or reader, listener, etc.) who will be delighted or not by what is seen, and who will be inclined, in a more or less systematic way, to assess, comment upon, and criticize the object of scrutiny. We may well agree that the poet whose poems are forever locked in a drawer is indeed a poet, and that the painter

---

1. Michael Oakeshott, *Experience and Its Modes* (Cambridge: Cambridge University Press, 1985), p. 10.

whose work likewise never sees the light of day is without doubt a painter, while nonetheless recognizing that such conclusions are absolutely and entirely hostage to the concept of poetry as something to be read, and painting as something to be seen, by others. If poems were never shared and paintings never shown, then there simply would be no such things, hidden or otherwise. Politics similarly is a matter not just of making decisions but also of the socio-historical contexts in which such decisions occur, the various dispositions that inform and influence decision makers, the consequences of decisions, and the like. These things are internal to, are aspects of, political activity; without them, politics would not be politics.

There is, I believe, a certain tendency to treat judgment—wherever it appears—in the abstract, to seize upon this or that particular aspect as somehow both characteristic and definitive, and to turn an account of that aspect into an account of the whole. Such an approach can never be satisfying, for our intuitions about a thing invariably reflect, however implicitly and inchoately, the full range of our experience with it. They are necessarily attendant to its complexity, its concreteness, and hence will never be satisfied with an interpretation that is partial and skewed and that fails, as a consequence, to do full justice to its subject.

I think this is the case with the approaches to linguistic communication that we have been considering. The theories of implicature, rule-following, and situated interpretation outlined in the previous chapter are, I believe, extremely helpful. They point to essential, ineliminable features of language usage. They fail, however, to treat the topic of conversation in its fullness, its concreteness. Insofar as linguistic communication presents a useful model for dealing with judgment in general, they fail thereby to suggest a complete and satisfying understanding of judgment itself.

I

As we have seen, the burden of speech-act theory is, in part, to show that the meaning of an utterance is not reducible to its propositional content. Sense and reference do not tell the whole story. I have argued, further, that this implies a noninferential account of linguistic communication. In important respects, successful conversation involves judgments that cannot be analyzed in terms of our tripartite model. But the precise focus of such a conclusion remains uncertain.

For there is always more than one person involved in any communicative exchange—an utterer and an audience—and it is not immediately evident that what is true for the one is also true for the others.

Now it seems clear that the implicit focus of our argument has in fact been on the hearer, the person to whom the speech act has been directed. For the argument has been about judgments of meaning, and it is the hearer who most obviously renders such a judgment. Our account indicates that the hearer often cannot be said to have deduced or otherwise reasoned toward the meaning of an utterance simply from the words uttered. The hearer, like Wittgenstein's rule-follower, grasps the meaning of an utterance noninferentially, "in a flash."

But I think that this conclusion is applicable to the utterer as well. Insofar as the utterer is utilizing the tools of language in order to perform a speech act, and insofar as that act is not reducible to its propositional (i.e., logically analyzable) content, it would seem that the utterer's participation is equally noninferential. Such a conclusion very much comports with our standard intuitions. Just as we typically understand utterances in a flash, without systematic analysis and interpretation, so we utter them in the same way. Sometimes we may choose our words with care and even calculate scrupulously their effect, but more often, the speaker's linguistic activity seems to be as unreflective and automatic as that of the listener.

Much the same kind of story can be told with respect to the theory of conversational implicature. Again, the focus seems to have been on the hearer, and our conclusion is that this individual invokes no algorithm and undertakes no systematic analysis in comprehending an utterance. The utterance and its implicature are instantly, immediately understood for what they are. But once more, this seems equally to describe the character of the conversational act itself. The utilization—including the deliberate flouting—of the principles of conversation, as outlined by Grice, often does not occur reflectively and self-consciously. It simply occurs.

If, then, A says, "I want to have a serious discussion now about our relationship," and B responds by saying, "Hey, how about those Mets?" we shall conclude that normally B's utterance is both apprehended and rendered noninferentially. Even if the utterance has been carefully weighed and considered, even if B thought very clearly about a suitable response, it is nonetheless quite possible, perhaps even likely, that this weighing and considering would not pertain to the exact words of the utterance itself. B may well have consciously determined that for some reason he didn't want to talk about "our relationship," may have explicitly concluded that the subject should be changed or the issue not directly broached, and may have consciously decided that a good way to express this view would be deliberately to say something "irrelevant." But even given all of this, it is most likely that that particular irrelevant response—out of the infinite range of possible irrelevant responses—came to and was uttered by B not through some process of deliberation and analysis but simply intuitively and automatically.

In sum, the noninferential character of any speech act pertains to the activity of both the utterer and the hearer. But what about an interested third party? Imagine that there is a third person, C, in the group with A and B, and imagine that C knows very little about A and B, knows even less about their relationship, is a non-native and inexperienced—though grammatically well-schooled—speaker of English, and has no idea about who or what the Mets might be. In such a circumstance, it is, I think, quite likely that C would not understand the implicature of B's utterance. B may have known this in advance and intended to make a quasi-private response to A, that is, a response that C would hear but not comprehend. Alternatively, B may have been ignorant of C's background and hence may have assumed that C would understand things perfectly; in such a circumstance, the response, though intended primarily for A, may also have been made for C's benefit. But in either case, it would often be highly appropriate for C to ask at this point, perhaps with a slightly puzzled smile: "Excuse me, I did not quite understand that."

Such a situation generally requires that B—and A as well—be able to reconstruct for C the logic of their exchange. It would be very helpful if, by coincidence, a knowledgeable and well-trained Gricean should happen to appear at that very moment, grasp the situation, and offer to describe for them the theory of conversational implicature. Short of that, however, it is still perfectly natural to expect both A and B to be able to explain B's response successfully. This might involve uncovering the linguistic "deep structure" of the utterance, as recommended by a number of speech-act theorists.[2] But it would necessarily involve a great deal more, including, for example, describing who the Mets are, acknowledging that A and B know very well who the Mets are, demonstrating the evident irrelevance of the Mets

2. See pp. 162–64 above.

to the question of *A*'s relationship to *B*, sketching a few salient features of that relationship, and presenting some version—however rough—of Grice's principle of relevance and its flouting. In short, it would require reconstructing those arguments on the basis of which *A* and *B* can justifiably claim to have correctly judged the meaning of "Hey, how about those Mets?" All of this would be easy enough to accomplish. Of course, external circumstances—time pressure, xenophobia, anti-intellectualism—might make *A* and *B* disinclined actually to do so. It would, however, be most peculiar if, given the appropriate circumstances, they could not explicate their exchange in an enlightening and highly satisfactory manner.

Let us assume that *C* now understands *B*'s response. But the nature of this understanding is quite different from the original understanding of *A* and *B*. It is based on a more-or-less thorough reconstruction of the logic of the exchange, and the upshot—the meaning of *B*'s response—is in some sense entailed by or otherwise inferable from the materials of that reconstruction. In other words, *C* is able consciously and explicitly to identify a rational connection between the premises of the exchange and the meaning of the utterance in question. But by providing *C* with this understanding, the character of *A*'s and *B*'s own understanding has changed as well. While their original judgments were indeed noninferential, they have now confirmed and recast those judgments through a process of rational reconstruction, so that they too have become explicitly aware of the logic of their exchange.

I wish to say three things about this example. First, the introduction of a third person, *C*, is by no means adventitious. Obviously, human communication involves third (and *n*th) persons much of the time; the example is hardly peculiar. But more important, it also leads us to consider in more detail the general possibility that an implicature has not been understood. I believe that this possibility is an ever-present feature of human communication, no matter how many individuals are involved or who those individuals might be. The utterer can never be entirely sure that the hearer will get the message. Perhaps the utterer is unwittingly using a word or expression that the hearer is unfamiliar with; perhaps the flouting of a conversational principle is so unexpected and extreme that the hearer is thrown into temporary confusion; perhaps the hearer is just not thinking clearly today. In all such cases, it is very possible that the hearer, not just some third party, will ask with a puzzled smile: "Excuse me, I did not quite understand that." Such a possibility can never be completely ruled out. There is no way to be absolutely sure that an implicature will be successful. But whenever a breakdown occurs, one has a certain responsibility (at least with respect to the ideals of communication itself) to explain one's meaning through a kind of rational reconstruction. This responsibility is, I believe, inherent in the utterer's role. To say something meaningful is to know what one is saying and, if circumstances allow, to be able to explain it.[3] The capacity to provide such an explanation is, in principle, a necessary and constitutive feature of any conversational act.[4]

Second, it will do no good to object that this places an unrealistic and excessive demand on language users. As indicated above, circumstances may make individuals unmotivated or even ill prepared to explicate thoroughly their conversational acts. But such circumstances pertain less to the inherent *capacity* to explain than to the *inclination* or *opportunity* to do so. The fact that someone is distracted, tired, impatient, drunk, ignorant of Gricean pragmatics, and the like, does not mean that he or she is intellectually incapable of offering a sound explanation.

To see this more clearly, consider what it would mean if one truly were unable to explain the meaning of one's own utterance. Assume that we have created propitious circumstances. The utterer is suddenly eager, alert, and sober, has been taught Grice, and is genuinely interested in offering—perhaps with some coaxing and guidance—a satisfactory reconstruction. Inclination and opportunity are highly favorable. If in such a situation the person is still fundamentally unable to explain the utterance, then I think we would be inclined to doubt that he or she had made a meaningful utterance at all. The individual would have been, rather, in the position of Searle's "translator"—someone who has performed mere mechanical manipulations without having any idea about their meaning.

Third, it might be suggested that the notion of a rational reconstruction begs the question, for any such reconstruction will itself depend on the use of language, which, as we have seen, is often a noninferential endeavor. The reconstruction will very possibly be engaged

3. I use the word "meaningful" here in the sense of Grice's "non-natural" meaning. See H. P. Grice, "Meaning," *Philosophical Review* 66 (1957), p. 383.

4. For a rather different but, I think, not incompatible approach to these issues, see Jerrold J. Katz and D. Terence Langendoen, "Pragmatics and Presupposition," *Language* 52 (1976), pp. 9–14.

in and understood intuitively, immediately, in a flash. Thus, to reconstruct is only to push the automatic, intuitive feature of communication back one step, to the level of reconstruction. Of course, we might be able to reconstruct the reconstruction; but that, in turn, would call for further reconstruction, and so on. Again, explanations must somewhere come to an end.

This seems to me correct, but it in no way obviates the claim that *C*'s understanding of *B*'s utterance, based on a thoroughgoing explanation, has a different character from the original, intuitive understandings of *A* and *B* themselves. Because of the process of reconstruction, *B*'s utterance has become rationally explicated. That explication itself may depend on further, as yet unexplicated premises, and those premises may, at some point, be inexplicable, but this is certainly not the same as saying that *B*'s utterance is inexplicable. It may be that we cannot dispense with intuition, but this does not mean that everything is intuition. The fact that explanations must end does not mean that nothing can be explained. Explanations may never be final and complete, but they remain explanations nonetheless.

Our example suggests, then, that the capacity rationally to reconstruct an exchange is an essential and intrinsic part of the exchange itself, even if such a reconstruction does not actually take place. This in no way refutes the accounts of Austin, Searle, and Grice regarding the noninferential nature of much conversation. Rather, it argues only that this noninferential feature is but one aspect of conversation, and that a fully concrete interpretation must take into account the fact that conversationalists are, in principle, capable of rationally reconstructing their exchanges. Stated otherwise, speech acts and implicatures are necessarily inferential, though often only prospectively.

This analysis provides an instance, I believe, of Ryle's famous distinction between *knowing how* and *knowing that*, although his account of that distinction requires some substantial modification. According to Ryle, *knowing that* something is the case is a matter of having and understanding propositions of some kind, and generally implies grounds or reasons for accepting those propositions; *knowing how* to do something is a matter of skill and ability and does not at all imply that the performer has explicitly considered and analyzed any proposition. For example,

> [r]ules of correct reasoning were first extracted by Aristotle, yet men knew how to avoid and detect fallacies before they learned

his lessons, just as men since Aristotle, and including Aristotle, ordinarily conduct their arguments without making any internal reference to his formulae. They do not plan their arguments before constructing them. Indeed if they had to plan what to think before thinking it they would never think at all; for this planning would itself be unplanned.[5]

According to the analysis presented above, engaging successfully in conversation is typically an instance of *knowing how* to do something. Rationally reconstructing that conversation is an instance of *knowing that* something is the case, that is, propositional knowledge.

Ryle uses this distinction to reject the "intellectualist" fallacy of claiming that all successful action is attendant to a prior consideration of propositions. He is surely correct in this. However, he wants also to distinguish "intelligent" performance (*knowing how*) from merely mechanical, lucky, habitual, organic, or instinctive performance. This is a crucial step. It suggests, I think correctly, that we do indeed need some positive account of activities that are importantly noninferential but that are also different from the mindless physical movements of machines and animals. It is here that Ryle's formulation needs to be modified.

He argues that "the well-regulated clock keeps good time and the well-drilled circus seal performs its tricks flawlessly, yet we do not call them 'intelligent.'" We do not, for example, claim that the clock or the seal has good judgment. We might want to say that the seal "knows how" to perform its tricks, but this is different from human know-how.

---

5. Gilbert Ryle, *The Concept of Mind* (New York: Barnes and Noble, 1960), p. 30. For an apparently independent but quite similar formulation, see Stanley Fish, "Dennis Martinez and the Uses of Theory," in *Doing What Comes Naturally: Change, Rhetoric and the Practice of Theory in Literary and Legal Studies* (Durham, North Carolina: Duke University Press, 1989), pp. 372–398. History has proven Stanley Fish to be a very unreliable judge of baseball talent, as evidenced by the events of July 28, 1991. Ryle's general distinction seems to me related to the distinction between the logic of discovery and the logic of justification, as outlined most famously by Reichenbach and Popper. A similar formulation can be found in Poincaré's treatment of mathematical reasoning. Poincaré distinguishes the subliminal ego of mathematical discovery and the conscious ego of mathematical analysis. He attributes one of his own important discoveries—a "sudden illumination"—in large part to black coffee and insomnia. See Henri Poincaré, *Science and Method* (New York: Dover Publications, 1952), pp. 46–53.

Persons who *know how* to do things are intelligent, and according to Ryle this means above all that they are "ready to detect and correct lapses, to repeat and improve upon successes, to profit from the example of others and so forth."[6] This, in effect, is Ryle's definition of intelligent performance. But it seems that repeating and improving upon successes is in fact precisely what a trained seal does. Moreover, in this advanced technological age we are quite familiar with gadgets that at least appear to be constantly detecting and correcting their own lapses: self-focusing cameras, missiles that home in on targets, thermostats, and the like. It would be strained at best, and more likely simply metaphorical, to call the seal or the clock "intelligent," but repeating, improving, detecting and correcting do not at all get at the feature of intelligence that we are interested in.

Our treatment of conversation ("Hey, how about those Mets?") suggests, I think, a much more plausible approach to intelligent performance. *Knowing how* does presuppose, albeit only prospectively, a certain element of *knowing that,* namely, the capacity retroactively to explain or account for one's successful action. This is not to commit the intellectualist fallacy, for again it seems absolutely clear to me that intelligent performance need not be attendant to a prior consideration of rules, propositions, and principles.[7] But the difference between the behavior of a seal and the intelligent action of a human is precisely that we fully expect the human, though not the seal, to be capable of offering a *post festum* account of his or her deed—a rational reconstruction. Intelligent performance is at least prospectively propositional.

I believe that this general insight applies with equal force to the other aspects of intelligent, noninferential performance that we have encountered. Wittgenstein's claim that we grasp rules "in a flash" is perfectly consistent with the notion that such grasping nonetheless presupposes the capacity to provide satisfactory *post festum* explanations. The fact that understanding and following a rule is noninferential does not mean that we cannot reconstruct the logic of the rule and

6. Ryle, *The Concept of Mind,* pp. 28–29.

7. Indeed, as Ryle points out (ibid., p. 30), at least some intelligent performance *must* precede any rational analysis: "[I]f, for any operation to be intelligently executed, a prior theoretical operation had first to be performed and performed intelligently, it would be a logical impossibility for anyone ever to break into the circle." Ryle, like Wittgenstein, is calling our attention to the infinite regress of interpretations.

hence justify our action as being consistent with it. Such a reconstruction inevitably alters somewhat the nature of our grasp of the rule. A native speaker of English who is not self-consciously aware of the difference between the genitive and dative cases may nonetheless be able to employ with absolute precision the linguistic rules pertaining to these cases. This in no way debars us from subsequently explaining to the person those rules. Once we have done so (i.e., given him a lesson in grammar), he will understand the rules in a new way, discursively or propositionally. The person will both *know how* to use them and *know that* certain propositions about them are true. His linguistic performance may well remain unchanged, and will certainly be unimproved, since he was previously able to follow the rules with absolute precision. But he might now, from time to time, employ those rules in an inferential rather than noninferential manner, and he would certainly be better prepared to explain in detail why one particular linguistic construction is correct and another is not.

It does seem to be true, following Wittgenstein, that the interpretation of the rules can never be final or complete. For that interpretation will itself be subject to interpretation, and at some point interpretation must come to an end. But again, this does not mean that an interpretation is not an interpretation. An individual who is well prepared to explain the genitive and dative cases has a different kind of purchase on those cases from an individual who knows only how to use them. We might indeed want to say that both individuals understand the rules (see below), but surely they do so in different ways. The mere fact that the first individual's explanation is itself eligible for explanation does not mean that his understanding is identical to that of the second individual. The explanation—in this case derived from the grammar lesson—does not simply dissolve into nothingness.

This example raises a further question about *knowing that*. We have argued that *knowing how* to do something presupposes the capacity to offer a rational reconstruction. But did our English speaker really have that capacity prior to receiving a lesson in grammar? Did he in any sense *know that* certain propositions about the genitive and dative cases are true? If not, can we then say that he engaged in an intelligent performance without having had the capacity to explain his deed *post festum*? I think this (implicit) objection will not work, for the fact is that we do necessarily attribute such a capacity to the speaker. In a sense, the grammar lesson merely explains to the individual what he already understands. One already grasps perfectly well the rules that one is invoking; one *knows that* certain propositions about them are true. One lacks only the conceptual materials or, indeed, the terminological apparatus to make that understanding explicit. The statement of a grammatical rule is a general description of linguistic practice. It does indeed illuminate such practice; it can help to guide and justify particular linguistic acts; and it can render our understanding systematic and discursive. But it also presupposes a great deal of knowledge that is not explicit. Our speaker of English is roughly like Meno's slave boy. We are able to elicit from him a satisfying interpretation only because he is in a sense already in possession of that interpretation, albeit only tacitly. For him, discovering the correct explanation is not like discovering America; it is not a new fact about the world that comes entirely out of the blue. It is, rather, the illumination, clarification, or elaboration of a proposition that in some sense he was already in secure possession of.

There are, therefore, two kinds of *knowing that.* In one case, it involves an understanding that is tacit, inarticulate, unself-conscious; in the other case, it involves an understanding that is explicit, manifest, reflective. Intelligent performance is, so to speak, utterly indifferent as to whether propositional knowledge is tacit or explicit; *knowing how* requires only that one have *at least* tacit knowledge of the relevant propositions, such as they may be. Nonetheless, the distinction between tacit and explicit understanding is crucial. For explicit understanding is, as such, directly eligible for critical scrutiny and analysis. It can be codified and systematized, communicated and taught, and is immediately available for rational assessment and evaluation. Tacit understanding is only indirectly available for such analysis. One can have no critical purchase on it until it is rendered explicit.

The implications of this for the *knowing how/knowing that* distinction are substantial. We have argued that *knowing how* presupposes a certain kind of *knowing that,* namely, the capacity to provide rational reconstructions. We have now shown that *knowing that* may be either tacit or explicit. It seems clear, moreover, that much and probably most *knowing that* is indeed quite tacit, and we may conclude, therefore, that there is often a close connection between tacit knowledge of propositions, on the one hand, and intelligent performance, on the other. But this certainly does not imply that knowing how is identical or reducible to, or the product of, a kind of tacit knowing that. We must without exception attribute to any intelligent performer an understanding, however inexplicit, of what he or she is doing, and a capacity to render that understanding explicit. But one should not infer from this that intelligent performance is necessarily informed by, based on, or in any other way causally related to knowledge of propositions, tacit or otherwise. Just as we might plausibly agree that every human has a body and mind without being able to understand the connection between them, so I here propose that *knowing how* and *knowing that* are constitutive elements of intelligent performance despite the fact that I cannot otherwise specify in any way the nature of their interdependence. Indeed, I doubt that such a specification is possible. *Knowing how* is, I think, inherently mysterious. To discover certain of its presuppositions (e.g., that it presupposes some propositional knowledge) is not to account for the fact that some people have it and others do not, that the same person has it at certain times and not at others, that occasionally our efforts to learn it succeed and occasionally they fail.

II

The analysis thus far suggests the rudiments of a theory of linguistic judgment. Such judgment is typically a species of intelligent performance. As such, it is often intuitive and immediate, and hence not at all—or, at least, not primarily—the product of inferential reasoning. We either *know how* to do it or we do not. But it also necessarily presupposes a capacity to reconstruct the judgment rationally. Such a reconstruction cannot be a retracing of the inferential steps involved in making the judgment since, in principle, there were no steps; the judgment was immediate. Nonetheless, we require any intelligent performer—any judge—to be able to explain, after the fact, the rationality of the judgment. We might say, in a somewhat Kantian vein, that such a rational reconstruction describes the steps that the intelligent performer *would have* followed if the performance had been conducted in a self-consciously inferential manner. It describes, perhaps, the ontology rather than the psychology of judgment.

All such *post festum* accounts will, of course, depend upon certain further judgments that are intuitive and immediate. While these may themselves be subject to rational reconstruction, at some point *post festum* explanation must stop. But the fact that rational reconstruction can never be final and complete does not at all suggest that it is futile, useless, unsatisfying, or dispensable. To the contrary, the capacity to reconstruct rationally is an internal and necessary aspect of that concrete manner of activity that we have called linguistic judgment.

This account is perfectly applicable, *mutatis mutandis,* to the hermeneutical theory of intelligent performance. As we have seen, hermeneutics can be understood as the (perhaps unwitting) fulfillment of Anglo-American language philosophy insofar as it helps us to account for the tacit, intuitive knowledge implicit in speech acts, implicatures, and rule-following in general. Searle, Grice, and Wittgenstein all advert to the communal contexts, background conditions, or forms of life that provide the essential foundations for successful, meaningful communication. Hermeneutics seeks to analyze those foundations, and does so largely in terms of categories such as tradition, horizon, and prejudice. The tacit understandings essential to conversation, and to any intelligent performance (e.g., following a cookbook recipe), are matters of traditionally derived and historically transmitted prejudices—unstated assumptions, prejudgments, conceptual materials that establish, however discreetly, the bases of a form of life. These prejudices are constitutive of our capacity to think and act intelligently and comprise an implicit and unarticulated store of intuitive knowledge.

It is a fundamental insight of the hermeneutical tradition that the element of *knowing that*—which, as we have seen, is a necessary precondition for all intelligent performance—is itself composed of propositions that invariably emerge out of and reflect a historically specific culture. But Jürgen Habermas, a deeply sympathetic student of hermeneutics, has pointed out that we can accept all of this and still recognize the possibility that prejudices can be "thematized." One can become cognizant of one's own prejudgments and intellectual presuppositions. This, in turn, radically changes the nature and status of those prejudices. A prejudice revealed is a prejudice suddenly available for inspection, analysis, evaluation and, ultimately, dissolution: "[A] structure of preunderstanding or prejudgment that has been rendered transparent can no longer function as a prejudice."[8] If I finally become aware that I have been looking at the world through rose-colored glasses, then I am also finally able to consider the possibility that I

---

8. Jürgen Habermas, "A Review of Gadamer's *Truth and Method*," in *Understanding and Social Inquiry,* ed. Fred R. Dallmayr and Thomas A. McCarthy (Notre Dame: University of Notre Dame Press, 1977), p. 358.

might take those glasses off and see the world differently. For Habermas, of course, the political implications of this are significant. The notion that we are unavoidably trapped within a given intellectual horizon of prejudices and prejudgments appears to have strongly conservative implications regarding possibilities for social progress and serious change.[9] The idea that we can examine our own prejudices is, to the contrary, liberating. It suggests the possibility of a genuine critical understanding whereby the spell of the merely given—whether historical, linguistic, psychological, or sociological—can be broken, and the power of independent reason unleashed.

Gadamer has an extremely strong response to this.[10] To take hermeneutics seriously, as Habermas claims to, is to recognize that thinking itself is impossible without prejudices. As we have seen, there is literally no such thing as pure perception or pure thought; all mental life emerges out of, and is made possible by, an intellectual horizon that alone can provide us with the indispensable materials of thought—pregiven concepts, tacit understandings, constitutive premises. Even more radically, "it is our prejudices that constitute our being."[11] It is therefore impossible to believe that we could have independent purchase on our prejudices. For all thought about prejudices will itself be rooted in prejudice. Prejudices are, to be sure, fluid and unstable; horizons are permeable and unfixed. Change is in fact a fundamental feature of intellectual life understood in hermeneutical terms; thus, hermeneutics is not at all a doctrine of conservatism, stasis, or blind obedience to authority.[12] But to believe that we can escape our prejudices and subject them to independent rational scrutiny is to misconceive the very idea of human cognition. All thought is embedded in and shaped by tacit and unavoidable, though historically vari-

9. Jürgen Habermas, "On Hermeneutics' Claim to Universality," in *The Hermeneutics Reader,* ed. Kurt Mueller-Vollmer (New York: Continuum, 1985), pp. 313–316.

10. Hans-Georg Gadamer, "On the Scope and Function of Hermeneutical Reflection," in *Philosophical Hermeneutics* (Berkeley: University of California Press, 1976), pp. 33–35.

11. Hans-Georg Gadamer, "The Universality of the Hermeneutical Problem," in *Philosophical Hermeneutics,* p. 9.

12. Gadamer, "On the Scope and Function of Hermeneutical Reflection." p. 31. For a critical discussion, see Georgia Warnke, *Gadamer: Hermeneutics, Tradition, and Reason* (Stanford: Stanford University Press, 1987), p. 106.

ous and occasionally unstable, prejudgments. Habermas's effort to deny this amounts to an enormous category error.

Our analysis of intelligent performance suggests, I believe, a sensible and persuasive approach to this controversy which shows that Habermas and Gadamer are, in an important sense, both quite correct. Prejudices are typically in the background and are invoked intuitively, immediately, and unreflectively. To the extent that judgments—linguistic or otherwise—are necessarily based on them, they too are intuitive and immediate, much like the correct but unself-conscious application of rules governing the genitive and dative cases. But like those rules, prejudices most certainly can be uncovered and subjected to systematic analysis, and it seems impossible to deny that this kind of analysis changes quite dramatically their status. To thematize and explicate them is, in a sense, to reconstruct rationally the thought processes that gave rise to them. What was merely an implicit *knowing that* now becomes explicit and, again, is suddenly eligible for evaluation and revision. Any such analysis will itself depend on further prejudices. Prejudice is constitutive of thought, and there is no way of getting around that. No analysis of prejudice can ever be exhaustive since it will always itself be prejudicial in some way. Thus, for Gadamer as for Wittgenstein, analysis necessarily comes to an artificial end. But this in no way nullifies Habermas's central claim that a prejudice revealed is, in some sense, no longer a prejudice. If my discovery that I have been looking at the world through rose-colored glasses, is based on further, as yet unspecified preunderstandings about (say) colors, glasses and the existence of an external world, this does not at all alter the fact that my discovery is genuine and that I may, as a result, be very much enlightened by it.

Consider our conversational example in light of this account. *B*'s utterance, "Hey, how about those Mets?" is recognized and comprehended on the basis of certain preunderstandings characteristic of the community of which *A* and *B* are a part. Those preunderstandings would include a notion of who the Mets are. To reconstruct the utterance rationally would require making explicit that understanding of the Mets, and this, of course, could lead to new utterances such as "The Mets are a baseball team that plays in New York." But such an utterance, though usually comprehended in a flash, would itself be based on a further and enormous range of communal preunderstandings involving, for example, the meaning of the concept *baseball team*, which would presuppose, in turn, an understanding of baseball, which would presuppose understanding the concept *game*, which would presuppose understandings about, say, the laws of physics, human psychology, and arithmetic, and so on. The list of such presuppositions is always inexhaustible, and this means that any cognitive act is necessarily based on a set of unanalyzed, unexplicated prejudices. The degree to which prejudices *are* uncovered, exhibited, and subjected to analysis, however, is the degree to which our action may become *comparatively* unprejudiced and explicated, and hence readily available for rational assessment and critique.

The hermeneutic tradition, suitably amended in this way, thus proposes what might be called the relativization of Platonic *anamnēsis*.[13] Intelligent performance does indeed depend upon a deep structure of preunderstanding, an often tacit *knowing that* certain propositions about the world are true. This knowledge can be "recollected," rendered explicit, and made available for critical evaluation. What is recollected is not primarily, as for Plato, a realm of eternal and immutable ideas but, rather, the historically and socially generated way of seeing things characteristic of a culture. For the hermeneutician, all intelligent performance—all judgment—necessarily occurs internal to a horizon. But this difference with Plato is, I believe, overshadowed by the more fundamental similarity: to think and act like a human requires the capacity to remember and reconstruct those underlying principles and preconceptions that make thought and action possible. If the process of *anamnēsis* is never complete, if recollection involves an ongoing and unending quest for finitude in an infinite realm, then this is a comment less on the nature of truth and knowledge than on limits inherent in the human condition.

III

We may now begin to describe the features of a coherent concept of judgment. This concept reflects many of the seemingly contradictory formulations that we have outlined thus far, but shows those contradictions to be only apparent. It is, I propose, a faithful rendering of our intuitions about intelligent performance and about the processes by which we relate particulars and universals; hence, it stands as a satisfactory account of what we mean when we talk about judgment. As such,

13. The now-standard treatment is to be found in 2 of Martin Heidegger's *Sein und Zeit* (Tübingen: M. Niemeyer Verlag, 1967).

it provides an understanding of the notion of good judgment with respect to the entire gamut of affairs in which judgment is required, including political affairs. Among its salient features are the following.

1. Judgment involves a kind of insight. By insight, I mean a capacity to perceive immediately certain features of the world, to become acquainted with those features without having to rely on inferential processes. That there is such capacity can only be presupposed, not proved; there is no definitive argument against the skeptic who would deny its existence. Nonetheless, if there is such a thing as reliable judgment, then this requires that there be a faculty of insight. The capacity immediately to perceive certain features of the world is, roughly, a transcendental condition of judgment.

Experientially, the prototype for this kind of insight is sense perception, for example, the perception of colors or sounds. My awareness that the fire engine is red is immediate and nondiscursive. I do not enumerate the steps by which I conclude that it is red, for it seems to me that there are no steps. The experience is direct, automatic, and instant. This does not mean that it is unconditioned. As we have seen, the hermeneutic tradition argues that there is no pure perception, that all perception is embedded in structures of meaning that incline me to attend to certain things and not others, and to do so in certain ways and not others. We can accept this and still insist that perception is immediate and noninferential. For just as we do not ordinarily think about the physical mechanisms by which perceptions are registered in our minds (even to the degree that we understand those mechanisms), so we do not ordinarily and selfconsciously reflect upon the structures of prejudice and preunderstanding that give shape and direction to our perceptual activities. The positivist/physicalist and hermeneutic/mentalist traditions agree on this if nothing else: that sense perception is a noninferential process.

Theoretically, the prototypical formulation of the faculty of insight is, as we have seen, the Aristotelian idea of *nous*. Indeed, with Arendt, we translate *nous* precisely as "insight," and we have identified in Aristotle two species of it—insight into the first principles of science and insight into the identifying features of particular things. We already know that Aristotle explicitly draws an analogy between insight and sense perception, referring to *nous* in terms of the "eye" of the soul and implying that it shares with visual perception the fact that it operates immediately. We have also seen that this kind of analogy recurs time and again in the literature on judgment. For Shaftesbury, the "*je ne sçay quoy*" that produces "good taste" involves a certain "eye" for the beautiful, while for Hutcheson aesthetic judgment involves a particular "constitution of our sense."[14] Kant's aesthetics invokes a notion of common *sense* described explicitly in terms of an immediate apprehension of aesthetic objects, and it is no accident that this notion, with similar implications, is taken up by writers on judgment as diverse as Gadamer, Arendt, and Rorty.

2. The fact that we can neither account for nor prove the existence of insight does not present insuperable difficulties for a theory of judgment. The analogy with sense perception is especially useful in this respect. It seems clear that reliable perception of color does not require a knowledge of the mechanisms by which such perception works. We may well have by this time a true theory of optics that helps explain how we are able to perceive and distinguish various colors. But the capacity so to perceive was well established and uncontroversial long before the development of optical science. Perceptions of color were made reliably and were accepted as such, and for very good reasons, before there were any plausible theories of how this happens. Indeed, in a sense this is still the case, since the vast majority of people today, most of whom are reliable color perceivers, are ignorant of optical science. Moreover, such a science is itself necessarily limited as a theory of perception, since it cannot explain how it is that perceptions of color actually come to be part of an individual's consciousness. The physics of light and the biology of the eye and the brain are not sufficient to account for the fact that we reflect on and talk about color. Thus, we do not need to understand how sense perception works in order to believe in the reliability of sense perception.

We know that making distinctions among colors is sometimes a difficult, even deeply unreliable process (as anyone who has looked at paint chips can attest). But the fact that there are hard cases and that color perception is imperfect is entirely consistent with believing, as most of us do, and for good reasons, that people generally can perceive colors with an acceptable degree of reliability and discrimination. The fallibility of sense perception in particular cases does not provide strong grounds for being skeptical about sense perception in general.

These arguments apply as well to other kinds of intuition. For

14. See Chapter 2, pp. 128–30.

example, we cannot fully explain the insight that something cannot be p and not-p at the same time or that every effect is preceded in time by its cause, yet we routinely, unproblematically, and for good reasons accept them as bases for reliable logical and empirical inferences. The principles of logic sometimes involve insights that are difficult to detect and are, as a result, controversial and often misunderstood; but again, this is no reason to call logic a fraud. What is true of sense perception is, therefore, true of insight in general. The faculties of *nous* upon which we base the idea of good judgment are not well understood, and are almost certainly fallible, but these are not sufficient reasons to deny their existence.

3. Insight and judgment can in one sense be taught and in another sense not. Much depends on our notion of education, and again the analogy with sense perception is useful. There are, to pick one example, limits to our understanding of how the ear listens to music. But there is no question that the ear can be trained. It is trained not through a process of systematic and self-reflective analysis; a complete understanding of aural science in and of itself does not enable one to hear better. Rather, ear training typically occurs through a curriculum of trial and error. The student hears a series of intervals and is unable to distinguish accurately among them. After repeated listening and instruction as to which interval is which, the distinctions gradually become more pronounced and their identities clearer until, finally, the student becomes adept at identifying with extraordinary ease an increasingly complex range of tonal relationships.

How does this happen? In one sense, we know the answer quite well. Ear-training techniques are venerable and well established. Themselves products of trial and error, there can be no doubt about their effectiveness. If we ask how the ear gets trained, the answer is simply that it gets trained through the application of such well-known techniques. In another sense, though, we do not know the answer very well at all, since we are not entirely sure how or why ear-training techniques work. The mechanism by which the brain comes to discriminate previously indiscriminate intervals and the mind comes to be conscious of those intervals is known only imperfectly, if at all. It may be that the tools of cognitive science will eventually help us to understand this better. But even so, such an understanding would not contribute directly to our ability actually to hear the intervals; hence, it would not make us any more willing to believe that ear training works. For again, ear training occurs quite satisfactorily without any recourse to systematic scientific analysis, whether aural or cognitive.[15]

In the *Republic*, Plato deals with two quite discrete educational protocols. The first is described in Books 2 and 3 and involves the training of the guardians. Through a rigorous process of habituation, censorship, and physical culture, potential guardians learn to distinguish friends from enemies and to acquire dispositions and temperaments suitable to governing the *kallipolis*. But in Book 7 a rather different kind of education is described, one appropriate not for guardians but for philosophers and aimed not at instilling good habits but at providing a systematic discursive understanding of true propositions about the world.[16] In the vocabulary that we have been using, the first system of education enables its students to *know how* to do certain things, the second to *know that* certain things are true.

When we say that insight can be taught, that people can learn to be good judges just as they can learn to recognize musical intervals, we generally rely on education in the first sense. Through habituation and the proper kinds of experience, we can acquire or sharpen the faculty of insight that permits us to judge things correctly. Education in the second sense cannot offer this; insight is not the fruit of discursive inquiry. We are sometimes inclined, as a result, to deny that such insight is possible. But, as we have seen, that conclusion is simply not warranted. The inefficacy of the second kind of education with respect to *knowing how* does not at all compromise that of the first kind of education, and this is, in principle, as true for *knowing how* to judge matters of aesthetics or law or politics accurately as it is for detecting musical intervals.

4. The faculty of insight is *common* but it is not *plebiscitary*. When Kant talks about common sense, the word "common" here does not mean "ordinary" or "familiar"; nor does it simply mean "popular" or "frequent." Common sense beliefs are not necessarily the beliefs that

15. For an exhaustive outline of the psychological literature on learning, see the first part of Barry Schwartz and Daniel Reisberg, *Learning and Memory* (New York: Norton, 1991).

16. For a discussion, see Peter J. Steinberger, "Ruling: Guardians and Philosopher-Kings," *American Political Science Review* 83 (December 1989), pp. 1217–1220. The distinction between these two kinds of education is made with particular clarity in the discussion between Socrates and Hippocrates at the beginning of the *Protagoras*. The *Protagoras* itself may be thought of as a commentary on this distinction.

most people hold at a particular time; nor are they even the beliefs that most people in a particular community hold at a particular time. Rather, common sense refers to a faculty that is widely shared by the members of a community, but that is not always cultivated, and not always employed, with appropriate care and attention. It is common in that it describes a generalized capacity, the fruits of which, when it is properly implemented, will also be general. But as such, it describes only a potentiality, the actualization of which depends on other factors.

Our musical common sense tells us that a simple chord composed of a B-flat above a C-natural (a "C-dominant" structure) has a certain kind of sound that tends to resolve into a chord having a different kind of sound (an "F-major" structure). It seems that some people can recognize this instantly and intuitively, even if they do not at all understand it theoretically. Many others, probably most, can hear it only after a program of ear training, while still others—those who are truly tone-deaf or suffer from some physical impairment—can perhaps never hear it. Moreover, it may be the case that the vast majority of people in a particular community have only moderate musical ability and have not had the benefit of ear training; they are trainable but as yet untrained. These people will not recognize the peculiar kind of sound characteristic of dominant structures and will not recognize its tendency to resolve into sounds characteristic of major-chord structures. When they listen to such sounds, they are apt not to be able to identify them; when asked certain questions about them, they are quite likely to answer those questions incorrectly. Their answers, taken together, will constitute a plebiscite that summarizes accurately the beliefs of the majority. Those beliefs will not be simply incorrect. They will violate the community's common sense and hence will fail to comport with the beliefs that the majority would have had if widely shared capacities had been cultivated and consulted.

Similarly, it is not at all unusual in political contexts to say that some large group of people, even a majority of the people, failed to exhibit common sense. The kind of mob behavior famously described by Gustave Le Bon reflects the capacity of a crowd, and the individuals who compose it, to lose touch momentarily with common sense.[17] But

17. Gustave Le Bon, *The Crowd: A Study of the Popular Mind* (London: T. Fisher Unwin, 1921). Le Bon talks about the "intellectual inferiority" of crowds and tells us that crowds "may be animated in succession by the most contrary sentiments, but they will always be under the influence of the exciting causes

such behavior need not be momentary. The majority of Germans who supported Hitler were not replacing a new common sense with an old one; for profound sociohistorical reasons, they were systematically and recurrently violating their own shared common sense and hence living a prolonged and agonizing contradiction. Indeed, in some influential accounts the failure to recognize and act according to the tenets of common sense is a most common feature of human beings. It is, by hypothesis, the norm rather than the exception. Without accepting this hypothesis, we can nonetheless stipulate that the concept of *common sense* does not describe a kind of empirical average, and there is no necessary tendency for commonsense beliefs to comport with the beliefs that people actually hold. Rather, common sense refers to a capacity, widely if not universally shared by some population, that implies certain beliefs which the members of that population ought to hold and act on if they are to exercise properly that common sense.

Thus, when we say of Joe that he "lacks common sense," we often do not mean that he lacks the faculty of good judgment. Rather, we mean that for some reason he is not exploiting his faculty properly, with the result that his judgments are bad. Again, we make this determination not because his decisions fail to conform to those of the statistical majority; rather, our criteria involve some independent notion of what, in the particular circumstance, common sense implies.

5. Some people are color-blind, while others are unusually good at discriminating between colors; some are tone-deaf, while others have perfect pitch. The reasons for these differences are not always known, but such differences are nonetheless a fact. They suggest not that sense perception is unreliable, but only that there is a hierarchy among sense perceivers. This is true, by analogy, for judgment as well. The fact that we cannot account for the difference between people of good judgment and bad inclines us to believe that the very idea of good judgment is a phantasm. But the premise does not entail the

---

of the moment. They are like leaves which a tempest whirls up and scatters in every direction and then allows to fall" (pp. 41–42). Moreover, "the arguments they employ and those which are capable of influencing them are, from a logical point of view, of such an inferior kind that it is only by way of analogy that they can be described as reasoning" (p. 73). The emphasis in these and other passages is on rationality and irrationality construed in the broadest possible terms. Indeed, Le Bon's book is, in effect, a systematic description of the loss of common sense.

conclusion. The fact of good judgment, like good sense perception, is entirely consistent with the fact that we cannot fully explain why some people have it and some do not.

There are, according to our intuitions, at least two general kinds of reasons that account for such differences. In certain cases, a deficiency or abundance of common sense is thought to be a natural attribute, like color blindness. Thus it may be that Jack, unlike Joe, really does lack the faculty of common sense and that he is in some important respect ineducable. In other cases, though, differences in insight are attributable to circumstantial considerations, including especially exposure to the kinds of experiences—systematic or otherwise—that help to educate and nurture our faculty of judgment. Again, Joe's failure might be attributable to educational deficiencies, and these in turn can be the result of various factors: a sheltered upbringing, poor schooling, massive propaganda, Joe's own indolence, and the like.

The moral implications of such a failure are not always clear. We are apt to believe that individuals ought to develop all of their capacities to the fullest.[18] But surely this is both unnecessary and impossible. Most people would regard as quite trivial the inability to identify C-dominant sounds, and properly so. Nothing of direct moral consequence rests on this, and there is, for most of us, no great need to develop ours musical insight. Moreover, there are often other faculties that one would prefer to cultivate and, given the limited amount of time and energy in any person's life, one must pick and choose. There are, after all, only so many hours in a day. The decision to embark on a program of musical training might well mean that some other faculty will be left uncultivated. The need to choose which faculties to develop is a simple fact of life, something that we face all the time, and does not, in and of itself, present any great moral difficulty.

Of course, some of us might choose not to cultivate our faculty of common sense, but even this should not be censured uncritically. To display a paucity of common sense is certainly a serious problem, but perhaps it is somewhat less so for, say, an unusually talented artist who chooses to devote all of his or her energies to a particular muse. Such an individual, having an attenuated faculty of common sense, will often be at the mercy of the practical world, unable to attend properly to the regular affairs of human existence and prone to mak-

18. See John Rawls's discussion of the "Aristotelian Principle" in his *A Theory of Justice* (Cambridge: Harvard University Press, 1971), pp. 424–433.

ing the most unfortunate of judgments. If, however, the result is also an extraordinary artistic achievement of some kind, then this is a choice which, however rash and unreflective, might prove to be most salutary indeed.

But would not such a choice itself be evidence of a well-developed faculty of common sense? Would it not be a matter of good judgment for the potential genius to choose a life of monomaniacal dedication? In fact, I think this is highly unlikely. For such choices are often less matters of common sense and good judgment than desperate and bizarre leaps into the unknown. If they occasionally result in extraordinary accomplishment, more often they end in unproductive, unsatisfying, and even ruined lives. The unwritten annals of the anonymous are undoubtedly filled with people of genuine talent who, lacking both good judgment and good luck, reached for greatness and failed miserably, having produced nothing of value for themselves or anyone else.

In sum, the faculty of insight or common sense that allows for good judgment is, like the faculties of sense perception, more acute in certain people than in others. We believe that these differences are sometimes natural and innate, sometimes a matter of circumstance and choice. Sometimes the circumstance or choice that results in a deficiency of common sense need not be censured if, as often happens, the upshot is that some other important faculty is allowed to develop in special ways. Our concept of insight is thus hierarchical, even elitist, but the political and ethical consequences of this are by no means obvious.

6. The faculty of insight, though perhaps a natural attribute, invariably operates within a context of meaning. Such a context is composed of those conceptual materials—assumptions, prejudices, and shared understandings, tacit or otherwise—that lend shape and substance to our encounter with the world. Our immediate perception of the world, our commonsense appropriation of it, is at once constrained and enriched by such materials. They provide the direction, background, and resonance without which insight would be, at best, aimless and unintelligent.

There are at least two versions of this general claim. The first is essentially prescriptive: common sense should follow, should permit itself to be influenced by, established conventions and presuppositions. Failing this, the faculties of human insight, through lack of proper guidance, are apt to become deeply misguided, and to render judgments that are inappropriate, irrelevant, and even tragically imprudent. For instance, the political appeal of abstract universal principles as opposed to established and proven traditions often leads to an ideological politics. History shows that such a rootless politics, unconnected with shared experiences and understandings, often leads to practices that horrify us precisely because they fail to comport with our assumptions about what is and is not proper. Gas chambers are a case in point. They are the result of an ungrounded and malignant ideology that inappropriately and unjustifiably "supplies in advance of the activity of attending to the arrangements of a society a formulated end to be pursued."[19] They are the result, as well, of an equally disembodied science involving the "absolute renunciation of the senses," a science that threatens to create "a dream world where every dreamed vision man himself produces has the character of reality only as long as the dream lasts."[20] Disembodied thought is inimical to, and leads to the destruction of, judgment properly understood.

The second version of our claim is that the contextualization of insight is simply unavoidable. This formulation is not prescriptive; rather, it is a description of the way insight necessarily operates. As we have seen, the hermeneutic school asserts that there is no such thing as "pure perception." Even the most basic and unproblematic of sense experiences are embedded in and derive an important part of their identity from established structures of meaning. This argument is straightforwardly generalizable to all of our faculties of judgment. Given structures of meaning are necessary preconditions for all cognition, and the employment of insight and common sense, as a cognitive activity, is unavoidably dependent upon such structures. We have argued that such a view has its roots in Aristotelian ethics (as interpreted by Martha Nussbaum, among others). It is related, in some respects, to the kind of holism often associated with Quine. But in its most radical and influential sense, it is essentially a Heideggerian view, especially as taken up and elaborated in the writings of Gadamer and Rorty.[21] It holds that human insight is both limited and liberated by

19. Michael Oakeshott, "Political Education," in *Rationalism in Politics* (London: Methuen, 1981), p. 116.

20. Hannah Arendt, *The Human Condition* (Garden City, New York: Doubleday, 1959), pp. 260–261.

21. It is Rorty, of course, who draws our attention to this connection between the otherwise deeply disparate views of Quine (along with Sellars, Davidson, and Kuhn among others) and the neo-Heideggerians. See Richard

structures of meaning, and that common sense therefore necessarily reflects the particular conceptual or cultural situation out of which it emerges.

Gadamer's work, as a prototypical example of this second formulation, demonstrates graphically at least one of its perplexities. For although Gadamer insists on the inexorability of context, his writing also has the aspect of a *kulturkritik* which seems to assume that disembodied thinking, though intellectually and socially disastrous, is nonetheless a genuine possibility.[22] How can one worry about decontextualized thought and still maintain that context is unavoidable? I think the answer is that hermeneutics, properly formulated, is criticizing not disembodied thinking (for there can be no such thing) but the illusion of disembodied thinking. We fail to judge correctly when we fail to reflect on or make note of the otherwise tacit contexts that invariably shape our judgment. Such reflection, of course, would render those contexts no longer tacit and, as we have seen, would make them available for criticism and revision. Moreover, criticism of this kind would in itself depend upon still other unexamined presuppositions, and so on *ad infinitum*. But the absence of such a process—a process of critical dialogue—is precisely what worries the hermeneutician. The hermeneutical *kulturkritik*, suitably reformulated, thus requires that common sense involve an important and illuminating but, at the same time, endless and unceasing effort to uncover and examine the various pre-understandings upon which it is based.

7. This is merely another way of restating the conclusion that we came to earlier: The exercise of judgment, as a species of intelligent performance, absolutely presupposes the capacity to provide satisfactory *post festum* explanations. Rational reconstruction is, at least prospectively, a necessary feature of the faculty of insight.

We have seen that following a rule of grammar (i.e., *knowing how* to use the language) necessarily involves a capacity, however latent, to reconstruct that rule. Someone who employs correctly the dative and genitive cases *knows that* certain propositions are rules of grammar, even though that knowledge may be only tacit, inarticulate, and unselfconscious. The faculty of insight or common sense allows one, either as speaker or hearer, to identify the cases correctly without actually

---

Rorty, *Philosophy and the Mirror of Nature* (Princeton: Princeton University Press, 1979), for example, pp. 169–173, 259–261, and 268–273.

22. See Chapter 3, footnote 76.

reconstructing the rules upon which they are based, but we would find it absurd to think that he or she lacks the capacity to "recollect" and reconstruct those rules. If we were to discover that the person in fact does not have this capacity, then we would doubt that this person is really engaged in the intelligent activity of using a language.

We have seen, further, that the analysis is equally applicable to such complex linguistic tasks as understanding the illocutionary force or implicature of an utterance. But in fact, this dual capacity—the capacity of insight and the capacity to reconstruct—is, I believe, a feature of all intelligent performance requiring judgment. Consider the case of jurisprudence. Theorists of legal reasoning have long argued that formulating constitutional law cannot be a straightforwardly inferential matter, but depends decisively on a noninferential faculty of insight or common sense. It is not a matter of subsuming algorithmically, as in our tripartite model, the facts of a case under the appropriate legal doctrine. In Levi's well-known formulation, the task of the judge is to find similarities and differences among a variety of cases. There is and can be no deductive rule for such a finding; the process is noninferential, intuitive, dependent on insight or common sense. Once similarities or distinctions have been identified, then it may be possible to formulate a legal rule. But this rule will be of only limited utility, since the next case to be considered, involving new and unique particulars, will again require judgments of similarity and difference that cannot be made inferentially and that may well imply a brand-new rule.[23]

Levi's discussion, along with those of Frank, Cardozo, and others, sensitizes us to the inadequacies of the tripartite model with respect to legal reasoning. But what such theorists perhaps underemphasize is the absolute necessity of *post festum* explanations.[24] We expect our judges to be able to justify their decisions in rational terms. This expectation is both appropriate and, I think, conceptually necessary. Imagine a judge who simply cannot account in any way for his or her

23. Edward H. Levi, *An Introduction to Legal Reasoning* (Chicago: University of Chicago Press, 1949), especially pp. 1–27.

24. This underemphasis can be explained in terms of the central theoretical goal of writers such as Levi and Frank, namely, to discredit the older, deductivist account of legal reasoning as outlined, for example, by John Austin. For an overview, see Lief H. Carter, *Reason in Law* (Boston: Little, Brown, 1979).

decision. Such a judge has not rendered a judgment at all. Something else has occurred. The judge's "decision" is more like a nervous tic, a biochemical reaction, a mechanical response to an external stimulus; it is the behavior of an animal or a machine, not an intelligent performance. Levi is almost certainly correct: the activity of constitutional interpretation is a matter of *knowing how* and involves a faculty of insight that does not proceed inferentially. But again, this *knowing how* presupposes a *knowing that,* however tacit and implicit it may be, and we expect to see evidence of this in the judge's effort to reconstruct the decision rationally, often in the form of a written opinion that operates in terms of inferences and propositions.

The activity of aesthetic judgment has, I believe, a precisely identical structure. The art critic neither employs nor can provide a foolproof method for identifying works of great merit. Kant is certainly correct: evaluation is, in the first instance, a matter of reflective rather than determinate judgment. It depends upon a faculty of insight that has been trained through an appropriate experiential curriculum and that invariably reflects, at least to some degree, established standards and dispositions. But the critic cannot simply look at a painting and say, "Beautiful." We require, again, an explanation, a reconstruction that provides us with reasons that will allow us to *know that* the work has merit. These reasons may well not be definitive; the task of rational reconstruction is, in part, precisely to allow us to evaluate and assess a judgment and to invite us either to offer a new judgment or to accept the old one on different grounds. This, however, is hardly peculiar to the aesthetic realm. It is as true for the hardest of the "hard sciences" as it is for art: there is, in all likelihood, no absolute and final *knowing that* something is the case. But this in no way vitiates our conceptual claim. Aesthetic judgment requires a *post festum* accounting. Indeed, such an accounting is precisely what critics do when they write what we aptly and appropriately call their "criticism."[25]

25. As implied in Chapter 2, the necessity for rational reconstruction is quite consistent with Kant's aesthetic theory, especially in the light of his insistence on the distinction between judgments of taste and judgments of sense. The former allow for some kind of *post festum* argumentation; the latter do not. On the other hand, my overall view clearly is informed by a far broader and more generous notion of what counts as cognitive, a notion that reflects the influence of contemporary holism in its various forms—Heidegger and Gadamer as well as Wittgenstein and Quine—and that is quite different from what we find in Kant's philosophy. My rejection of Kantian noncognitivism

All of this is, in my view, equally true for political judgment. Machiavellian *virtu,* Tocquevillian deliberation, Nietzschean aesthetics—such notions reflect a deep understanding that judgment in politics is fundamentally noninferential. This holds as well, only more explicitly, for the pursuit of intimations described by Oakeshott and the *sensus communus* described by Arendt. But to these various formulations we must add what I take to be an absolute conceptual requirement: The decisions of the public realm require explicit and rational justification. The citizen, the delegate, the prince—all must be prepared to account for their choices and actions. Political judgment, like any species of intelligent performance, presupposes a capacity to adduce after the fact some kind of propositional calculus involving, as any such calculus must, both the opportunity and the obligation to engage in a process of rational evaluation and critique.

8. These various features apply to the concept of intelligent performance per se. But judgment is a certain variety of intelligent performance. As such, it is characterized by a particular kind of rational reconstruction, the precise nature of which follows quite directly and straightforwardly, I believe, from everything that we have said thus far.

Judgment is, by definition, the activity in which particulars are subsumed under or otherwise connected with universals. In conversation, a particular grammatical utterance is judged to be (or not to be) an instance of the genitive case; in a court of law, a particular event is judged to be legal; in aesthetics, a work of art is judged to be beautiful; in public affairs, a policy is judged to be prudent. These various universals—genitive case, legal, beautiful, prudent—are, of course, merely illustrative. In each realm of judgment, an enormous range of universals may come into play, but in all cases, their application to particular things requires, like intelligent performance in general, both *knowing how* to do something and an at least tacit *knowing that* certain propositions are true. Specifically, the judge must have both a faculty of insight (which provides a kind of immediate access to the individuating features of particulars and the relevant characteristics of

---

with respect to art is, in a sense, representative of my entire effort to undermine what I have been calling the dichotomy of judgment. Aesthetic judgment is no more and no less cognitive than any other kind of intelligent performance. All such performance presupposes both the faculty of insight and the capacity rationally to reconstruct.

universals) and also the capacity, at least prospectively, to uncover and explicate underlying propositions, thereby describing what the process of judgment would have been like if it had been inferential.

What could such a description be, other than that it involves precisely our tripartite model of judgment? To reconstruct rationally a judgment means nothing less than (1) describing the conceptual features of the universal being invoked, (2) specifying at least some of the relevant individuating characteristics of the particular things being judged, and (3) demonstrating some connection between them such that predicating the universal of the particular is shown to be justifiable. The jurist, for example, must provide a coherent account of a legal principle, identify and describe the relevant features of a particular case, and demonstrate through some rational argument that the two are connected in a specifiable way. It is highly doubtful, of course, that this describes accurately the *psychology* of judicial decision making, but it is, nonetheless, the distinctive and peculiar form of rational reconstruction with respect to judgment in law. As such, it is equally applicable, *mutatis mutandis,* to all problems of judgment.

The tripartite model is not, then, a description of how judgment typically occurs; rather, it sets forth the structure that any appropriate reconstruction must have. As such, it describes a constitutive feature of that concrete species of intelligent performance that we are calling judgment.

IV

We have seen that our concept of insight or common sense, as a feature of judgment and intelligent performance, absolutely requires the capacity of rational reconstruction. But we must not lose sight of the underlying character of all such reconstruction, namely, that it involves a kind of recollection, or *anamnēsis*. In reconstructing the steps that would have been taken if the judging process had been inferential, the intelligent performer is recalling and making explicit those historically and socially generated premises and propositions that constitute the conceptual and theoretical foundation for any human action. The jurist who must discover differences and similarities among cases does not do this out of thin air; nor can we be confident in saying that those decisions reflect timeless, transcendent truths about the world. Rather, juristic insight emerges out of a traditional and established structure of preunderstandings. This structure determines, at least in part, what the judge takes to be the conceptual features of laws *qua* universals and the individuating characteristics of events *qua* particulars. To reconstruct the judge's insight rationally, then, is precisely to make those preunderstandings explicit and manifest, to uncover them and put them on the table, so that they can be assessed and evaluated. The jurist is, in this respect, every bit like the statesman, the language user, the aesthete. Judgment of whatever kind is embedded in, and must be reconstructed in terms of, its tacit intellectual contexts.

But does politics—or language, aesthetics, and the like—really need or even benefit from judgment understood in this way? Suppose we find in our midst a most unusual creature, a kind of mystical idiot-savant—let's call this character "Malabar"[26]—who somehow has an ability to make political decisions that always turn out for the best, but who has absolutely no capacity to reconstruct those decisions. Would not such a creature be a highly reliable guide to political action? And does it matter that the judgments of this Malabar would not really be judgments at all? The fact that they would not fit our criteria for intelligent performance would not affect in any way their reliability. Why, then, do those criteria count for anything?

There are, I believe, at least three strong responses to such a question. First, the idea of an unintelligent creature whose decisions always turn out for the best presupposes that the quality of outcomes is somehow self-evident or predetermined. This is almost certainly not the case. A central task of political judgment is to determine not simply the means to attain some end but the appropriateness of the end itself. Machiavelli's prince has insight into political strategy, but this insight is informed by an even deeper insight into the meaning and purpose of political society and political rule. The universals that one predicates of political particulars—prudence, justice, interest, and the like—necessarily reflect such an insight. Thus, the concept of judgment in politics is not just a matter of technique. It involves an intuition about the peculiar role that political life can and should play in the pursuit of human flourishing. Do the "decisions" of Malabar really turn out

---

26. See D. H. Lawrence, "The Rocking-Horse Winner," in *The Portable D. H. Lawrence* (New York: Viking Press, 1947). For obscure rhetorical reasons, I have substituted the name of the prediction for that of the predictor.

for the best? That is importantly a matter of judgment, and is something that Malabar, utterly lacking in judgment, cannot decide.[27]

Second, even if one could stipulate at the outset some set of desirable ends that Malabar could reliably achieve for us, the fact remains that *we* would have, and would always have, the decision as to whether or not to follow Malabar's recommendations. This would necessarily require judgment on our part. As such, it would depend on *our* having the insight that the recommendations in question really are reliable. And this insight, like any other, would call for a rational reconstruction of some kind. At a minimum, we would have to point to the track record and, together with some kind of probabilistic analysis, provide an account of why we should do what Malabar tells us to do. But further, we would also be required to determine, to the degree possible, exactly why Malabar is so successful, to arrive at some scientific explanation that would convince us that what we are doing has a rational warrant. This might not occur right away. For practical reasons, we might provisionally decide to go along with Malabar on a hunch, pending a fuller investigation. Indeed, we might put off such an investigation indefinitely. But as intelligent performers, we must nonetheless be prepared to seek a rational justification for our choice if and when the issue arises. We must, in other words, seek for ourselves the kinds of connections between the particulars at hand and the relevant universals that would justify independently the choice of this action or policy over that.

All of this means that we could not really dispense with judgment, and that any judgment would be entirely ours. Decisions would be made not by Malabar but by us, insofar as we would choose to accept or reject Malabar's recommendations. On this account, then, Malabar is merely a kind of natural phenomenon which we interpret and utilize according to our own common sense.

Finally, and relatedly, the need for rational reconstruction points to the fact that political judgment—and, indeed, judgment in general—is a public matter requiring a kind of mutual understanding based on common sense. In this connection, certain themes in contem-

27. For a famous discussion of means and ends in a somewhat similar context, see J. R. Bambrough, "Plato's Political Analogies," in *Philosophy, Politics, and Society,* ed. Peter Laslett (Oxford: Blackwell, 1956.)

porary epistemology may be instructive. According to the so-called externalist approach to knowledge,

> the epistemic justification or reasonableness of a basic empirical belief derives from the obtaining of an appropriate relation, generally construed as causal or nomological in character, between the believer and the world. . . . This relation . . . would thus provide, for anyone who knew about it, an undeniably excellent reason for accepting the belief. But according to externalism, the person for whom the belief is basic need not (and in the crucial cases will not) have any cognitive grasp of this reason, or of the relation that is the the basis of it, in order for his belief to be justified.[28]

As long as there is a correspondence between belief and world, the person holding the belief can be said to have knowledge despite being entirely unable to account for it.

Much depends here on how we characterize knowledge itself as a feature of cognition. But insofar as we describe it in the context of intelligent performance, knowledge cannot be a purely private matter but is embedded in shared structures of meaning that give sense to knowledge claims. This implies that such claims are in certain respects public. Knowledge must be recognized as such, and in order to be recognized there must be, at least prospectively, an account that *some-one*—though perhaps not the believer himself—can provide by way of rational reconstruction. The externalist approach often fails to consider adequately this aspect of knowledge and hence fails to give sufficient attention to the central role of explicit and public justification.

It is much the same with political judgment. Malabar's "insights," insofar as they resist rational reconstruction, are purely private and hence do not count as judgments at all. The need for rational reconstruction reflects the idea that the faculty of judgment is a matter of *common* sense, that it is invariably shaped and directed by a shared conceptual and theoretical vocabulary, and that any particular judgment must therefore be available for analysis and evaluation.

But what constitutes an adequate rational reconstruction? It is difficult to provide a general and abstract answer to this question, but an

28. Laurence Bonjour, *The Structure of Empirical Knowledge* (Cambridge: Harvard University Press, 1985), pp. 34–35.

example may point to certain important desiderata. Let us reconsider in greater depth Searle's Chinese room example (mentioned briefly in Chapter 3), this time somewhat reformulated.[29] I have been given the task of translating some Chinese text into Arabic. I have no knowledge at all of either Chinese or Arabic; English is my only language. My taskmaster, however, has provided a complete set of English-language instructions of the following kind: whenever I see a particular configuration of characters in the Chinese text (squiggles, the meanings of which are entirely opaque to me), I am to produce a different configuration (more squiggles) that is, I am told, composed of Arabic characters. The instructions say or imply absolutely nothing about the meaning of the various characters or words. There is no semantic connection between the rules I am to follow, which are written in English, and the non-English text I am translating. Despite this, and assuming that the instructions are indeed complete and accurate, the result will be for many purposes an acceptable translation.

Following Searle, we want to say that, despite the success of my translation, I clearly do not know Chinese or Arabic, and therefore I am in a very different position and have performed a very different task from that performed by someone who is fluent in both Chinese and Arabic and who can really translate from the one to the other. In Searle's account, I have performed certain purely formal syntactic operations, and one cannot get semantics from syntax. The person who is fluent in both Chinese and Arabic, on the other hand, knows what the words mean and hence is truly engaged in an act of translation. Now I want to say, further, that I am in an important sense also unable to reconstruct rationally my (putative) act of translation. I cannot account for or explain the translation that I have produced, and therefore I have not been engaged in an intelligent performance at all.

There is an obvious sense in which this is false. I can rationally reconstruct my decisions simply by pointing to the rules that the taskmaster has provided and explaining how each decision comported with those rules. This, however, would be sufficient to explain and justify only the activity of making squiggle-to-squiggle correlations. It would involve a reconstruction of squiggle-correlation, but not of

29. John Searle, *Minds, Brains, and Science* (Cambridge: Harvard University Press, 1984), pp. 32–41. My reformulation is designed to make the case more graphic and is, as far as I can tell, entirely in the spirit of Searle's original.

linguistic translation. To see this, consider that there is in fact no good reason why I would necessarily know that I was involved in an act of translation at all. The rules that I followed need not mention the Chinese and Arabic languages; they might simply describe squiggle-correlations, and I might be free to interpret these in any number of ways, for example, as involving a kind of game, blueprint, or psychological test. It is impossible, then, that my rational reconstruction—involving demonstrable compliance with the rules—could serve as an adequate account or explanation of a *translation;* in and of itself, it could not even show that a translation had taken place. It might still be a fine rational reconstruction, but it would be a reconstruction of a quite different kind of intelligent performance, namely, squiggle-correlation.

Perhaps, though, I do have good reason to believe that I have been involved in an act of translation. Let us say that the rules specify that they are designed to translate Chinese into Arabic, that my taskmaster does indeed know how to formulate such rules, that the particular formulation that I have is a sincere and informed effort to produce an accurate translation, and that I have strong independent grounds for believing all of these things to be true. Would my account—demonstrated compliance with the rules—now constitute an adequate reconstruction of an act of translation? I think not. I could certainly explain and justify my belief that the translation is, in fact, a translation, and that my own deeds contributed to a successful outcome. But such a reconstruction would not provide an explanation of the translation itself. For in order to explain why one set of squiggles corresponds semantically to another, one has to understand the meanings of the squiggles. I have no such understanding and therefore cannot provide an appropriate explanation. In effect, my rational reconstruction, now based on both compliance with the rules and my justified belief that the result will be an accurate translation, really comes down to this: I judge that my *taskmaster* can provide a rational reconstruction of the translation, and I can offer arguments that will explain *that* judgment. The implication, then, is that the taskmaster is really doing the translating, not I. I am merely functioning as a mechanical device for making manifest the fruits of a translation that is actually embedded in and entailed by the rules themselves.

Rational reconstructions must therefore be adequate in terms of the specific kind of judgment one is seeking to explain. Simply adverting to a mechanical procedure will not suffice, unless it is the mechanical procedure itself that needs justification. With respect to legal, aesthetic, and political judgment, then, the capacity to reconstruct rationally means the capacity to provide explanations that operate in terms of the peculiar and defining substantive features of each. Such explanations will tell us exactly why the features of a particular case are connected in specifiable ways to the characteristics of concept, rule, or principle. This is merely another way of saying that any particular species of intelligent performance requires a *knowing that* certain propositions characteristic of that species are true.

A final question remains: Does the requirement of rational reconstruction mean that our analogy with sense perception breaks down? After all, we perceive colors and sounds quite well without ever seeking to explain how this works. If a prospective *post festum* accounting is necessary for judgment and not necessary for sense perception, then the similarity between the two is perhaps more limited than we have thus far suggested.

This in fact seems to be true enough, but it certainly does not involve any serious problems for our argument. For on such an account, sense perception, in and of itself, is just not a type of intelligent performance at all. We believe that animals perceive at least as well as and often much better than we do, and this does not turn them into intelligent actors. They are, rather, parts of the natural world of cause and effect, and to the extent that we have animal natures we are, of course, part of that world as well. Now the difference between humans and animals may well be the oldest topic of Western philosophy. But at least one way of articulating this difference is to note that, as creatures capable of intelligent performance, humans may be able to think about and rationally reconstruct at least some of their sense perceptions, that is, to engage in a kind of second-order thinking.[30] In our musical example, the ability to perceive that a C-dominant structure resolves into an F-major structure is, as these phrases themselves indicate, capable of being reconstructed in terms of an elaborate conceptual and theoretical system that helps us to account for and explain just what it is that we are hearing. This explanation can, in turn, be supplemented by further investigations involving, for example, the overtone system, the neuropsychology of musical perception, and more generally the physics of music, all of which have substantial and important

---

30. Peter J. Steinberger, *Logic and Politics: Hegel's Philosophy of Right* (New Haven: Yale University Press), pp. 165–176.

literatures. The capacity of humans to engage in these kinds of analysis and to reconstruct, thereby, their sense perceptions is what turns an animal activity into an activity of judgment.

It may be objected that such analyses can never be definitive, that there is an element of sense perception that will always be beyond explanation. But it should be clear by now that this kind of claim, far from being a criticism, is in fact an important and integral feature of our concept of judgment. Rational reconstruction is necessarily limited. It always invokes and relies on judgments that themselves require a rational reconstruction which in turn invokes and relies on judgments, and so on. The resulting infinite regress means that explanations must somewhere stop, not because they are complete but for the very opposite reason: they can never be complete. Thus, for example, our insight that the principle of contradiction is true, though it can be explicated and exemplified in an unlimited number of ways, will always in the end be irreducible; either we "see" it, or we do not. But again, this does not mean that explanations are not explanations, and it does not mean that the faculty of insight is no different from animal instinct. The capacity to provide an account, to reconstruct rationally, to describe the steps that we would have taken if our process had been inferential—this capacity makes all the difference.

V

I have described what I believe to be some basic features of our concept of judgment. Judgment involves a kind of noninferential faculty of insight or intuition, roughly equivalent to Aristotelian *nous*. Like sense perception, this faculty may be recognized and acknowledged as reliable despite our inability to understand fully how it operates. It can be nurtured and improved through an appropriate educational curriculum, though this curriculum will largely be a matter of habituation and experience rather than discourse. The faculty is common—it is a faculty of common sense—but it is not plebiscitary; as such, it is widely shared in any community, but it is not always cultivated and employed in an appropriate manner. For either innate or experiential reasons, the faculty of insight is more acute and reliable in some individuals than in others. But in all cases, it is embedded in and invariably operates in light of the often implicit conceptual and theoretical materials that compose the intellectual foundations of a culture. The exercise of this faculty absolutely presupposes a capacity to reconstruct those foundations rationally, to describe the implicit element of *knowing that* which is required if there is to be a genuine *knowing how*, to "recollect" (*anamimnēskō*) the tacit, socially and historically generated propositions about particulars and universals that one would have employed if the process of judgment had been inferential. This last feature is indispensable. Without the capacity to reconstruct, we would be unable to distinguish judgment as intelligent performance from the brute occurrences of nature; without the actual fact of reconstruction, and the criteria of evaluation implied therein, we would be unable to distinguish genuine perspicacity from mere invention, good judgment from bad, claims that are serious and substantial from those that are trash.

But taken together, these features still do not describe fully the character of judgment as we understand it. For judgment is necessarily "judgment of " something, and that something is, I believe, always and invariably someone else's judgment. This may seem to be a surprising conclusion, but in fact it follows from the argument as thus far presented. We have said, to be sure, that judgment is the activity in which universals are predicated of particulars. But this, in and of itself, can be misleading. For strictly speaking, a judgment is never directly or even primarily a claim about the relationship between a natural particular and a universal; it is, rather, a claim about such a claim. In this sense, as we shall see, to judge is to participate in a kind of dialogue with the object of judgment itself.

Consider again the case of linguistic interpretation. When I claim that your utterance, "Hey, how about those Mets?" falls under the Gricean category of *flouting a conversational principle*, I appear to be saying that this particular and individuated event (*P*) can be classified as an instance of some identifiable universal (*U*) which tells me, ultimately, what the utterance means. In short, I seem to be predicating *U* (flouting) of *P* (the utterance). But I think I am primarily doing something rather different. For when I make such a claim about your utterance, I am in the first instance claiming that my judgment is a faithful rendering of *your* judgment. In predicating *U* of *P*, I am really saying that *you* are predicating *U* of *P*. In the instant case, my interpretation of "Hey, how about those Mets?" is in fact a judgment about your interpretation of the same utterance, your own utterance.

This is so because the utterance "Hey, how about those Mets?" is an intelligent performance. To understand it properly is to understand it as such. But this in turn means that my judgment of it must focus on the prospective rational reconstruction that is, as we have seen, a constitutive feature of any intelligent performance. In other words, I must look primarily, though perhaps only intuitively, at the underlying propositions that form the bases of your intelligent performance, and these, of course, are propositions that you must hold, at least implicitly, if the intelligent performance is indeed yours. Moreover, some if not most of those propositions will bear directly on the question of whether or not "Hey, how about those Mets?" is a case of flouting; if this were not the case, one could hardly reconstruct the performance in any satisfying way. These propositions would therefore amount precisely to a judgment about the utterance with respect to the universal in question: they would be propositions that you hold about the relationship between U and P. Thus, my interpretation would really be a judgment about your judgment; hence, it would be what we may call a "second-order" judgment.

In order for me to make such a judgment, I must of course have an insight into certain particulars. But the particulars in this case would involve primarily *your* implicit sense of your own words; my insight is an insight into your particular insight. It is because I sense what the words "Hey, how about those Mets?" mean to you that I judge the utterance to be an instance of Gricean flouting. I am judging not simply an independent and natural particular thing in the world, but another individual's own (implicit) understanding of an intelligent performance. Thus, when I conclude that P is a case of U, I am claiming primarily that this is your claim.

But what if you have not in fact articulated such a claim? What if you do not manifestly believe that the utterance is a case of flouting? Can my judgment then really be about your judgment if you have not explicitly rendered this judgment at all? There are at least three possibilities here. First, your failure to believe self-consciously that P is a case of U may simply indicate that you have not yet rationally reconstructed your own judgment. You have not come to grips with your own intelligent performance; hence, you are not explicitly aware of the meaning of your utterance. Some instruction from me—a lesson in Gricean pragmatics, perhaps—might, in the appropriate circumstance, suffice to clarify or make manifest exactly what it is that you have done. In a sense, then, the claim that P is a case of U really is your own judgment, whether or not you are aware of it, and my claim is essentially a claim about that judgment.

A second, related possibility is that you have indeed reconstructed your performance but have done so inaccurately. You may, for example, have mistakenly used a false theory of pragmatics, thereby misconstruing the function of your own utterance. Your reconstruction is not entirely accurate; it will not stand up to systematic scrutiny. Of course, implicitly you know exactly what the utterance is all about, just as Meno's slave boy knows the Pythagorean theorem, but because of your theoretical error, you are as yet unable to articulate that understanding. Again, a lesson in Grice might serve to make evident your own deep understanding and hence demonstrate to you what your own real judgment is. My judgment is therefore a claim about your *real* judgment and hence about the deep structure of your intelligent performance, despite what you happen explicitly to believe.

Finally, it may be that my judgment is in error. Perhaps Grice is wrong, or perhaps my insight into the sense of your utterance is faulty. Judgments are, by definition, eligible for critical analysis and evaluation, and this means that they may be mistaken. Again, reconstruction per se is not enough; it must be rational. It may turn out, then, that P is not in fact a case of U, but this does not in any way alter the fact that my judgment is primarily and directly about your (perhaps implicit) judgment regarding P and U. It is, again, a second-order judgment.

But if my judgment is primarily about your judgment, does this not suggest that your judgment—P is a case of U—must be a first-order judgment? And would that not mean that my assertion above, that all judgment is primarily about judgment, is necessarily false? I think such a view is untenable. For in fact, your claim that P is a case of U is in the first instance a claim about what you think *my* judgment is or will be. You utter the words "Hey, how about those Mets?" in the belief that, given the appropriate circumstances, I will judge those words in a certain way. I will see, however implicitly, that they are a case of flouting. Again, your belief that I will come to see this may itself be only implicit. It may be an unarticulated insight into my equally unarticulated insight, an intuitive sense about what is or will be my intuitive sense of those words.[31] But in either case, it will be primarily a judgment about a judgment. Thus, both of our judgments involving

31. Even if you think that I am and will continue to be constitutionally unable to understand your utterance, the fact of the utterance presupposes that *someone* could at sometime understand it and that you are, as a result, making a second-order claim.

the utterance are basically second-order judgments and pertain primarily to one another, rather than to the discrete, isolated fact of the utterance itself. But this conclusion seems to fly in the face of an apparently obvious asymmetry between your judgment and mine. Imagine that you believe that I will see "Hey, how about those Mets?" to be a case of flouting. Imagine, further, that I just do not and never will see it that way. Perhaps, then, your judgment regarding my judgment is mistaken. But are you not also in a special situation vis-à-vis the utterance itself, so that you can say with absolute certainty: "Perhaps I misjudged you; you, in fact, do not understand my utterance to be a case of flouting. But the most important fact is that your judgment is wrong. For I did indeed intend the utterance to be a case of flouting, and that, therefore, is exactly what it is"? In other words, you, as the utterer, seem to be uniquely situated to render a definitive judgment of the utterance—a first-order judgment.

This objection is wrong on several counts. First, it assumes that the utterer is necessarily privileged with respect to his or her own intentions. Such an assumption may seem plausible enough, but a century or more of sociological and psychoanalytical theory ought to have made us at least somewhat skeptical. Indeed, some conclude that individuals are actually *least* able to understand their own deepest intentions. Even simple intentions, like the intention to flout a principle of conversation, may be less immediately evident to the utterer than to the hearer or to some third party.

More important, the objection assumes that the meaning of an utterance is reducible to the intention of the utterer. Without in any way taking sides on the broader question of intentionalism, we can say with some confidence that utterances operate within a structure of conventions and principles—syntactic, semantic, and pragmatic—that ultimately determine meaning. We may finally decide (*pace* Marx, Freud, et al.) that the utterer does have some special access to the intentions behind an utterance, and that would surely be an important fact. But it would not always be determinative. This is clear in the case of semantics. If, in Paris, I intend to order a steak by uttering the words "*Je voudrais la livre*," my intention neither overcomes my ignorance of French nor alters the meaning of the word *livre*. If, in New York, I intend to call Patton brave by saying, "Patton was pusillanimous," again this shows only that I do not know the meaning of "pusillanimous" and that there is a contradiction between the meaning of what I said and my intended meaning. It is much the same with pragmatics.

Your intention to flout a Gricean principle does not at all indicate that you actually have done so. To determine this requires reference to a structure of shared understandings and conventions that stand apart from your own particular intentions. With respect to this structure, utterer and hearer are generally in the same boat. The question of whether or not P is a case of U is, in principle, the same for both.

If there is, therefore, an asymmetry between you and me with respect to P and U (and there surely is *some* kind of asymmetry), this does not in and of itself show that your claim must be primarily a first-order judgment. Of course, neither does it show that it *cannot* be such a judgment. In fact, though, I believe that it cannot be, at least not primarily. For a claim about "Hey, how about those Mets?" is a claim about part of a conversation; as such, it must be directly a judgment about the utterance's function in that conversation, and this is determined by the judgments—actual or prospective, express or implicit—of the individuals participating in the conversation. In other words, your judgment regarding your own utterance is hostage to my fully reconstructed and rational understanding of it. Again, my conscious beliefs about the utterance may be mistaken; I may have failed to reconstruct my judgment, or may have failed to do so rationally. If, however, I am able and disposed to judge your utterance, to reconstruct that judgment rationally, and to see that my reconstruction holds up under critical scrutiny, then the result of this process must in fact determine for you what the utterance is.

Consider the implications if this were not so. Imagine that you, in conversation with me, conclude both that P is a case of U and that, despite this, my judgment is that P is not a case of U. Assume further that the latter claim is not simply that my express beliefs about P are wrong but that my beliefs, once completely and rationally reconstructed, evaluated, emended, and perfected, are still wrong. Your best, fully reconstructed judgment is that P is a case of U; my equivalent judgment demurs. The result is not simply a disagreement but a hopeless contradiction. You may want to deny that there is a contradiction by pointing to the fact that my judgment is simply mistaken. The utterance, after all, is your utterance, and if you conclude that P is a case of U, then that is what it is. My judgment does not really count. But if the deep structure of my beliefs is such that I truly judge that P is not a case of U, then our insights and presuppositions are so disjoint that we could not even have a conversation with one another (at least not involving P and U). You certainly cannot prove me wrong

about P and U, since my judgment—insofar as it has been fully reconstructed and satisfactorily evaluated—is attendant to the communally
generated assumptions or preunderstandings that make it possible for
me to think in the first place. But more importantly, my judgment is
precisely all that you should be interested in. For if you have genuinely
made an utterance, then you are seeking to participate in a conversation, and your understanding of that utterance can occur only in that
light. The logic of your own intelligent performance requires that your
putative judgment about the utterance is, when separated from mine,
largely irrelevant. Your insistence that P is a case of U and your claim
to be engaged in conversation with me are, when juxtaposed to my
rationally reconstructed claim that P is not a case of U, internally
contradictory. If, then, we are to have such a conversation, your judgment about the relationship between P and U must really be a claim
concerning my judgment about that relationship—a claim about how
I will understand P and U, at least in the proper circumstances. It is,
therefore and necessarily, a second-order judgment.

VI

From a second-order judgment we can, to be sure, derive a first-order
judgment. If you and I agree that P is a case of U, and if that agreement reflects the deep structure of our cognitive resources, then for
all intents and purposes P is indeed a case of U. But, perhaps paradoxically, that first-order claim is actually attendant to, and derivative
of, the second-order claim. It is not itself the focus of the faculty of
judgment but, rather, a happy by-product. The *effect* of judgment is
that universals are predicated of natural particulars: *utterances flout,
Churchill is a statesman,* and so forth. But judgments are primarily *of*
one another.

A number of epistemological claims follow more or less directly
from the concept of judgment as it has been outlined thus far. Judgment is indeed a matter of predicating universals of particulars. However, our access to particulars is necessarily dependent on intellectual
faculties that are embedded in and hostage to larger structures of
meaning. Such structures must be already in place, so to speak, if
perception, properly understood, is to occur. Raw feels are not perceptions. The sensory life of an amoeba, composed entirely of such feels,
is, we have presupposed, different from the perceptual experiences of
humans precisely because the latter emerge out of and are shaped by

an available conceptual apparatus, a reservoir of established meanings. There is, we have seen, no such thing as pure perception, and this means that judgments are invariably interpretations, based on and informed by a presupposed set of meaningful understandings.

Structures of meaning are reflective, in turn, of social or interactive structures. This is because concepts, as repositories of meaning, necessarily emerge out of the disposition to communicate intelligently and reflectively, and are sustained by communicative habits. If there were no such dispositions and habits, there would be no need for, and no opportunity for, meaningfulness. A concept can have no conceivable function or foundation other than to serve as a basis for intelligent interaction. But communication itself presupposes a *shared* universe of discourse that allows for mutual intelligibility. We can communicate successfully only to the degree that we employ and are governed by a common set of meanings and preunderstandings. Thus, a conceptual apparatus is never the peculiar, idiosyncratic, and private possession of a discrete and isolated individual. All of our perceptions and judgments reflect conceptual materials that are in some sense prior to those perceptions and judgments, that exist "out there," and that transcend, therefore, the purely sensory life of the individual.

The idea is Hegelian, although it adverts to the very notion of *anamnēsis* upon which we have previously relied. Meno's slave recollects not a private, idiosyncratic truth but a truth of reason that exists independently of all reasoning creatures and to which such creatures may, in certain circumstances, have common access. Such a truth provides the indispensable context for all meaningful thought. In Hegel, this general notion acquires a historical dimension. *Geist*, best translated as "mind," is the complete and coherent compendium of all rational propositions. It describes nothing other than the full content of intellectual life. As such, its existence is independent of all particular mental beings. We are mere vehicles of *Geist*, and our intellectual lives—including our judgments—are simply emanations of this preexisting intellectual realm. It provides for us our preunderstandings, our prejudices. To the degree that we are able to uncover or recollect those prejudices, we can participate in the historical process by which *Geist*, originally shrouded in the superstition and neglect of infancy, becomes mature and explicit, and hence comes to be fully aware of itself. For the hermeneutic tradition, this general notion remains historical but loses altogether its teleological character. Structures of meaning define neither a fixed core of immutable truth nor stages in the self-unfolding of such a truth, but the more-or-less stable prejudices of a particular culture existing in a particular time and connected only fitfully, if at all, to other cultures. These structures or horizons perhaps lack the grandiose and sublime character of Platonic and Hegelian mind. But their effect is essentially similar, insofar as they and they alone provide the necessary element of *knowing that* upon which every one of our perceptions and judgments is authorized.

The implications of such a view are quite decisive for the idea of judgment. Certainly the purpose of any judgment is twofold: to assert a valid claim about the world and to communicate that claim in an intelligible manner. These aims, though distinct, are deeply bound up with one another, since each fundamentally relies upon independent and authorizing structures of meaning. Again, the communicability of judgment is determined by the degree to which individuals share an already available conceptual apparatus. But the validity of judgment is largely determined in the same way. In the *Meno*, for example, the slave's conjectures are assessed in terms of the degree to which they comport with a shared universe of discourse that identifies certain claims, and not others, as making sense. If the slave utters nonsense, then this shows the invalidity of his views. It is similar with Hegel. Validity is a function of the progressive self-disclosure of *Geist*. As this process unfolds, what was thought to be valid at one point in time eventually becomes incoherent and nonsensical, and hence loses—for that reason and that reason alone—its claim to validity.

This kind of criterion is, I believe, characteristic of judgment per se. Meaningfulness is ultimately a standard not only of communicability but of validity.[32] As we have seen, "68 plus 57 equals sour-tasting" is invalid *because* it is unintelligible. We have also seen, to be sure, that "68 plus 57 equals 115" is initially quite intelligible despite being incorrect. But its intelligibility absolutely presupposes its corrigibility. Once it is evaluated in terms of our shared understandings and assumptions about numbers and addition, then someone who has been privy to and has evidently understood such an evaluation and who continues to hold that "68 plus 57 equals 115" is saying something that is entirely unintelligible and hence invalid. In all such cases, the central role played by independent intellectual structures—shared horizons, universes of discourse (historically variable or otherwise), tacit

32. Jürgen Habermas, *Der philosophische Diskurs der Modernen* (Frankfurt: Suhrkamp Verlag, 1985), pp. 364–365.

and presupposed *knowing that* certain propositions are true—means that communicability and validity are merely two sides of the very same coin.

A judgment is thus a hypothesis about what its own intellectual presuppositions entail. It asks a question of those conceptual and theoretical materials that control its own intelligibility. It is in dialogue with these materials, and the criterion of its validity is simply whether or not a successful, meaningful interchange has in fact taken place. If you claim that P is a case of U, then this is to propose that it makes sense to say that P is a case of U, at least in light of the larger structures of meaning out of which that claim emerges. Such a determination is at once a matter of validity and intelligibility. It ultimately occurs when an individual communicates—either actually or prospectively—with other individuals whose thinking depends equally on those same structures of meaning. Indeed, we may take this a step further. Communication among individuals is, in effect, nothing other than the active manifestation of a universe of discourse communicating with itself, examining through the words of those individuals its own implications, and determining thereby which claims about the world it can and cannot accept as valid.

For this reason, particular judgments, though always primarily second-order (i.e., hypotheses about intelligible agreement internal to a structure of meaning) are also necessarily, though indirectly, first-order judgments, since they purport to state valid propositions about the world. The fact that validity is a function of intelligibility should not obscure the fact that in making a claim about someone else's claim, I am in effect offering a hypothesis about how the world itself can be intelligible to us, how it can make sense, and hence how it must be interpreted. This feature of our concept of judgment, the intercalation of meaningfulness and knowledge, is, I believe, characteristic of all coherence theories of truth.

The argument suggests that the concept of judgment that we have been describing, including especially our emphasis on its second-order character, is not simply an artifact of the linguistic example ("Hey, how about those Mets?") with which we began. It holds for even the most basic of empirical judgments. When I judge that the leaf is green, I am invoking that established world of concepts that allows me to think meaningfully and reflectively about leaves and colors. That world is, of course, independent of me and is, as such, a world that I share with (say) you. In this sense, my judgment is primarily a claim about your judgment. For I am saying that in light of our shared intuitions regarding this leafy object before us, and our shared understandings of concepts such as leaf and green, *you* will conclude that the leaf is green. To be sure, such judgments are often made outside of any conventional conversational setting. Walking alone in the forest, I can still judge that the leaf is green. But in such a circumstance, I am really engaging in an imaginary—or, perhaps, prospective—conversation with someone else. By formulating the judgment as a judgment, by invoking socially embedded concepts and communally generated criteria, I am necessarily participating in a dialogue with one or more interlocutors who, for purely contingent reasons, happen to be absent. If this were not so, if I were alone in a rather more thoroughgoing sense, then there would be neither the need nor the ability to make a judgment, that is, to predicate universals of particulars. I would see green leaves, but I would not judge them. I would simply observe them, like an animal.[33]

In this sense, all judgment, in virtue of its second-order character, is by definition dialogic. In aesthetics, the critic seeks to interpret and judge not so much the work of art itself but the judgments of other individuals—including those of the artist—who would engage and seek to understand it. If the critic pronounces the work beautiful, then this is really to claim that *we* judge it to be beautiful, whether we self-consciously know it or not. If we do not yet believe it to be so, then we should join the critic in a dialogical process of rational reconstruction by reading, for example, his or her criticism, the purpose of which would be to help us discover or "recollect" our own true beliefs. Similarly, the jurist who decrees that an act was lawful is telling us that in light of our shared insight into certain acts and certain laws—in light of our common sense—*we* judge the act lawful; the jurist is merely the self-conscious and duly appointed vehicle for rendering a communal judgment. Or again, the statesman who decides that a particular policy is prudent is, in effect, claiming to articulate the collective, albeit tacit, wisdom of the community and is therefore making clear to us what are our own best judgments.

Even scientific judgment operates in this manner. Twentieth-century philosophers of science have convinced us that science is importantly a social/institutional enterprise. The investigation of nature

33. For a related discussion, see Richard Rorty, *Philosophy and the Mirror of Nature*, pp. 182–92.

is based on theories, concepts, and methods that are generated through processes of meaningful social interaction which are, in turn, institutionally situated and mediated. As we have seen in Chapter 3, a crucial implication of this is that the key relationship in science is not between scientist and object but between scientist and scientist. Scientists argue with one another, not with discrete physical objects, and this arguing—involving experimentation and replication, the presentation of findings and their critical reception—is the core of the scientific method. None of this suggests that science, or any other realm of judgment, is necessarily a radically relativistic endeavor. Our account of judgment is entirely compatible with the belief that sense perceptions are real, that observations have a certain indubitability, that at some level the data do not lie. It does suggest, though, that the interpretation of data presupposes a repertoire of concepts that are not entirely reducible to, and hence are importantly independent of, our brute sensations. It is with the scientist as with judges in general: sensations establish a perhaps stable and reliable substrate that nonetheless cannot truly be perceived and experienced without a structure of meaningful preunderstandings, which provide, in turn, the basis for judgment and dialogue. This account insists on the centrality of context, but is nonetheless entirely indifferent as to whether or not the process of judgment itself is cumulative and progressive.

In all cases, of course, those who are judged—the artist and the audience, the defendant and the legal community, the researcher, the legislator, the citizen—have a right and an obligation to judge in return. We must judge the judgments of the critic, the jurist, the scientist, the statesman. Immediate intuitions are tested vis-à-vis one another, and this requires uncovering and assessing systematically their underlying and prospective structures of inference. We must seek to reconstruct and evaluate insight, to participate, that is, in a potentially ceaseless process of perception and clarification, assertion and critique, the upshot of which, though inevitably provisional, is always of central importance to the conduct of human affairs.

VII

From this account we derive yet a further conclusion: Judgment *qua* dialogue occurs in two stages, or on two levels. At the first level, insight engages insight, *nous* encounters *nous*. Dialogue proceeds through the interplay of immediate, unreconstructed intuitions and does not invoke explicit and articulated inferences. Judgment at this level has the character of a *conversation*. At the second level, insight is given an explicitly rational form. Intuitions are reconstituted as inferential arguments, subject now to the rules and principles that distinguish valid inferences from invalid ones. Judgment at this level has the character of a *demonstration*.

Since judgment, as a species of intelligent performance, is a dialogic or communicative endeavor, its character can be ascertained by considering in more detail the distinction between conversation and demonstration, specifically by examining that distinction in the light of other schemes with which it shares some superficial similarities. We already understand well enough the concept of demonstration, insofar as it is embodied in the principles and exigencies of the tripartite model. What we need is a clearer account of conversation, and of its precise relationship to demonstration:

In Chapter 1, we discussed a particularly influential notion of conversation. According to Oakeshott, a conversation is "an unrehearsed intellectual adventure."[34] It is, as such, a model of noninferential thinking. For conversations do not proceed according to systematic methodological protocols. They are at once more playful and less rigorous:

> Thoughts of different species take wing and play round one another, responding to each other's movements and provoking one another to fresh exertions. Nobody asks where they have come from or on what authority they are present; nobody cares what will become of them when they have played their part. There is no symposiarch or arbiter; not even a doorkeeper to examine credentials. Every entrant is taken at its face-value and everything is permitted which can get itself accepted into the flow of speculation.[35]

Conversation is thus an improvisational art, a spontaneous activity in which participants—or, rather, their ideas—swirl among and about one another in a kind of civilized dance, seemingly random and unpredictable, yet at the same time decorous and restrained. To be a conversationalist is to be a kind of poet, someone attuned to and preoccupied

34. Michael Oakeshott, "The Voice of Poetry in the Conversation of Mankind," in *Rationalism in Politics* (London: Methuen, 1962), p. 198.
35. Ibid.

with ambiguity and nuance, hence uninterested in the hard distinctions and fixed protocols characteristic of inferential thought. Indeed, the voice of poetry itself is "preeminently conversable." Oakeshott juxtaposes this idea of conversation to what he calls "argumentative discourse," wherein participants engage jointly in systematic "inquiry" aimed at proving the truth of specified propositions.

By way of contrast, the contemporary theory of communicative action approaches such matters in a quite different way. There is the terminological fact that the word "conversation" (*Konversation*) in this theory is not differentiated from but is nearly synonymous with "argumentative discourse." Inquiries aimed at reaching mutual agreement regarding the truth of propositions about the world are called "conversations," and "argumentation is perhaps the most important special case of conversation."[36] In one sense, the disagreement with Oakeshott is *merely* terminological, since Oakeshott's notion of argumentative discourse, though adumbrated only in the most sketchy terms, is conceptually quite similar to what Habermas variously calls "argument," "praxis of inquiry," or "theoretical discourse," all of which are ultimately subsumed under the category of "conversation." But in fact, the theoretical differences go rather deeper in at least two respects.

First, Oakeshott's precise notion of conversation—a rarefied intellectual exchange composed of distinct and identifiable "voices"— seems to have no equivalent in the theory of communicative action. For Oakeshott, the voices of practice and science, politics and poetry, employ fundamentally different idioms. They speak in different dialects and with different accents; their encounter thus requires of them some effort at mutual translation, an effort that draws each out of its own special domain and into an open and uncharted field of interchange where it can freely explore, contemplate, and ultimately delight in the peculiar inflections of its interlocutors. As a sociological matter, conversation so defined is a rather rare occurrence, and this may help to explain why such a notion is largely missing from the theory of communicative action. Its importance for Oakeshott can hardly be overstated, since in his view it describes nothing less than "the appropriate image of human intercourse." But for Habermas, it does no such thing. For him, the appropriate image of human intercourse is embodied, rather, in an "ideal speech situation." This situa-

---

36. Jürgen Habermas, *Theorie des kommunikativen Handelns* (Frankfurt: Suhrkamp Verlag, 1981), vol. 1, pp. 435–440.

tion shares with Oakeshott's conversation a certain freedom of exchange and openness to a diversity of perspectives. But it differs pointedly in being an enterprise concerned above all with justifying propositions about the world. According to Oakeshott, the participants in a conversation are "not engaged in an inquiry or a debate; there is no 'truth' to be discovered, no proposition to be proved, no conclusion sought. They are not concerned to inform, to persuade, or to refute one another."[37] Yet these are precisely the aims and activities characteristic of individuals who find themselves in Habermas's ideal speech situation.

Second, the notion of conversation in the theory of communicative action is itself embedded in theoretical distinctions quite different from those that we find in Oakeshott. As a species of "communicative action," conversation is oriented to "reaching understanding" and is to be sharply distinguished from all forms of "strategic action," which are, by definition, oriented to "success."[38] This distinction—understanding versus success—does not jibe well with Oakeshott's metaphysics, according to which communicability and success are, in various ways, equally characteristic of all manners of thought. Poetry yields delight; science, coherence; and practice, accommodation. These are varieties of success, and each depends upon and is bound up with the possibility of communication and mutual understanding. Moreover, within Habermas's category of communicative action, conversation as argument or discourse is understood to be a "reflexive" form of communication in contradistinction to the "naive" forms of everyday communicative behavior. Discursive conversation is systematic inquiry into the validity of truth claims, while naive interaction is something far less substantial.[39] The implication is that "it is via discourse or argument rather than through everyday 'naive' forms that parties to communicative action operate reflectively."[40] For Oakeshott, on the other hand, the voices of conversation are heard in everyday interaction as well as in more refined venues. They define the parameters of a cul-

37. Oakeshott, "The Voice of Poetry in the Conversation of Mankind," p. 198.

38. Habermas, *Theorie des kommunikativen Handelns*, vol. 1, pp. 377–397 and 440–452.

39. Ibid., vol. 2, p. 114–115.

40. James Johnson, "Habermas on Strategic and Communicative Action," *Political Theory* 19 (May 1991), p. 186.

ture, whether highfalutin or otherwise. Indeed, Oakeshott is, as a rule, rarely so impressed by the differences between the ordinary and the exceptional.[41]

Habermas describes two other kinds of communicative activity: "normatively regulated action," which aims to achieve consensus regarding ethical principles, and "dramaturgical action," in which an individual "reveals to a public an experience to which he has privileged access."[42] These might be thought to correspond, respectively, to Oakeshott's practical and poetical voices. In fact, any such claim would be superficial and misleading. For Oakeshott, the practical voice is the voice of desire; it speaks a Hobbesian language and seeks not so much principles of ethics as convenient and tangible structures of accommodation. In contrast, "normatively regulated action," as described by Habermas, is oriented to reaching principled and universalizable agreement about the kinds of behavior that should be considered morally upright; it contemplates an ongoing commitment to rational and abstract ethical discourse. In this sense, Hobbes and Kant, and their twentieth-century heirs, do not simply present alternative ethical theories but deeply discrepant understandings of what it means to regulate human conduct; hence, they present fundamentally different notions about the nature and purpose of ethical inquiry itself. Similarly, Oakeshott's poetical voice is a voice of pure contemplation and intellectual delight, utterly devoid of ulterior purpose, perfectly disinterested, and dedicated only to the consideration of images that are valued simply and solely on their own account, whereas dramaturgical action, as conceived by Habermas, is rooted in the most primitive and tangible of human interests, namely, the desire of the ego to articulate and

41. This may seem somewhat suprising in light of Oakeshott's political views, and he is hardly insensitive to the special claims of exceptional ability and genius. But his brand of conservatism emphasizes, in part, the continuity of traditions that resonate through the entire life of a culture. Not everyone employs the voices of conversation with equal depth and skill, but one hears those voices—even the poetical—in the most unlikely of settings. They comprise the intellectual infrastructure of a culture. On the other hand, the actual active engagement of those voices with one another—conversation, properly understood—is unfortunately an all-too-rare occurrence.

42. Habermas, *Theorie des kommunikativen Handelns*, vol. 1, p. 436.

impress upon others its own individuality and subjectivity as manifested in needs, wants, hopes, and the like.[43]

In trying to make some sense of these various notions, Dallmayr proposes a rather different formulation.[44] "Conversation" is to be understood as the "broadest or most ample type of communication" in which individuals seek "to achieve mutual understanding . . . relative to respective horizons of experience and subject matters of joint concern." Dallmayr indicates that this idea is synonymous (or nearly so) with Gadamer's theory of linguistic interchange, Oakeshott's idea of conversation, Oakeshott's idea of practical language, and Rorty's notion of "ordinary hermeneutics." Since these are four substantially different things—hardly synonymous with one another—it is not at all clear that the discussion can move us in the right direction. More helpfully, Dallmayr distinguishes conversation from three other communicative modes: (1) "discourse," used in Habermas's sense to refer to systematic rational inquiry into propositions about the world; (2) "everyday talk" (or "chatter"), roughly equivalent to what Habermas calls "naive conversation"; and (3) "poetry," explicitly understood not in Habermas's sense of dramaturgical action but in terms of "a heightened openness to strangeness and unfamiliarity" which, Dallmayr claims, is the essence of Oakeshott's poetic voice. This typology appears to take no specific account of expressive or dramaturgical communication, political or prudential interaction (as in Oakeshott's voice of practice), or inquiry aimed at establishing ethical principles (what Habermas calls "normatively regulated action"). It does suggest a plausible way of integrating and making coherent certain otherwise quite disparate theoretical materials, but it also runs the risk of ignoring or obscuring the very different aims of Oakeshott and Habermas and undermining the intellectual richness that such a difference implies.

To these discussions of conversation one might add several others, notably Gadamer's account of the "I-Thou" character of communica-

43. If Oakeshott's ethics are, in the broadest sense, Hobbesian, and Habermas's Kantian, then one might almost suggest that in aesthetics it's just the reverse. Upon reflection, the reader may find this suggestion rather less bizarre than it initially appears to be.

44. Fred R. Dallmayr, *Polis and Praxis: Exercises in Contemporary Political Theory* (Cambridge: MIT Press, 1984), pp. 214–217.

tion, Arendt's treatment of logical reasoning, cognition, and thinking, Rorty's appropriation of the Kuhnian distinction between normal inquiry and abnormal discourse, and Dworkin's analysis of "conversational" and "constructive" interpretation.[45] Again, we must beware of treating such discussions as merely alternative and rival accounts of the same phenomena, and of overlooking thereby the sense in which they may be dealing with entirely different and unrelated realms of meaningful interaction. But however this may be, and at the risk of being equally procrustean, I believe that they all suffer from a similar and by now familiar defect. For each merely recapitulates, in one form or another, what we have called the dichotomy of judgment. As a result, each fails to see that this dichotomy presents a false opposition, turning a useful analytic distinction into an incoherent contradiction and failing thereby to understand the fundamental and concrete integrity of judgment itself.

Systematic rational inquiry aimed at demonstrating inferentially the truth of propositions about the world represents a kind of touchstone for every account of conversation, though different authors employ it in quite different ways. For Oakeshott, as we have seen, such inquiry—"argumentative discourse"—is precisely what conversation is not. Not only does the multivocal conversation of mankind generally abjure systematic argument,[46] but the individual voices themselves proceed in a largely noninferential manner. Even the voice of science emerges "not as an array of marvellous discoveries, nor as a settled doctrine about the world, but as a universe of discourse, a way of imagining and moving about among images."[47] Similarly, for Gadamer, systematic inferential thinking invokes "method" in the narrowest and most pejorative sense; as such, it either foolishly ignores or willfully undermines the interpretive attitude out of which alone true understanding emerges. Arendt juxtaposes the freedom and openness of thinking to the deadening rigidity and slavishness of logical reasoning and cognition, while Rorty views abnormal discourse, rather than normal inferential inquiry, as an appropriate model for

45. Ronald Dworkin, *Law's Empire* (Cambridge: Harvard University Press, 1986), pp. 49–53.

46. Although, as Oakeshott notes, any conversation may contain argumentative passages.

47. Oakeshott, "The Voice of Poetry in the Conversation of Mankind," p. 213.

meaningful communication and edification. Such theorists insist on the opposition and incompatibility between inferential and noninferential thought—between, roughly, Platonic *technē* and Aristotelian *phronēsis*—and, faced with the either-or implicit in such a distinction, choose the latter.

Habermas accepts the same opposition, but makes a different choice. He regards rational discourse as the model for conversation, and contrasts it to the unsystematic, noninferential, and hence irrational character of naive communication. In ordinary, everyday interchange, propositions are offered and acknowledged immediately, without argument; hence, they are not subject to rational scrutiny. As a result, such interchange is peculiarly susceptible to distortions rooted in the particular interests and ideologies of interlocutors and exacerbated by the unequal distribution of social and communicative resources. Habermas thus insists on "a sharp conceptual distinction between everyday exchanges and rational-discursive communication."[48] The immediate, intuitive nature of ordinary give-and-take is no virtue. Indeed, it poses a substantial danger, and this prompts Habermas to contemplate an ideal speech situation in which putatively rational inferences are adduced, specified, and systematically evaluated.

In devaluing everyday discussion, Habermas (somewhat surprisingly) echoes a position argued most strenuously by Heidegger. According to Heidegger, much of everyday communication is a matter of "idle talk" (*Gerede*), and while he claims not to be using this term in a disparaging sense, his account is hardly an admiring one.[49] Idle talk is a kind of groundless gossip that tends to take on a life of its own, separate from and unconcerned with the "entities" that it purports to be treating. It acquires "an authoritative character" despite the fact that it is saying nothing of consequence and certainly nothing that is true. In so doing, it substitutes a false understanding for genuine knowledge, cutting us off from the things in which we are really interested; it thereby "discourages any new inquiry and any disputation, and in a peculiar way suppresses them and holds them back."

48. Dallmayr, *Polis and Praxis,* p. 241.

49. Heidegger, *Sein und Zeit,* 35. (Dallmayr prefers to translate *Gerede* as "chatter.") The fact that idle talk, as a feature of "fallenness," is an unavoidable and even constitutive element of "Being-in-the-world" does give it a certain ontological significance, but this does not change the pejorative tenor of Heidegger's treatment of it or its ambiguous relationship to authenticity.

Against these various positions, our argument—culminating in a distinction between *conversation* and *demonstration* as constituent features of judgment *qua* dialogue—at once preserves and annuls the dichotomy of judgment, ultimately dissolving its apparent oppositions and disclosing, thereby, the underlying and fundamental coherence of the concept of judgment.

Consider the following brief fictional exchange, which might have been overheard in a lounge at the 1952 convention of the American Political Science Association. The interlocutors, let us suppose, are sitting comfortably at a small table, sipping aperitifs:

A: "I do believe that the Democrats have a good chance. Stevenson is a brilliant orator."

B: "He's an intellectual—an egg-head—running against a hero."

A: "He's from Illinois. The heartland decides elections in this country."

B: "Yeah, Ike's really a far-out Eastern liberal. Anyway, a hole in your shoe isn't going to make you the darling of middle America."

A: "Democrats are the majority party."

B: "Majority parties always win? Dewey almost won, and should have."

There are many ways of construing such an exchange, depending in part on its precise circumstances and the nature of the interlocutors. If we assume that it involved two well-informed political scientists who also happened to be personal friends, then we may plausibly conclude that it was a most casual and even desultory discussion, engaged in not for some explicit didactic or forensic purpose but simply to pass the time in a not unpleasant way. It is an example of "idle talk" or "chatter," an excerpt from what we would normally and, I think, quite correctly call a "conversation."[50] As such, it has several notable and characteristic features.

---

50. In the light of ordinary language, Oakeshott's use of the word "conversation," and Habermas's use of *Konversation,* are surely, and not accidentally, eccentric. Some readers may doubt that an exchange about electoral politics between two college professors could be an example of everyday chitchat. But I believe that one could simply substitute for this example an infinite number of conversations having a perhaps more homely content but otherwise identical properties. Consider the following:

A: "I do believe that Jenny will pick John over Jeff. He's so good looking."

B: "An insurance salesman can't compete with a doctor."

To begin with, it is replete with Gricean implicatures. The most obvious example is "Yeah, Ike's really a far-out Eastern liberal," a clear case of flouting. But nearly every response has an intended meaning other than, or in addition to, its literal meaning. "He's an intellectual" suggests that the Democrats will lose. "A hole in your shoe" refers, without actually saying so, to a specific campaign incident that occurred in Pontiac, Michigan. "Majority parties always win?" indicates that majority parties do not always win. Generally, then, the responses, taken literally, do not follow one another in a strictly logical manner.

Moreover, the success of the conversation involves no self-conscious and systematic effort at drawing inferences. Utterances are immediately and unreflectively uttered and understood. Responses are offered, and comprehended, without making explicit linguistic connections or explanations. Nobody says "but," or "I disagree," or "on the other hand." Transitions are almost entirely tacit, yet it is quite clear who thinks what.

It also seems highly unlikely that the exchange involves any transfer of new information. When *A* says that Stevenson is "from Illinois," it is virtually certain that *B* already knows this fact (as well as its general significance), already knows that *A* knows it, and knows that *A* already believes both that *B* already knows it and that *B* believes that *A* already knows it. This is plausibly true of every fact mentioned in the excerpt; both interlocutors know perfectly well that everything said is new to neither of them. Yet they persist in saying those things, and do so without a hint of embarrassment or strangeness. One clear implication is that neither of the interlocutors is trying primarily to persuade the other about the upcoming election by presenting some new and decisive piece of information. Indeed, despite the fact that they disagree, it is equally unlikely that they are trying primarily to persuade each other through the force of rhetoric; for this is, at best, light banter or benign chitchat, perhaps rather languid, perhaps not, but hardly a

---

A: "John goes to church. She's very religious."

B: "Yeah, Jeff's really a far-out atheist. Anyway, hanging a cross around your neck doesn't make you a saint."

A: "Jenny's parents are crazy about John."

B: "Kids always do what their parents want? Barbara almost married Walt, and should have.".

Everything that will be said about our Eisenhower-Stevenson example would apply equally to this one.

matter of passionate intellectual debate.[51] We would not want to dignify it with the phrase "conversation of mankind," nor is it a serious effort at generating "empirical theoretical knowledge of the world." Nonetheless, I believe that it can serve us quite well as a model of conversation in at least the following respects.

1. The conversation is a dialogue between individuals trying to understand each other. They are successful because they *know how* to do this, and this means that they are able to employ a certain faculty of insight that provides each with an immediate, intuitive understanding of various utterances.

2. Each such faculty is embedded in and informed by a set of implicit preunderstandings. The preunderstandings of *A* are necessarily different from but overlap those of *B*. They are different because *A* and *B* are distinct individuals whose experiences, or "effective histories," are necessarily different. This is what makes the faculty of insight and interpretation necessary. But their preunderstandings also overlap, for if they did not—if their horizons were utterly discrepant and incommensurable—then no conversation between *A* and *B* could take place. This is what makes insight and interpretation possible. The relationship between those horizons is different from that between my horizon and Plato's, or between my horizon and an Azande's, but these are merely differences of degree. The amount of overlap may be greater or smaller, depending on the amount of cultural and historical distance; hence, achieving mutual understanding may be easy and expeditious or difficult and laborious. But interpretation always involves at least some distance to be bridged, and also some solid points of contact on the basis of which bridges may be built.

3. Since *A* and *B* are not trying primarily to persuade one another or to exchange new information, we are inclined to wonder about the purpose of such a conversation. Of course, there are many possibilities. *A* and *B* may simply be trying to while away the time, or they may be attempting somehow to impress one another in order to obtain some extrinsic goal, or they may be hiding out in the lounge in order to avoid running into *C*. But all of these purposes—which are not mutually contradictory—could be equally well accomplished in many other ways and hence do not explain the peculiar and distinctive function of the conversation itself.

51. In many conversations there is no such disagreement, and it is therefore even less likely that persuasion would be a primary conversational goal.

It seems to me that only one explanation is really plausible. This casual conversation, in which the interlocutors are knowingly telling each other things that they already know, functions essentially to make further conversations possible. *A* and *B* are reminding each other of the information that they share and also, less explicitly, of their shared conceptual and theoretical premises. They are putting on the table for their mutual inspection and admiration some of those elements that allow them to be interlocutors. They are like the stamp collector who takes his collection out of its drawer and pores over it at his leisure, not to find anything new but simply to admire and enjoy, and to refresh his memory. Their relationship depends on the fact that their horizons, however discrepant, are overlapping, and they feel the need—as we all do from time to time—to reawaken and perhaps reconfirm this sense of mutual connectedness. When *A* says "He's from Illinois," something like the following is, in effect, being communicated: "We both know that Stevenson is from Illinois, but I just wanted to remind each of us that we share this bit of information (and almost certainly a mountain of related information) along with an elaborate if unstated conceptual and theoretical scheme that makes such information meaningful and pertinent to us, so that we may be confident that we can continue to have sensible conversations despite the fact that we haven't seen each other in six months and that, in part as a consequence of this, our experiences have not been identical."

Conversation is thus pursued for its own sake, its own perpetuation. The primary purpose is not to exchange new information or to persuade, nor is it to achieve any other external goal. It is with conversation as with genuine friendship: once the motivation becomes ulterior, the activity loses its defining character. Despite their great differences, Oakeshott and Arendt explicitly agree on this: Conversation as a form of thinking "is not an enterprise designed to yield an extrinsic profit."[52] Moreover, they agree that since conversation is essentially a matter of meaningful interaction, its primary focus is meaning itself— "to reestablish or nurture a tissue of meaning on the basis of which disparate persons can conduct with one another a coherent intellectual life."[53] In conversation, the intellectual foundations of conversation

52. Oakeshott, "The Voice of Poetry in the Conversation of Mankind," p. 198. See Hannah Arendt, *The Life of the Mind* (New York: Harcourt Brace Jovanovich, 1978), vol. 1, p. 64.

53. Peter J. Steinberger, "Hannah Arendt on Judgment," *American Journal of Political Science* 34 (August 1990), p. 812. See also Oakeshott, "The Voice

itself are put through their paces—exercised, reawakened, reinvigorated.

But to these various features of conversation—noninferentiality, embeddedness, nonulteriority, an orientation to meaning—we must add several others without which our conversation would be incomprehensible, at least as a case of intelligent performance.

4. Each of the interlocutors, A and B, must be capable of rationally reconstructing their exchange. This means that they must have the ability to articulate the tacit *knowing that* upon which they comprehend one another's utterance. When B says, "Yeah, Ike's really a far-out Eastern liberal," each must be prepared to present explicit grounds for believing that Ike is not a far-out Eastern liberal and that both are well aware that they know this. This might involve any number of facts: Ike is a nickname for Dwight David Eisenhower, he was born and bred in Kansas and later made his home in Western Pennsylvania, his express political views were moderately conservative, A is not a numbskull, is well versed in twentieth-century American history, does not suffer from amnesia, and the like. From the complete set of such facts, one could infer—rationally, perhaps even deductively—that "Yeah, Ike's really a far-out Eastern liberal" is an example of Gricean flouting and really means something like the following: "Dwight Eisenhower is a midwestern conservative who appeals to the heartland at least as much as Adlai Stevenson."

The conversation as it actually occurs is, thus, a structure of enthymemes. The *process* whereby each interlocutor judges the other's meaning is noninferential; there is no need to articulate suppressed premises. But the *logic* of the conversation, and of the judgments contained therein, absolutely requires that those premises be articulated and their entailments specified, at least prospectively.

5. This suggests, then, that each and every conversational move is eligible for critical evaluation. When B says "Yeah, Ike's really a far-out liberal," the sense of this presupposes agreement on two premises: Ike is not far-out Eastern liberal, and A and B both know that both of them know this. If either of these premises turns out to be controversial, then the meaning of "Yeah, Ike's really a far-out liberal" is up for grabs, and to the degree that the meaning of utterances is up for grabs, conversation becomes increasingly difficult. If A does not really

---

of Poetry in the Conversation of Mankind," p. 198, and Arendt, *Life of the Mind*, vol. 1, pp. 59–65.

know *B* that well, he might conclude that *B* is quite serious about Ike being a far-out liberal and is simply ignorant. Similarly, it might be *A* who is ignorant about Ike's geographical roots, in which case the utterance would be taken seriously for other reasons. In either circumstance, both *A* and *B* would be speaking on the basis of false inferences; they would fail truly to understand one another; their conversation would be a comedy of errors.

6. In an important sense, then, this conversation—and every other conversation—is oriented to truth. We have just said that conversation apparently focuses on meaning rather than truth. But we have also seen the intimate connection between meaning and validity. The importance of this connection should now be apparent. In conversing for the sake of conversing, interlocutors inevitably make reference to those shared truths on the basis of which their conversation is hypothetically possible. But the very fact that truths have been referred to means, at least in principle, that they are now available for inspection and assessment. To have a conversation, then, is necessarily to raise the question of what is true. Moreover, the answer to this question is, in an important sense, to be found precisely in conversation itself. For if the success of a conversation depends upon shared truths, then a truth can be taken as established to the degree that conversation successfully occurs. Our ability to understand one another and nod our heads jointly means that we agree about certain truths, so that we find certain statements to be valid and others not.

Of course, conversation does not presuppose that we agree about everything. In the example given, *A* and *B* disagree strongly about who will win the election; more generally, we can surely agree to disagree. But disagreements may in fact limit greatly the scope and nature of the conversation and may ultimately undermine it altogether. Imagine that at some point in our example *B* says to *A*: "You're mistaken, Stevenson is from Louisiana." Absent a handy reference book, *A* and *B* are now unable meaningfully to discuss an entire range of questions that depend on knowing where Stevenson is from—the regional implications of the election, Stevenson's past political record, the character of his natural constituency, and the like. It seems, to be sure, that the solution to this problem is to be found not in conversation itself but precisely in a handy reference; we should simply look it up. Even here, though, the testimony of the conversation is decisive. For imagine that our interlocutors find a political almanac and discover that Stevenson is indeed from Illinois. This would provide a basis for agreement and successful conversation if and only if both of them understand what a political almanac is and agree that there are overwhelming reasons to consider such a document authoritative. An individual who believes that Stevenson is from Louisiana might as easily believe that a political almanac is a random compilation of assertions, some of which are true, some not, or that it is the deceitful result of a conspiracy designed to hide the truth, or that it is written in code and needs to be deciphered by those who know the secret formula. Such an individual B might be able intelligibly to discuss many things with A—the weather, the virtues of *boeuf à la mode*, the fate of the Mets—but there are certain things about which they could not make mutual sense. I advert once again to the distinction, suggested earlier with respect to Wittgenstein, between claims that are incorrect and those that are unintelligible. Disagreement may involve an incorrect claim, in which case the criteria of corrigibility are internal to and provided by the conversation itself, or it may involve an unintelligible claim, in which case conversation essentially dies. In any event, the validity of conversational utterances is itself determined by and is a measure of the degree to which those utterances express shared truths.

Now it will be argued that the exigencies of conversation can hardly be the whole story. After all, Stevenson *was* from Illinois. If two interlocutors were to conclude otherwise, and this were to form the basis for a successful conversation between them, then that would certainly not make it right; indeed, one would have to wonder about just how "successful" such a conversation could be. Again, though, the objection confuses that which is incorrect with that which is unintelligible. If for some reason our conversationalists decide that Stevenson was from Louisiana, then they are simply saying something incorrect. Of course, this error is likely to lead to further errors in their conversation, errors that they share, but all of these could be easily enough corrected if some third or nth party (another political scientist, the author of an almanac, etc.) were to join the discussion. All such conversation, however, would presuppose an enormous, nearly infinite array of tacit agreements pertaining to, among other things, the identity of Illinois and Louisiana, the very nature of a state boundary, the role of the states in the federal system, the character of constituencies, the problem of state political culture, and the like. One can imagine interlocutors who knew literally nothing about all of this, who believed that location was important only in terms of climate and who decided, therefore, that Stevenson would win, or lose, simply because he came from a comparatively cold part of the world. For such individuals, the question of Illinois or Louisiana might be so alien as to be unintelligible. The question of its truth, therefore, would never even arise.

A crucial consequence of our analysis is that the sharp distinction between communication oriented to understanding and communication oriented to truth is untenable. Understanding and truth are inextricably bound together in conversational contexts; to the degree that one is at stake, the other is also necessarily implicated. It may be that conversation is pursued for its own sake, that is, to perpetuate the possibility of conversation itself. But this in no way denies the possibility that conversation is dependent on claims about what is true, claims that are, in principle, testable precisely to the degree that they permit successful communication. It may be that conversation occurs immediately, that understandings are shared intuitively and without recourse to explicitly drawn inferences. But this in no way denies that such communication presupposes an underlying *knowing that* certain propositions are true, a kind of knowledge that is always eligible for systematic analysis and reconstruction. It may be that conversation involves a kind of knack, a certain *"je ne sçay quoy"* that is learned through practice and habituation and that resembles and is perhaps a model for the peculiar kind of insight and skill characteristic of the *phronimos*. But this in no way denies that conversation is also a structure of enthymemes and that the logic of any conversation must always in principle be specifiable in terms that would satisfy a strict theoretician. In all of this, the fundamental and determinative fact is that assertions presuppose assertion conditions and that these in turn underwrite, at one and the same time, the successful exchange of meanings and the sharing of truth claims that such an exchange presupposes. A *conversation* is never simply that but is also, however implicitly and prospectively, a putative *demonstration* of truth.

I hypothesize that these conclusions pertain to all meaningful interchange. Consider the following example:

O-iodoanilides are easily introduced, stable precursors that permit the use of C-H bonds as precursors for radical formation adjacent to carbonyl groups in functionalized molecules. The intramolecular hydrogen-transfer reactions of these precursors are exceedingly rapid, and the resulting radicals can be used for standard radical addition and cyclization reactions. Finally, although removal is clearly a matter of concern, we have not yet extensively investigated the excision of the anilide auxiliary from the product. In two cases . . . , we successfully hydrolyzed the products to carboxylic acids under standard conditions (NaOH, THF/water, 100 degrees C, 12 h). In the long run, we believe that the design of modified *o*-iodoanilides will result in groups that are even easier to remove.[54]

This passage is not outwardly part of a conversation; it is excerpted from an article that appeared in a learned journal. It presents not an idle and desultory exchange between friends but a formal and technical summary of certain experimental results. Its original appearance was not (presumably) oral but written, and therefore its appearance here is rather closer to the original. The presentation is attendant to a systematic and specified process of fact gathering, and its conclusions are defended in terms of explicit and well-established processes of inference. In sum, one can hardly imagine an example of communication apparently more different from our previous one.

But in fact, I believe that the two are not so very different. The present passage, though not explicitly a conversation, is designed as a meaningful communication to be encountered by other individuals who will seek to understand it and who may very well have an opportunity to respond—perhaps by writing a critical comment for publication, perhaps in private correspondence, perhaps during a casual chat in the elevator at a professional meeting. We may be certain, moreover, that it is often read by individuals who understand its meaning immediately and intuitively, without having to make any explicit semantic or syntactic inferences. Such words and phrases as "*o*- iodoanilide" or "precursor" or "radical formation" are, for many of the article's interlocutors, apprehended in a flash. This, of course, presupposes further that such words and phrases are being used in accordance with assertion conditions that allow them to be intelligible in the first place and that reflect, in turn, a particular community of interpretation. A chemist who reads the article thus apprehends it much as *A* and *B* apprehend their mutual idle chatter about politics—automatically and unreflectively.

Obviously, our example also expresses, as did our previous one,

54. Dennis P. Curran, Ann C. Abraham, and Hongtao Liu, "Radical Translocation Reactions of *o*-Iodoanilides: The Use of Carbon-Hydrogen Bonds as Precursors of Radicals Adjacent to Carbonyl Groups," *Journal of Organic Chemistry* 56 (July 5, 1991), p. 4337.

certain truth claims that can be specified and examined critically. We may be inclined to say that this is more evident here than before. But if the processes of inference are, in the present case, perhaps more explicit, the passage is nonetheless still riddled with enthymemes or other inferential leaps that call for rational reconstruction. Indeed, the mere fact that I do not currently understand much of the passage, but could in time learn to understand it with the help of some chemistry lessons, shows that its authors and more experienced readers implicitly *know that* a vast storehouse of unstated propositions are true and could dredge up and exhibit those propositions if circumstances allowed. Like the first example, then, its communicative success is dependent upon assertion conditions in which communicability and validity are essentially and inextricably interwoven.

It is true that the passage in question seems to have a purpose quite different from that of our political conversation. Its apparent goal is certainly not to while away the time, nor is it to reawaken shared meanings and understandings on the basis of which further communication can occur. Its aim, evidently, is to transfer some information. Even here, though, differences between the two cases are more apparent than real, for one can easily imagine a pair of organic chemists discussing o-iodoanilides in casual conversation at a professional meeting, and doing so without believing that they are telling each other anything that they do not already know. One can also imagine that the authors of the article in question doubt that its findings will ever explicitly be examined or utilized by anyone else, and that its main purpose is not really to transfer information but to acknowledge and participate in a community of scholars, thereby helping to keep alive a tradition of inquiry and theoretical speculation out of which work of genuine consequence does sometimes emerge, however fitfully.

Our two cases of communication, despite outward differences, thus share some extremely important and fundamental characteristics. Each operates intuitively and immmediately, yet each also presupposes an underlying propositional structure—a structure of truth—involving inferences that can be rationally reconstructed. In each case, then, we need to distinguish the psychology of the act from its ontology. When we do this, we can see that each is, in fact, a conversation that, like all conversations, is bound up with—indeed, is part and parcel of—an implicit demonstration. Typologies that seek sharply to differentiate conversation from argument, idle talk from discourse, or meaning-oriented exchange from truth-oriented exchange fail to understand the deep unity of communicative action as a form of intelligent performance, of which intuition and inference are ever-present and ineliminable features.

VIII

If this analysis is correct, then the result is nothing less than the eradication of the dichotomy of judgment. As we have seen, judgment is dialogic—an intelligent process of communication, actual or prospective, about the relationship between universals and particulars. It is true that communicative acts, including judgments, differ in their shape and emphasis; their various outward appearances are obviously and self-evidently discrepant in many ways. But at base, they are fundamentally alike. Without exception they proceed noninferentially in terms of a certain *knowing how* to communicate, and they presuppose, at the same time, an elaborate structure of truth, a *knowing that* certain propositions about the world are true. In saying this, I deny the most important and constitutive premises upon which the dichotomy of judgment is based. But I also and simultaneously revitalize that dichotomy, now understood to describe not different varieties of communicative action but distinct yet inseparable features of all such action. The dichotomy reappears not as an opposition between discrete kinds of communication and judgment but as the depiction of an organic, internally differentiated whole characteristic of every communicative act. Casual conversations and scientific reports, art and art criticism, judicial decision making and political judgment all presuppose—as varieties of intelligent performance—faculties of insight and intuition that are bound up with principles of inference and proof, principles that reflect, in turn, established structures of truth and meaning on the basis of which any particular performance can be evaluated for coherence and intelligibility. It is in these terms, then, that I propose the complete and final sublation of the dichotomy of judgment.

The argument can be fruitfully restated in the light of certain distinctions suggested by Habermas. According to the theory of communicative action, different kinds of utterances "thematize" different kinds of validity claims. In the earliest important version of this theory (which I have somewhat modified), four such claims are specified: validity may be assessed in terms of comprehensibility, truth, sincerity, and appropriateness.[55] Certain utterances raise questions about syntax and semantics; we are unclear about what is being said, perhaps because we are not (fully) competent speakers of the language and/or because we are unfamiliar with certain words. Many questions of translation fall into this category. Other utterances thematize the issue of truth; we understand the meaning of a proposition, but we are unsure if it is true, and thus we are inclined to investigate the matter further by invoking an appropriate research protocol. Such a protocol might be as simple as turning around to see what is behind you or as complex as a full-fledged scientific study. Still other kinds of communication give rise to questions of sincerity: did the speaker speak truthfully, or was the utterance an act of dissembling, playful or otherwise? Problems of political rhetoric, ideology, and advertising often arise in this context, as do questions of judicial testimony. Finally, some utterances thematize the issue of appropriateness; certain statements that are perfectly acceptable in one circumstance are not acceptable in another. Such statements often call for judgments of taste, prudence, and moral rectitude.

Habermas's analysis is, in my view, extremely powerful, but it also runs the risk of overlooking an important feature of meaningful communication and judgment. For while different specific utterances often thematize only one or another of these validity claims, this is largely for contingent and accidental factors pertaining to the immediate, existential contexts of the utterance itself. In principle, and given the right circumstance, any utterance can be evaluated and criticized—and, ultimately, reconstructed—on the basis of all four types of validity.[56] A typology that categorizes utterances in terms of validity claims is likely to miss the underlying unity of all linguistic communication and hence to ignore the sense in which the dichotomy of judgment,

55. Jürgen Habermas, "Was Heisst Universalpragmatik?" in *Sprachpragmatik und Philosophie,* ed. Karl-Otto Apel (Frankfurt: Suhrkamp Verlag, 1982), pp. 175, 245–246.

56. For a broader criticism of Habermas's alleged separation of system and lifeworld, see Vicki Ash, "The Coupling of Lifeworld and System," xerox from the University of Colorado, 1991. The notion that all communicative actions could, in the appropriate circumstances, thematize any of the validity claims is, I am certain, well understood and accepted by Habermas himself. To my knowledge, though, he has not pursued this notion or its very important implications in any kind of systematic way.

properly understood, is annulled yet preserved in a more coherent and satisfying account of judgment itself.

For example, we may think that statements in a scientific journal generally raise only the question of truth and rarely thematize issues of comprehensibility, sincerity, and appropriateness. I think a little reflection will show this to be plainly false. Recent controversies about scientific fraud make it clear that the question of sincerity is very real indeed for the scientific community. Moreover, the fact that most readers of scientific journals can understand most articles only means that the linguistic conventions of science tend to be obeyed rather scrupulously, and when a nonscientist reads such an article, comprehensibility is thematized indeed. (If this were not so, then there would no "popular science" literature.) As to appropriateness, one may safely say that this issue tends to be decided at the editorial level; if we fail to find inappropriate articles in scientific journals, then this is almost certainly because legions of such articles have been weeded out at an early stage. An article appropriate for the *Journal of Organic Chemistry* is almost certainly unsuitable for *Scientific American* (or for *Time, Playboy, Mad, Reader's Digest,* etc.), and vice versa. We may safely suppose that such articles are submitted by authors and redirected by editors with great regularity. In principle, then, all scientific communications necessarily raise questions pertaining to all four validity claims. Sometimes these questions are more apparent and easily resolved than others, but in all cases a successful answer will depend upon, or amount to, a rational reconstruction of the *knowing that* upon which any such communication is based.

It is, I propose, the same with conversation in general. A casual discussion about Eisenhower and Stevenson plausibly raises questions of truth (well, was Stevenson from Illinois or wasn't he?) and comprehensibility (do we agree on what "Illinois" signifies?). Issues of sincerity are always lurking in the background ("Do you really think Stevenson can win, or are you just playing devil's advocate?"), as are problems of appropriateness ("There are two things, religion and politics, that even political scientists should not discuss, at least not over drinks"; or, even more simply, "Let's not talk shop.") The fact that such questions can be raised at any time suggests that the conversation must be always available, so to speak, for a rational reconstruction in terms of which we can discover suitable answers. Again, external circumstances will generally determine if and when a particular validity claim is thematized. If a visiting scholar from Bulgaria should join our political conversation, then the meaning of "Illinois" might very well become an issue; if, on the other hand, our interlocutors are joined by their five-year-old children, then the problem of appropriateness takes center stage. The point is that Habermas's validity claims are useful not in classifying different types of communication but in describing the kinds of issues, and the kinds of potential rational reconstructions, that are characteristic of each and every communicative act.

Judgment is thus the dialogical enterprise wherein universals are predicated of particulars. It is, as such, an intelligent performance that always proceeds through insight and intuition involving a certain *knowing how* to do something, but that also presupposes at the same time a capacity to reconstruct rational processes of inference involving a *knowing that* certain propositions are true. Insight and inference both emerge out of, and are shaped at every turn by, established structures of truth and meaning that provide criteria of intelligibility against which any judgment can be evaluated. The dialogue of judgment thus reflects assertion conditions which must be prior to and independent of judgment itself. These features pertain to all judgment, whether scientific or aesthetic, legal or literary, ethical or political. In this sense, judgment is of a piece.

In light of such a formulation, many of the difficulties and perplexities that we have encountered in earlier chapters simply dissolve. Plato's distinction between *technē* and *empeiria,* apparently so unsatisfying in its contradictory implications, can now be rehabilitated as a coherent and enlightening analysis of the two complementary sides of intelligent performance per se. The philosopher, though master of inference and rational judgment, unavoidably relies on insights that do not emerge out of, and may be irreducible to, structures of rational analysis, while the skilled rhetor, though undoubtedly an intuitive creature, can judge reliably only to the degree that rhetorical success admits of a rational accounting. The tangled knot of Aristotelian concepts, clustering around the central notion of *practical wisdom,* comes undone the moment we realize that *phronēsis* presupposes both a faculty of immediate, noninferential insight and a complementary virtue of *sophia* that allows its conclusions to be certified as intelligent. Determinate and reflective judgment do not characterize wholly different realms of human activity—the scientific and the aesthetic—but, rather, necessary and sufficient conditions for human cognition per se. The determinate judgment of the scientist presupposes certain reflective judgments about the nature of particular things, while the judgment of taste differs from mere appetite and inclination precisely because the judge is prepared rationally and systematically to defend the claim that this object is beautiful and that is not. In all such cases, the tripartite model is incorrect only because it purports to describe the whole of judgment; we jettison that model only at the risk of forfeiting entirely the very idea of intelligent performance.

Our account recognizes and warrants the intuition of those who insist on the *"je ne sçay quoy"* of judgment, those who—from Shaftesbury to Gadamer, from Kant to Anthony Lewis—refuse to reduce judgment to method, reject the intellectualist fallacy, and locate the source of good judgment in a certain insight, in an unfocusing of perception that allows for the free play of imagination, in the mental fog of meaningful deliberation or the heady boundlessness of poetic imagination, in a pot of black coffee and a sleepless night. But it undergirds this with an essential constitutive structure of rational inference. It insists on the intelligence of intelligent performance. It proposes, thereby, intellectual standards immanent in judgment itself, standards that are determinative of good judgment and that require of judgment, however formulated, that it acknowledge as authoritative the claims of reason.

Toward a Theory of Judgment in Politics

WHAT, THEN, of *political* judgment?

According to one school of thought, judgment in politics is a scientific endeavor, essentially homologous with judgment in natural science, ethical science, the science of human psychology, and the like. Principles of rational analysis and inference are as applicable to questions of politics as to any other. Politically relevant universals are predicated of particulars according intellectual protocols characteristic of rational judgment in general, as outlined by the tripartite model. There is, then, nothing very peculiar about political judgment as a mode of thought; it is distinguished only by its subject matter.

This view is shared by a diversity of theorists having sharply disparate notions of what rational knowledge involves. According to Plato, for example, the wisdom of the philosopher/king is rooted precisely in those qualities of abstraction or pure intellection that produce wisdom in general. The habits of mind that allow for an intelligent study of the heavens, mathematics, and the forms are of equal service regarding the affairs of the polis. Political knowledge is, therefore, simply a species of knowledge per se. It is true that the particulars of political life, as empirical things, cannot be known with the certainty of abstract entities. But Plato, in rejecting the doctrine of radical flux, must hold that they are relatively stable and accessible, for he believes that we can predicate universals of them with considerable reliability. Moreover, since all knowledge emerges from, and can be assessed in terms of, explicit and well-founded inferential procedures, this must be true of political knowledge as well. Thus, judgment in politics, like judgment in general, involves claims that are, at least in principle, capable of being demonstrated rationally.

Although Hobbes's view of how we can know and judge things could hardly be more different from Plato's, his account is similarly general in sweep, and associates the activity of the political actor and theorist with that of the natural scientist or mathematician. Wisdom in politics is, for Hobbes as for Plato, essentially of a piece with wisdom itself. It involves a scientific study of the nature of things, based on a materialist conception of the world, and relying on a systematic observation of physical bodies in motion. Such an account implies, further, that claims to political knowledge, like knowledge claims in general, must be justified according to standard methods of inference. Hobbes thus agrees with Plato, if only in this respect, that truth in politics is, like truth in physics and geometry, a truth of reason.

As we have seen, an alternative tradition postulates a deep discrepancy between the character of scientific knowledge and that of political judgment. Machiavelli's prince, Tocqueville's citizen, and Nietzsche's political genius all possess a special kind of insight into the affairs of the public realm that is not in any obvious way dependent on methods of rational inference and demonstration. To have this kind of insight is, roughly, to possess *phronēsis*. It is to be engaged in a process of reflective rather than determinate judgment, wherein political concepts—prudence, fairness, feasibility, constitutionality, and so on—are predicated of individual acts or outcomes without the benefit of rules or inferential methods, and hence without an opportunity for demonstration and justification. Such judgment does not rely on a rationally grounded and explicitly justified calculus or method. It is, rather, a pursuit of intimations, and this requires an adventure in free thinking—"the free play of the understanding and imagination"—uncoerced by the exigencies of logical or empirical fact and having as its goal not the discovery of some previously unknown truth but the elucidation of meaning.

It is a central thesis of this book that our concept of political judgment acknowledges and reflects both of these perspectives. Their mutual antipathies are, in fact, illusory. Rational/scientific and intuitive/noninferential theories merely elucidate different aspects of what is, properly understood, a single, concrete manner of thinking and acting. Taken separately, each proposes a useful but potentially misleading abstraction. Together, they describe the nature of political judgment in its fullness and depth.

The concept of political judgment is not merely an artificial and mechanical aggregate of these elements. The two sides of judgment— the intuitive and the inferential—are not tacked on to one another as a matter of convenience. Rather, they share a deep mutual dependence. This becomes apparent, I believe, only when each has been suitably reinterpreted and reformulated, a task to which the larger part of this book has been devoted. The peculiar kind of *insight* characteristic of political wisdom is shown to be bound up with an established structure of truth. It is a *knowing how* inextricably tied to a *knowing that,* an exercise of mind that makes sense only as part of a larger intelligent enterprise. The process of *justification* characteristic of political wisdom is shown to be a matter of *post festum* reconstruction. It relies importantly on conditions of intelligibility and is, as result, connected in essential ways to a faculty of common sense. Political judgment, as a concrete manner of thinking and acting, is constituted by the organic interdependence of these elements. It is a complex, inwardly differentiated, but entirely coherent and self-sustaining whole.

Judgment in politics, like all human judgment, does indeed presuppose a kind of vision or perception that defies systematic, rational accounting. To see that a policy is prudent, or that a particular situation calls for a particular kind of solution, or that a certain political arrangement violates our sense of what is fair or legal or practicable— all of this requires an irreducible faculty of insight roughly analogous to that with which we perceive that an apple is red, or that a cause necessarily precedes its effects, or that a proposition cannot be true and not true at the same time. This faculty is almost certain to be unequally distributed. As with our other faculties of perception, some people have it in high degree, some not. Admittedly, it can often be improved. Political judgment—like any other kind of judgment—can be nurtured and honed, largely through a curriculum of experience, expert guidance, and habituation. But just as some people have perfect pitch, while others are tone-deaf, so do some individuals have a certain knack for the practice of politics that others can never acquire.

If a skeptic asks how we can prove that such a faculty exists, the answer, of course, is that we cannot. Nor can we demonstrate that it is teachable or that it is unequally distributed in the way that we have described. We state here not iron-clad truths about the world, but simply necessary features of our concept of political judgment. If we believe that there is such a thing as good judgment in politics, then the availability of such a faculty, along with the various features that we have outlined, must be presupposed on pain of contradiction.

Our understanding presupposes, further, that political judgment, though importantly a matter of immediate insight, is not simply that. For it is also a species of intelligent performance. This means, first, that it is always and invariably embedded in and informed by an established structure of meaning or truth. Insight is never pure, but necessarily emerges out of a socially and historically generated set of prejudices or preunderstandings about the world. These preunderstandings transform mere sensation into experience, hence give perception a direction and a significance that unavoidably reflects the exigencies of a particular social order. The sense of political judgment is, thus, a common sense; and while the majority of people at a given time may violate its dictates, common sense nonetheless establishes indispensable criteria with which we can evaluate the coherence and legitimacy of particular thoughts and actions.

It is here that we find perhaps the key to our concept of political judgment. Any such judgment is, in principle, defeasible. It is available for critical scrutiny and may, upon inspection, turn out to be unsupportable. This characteristic is traceable directly to the fact that political judgments are always embedded in a fabric of widely accepted propositions about political life. A political judgment always and necessarily implies, however tacitly, that it is faithful to and coherent with a structure of truth. To judge is inevitably to propose the hypothesis that the judgment itself best reflects that truth, whatever it may be. This fact confers upon the practitioner of politics both an opportunity and an obligation to test the hypothesis, to articulate, as well as possible, the relevant structure of political truth and determine to what extent it actually entails, or is even consistent with, the judgment at hand. By situating political judgment within a nexus of established political practices and understandings, we show it to be a species of intelligent performance. It depends on its contexts for its justification, and it requires of its author the capacity to reconstruct it rationally by demonstrating exactly how it vindicates those contexts.

Specifically, the author of a political judgment, as an intelligent creature, must be able to reflect upon and offer an account of the shared structure of meaning and truth that composes, in part, his or her political horizon. This account will provide more-or-less determinate concepts of a political nature that can then be predicated of particular political situations. To render a political judgment is to presuppose the capacity to make such a predication justifiably, albeit retrospectively. In short, it presupposes the capacity to invoke the tripartite model by (1) specifying the features of concepts that derive from a shared structure of political truth, (2) identifying the distinguishing characteristics of particular situations, and (3) describing a demonstrable and explicable connection between conceptual features and particular characteristics.

If all political judgments emerge out of a structure of truth that establishes grounds for their legitimacy, how can some judgments be faulty? The answer, in part, is that structures of truth are invariably complex. They reflect the gamut of our tacit understandings of the world, some of them directly political, some not. Insofar as they provide the ground out of which our common sense emerges, they may sometimes seem to send conflicting messages. Indeed, while coherence is an internal regulative principle for any structure of truth, it is also a goal rather than an established fact. To discover that we have resolved all of the tensions and contradictions inherent in our preunderstanding would, according to some influential accounts, be to approach the full flowering of Absolute Mind and hence to entertain seriously something like the end of history. In the absence of this, even perfect fidelity to certain aspects of a structure of truth might well mean violating other, perhaps preponderant aspects. The result will be a judgment that is flawed in terms of its own background conditions.

In addition, our capacity for political perception is almost certainly fallible. Perfect pitch is rarely if ever really perfect; even an "unerring" sense of political prudence is liable to err from time to time. Occasionally, then, we will fail to predicate universals of particulars correctly, simply because we have misperceived the latter. But our intellectual limitations go well beyond this. For even if our perceptions are entirely accurate, we may simply make discursive errors in relating particulars to universals. The literature in cognitive science is replete with examples of "logical illusions" (analogous to optical illusions) that demonstrate the imperfections of the human mind as an instrument of reason. Thus, the complexity of background conditions together with the frailty of our faculties means that we will sometimes, perhaps often, produce judgments that fail to comport satisfactorily with the larger force of our own prejudices and preunderstandings.

Again, we are obliged to test our political judgments, and therefore our political perceptions. But this testing is of a certain kind. For political judgments are necessarily, and in the first instance, claims about how other potential judges will see things. They are dialogic acts, judgments about judgments, either actually or prospectively, and depend for their legitimacy on the capacity of political judges to understand one another. This means, first, that judgment in politics presupposes membership in a political community. Such a community is invariably based on a structure of *political* meaning and truth that determines what kinds of claims will be intelligible and valid. To judge in politics is thus to participate in a community and to help that community recall exactly which claims it regards as valid and sensible. The dialogic nature of political judgment means, second, that the overriding criterion of judgment is meaningfulness. To the degree that a judgment comports with a structure of established political understandings, it is intelligible; that is, other judges can comprehend it, and this in turn lends the judgment the most important kind of authority that it can have. A judgment is valid insofar as it is, or can be, coherently recognized as such. Such a view does not give ultimate and total authority to the weight of mere opinion; for again, opinion and common sense need not be in conformity. But it does suggest that political judgments are hostage to a set of political understandings or presuppositions which, upon reflection and reconstruction, provide the basis for any political claim that purports to be true.

Political judgment is, thus, primarily second-order judgment. Any such judgment is a hypothesis about intelligible agreement internal to a structure of political truth or meaning. Of course, given our claims regarding the interdependence of meaningfulness and knowledge, intelligibility and truth, to offer a second-order judgment in politics is also to offer a first-order judgment. It is to assert a claim about how we must jointly interpret and make sense of this or that aspect of the political world. As such, it is a preeminent feature of any political action that we would wish to call intelligent.

I

In Chapter 1, we encountered three iterations of a thesis about political judgment. Each of these was found wanting, largely for failing to describe political judgment as anything other than indescribable—a kind of ineffable, indeterminate knack. Despite this, each was also found to reflect our own deep intuition that political judgment is not a phantasm but a genuine, truth-producing manner of thinking that is, at the same time, quite unrelated to standard modes of rational thought.

Our ambivalence toward these three iterations should now be dissolved. For the analysis has uncovered a concept of judgment, in politics as elsewhere, that does full justice to their prima facie appeal while providing them with a new-found and quite substantial grounding. This means, I believe, that each iteration—in each of its versions—in fact does contain, but only in a concealed and implicit way, the full and satisfying concept of political judgment that we have here derived. Their authors, like Meno's slave boy, somehow understand the nature of political judgment but have been, for various reasons, unable properly to articulate that understanding. They have described accurately the outward appearance of political wisdom, but have failed to uncover its inward articulation, its structure, its ontology. Our task, then, is to engage in our own process of rational reconstruction, whereby the tacit foundations of the three iterations can be brought to light.

Consider Oakeshott's claim that political judgment is a matter of pursuing intimations in the context of "attending to the arrangements of society." He offers the following example:

> [T]he legal status of women in our society was for a long time (and perhaps still is) in comparative confusion, because the rights and duties which composed it intimated rights and duties which were nevertheless not recognized. And, on the view of things I am suggesting, the only cogent reason to be advanced for the technical "enfranchisement" of women was that in most other important respects they had already been enfranchised. Arguments drawn from abstract natural right, from "justice," or from some general concept of feminine personality, must be regarded as either irrelevant, or as unfortunately disguised forms of the one valid argument; namely, that there was an incoherence in the arrangements of society which pressed convincingly for remedy.[1]

We see much here that reflects faithfully and explicitly the concept of political judgment, properly understood. The original judgment that women should be permitted to vote involved an insight. This insight

---

1. Michael Oakeshott, "Political Education," in *Rationalism in Politics* (London: Methuen, 1984), p. 124.

pertained to the structure of meaning or truth that made up, in part, a common sense. Common sense had manifested itself in a set of understandings and agreements about the nature of women the effect of which was that "in all or most other important respects they had already been enfranchised." We intuited or intimated this fact about our background understandings and hence discovered the further fact that the political disenfranchisement of women simply made no sense in the light of those understandings. In other words, our common sense told us what, perhaps, the explicit beliefs and opinions of the majority did not, namely, that women should have the right to vote. Oakeshott thus understands rather clearly that wisdom in politics involves a faculty of judgment—a kind of *knowing how*—that is deeply rooted in a sociocultural horizon or form of life, that might nonetheless be at variance with expressed public opinion, and that proposes a policy that is at once obvious to those who see it and indefensible to those who do not.

But for Oakeshott, this essentially exhausts the character of political judgment. In particular, by emphasizing the pursuit of intimations, he explicitly denies the rational, "intellectualistic" features of our concept of judgment: "[W]hat we have to do with is something less imposing than logical implications or necessary consequences."[2] His argument for this is extremely weak. His central claim is that there is "no piece of mistake-proof apparatus by means of which we can elicit the intimation most worth while pursuing." In a subsequent postscript, he repeats this position: "Do you want to be told that in politics there is, what certainly exists nowhere else, a mistake-proof manner of deciding what should be done?"[3] We have seen, however, that the process of rational reflection, and the absolute requirement of all intelligent performance for systematic justification, does not at all presuppose infallibility. Our analysis of judgment in linguistic communication shows what we already know, namely, that mistakes are always possible. But the frailties of rational argument do not mean that rational argument is a myth. Indeed, the very possibility of error suggests, in and of itself, the need for rational reconstruction and justification, however open-ended that process may be. It suggests, as well, criteria for distinguishing errors of incorrectness from "errors" of sheer unintelligibility—differentiating mistakes on the one hand from utter nonsense

2. Ibid.
3. Ibid., p. 136.

on the other. Oakeshott's complaint about the demand for a mistake-free apparatus is thus a red herring. Nothing that he says justifies his implicit claim that political judgment is purely intuitive, for error and argument go hand in hand.

Indeed, much of what Oakeshott actually says shows that his theory does indeed presuppose, albeit only tacitly, the full, concrete account of political judgment, as here developed. He insists that the pursuit of intimations, though not mistake-free, does involve "argument" of some kind.[4] He insists, further, that such a pursuit necessarily involves the political actor in a kind "conversation."[5] He fails, however, to uncover and articulate the fact that all argument and all conversation necessarily presuppose a recoverable structure of meaning or truth that allows for and, indeed, encourages an activity of rational reconstruction whereby particular argumentative or conversational moves can be assessed and validated. He thus fails to see that his own criterion for political wisdom—coherence—is a criterion of logical implication or entailment. A judgment is to be evaluated in terms of its coherence with an established structure of meaning or truth, and such coherence can be established only through a process of reconstruction governed by standard principles of rational inference. The fact that such a process is not infallible and the related fact that it is likely to be never-ending are, as we have seen, no argument against the theory of political judgment that we have proposed.

Thus, Oakeshott's judgment that women should have the right to vote expresses a truth to be intuited or perceived, but also to be explicitly and rationally justified in light of the established structure of truth out of which it has emerged. It is a judgment about a judgment, a political thinker's claim about how his fellow citizens would view the question of suffrage if they were faithful to their own common sense. As such, it is fully eligible for systematic analysis and evaluation according to quite rigorous standards of intelligibility and coherence.

Consider, similarly, a central theme of Arendt's political thought, namely, the banality of evil as embodied in Eichmann. Arendt accuses

4. Ibid., p. 134.

5. Ibid., p. 125. Oakeshott's claim here that judgment involves "a conversation, not an argument" literally contradicts what he says on p. 134. Presumably, he is using the word "argument" in more than one sense. My claim, on the other hand, is that even the loosest argument, if it is to be an argument at all, must be eligible for a standard kind of rational analysis and evaluation.

Eichmann of poor judgment. This may initially strike the reader as an extraordinary understatement; Eichmann's offense must have been rather more serious than that. But for Arendt, poor judgment is a deadly serious business. It is, in certain circumstances, the *sine qua non* of evil in the modern world. Her argument for this is based on an account of the relationship between "thinking" and "judging," as described in Chapter 1 above. Arendt explicitly indicts Eichmann for thoughtlessness—an inability to engage with others in the kind of ongoing and unconstrained inquiry into meaning that is, for her, the core of thinking, properly understood. Time and again, she refers to his failure to engage in anything remotely like a critical dialogue, and recounts his constant reliance on "stock phrases." He embraced and absorbed the "language rules" characteristic of the Nazi regime, which for him took the place of reflection: "[O]fficialese became his language because he was genuinely incapable of uttering a single sentence that was not a cliché."[6] Most importantly, his inability to speak "was closely connected with an inability to *think*, namely, to think from the standpoint of somebody else."[7] We have seen, though, that thinking is, for Arendt, the foundation of political judgment, that judging is, in fact, the particular form that thinking takes in the political world. Thus, Eichmann's inability to think is both the cause and the evidence of his lack of political judgment, and to lack such judgment thoroughly and entirely is to be evil or, at least, to be unable to resist the blandishments of evil when they present themselves.

A close reading of *Eichmann in Jerusalem* suggests, further, that Eichmann's inability to think was precisely an inability to carry on a dialogue with the structure of meaning and truth that composed his own culture. For while anti-Semitism was hardly new to Germany and Austria, the fact is that Eichmann's world very much presupposed the knowledge that Jews per se were not bestial or monstrous—were not base and malevolent creatures of an exotic and entirely alien nature, eligible for eradication—but were in fact human beings. In Arendt's account, Eichmann himself quite naturally shared this conviction. He had Jewish relatives by law. Some of these had helped him obtain work before the war, and he was "properly grateful." He evidently also had a Jewish mistress in Vienna, and he repeatedly emphasized at the trial,

6. On "language rules", see Hannah Arendt, *Eichmann in Jerusalem* (New York: Viking Press, 1968), pp. 85, 145.
7. Ibid., p. 49.

persuasively to Arendt, that he "had no hatred for Jews." He explained this by saying that "my whole education through my mother and my father had been strictly Christian"—implying that he had been raised on the principle of charity and brotherly love for all humans, including Jews.[8] Other Nazis reflected these larger cultural presuppositions, however perversely, by emphasizing the difference between German and non-German Jews and insisting on (relatively) humane treatment for the former, that is, "people who come from our own cultural milieu."[9] It is no accident that official and legal discrimination against Jews in Germany required specific acts (e.g., the Nuremberg Laws of 1935) that overturned existing and established rights and protections.[10]

Eichmann's thoughtlessness put him, like much of his generation, out of touch with these background assumptions. He was unable and indisposed to compare public opinions and official actions regarding Jews to the deeper truths of the culture of which he was a part. He was, for this precise reason, utterly bereft of judgment. Of course, Nazism as a whole embodied the very same thoughtlessness on a grand scale. An entire society had given up its critical faculty, and this because it had forfeited any and all ability to make contact with its own common sense. The result was a massive loss of insight and the temporary end of culture itself, leaving only a blind and rootless aggregation of people profoundly ignorant of right and wrong.

The accuracy of Arendt's account is not at question here. What is important is that her view of judgment in politics very much reflects many of the ideas that we have described above. Like Oakeshott, however, she fails to explicate the underlying premise of her own work, namely, that the disjunction between Eichmann's opinions and the common sense of German civilization is something that can be identified, articulated, and demonstrated. To judge correctly, and hence to engage in thinking properly understood, is to undertake an intelligent performance the adequacy of which can be established only through

8. Ibid., p. 30.

9. Ibid., p. 96.

10. Surely the incoherence of anti-Semitism in the light of larger cultural understandings is Shylock's point as well: "If you prick us, do we not bleed? If you tickle us, do we not laugh? If you poison us, do we not die? And if you wrong us, shall we not revenge?" (Shakespeare, *Merchant of Venice*, Act 3, Scene 1).

rational reconstruction. We may not be able to know just why Eichmann was so blind to the commonsense truths of his world, but his blindness can be demonstrated simply by comparing—logically and systematically—the substance of his words and deeds with the array of presuppositions clearly implicit in the quite advanced and highly cultivated society that had once been Germany. Such a demonstration is absolutely essential to Arendt's story, for without it her view of Eichmann's thoughtlessness would be mere assertion and would, as such, have no intellectual privilege over thoughtlessness itself. Her own capacity to judge Eichmann involves precisely the kind of intelligent performance of which Eichmann, for whatever reason, was incapable.

The plausibility and persuasiveness of Oakeshott's and Arendt's approaches to political judgment is thus to be found in the suppressed premises of each. These premises pertain to the intellectual core of an endeavor that seems, from outward appearances, to defy any kind of systematic accounting, but that is shown, upon sustained inquiry, to be a complex and concrete manner of thinking and acting deeply dependent on standard methods of rational inference. Such a view manifests itself throughout the political ontologies of action and conversation that make up our Third Iteration of a thesis—from the question of Eichmann to the problem of American foreign policy and the Vietnam war,[11] from the isolated issue of women's suffrage to the very idea of a regime understood as a "moral relationship" and designated by the term *societas*.[12]

Our Second Iteration of a thesis rests upon a similar foundation of suppressed premises. In Machiavelli's telling, for example, Francesco Sforza was a person of extraordinary political ability—a prince of "great courage and high ambition" who had the insight "to make himself beloved and feared by the people, followed and reverenced by the

11. Hannah Arendt, "Lying in Politics," in *Crises of the Republic* (New York: Harcourt Brace Jovanovich, 1972). Arendt writes: "Reading the memos, the options, the scenarios, the way percentages are ascribed to the potential risks and returns . . . of contemplated actions, one sometimes has the impression that a computer, rather than 'decision-makers,' had been let loose in Southeast Asia. The problem-solvers did not *judge;* they calculated" (p. 37). We see in this essay both Arendt's deep skepticism about the utility of rational analysis and the utter and inevitable dependence of her view of judgment upon it.

12. Michael Oakeshott, *On Human Conduct* (Oxford: Oxford University Press, 1990), pp. 201–202.

soldiers. . . . severe and kind, magnanimous and liberal."[13] But though Sforza's rise to power may reflect a certain indefinable *knowing how*, a knack that any would-be politician should seek to imitate and cultivate, we must also think of his political activity as a species of intelligent performance undertaken by a man of intellect whose insights by definition reflected a rational and recoverable, albeit unstated and unrecognized, structure of truth—a *knowing that* the world, and the people who compose it, are of such a character that certain actions are likely to succeed where others will not. Sforza sees, for example, that citizens will regard some acts of cruelty with respect and even admiration; they will, perhaps perversely, come to judge such acts in a positive light. Sforza "knows" his compatriots, and this allows him to judge their judgments accurately. Thus, he knows that sometimes he should be cruel. His presumed failure to articulate the source of this knowledge in no way compromises the claim that, with the benefit of appropriate questioning and in suitable circumstances, he would be able to reconstruct a rational and compelling explanation of his success.

Similarly, Tocqueville's deliberative citizen brings to bear on issues of communal concern a faculty of common sense and, in particular, an understanding of how his fellow citizens will judge things. This allows each and every decision to enjoy, at least prospectively, a *post festum* reconstruction, thereby demonstrating that the public realm is governed not by the aimless guesses of an untutored mob, nor by an occult and providential unseen hand, but by an assemblage of intelligent persons who know, though only tacitly, that they are together acting and judging in a rational and justifiable manner. In a similar way, *mutatis mutandis*, Nietzsche's political genius, far from being a kind of otherworldly demiurge, in fact subjects the world of affairs, and the judgments that compose it, to the most rigorous intellectual discipline—a discipline perhaps beyond the ken of the average mind but reflective, nonetheless, of the deepest and most enduring representations of an established form of life. For all of these writers, of course, political judgment has an important noninferential element. The prince, the citizen, the political aesthete do indeed have an acuity of vision or insight that permits them to make discriminations with more than the usual speed and accuracy. The existence of such an ability, though not itself easily detected or demonstrated, is a matter of accepted, stipulated fact. But again, its existence is not in spite

13. Machiavelli, *The Prince*, Chapter 7.

of but, in fact, inextricably connected to a realm of systematic and reconstructable intellectual endeavor. Machiavelli, Tocqueville, and Nietzsche fail to acknowledge and examine this fact. It remains, nonetheless, an indispensable if well-hidden presupposition of everything that they say, and of all theories of political judgment that ring true.

And thus, Robert Bork's qualifications for public service are profoundly dependent on the theoretical power of his views. We may not be satisfied with the state of his theorizing. We may believe, for example, that he has mistakenly reconstructed his own opinions, that his account, analysis, and defense of the positions he has taken do not reflect adequately the implications of those positions and their consequences. But it is not enough for us simply to conclude, with our First Iteration, that he therefore has bad judgment. For the question of judgment requires that we confront Bork precisely in theoretical terms, that we engage with him in a dialogue or conversation about the alleged connection between his opinions and the structure of truth out of which they arise. If Bork consistently misjudges and misperceives, then this is something that we must demonstrate after the fact, through a rational reconstruction of his decisions wherein the soundness of his analyses, whether tacit or otherwise, can be systematically evaluated.

It is, I think, no accident that we expect Supreme Court justices to write opinions. We understand that their effectiveness as judges depends on their insight into the facts of particular cases and on a knowledge of how those cases would be judged and evaluated by persons of common sense. We understand, further, that such cases often present confusing problems, and that unusual perspicacity is sometimes required in distinguishing the important features of a case from the unimportant ones. We understand, finally, that there is no clear method, no rational rule, for making such distinctions in the first place. Judging is indeed a matter of *knowing how*. But we also require our judges to be intelligent performers, and this means that we expect them to explain their decisions in the light of established and shared assumptions about how the world works. We expect them to participate with us in an ongoing dialogue about cases and about the law in which standards of right and wrong, coherence and contradiction, common sense and nonsense play an absolutely central role. If we suspect that such a dialogue will never end, and that its interlocutors will sometimes make mistakes and misunderstand one another, this does not justify our casting aside what is, in the end, a constitutive and quite salutary feature of political judgment and political life.

II

The account that I have presented is, by design, an effort to make explicit, and discover the logic of, our own deep intuitions about the concept of political judgment. Just as judgment itself presupposes a capacity for rational reconstruction, so does the theory of judgment similarly rely on a process of explication and justification whereby tacit understandings are brought to light and reformulated in rational terms. The accuracy of the theory rests, therefore, on the degree to which it comports with the gamut of our unstated presuppositions about what it means to judge in politics.

In at least three respects, it may seem that the theory is seriously counterintuitive and hence vulnerable to very strong objections. In fact, I believe that these objections will prove to be groundless. Nonetheless, they raise important issues that merit now at least some serious consideration.

1. As indicated in Chapter 1 above, we are inclined to think that there is often a great difference between a capacity for political judgment on the one hand and intellectual or theoretical ability on the other. In the face of this, however, we are now asked to contemplate a notion of political judgment that is, in many crucial respects, frankly intellectualistic. The quality and reliability of any judgment, whether that of Sforza, or Bork, or the ordinary citizen, is said to depend importantly on some kind of systematic theoretical accounting and hence on the authority of the abstract, speculative intellect. Given our intuitions, then, it may appear that I—an intellectual—have placed too heavy an emphasis on our rational faculties. The *phronimos* has become, perversely enough, a philosopher.

It should be clear, though, that the theory of judgment, however intellectualistic it may be, does not fall prey to the "intellectualistic fallacy" as described, for example, by Ryle. It does not argue that political wisdom is reducible to some sort of rational calculus. For again, to judge in politics is to invoke a kind of insight—a faculty of *nous* or common sense, a certain *knowing how*, a *"je ne sçay quoy"*—the mechanisms of which defy analysis. The precise empirical psychology of political insight is, at best, a matter for cognitive scientists to puzzle over; at worst, and more likely, it is a permanent mystery. But in either case, it is to be distinguished from the methodical, step-by-step manner of thinking that characterizes all forms of inferential reasoning.

Political judgment also presupposes, on our account, a structure of meaning and truth, a *knowing that,* which is eligible for, and indeed implicitly demands, *post festum* analysis. Without this, political judgment would entirely cease to be what we firmly believe it to be, a species of intelligent performance. But this does not contradict in any way our intuitions about insight and intellect. For we do not require that Sforza or Bork or the wise democratic citizen be a philosopher in the original sense, namely, a professional lover of truth whose life is devoted to the contemplation of those verities that constitute the core of human wisdom. Rather, we simply presuppose that there must be some substantial connection between judgment and truth and that the person who consistently makes good political decisions does so not through sheer accident but in such a way that the results can be systematically justified. The *phronimos* is, like each of us, a lover of truth indeed, though not a professional one. As an intelligent performer, he or she must care about the truth, and must therefore be prepared to participate with others—perhaps under the goading and guidance of professional truth seekers—in a process of reconstruction whereby the validity of particular judgments can be demonstrated and displayed. Politics is not philosophy, but it does presuppose the possibility of philosophical analysis.

The recurrent tendency of our political civilization to be impatient with philosophy, described in the sixth book of Plato's *Republic* (488a–489b) and documented in the writings of Machiavelli, is no argument against this view. It merely reveals a failure to recognize and acknowledge civilization's own foundations. Politics and truth may not always make happy partners.[14] But politics without any interest in and connection to the truth is not politics at all; it is, rather, an uncivilized event of nature. In this sense, anti-intellectualism in politics, like the anti-Semitism of Eichmann's Germany, is simply a sign of incoherence, the symptom of a culture out of touch with itself.

2. It will be be argued, perhaps paradoxically, that the concept of political judgment, however intellectualistic in orientation, also pre-

---

14. For a quite brilliant formulation of this issue, see Hannah Arendt, "Truth and Politics," in *Between Past and Future* (New York: Viking Press, 1968), pp. 239–249.

supposes a kind of epistemic relativism that is inimical to the very idea of judgment. For if political judgment is anything serious, it must have an objective grounding. Only this could allow us to distinguish arbitrary and unsupported preferences on the one hand from sound judgments on the other. But by basing political judgment on socially and historically generated traditions and structures of meaning, the account that has been developed here may seem to call into question the objectivity of judgment and hence the possibility that we can be justified in distinguishing good judgments from bad.

It is quite clear that the concept of judgment has strongly relativistic implications. But this is equally so for most other theories of truth and justification that rely primarily upon notions of coherence. These theories recognize, however implicitly, that truth claims are necessarily made within a particular universe of discourse. Such a universe establishes conditions of intelligibility that allow questions to be posed and answered in a comprehensible manner. Questions and answers have a meaning and reality specific to—relative to—a particular universe of discourse. But this suggests, further, that there is no possibility of asking truly critical or radical questions about the framework itself, for to ask such questions would require standing outside of the framework, and from such a position no questions can be intelligibly thought, much less asked and answered. Thus, whether a particular decision shows good political judgment will depend greatly upon the presuppositions inherent in the particular structure of political meaning out of which it has emerged.[15]

The relativism of political judgment has, however, two further features, and these help to preserve for it a crucial sense of objectivity. First, no particular structure of political meaning can be entirely closed and completely isolated from other similar structures. As we have seen, the Gadamerian idea of "fusion" proposes that horizons are porous and fluid; they overlap with other horizons, and this permits meaningful communication whereby the claims of one can be successfully translated into those of another. The concept of political judgment embraces this precise notion. Any universe of political discourse invariably has a history of its own, and this means that it is connected in important ways with structures that may seem to be chronologically

15. For a discussion, see Barry Stroud, "The Significance of Scepticism," in *Transcendental Arguments and Science: Essays in Epistemology*, ed. Peter Bieri, Rolf-P. Horstmann, and Lorenz Kruger, (Boston: D. Reidel, 1979).

and sociologically quite alien. Thus, for example, the views of Plato, Aristotle, or Machiavelli regarding political wisdom are fully eligible for interpretation and evaluation in the light of our own political prejudices, precisely because our views are genealogically connected to, and overlap with, theirs. Since the universe of political discourse out of which our judgments emerge is itself a product of, and is bound up with, its "effective history," contemporary views of political judgment do not reflect a narrow and parochial vision but, rather, a set of prejudices that represent much larger sociohistorical developments.

Second, the fact that political wisdom is specific to a tradition is, in and of itself, entirely incompatible with radical relativism of a solipsistic nature. For every tradition, as a community of interpretation, imposes restrictions on the kinds of judgments that each member of that community can make. These restrictions—which we have called intelligibility conditions—require that political judgments be evaluated in terms of criteria implicit in a shared form of life, criteria that, as such, far transcend the purely subjective idiosyncrasies of the individual. Indeed, such criteria determine that certain political judgments are simply impossible because unintelligible, and this establishes for political life an objective foundation. It establishes conditions whereby certain political judgments cannot be (intelligibly) refuted; and an irrefutable judgment—a judgment that cannot be coherently denied—is a judgment that objectively commands assent.

3. Assuming that the analysis thus far is correct, readers may nonetheless be inclined to think that it fails to reflect adequately the peculiar and distinctive features of political life and hence fails to distinguish political judgment from judgment per se. Of course, I have insisted above that political judgment is merely a species of judgment in general. In so doing, I have followed the quite standard tradition of conceiving of politics as a manifestation of some other, more basic and irreducible kind of human activity—a philosophical practice, an economy of power, a set of social institutions, a quest for glory, a process of deliberative interaction, an art form, and the like. But certain writers, some of whom we have considered, some not, have claimed that politics is *sui generis,* that it is itself a foundational kind of endeavor unlike any other and characterized by a unique set of attitudes and activities. For Dewey, the distinctively public nature of politics creates a special set of problems and opportunities that are not to be found in any other field of human endeavor. For Arendt, political action is uniquely characterized by natality, unpredictability, narration, and

immortality, and this requires us to distinguish political life, truly understood, from the pretensions and vicissitudes of the merely "social."

In my view, the realm of the political, as we standardly conceive of it, presupposes certain activities that are, if not unique to politics, then at least associated with it more closely than with any other realm. Politics is, after all, the art of the possible, and this suggests a particular emphasis on processes of negotiation and accommodation, the play and balance of interests, and the exercise of influence and power, including rhetorical power; it involves the need to arrive at decisions about complex matters involving large numbers of disparate agents under circumstances that do not always allow for a deliberate and careful consideration of alternatives; it trades on the nearly complete gamut of social, psychological, and material impulses, and renders outcomes that have, as a result, a peculiar stamp of authority—all of which, taken together, describes a distinctive field of human activity. None of this, however, exempts political life from the requirements of judgment, broadly conceived. The particular facts of politics are like no others; they do indeed describe a unique area of experience. This may well mean, in turn, that politics requires a distinctive faculty of perception, a uniquely political *nous,* one especially suited to that range of particulars. But this kind of specialization is almost certainly true of all areas in which human judgment is required. The ability to hear sounds is different from, and probably unrelated to, the ability to see colors; but such a difference, rooted in a difference of particulars, is perfectly consistent with saying that music criticism and art criticism are equally and similarly matters of judgment, understood as an intelligent activity whereby universals are predicated of particulars in a manner that is eligible for retrospective analysis and evaluation. The concept of judgment does not deny the varieties of judgment. It claims, though, that such varieties differ largely in terms of the particulars involved, along with the perceptual faculties associated with those particulars, while the underlying logic of judgment is universal.

Thus, the concept of judgment does not at all deny the distinctiveness of the political enterprise. It insists, however, that judgment in politics is indeed a species of judgment in general, and that the protocols by which we make political judgments are unique in their details but not in their basic structure. Political judgment is a type of intelligent performance. As such, it is hostage to, and explicable in terms of, the larger facts of thought and action that distinguish human endeavor itself from the merely natural world in which it occurs.

III

In condemning Eichmann for thoughtlessness, Hannah Arendt seems to have drawn a close connection between political judgment and morality: Eichmann's inability to judge is a symptom of moral decadence. Elsewhere, though, she denies any such connection. Indeed, she implies that a genuine moral agent who brings to the public realm a firm commitment to (say) the categorical imperative is at best an ingenue and at worst a fool, destined to be devoured by the rough and ready world of politics.[16] This general question of judgment and morality manifests itself as well in Machiavelli's treatment of Sforza. The Duke of Milan may have been a good judge in politics, but he also pursued his political goals with a kind of callous brutality hardly reminiscent of moral righteousness, standardly conceived. We are thus inclined to ask whether the concept of political judgment, as here defined, is in any sense an ethical category.

The answer depends, I believe, upon the particular structure of meaning and truth from which any such judgment emerges. To judge is to exercise a faculty of common sense internal to a form of life. But, as we have seen, forms of life, and the structures of truth that characterize them, are not of a piece. Each reflects its own effective history; hence each proposes a structure of truth that may well be distinctive and unique, an artifact of a particular time and place.

It is certainly true that some such structures understand the political realm as, at least in principle, profoundly moral in nature, governed by and directed toward the highest ethical values. Such a perspective will surely be familiar to most of us, heirs of a humanistic tradition. Even Machiavelli's embrace of Sforza's cynical, hard-bitten politics reflects, I believe, a tragic moral sensibility; the suffering caused by the prince is the inevitable price that we pay for achieving

---

16. Hannah Arendt, *Lectures on Kant's Political Philosophy* (Chicago: University of Chicago Press, 1982), pp. 17–22 and 46–51. Arendt adverts, here and elsewhere, to a distinction between "actor" and "spectator," identifying the latter with judgment of a moral rather than political nature. While such a distinction is certainly plausible and important, it should not be confused with actors and spectators internal to the political process, who must necessarily be engaged in political judgment of some kind.

the greater good of peace and order.[17] But we can perhaps imagine other worlds, or other societies, in which the public realm is denuded of any moral significance, where politics is understood to be a purely instrumental or technical endeavor—a kind of higher-order house-keeping—separate from and unaffected by the moral exigencies of personal conscience and private life. Along these lines, certain Christian writers, convinced of the comparative insignificance of life on earth and concerned only with matters spiritual and divine, assigned to the temporal order a peripheral role at best, and counseled obedience to secular rulers not because it was inherently the right thing to do but only because it provided a peaceful setting conducive to serious prayer and pious contemplation.

The concept of political judgment is, as far as I can tell, essentially neutral on such questions. Good judgment in politics is a matter of rendering claims and making decisions that are consistent with and authorized by the preponderant assumptions and tacit beliefs of a sociocultural tradition. If those assumptions and beliefs require that political decisions pass a test of moral legitimacy, then judgment in politics is likely to involve ethical criteria; if not, not. The question of morality and judgment depends, therefore, on particular understandings of the nature and purpose of politics, and these are, at least up to a point, matters of historical, not philosophical, fact.

The theory of political judgment is not a full-blooded political theory in the traditional sense. It does not prescribe, or even imply, specific political arrangements, procedures, or policies. It is, moreover, indifferent as to the purposes of political society. It is content to leave such questions to the vicissitudes of history, and accepts with equanimity the variety of political practices and judgments that history may produce. It recoils from prescribing specific standards. It insists only that some such standards must be in place, and it proposes that political life be characterized to a significant degree by habits of analysis and discourse, by a ready disposition to engage in rational reconstruction, guided always by the requirement of coherence.

The concept of political judgment implies that judgment itself is,

---

17. The complexity of Machiavelli's views on this question cannot be grasped without considering his treatment of Agathocles the Sicilian (*The Prince*, Chapter 8.)

and must be, a central and persistent feature of political life. There is, as a result, an apparent tension between that concept and various influential theories of politics and society that counsel us to be as little judgmental as possible. Such theories conceive of politics as an "art of separation,"[18] a structure of mutual toleration wherein individuals, either from indifference, prudence, or respect, refrain from subjecting one another to constant analysis and evaluation. Political society, so conceived, is a fabric of accommodation. It aims not to assess, improve, and correct the motives and actions of individuals and groups, but to establish a moral and ideological climate, supported by an infrastructure of power, that permits a maximum range of independent thought and movement unaffected, to the degree possible, by an economy of approval and disapprobation, official or otherwise. Against this, the concept of political judgment, and the very language with which I have presented it, may seem to suggest something quite different—a politics of relentless mutual examination leading to a dominion of total institutions in which every thought and every deed is subject to critical scrutiny and is eligible for the ministrations, at once benign and ruthless, of society's censorial apparatus.

This characterization is quite correct and, at the same time, utterly inapposite. Above all, it fails, I think, to make contact with certain unavoidable facts of social existence. The concept of political judgment does, indeed, propose an unceasing and habitual reliance on analysis, reconstruction, and evaluation. This, however, is not peculiar to politics; it is, rather, a defining feature of human endeavor insofar as it is intelligent. Our active engagement with the world is bound up with our thinking about it, and this, in turn, is a matter of constantly making and attending to distinctions, and hence of predicating universals of particulars, however unself-consciously. We work our way through the world by mapping it conceptually, and all of our mappings are necessarily available for, indeed call out for, rational reconstruction, whereby their suitability can be discussed and evaluated. To deny this is to deny the most salient and distinguishing features of humankind; to abjure it, if such a thing is possible, is to renounce our capacity for intelligent performance.

The political realm defines one of these conceptual maps. It is, as such, a structure of discriminations and judgments. This is true

18. Michael Walzer, "Liberalism and the Art of Separation," *Political Theory* 12 (May 1984), pp. 315–330.

regardless of its particular configuration. Some judgments may call for a vigorous exercise of the public authority, others for a policy of laissez-faire. But in all cases, the decision to act or not, to interfere or ignore, presupposes a complex of determinations, each of which represents an intelligent and reconstructable claim about political reality.

Consider, for example, a decision not to regulate actively a particular segment of the economy. Such a decision would necessarily reflect judgments every bit as substantive and directive as those that would have led to an opposite decision. For in choosing not to regulate, we would have determined that the various possible outcomes in that segment of the economy are all more-or-less acceptable to us. Our decision not to prescribe outcome *A* over outcome *B* (and vice versa) is not a decision to eschew prescription altogether; rather, it entails a quite direct and explicit prescription in its own right, namely, "either *A* or *B*." In this sense, of course, the absence of overt regulation is a nontrivial kind of regulation. The polity simply arrogates to itself the choice of whether to regulate through active involvement or benign neglect. In either case, the economic activity in question proceeds only at the intelligent and thoughtful sufferance of the public authority.

To tolerate, to leave alone, to separate or quarantine—all of this is a matter of judgment. The decision to be "as little judgmental as possible" is, thus, a linguistic deception. Such a decision does not minimize judgment per se but, at best, only a particular kind of judgment. We decide, for example, not to judge another person's moral views; we do so, however, not in the absence of judgment altogether, but precisely because we have come to the political judgment that this is the prudent thing to do. And such a judgment is itself necessarily based on the prior judgment that the other person's moral views, whatever they may be, fall "within the pale," so that however much we may disagree with them, we also believe that they are sufficiently harmless as to be tolerable.

The ubiquity of judgment thus provides no argument against, and in no way contradicts, principles of liberalism and the art of separation. In this sense, the concept of political judgment is utterly nonpartisan. At the same time, though, it provides an unusually clear-eyed appreciation of the ever-present hazards of political life. For political judgment is, at one and the same time, the unique solution to and the ineluctable source of pathological politics.

The formal arrangements of political society, whatever they may be, can never substitute for argument, analysis, and rational reconstruction. In particular, the insidious and emergent claims of tyranny will not disappear if only we try to be as little judgmental as possible. Those claims must be taken for what they are: judgments to be uncovered, explicated and, in the best of circumstances, disproved. It is thus true that the very tools of intolerance and censure—habits and mechanisms of observation, discrimination, and evaluation—are equally the tools with which to defend prudence and good sense. But this only demonstrates with particular clarity the unavoidably tragic character of political life.

I use the word "tragic" here advisedly. Tragedy is, I think, a feature primarily of situations rather than individuals. The great figures of classical literature—Agamemnon, Kreon, Pentheus—were tragic not from any peculiar defect of character, but because they found themselves in circumstances that both required and prevented virtuous action. Each faced a quite literal moral paradox. Each was forced to choose from a range of alternatives, none of which was in any way morally acceptable. As a result, and despite their own heroic efforts, each faced inevitable doom.

The universal tragedy of politics is similarly written into the very nature of political life. For as political actors, we too face a moral paradox. Either we flee, in the name of "separation," from the responsibilities of intelligent endeavor, in which case we give ourselves up to the barbarism of irrational cause and effect, or else we acknowledge and accept the ubiquity of judgment, in which case we expose ourselves to the ever-present possibility and, indeed, the virtual long-term certainty of catastrophic misjudgment. In the face of this, we are forced, I think, to take the risk, to struggle for insight and enlightenment, knowing full well that our faculties are frail, our decisions will often be in error, and our future will, as a result, resemble all too closely our past.

Our proper ambition is to forestall the inevitable, to seek temporary triumph over inexorable *fortuna,* and this requires, I believe, a particular reliance on those individuals, perhaps many, perhaps only a few, who are peculiarly well suited, through nature and circumstance, to cast upon the dim, disorienting landscape of the public realm the cold light of critical reason. As skilled practitioners of political judgment, such individuals are at once our scourge and our only hope.

INDEX

Action, political. *See* Arendt,
Hannah: theory of political
action
Addison, Joseph, 128
Aesthetics. *See* Art and aesthetics
Anamnēsis: in hermeneutics, 193,
226; and intelligent performance, 221, 240–41; and universes of discourse, 254–55
Anaxagoras, 115, 117
Arendt, Hannah, 44; on common
sense, 67–69, 85, 239; on contemplation, 48–49, 61–62, 65;
on Eichmann, 289–92, 300;
influence of, on political theorists, 73–75, 79–82; on judgment in politics, 62, 64–69,
75–76, 78–79; compared with
Kant, 146; on logical reasoning,
63; view of Machiavelli, 21–22,
57n; role of mental faculties in
action, 61–63; theory of mental
faculties, 62–67, 264, 269; on
nous, 227, 228; compared with
Oakeshott, 57–61; on philosophy and politics, 48, 51, 60–61;
theory of political action, 47–52,
58–61, 65–69; and rational reconstruction, 289–92; on thinking, 62–63, 64–65, 68–69; on
truth, 65–67; on willing, 62
Aristotle, 13, 217–18, 298; on communities of interpretation, 199;
on deliberation, 110–12; ethical
theory of, 113–15, 123–25, 235;
on judgment, 128, 130, 147–48,
149–52; compared with Kant,
144; on types of knowledge,
119–25; on necessity and choice
in judgment, 109–12; philosophy
of mind of, 106–27; on *nous*,

119–27, 227; on particulars,
115–17, 125–27; on *phronēsis*
and *sophia*, 106–12, 113–22, 153,
154, 156, 167, 279; view of science, 109–15, 117, 23; on *technē*,
107–8
Art and aesthetics: as a concrete
activity, 211–12; and ethics,
145–46; in Gadamer, 187–92,
196–98; in Hutcheson, 129;
Kant's theory of, 133–46; in
Machiavelli, 22–24; in Nietzsche,
37–42; as a political metaphor,
34; modern theory of, 127–49,
154, 167; and rational reconstruction, 238; in Shaftesbury, 128–
29, 145
Augustine, 11
Austin, J. L., 186, 208, 217; on
speech acts, 159, 163, 168

Barber, Benjamin R., 83–88
Beauty: as indeterminate concept,
in Kant, 134–36. *See also* Art and
aesthetics
Beiner, Ronald, xi
Benjamin, Walter, 195–96
Bentham, Jeremy, 11
Berkeley, George, 54
Bernstein, Richard J., xi
Betti, Emilio, 187n
Bork, Robert, 1, 4, 6, 294–95
Burke, Edmund, 53, 128

Cardozo, Benjamin, 237
Carnap, Rudolf, 183
Civic humanism, 25. *See also* Machiavelli
Common sense: Arendt's theory of,
67–69, 85, 239; and democracy,
34; as differentially distributed,